D1553728

Mr. Chairman

★ ★

BLISS INSTITUTE SERIES

Bliss Institute Series

John C. Green, Editor

William L. Hershey and John C. Green, *Mr. Chairman: The Life and Times of Ray C. Bliss*

Douglas M. Brattebo, Tom Lansford, Jack Covarrubias, and Robert J. Pauly Jr., editors, *Culture, Rhetoric, and Voting: The Presidential Election of 2012*

Douglas M. Brattebo, Tom Lansford, and Jack Covarrubias, editors, *A Transformation in American National Politics: The Presidential Election of 2012*

Daniel J. Coffey, John C. Green, David B. Cohen, and Stephen C. Brooks, *Buckeye Battleground: Ohio, Campaigns, and Elections in the Twenty-First Century*

Lee Leonard, *A Columnist's View of Capitol Square: Ohio Politics and Government, 1969–2005*

Abe Zaidan, with John C. Green, *Portraits of Power: Ohio and National Politics, 1964–2004*

Mr. Chairman

★ ★

The Life and Times of
Ray C. Bliss

William L. Hershey
& John C. Green

University of Akron Press
Akron, Ohio

All Material Copyright © 2017 by The University of Akron Press
All rights reserved • First Edition 2017 • Manufactured in the United States of America.

All inquiries and permission requests should be addressed to the publisher, The University of
Akron Press, Akron, Ohio 44325-1703.

21   20   19   18   17   5   4   3   2   1

ISBN: 978-1-629220-41-3 (cloth)
ISBN: 978-1-629220-42-0 (ePDF)
ISBN: 978-1-629220-43-7 (ePub)

LIBRARY OF CONGRESS CATALOGING-IN-PUBLICATION DATA

Names: Hershey, William L., author. | Green, John Clifford, 1953– author.
Title: Mr. Chairman : the life and times of Ray C. Bliss / William L. Hershey and John C. Green.
Description: First edition. | Akron, Ohio : University of Akron Press, 2017. | Series: Bliss Institute
    series | Includes bibliographical references and index. |
Identifiers: LCCN 2017013389 (print) | LCCN 2017029398 (ebook) | ISBN 9781629220420 (ePDF) |
    ISBN 9781629220437 (ePub) | ISBN 9781629220413 (hardcover : alk. paper)
Subjects: LCSH: Bliss, Ray C. | Nixon, Richard M. (Richard Milhous), 1913–1994—Friends and
    associates. | Republican National Committee (U.S.)—Officials and employees—Biography. |
    Republican Party (U.S. : 1854–)—History—20th century. | Political party organization—United
    States—History—20th century. | Politicians—Ohio—Biography. | Ohio—Politics and
    government—1951– | United States—Politics and government—1961–1963. | United States—
    Politics and government—1963–1969.
Classification: LCC E840.8.B585 (ebook) | LCC E840.8.B585 H47 2017 (print) |
    DDC 324.2734092 [B] —dc23
LC record available at https://lccn.loc.gov/2017013389

∞ The paper used in this publication meets the minimum requirements of ANSI / NISO Z39.48–
1992 (Permanence of Paper).

Cover design: Tyler Krusinski. Cover photo: Associated Press Photo/Jack Thornell. © 1967
The Associated Press. Used with permission.

Mr. Chairman was designed and typeset in Centaur with Futura display by Amy Freels, with
assistance from Tyler Krusinski. *Mr. Chairman* was printed on sixty-pound natural and bound by
Bookmasters of Ashland, Ohio.

To Marcia Hershey, for all the good times we've had and more to come

To Lynn Green, a steadfast companion on a joyful journey

Contents

Acknowledgments

This book could not have been written without the help of many people. They include the staff of the Bliss Institute, particularly Janet Bolois and Jenni Fitzgerald, and generations of students, as well as the staff of the University of Akron Press, especially Jon Miller and Amy Freels. The following people were interviewed for the book and many agreed to be quoted in the text. We wish to thank these and many others for sharing their knowledge and memories of the life and times of Ray C. Bliss.

Stephen Ambrose
John Andrews
Alexander Arshinkoff
Gerald Austin
Frank Avren
William Ayres
James Baker
Kenneth Barker
John Ballard
Haley Barbour
Robert Bennett
John Bibby
Ellen Bliss
Amy Bragg
William Brock
Clarence J. "Bud" Brown Jr.
Helen Brown
Roy Browne
Hal Bruno

Rose Carlson
Cyndra Cole
Leroy Contie
Kellie Copeland
Madge Doerler
William Eells
Louise Palmer Earley
Robert Feldkamp
Ody Fish
Sy L. Fisher
Gerald Ford
Thaddeus A. Garrett Jr.
John Glenn
Ralph Goetller
Josephine Good
Walter J. Hickel
Clayton Horn
Robert Huckshorn
Elisabeth Hurley

Richard Hurley
Mrs. Howard Hyde
Robert Hynes Jr.
Raphael Jeter
Jefferson Keener
Herbert Klein
George W. Knepper
Charles Kurfess
John LaGuardia
John C. McDonald
Kent McGough
Keith McNamara
Mrs. J. Willard Marriott
John Mahaney
Clyde Mann
Della Mann
Howard Metzenbaum
Peter O'Grady
Robert Paduchik

Michael Pavick

Arthur Peterson

Ray Price

Janet Purnell

Roy Ray

Morris Reid

Ralph Regula

Frances Rex

James Rhodes

Norma Rios

Bernard Rosen

Gary Rosen

Don Ross

James Ruvolo

William Saxbe

John Sears

John Seiberling

Mary L. Smith

Daly "Tim" Smith

Harry Stein

Robert Taft Jr.

Mrs. Henry H. Timken Jr.

W. R. Timken Sr.

W. R. Timken Jr.

Roger Tracy

James Tilling

William Vance

David Eugene Waddell

Paul Weick

W. Richard Wright

Abe Zaidan

Prologue

In January 1981, Republicans streamed into Washington, DC, for Ronald Reagan's inauguration as president. There was much to celebrate for the Grand Old Party. Reagan had defeated the Democratic incumbent, President Jimmy Carter, in a landslide. Republicans had taken control of the US Senate and gained fifty-two seats in the US House of Representatives. The Watergate scandal that had forced Richard M. Nixon from the White House in 1974 seemed a distant memory.

Reagan's inauguration also coincided with another celebration: the fiftieth anniversary of the political career of Ray C. Bliss. Then seventy-three, Bliss had spent his entire adult life working for the Republican Party, serving as chairman at the local, state, and national levels. At one of the Reagan inaugural balls, Bliss and his wife Ellen held court while senators, representatives, and party officials came by to say thank you to "Mr. Chairman."

Bliss was a rare national party chairman who put his mark on political history. He was the first of the "Three Bs" of the modern Republican Party, a moniker suggested by columnist David Broder for three national chairmen—Ray Bliss, Bill Brock, and Haley Barbour—who put the party back together after major defeats.[1]

None of these setbacks was more challenging than Republican Barry Goldwater's landslide loss to Democrat Lyndon B. Johnson in 1964. Bliss took over the next year as national chairman of a demoralized and divided party. Pundits questioned whether the GOP was dead, a little more than a hundred years after its birth.

To rebuild the Republican Party, Bliss focused on the "nuts and bolts" of practical politics, strengthening and uniting the organization. A key feature was training party leaders in the ancient art and new science of electioneering. He expanded a system of direct-mail fund-raising from small contributors and used these funds to provide state and local parties with tools to get out the vote. Most importantly, Bliss created the Republican Coordinating Committee, a policy-making vehicle to accommodate the conservatives still steaming from Goldwater's defeat and the moderates who had done little to help prevent the loss. The committee developed a consensus on issues for upcoming campaigns. These innovations paid off at the ballot box. Just four years after the Goldwater debacle, the GOP won the White House in 1968 with Richard Nixon.

Bliss made a career out of organizing such comebacks. After the 1948 and 1958 elections, he helped Ohio Republicans recover from major defeats. His longtime friend and University of Akron official, W. Richard Wright, had a front-row seat for observing how Bliss liked to work. "In the realm of politics, he [Bliss] liked to take a situation that needed rebuilding," said Wright. "Bliss would use his organization to pick the candidates, put them in the right slots and then bring everyone together to win elections.... I think it was like writing a play for him," Wright recalled. "He could see what needed to be done, then he went about to do what was necessary to accomplish the goal."[2]

After the Watergate scandal devastated the GOP in 1974, a new Republican national chairman, William Brock, dusted off the Bliss methods—disregarded in the interim by President Nixon and his allies—and developed them further. These efforts led to the 1980 victories celebrated at President Reagan's inaugural.

At a personal level, Ray Bliss certainly was no Ronald Reagan. The bespectacled Bliss—plump and shy, his once-auburn hair turned gray, slicked back and parted slightly to the left of center—looked like the Akron insurance man that he was.

Bliss had no interest in self-promotion. He told people he was an "office chairman" focused on the nuts and bolts of elections, not a "speaking chairman" sharing the limelight with candidates.[3] A self-described "organizational man," he was committed to the party rather than to any particular candidate. "I got into politics because I believe in two strong parties," said Bliss. "I believe the two-party system provides us the best government."[4]

Bliss's devotion to the GOP reflected such broader purposes: "As for me, I still firmly believe, as I have believed for more than 30 years in politics, that the Republican Party offers the best hope for government which is efficient, yet economical; government that is alert to the changing times, yet guided by common sense; government which is compassionate to the needs of the people, yet wise in the execution of programs to meet those needs."[5]

Throughout his career, Bliss was bedeviled by the growing independence of candidates from the party organization. Goldwater and Nixon were good examples in his day, and the trend has continued after his career in both major political parties. It reached a peak with the Republican presidential nomination of Donald J. Trump in 2016.

Bliss's own political career had started humbly enough as an errand boy in a 1931 Akron mayoral race. He got the job after being expelled from the University of Akron in an alleged ballot box–stuffing scandal—an irony for a man who later would be known for his honesty and integrity. Bliss became chairman of the Summit County Republican Party in 1942 and of the Ohio Republican Party in 1949. He left both jobs in 1965 to become Republican national chairman. Bliss resigned the top post in 1969 and returned to his hometown of Akron, Ohio. Along the way, he ran winning campaigns in 1950, 1956, 1960, 1962, and 1968 that still serve as models for his successors.

Back in Akron, there was little trace of Bliss's national prominence in his insurance office. His walls were bare of the trademark of most political leaders—rows of pictures featuring him grinning and shaking hands with great and would-be-great Republicans. "If I have to put up pictures to convince people of my record and my career, I'm not interested," said Bliss.[6] What Bliss treasured was a cocktail, a juicy steak, and political talk at Akron's Diamond Grille, most often with a fraternity brother he had known since both were students at the University of Akron in the 1920s. And, just as much, Bliss enjoyed a quiet night at home sharing a bowl of popcorn with his wife, Ellen.

After Reagan's inaugural in 1981, Bliss had little time left to enjoy these pleasures: he died of a heart attack later that year.

This book traces Bliss's life and his remarkable fifty-year career in politics. The story begins and ends in Akron, Ohio.

Chapter 1

Akron, Ohio

Richard Nixon's election as president in 1968 should have been a time of triumph for Ray Bliss. As chairman of the Republican National Committee, he had helped engineer Nixon's victory just four years after Barry Goldwater's disastrous loss to President Lyndon Johnson in 1964. But almost as soon as the ballots were counted, Nixon began pressuring Bliss to leave his post. In an attempt to placate Bliss, the president offered to appoint him American ambassador to Denmark—the kind of post that appealed to Nixon. But not to Ray Bliss. If he couldn't stay on as national chairman, there was only one place he wanted to go—back to Akron.

"I went to school here [Akron]. I was raised here. The people of Akron helped make me a success. If I hadn't been a success here, what would I be?" Bliss asked rhetorically. "Nothing."[1] After leaving his position as national chairman in 1969, he lived in Akron until his death in 1981. The city where Bliss was born put an indelible stamp on his life. Although he lived in other places during his career, he never really *left* Akron. "Ray never lost the sense of being part of the local community," recalled Madge Doerler, Bliss's business and political associate. "He loved being with people, especially close friends."[2]

When Bliss was born in 1907, America was changing from a mostly rural and agricultural society to a largely urban, industrial one. Akron played a key role in this transformation. It was fast becoming the "Rubber Capital of the World," and tire production was a pillar of the new industrial economy.[3] The change was driven by a cycle of boom and bust, with rubber replacing Akron's previous industries. The city was first known as the "sewer pipe capital" of the country because of clay product manufacturing. Other businesses included grain milling (the origin of the Quaker Oats Company), matches (the roots of the Diamond Match Company), and farm machinery (eventually absorbed into International Harvester).[4]

These industries had, in turn, replaced Akron's original agricultural economy. Settlement in the area began in 1807, a century before Bliss's birth, and expanded with the opening of the Ohio and Erie Canal in 1826. Akron was incorporated as a city in 1836. Its name derived from the Greek word for "high"—appropriate for its geographic location at the high point of the canal.[5] The name also captured the city's economic aspirations. The canal was the "superhighway" of its day, and just like Akron's succession of industries, it was eventually replaced by railroads, and then roadways (and a demand for rubber tires). Economic change continued throughout Bliss's life, with the rubber industry declining in Akron as he retired from politics.

The boom-and-bust cycles were fueled by a steady stream of risk-takers. They built companies with their own money and what they could scrape together from investors. They had no guarantees of success, and the ventures often failed. The willingness of entrepreneurs to take chance after chance had a lasting impact on Bliss: "I happen to be a Republican because I believe in our form of government and the free enterprise system. This may sound trite to you. But I believe in the right of a man to do something in life if he is willing to work harder than his neighbor....I am a believer in the capitalistic system. I make no bones about it. I am a believer in a system that encourages initiative and expansion of business. I sincerely believe it."[6]

During Bliss's childhood, the rubber industry had been growing for more than forty years. In 1870, Dr. Benjamin Franklin Goodrich relocated his small rubber factory to Akron; it became the B. F. Goodrich Company in 1880. In 1898, local businessmen F. A. and Charles W. Seiberling started the Goodyear Tire and Rubber Company. In 1900, Harvey S. Firestone, a farm boy from southeast of Akron, opened the Firestone Tire and Rubber Company. General Tire was founded by local business leader William O'Neil in 1915.[7] These companies were part of the "managerial revolution" in American business. Along with innovations in technology, new business methods were adopted. Professional managers, trained in accounting, finance, and marketing, were increasingly hired to run companies more efficiently. By the late 1920s, the rubber companies had become corporate giants.[8]

Bliss admired the professional managers of Akron's rubber companies and of other industries across the country. He imitated them by applying many of the same techniques to modernize the Republican Party at the local, state, and national levels.

The "smell of jobs"—as civic boosters later referred to the sweet, sickly odor from the rubber plants—attracted workers to Akron. From 1910 to 1920, the city's population soared from 69,067 to 208,435. The rubber factories seemed to have jobs for everyone. By 1920, they employed nearly 70,000 workers. The factories ran twenty-four hours a day to keep up with the demand for tires.[9] There literally wasn't room for everyone who came to live in the Rubber City. It was easy to find a job, but nearly impossible to find a place to sleep. Akron drew the unwanted distinction of having more miles of unpaved streets than any city its size in the nation. "The streets are paved with people," one writer noted.[10]

Industrial booms brought prosperity, but the busts created hardships. Jobs in the rubber shops did not automatically translate into gains for the workers. The competition among the tire makers was cutthroat, and professional managers focused on the bottom line. They sped up production, changed work rules, and fired workers at will. As a consequence, tensions developed between labor and management. As early as 1900, workers began to organize unions, seeking higher pay and better working conditions. The first major strike came in 1913 at Firestone. Akron residents chose up sides between the strikers and management. When it was settled, the strike brought some improvements in working conditions, but foreshadowed often acrimonious labor-management relations.[11]

Although Ray Bliss never worked a day in the rubber shops, many of his relatives did. This connection helped Bliss find support for Republican candidates among working-class voters. Opposition to—and respect for—the political power of organized labor was a central fact of Bliss's career.

Akron's population explosion attracted new kinds of people. At its founding, Akron was dominated by English and Scottish migrants from Connecticut, followed by Irish and German immigrants after the Civil War. By 1900, the rubber industry attracted immigrants from central, southern, and eastern Europe in large numbers. Native migrants swelled the tide, including whites from Appalachia and African Americans from the South. Religion was part of the change. Akron's Yankee and German settlers had been predominantly Protestants, while many newcomers were Roman Catholic, Eastern Orthodox, Jewish, and evangelical Christians.[12]

The city's early settlers formed tight-knit communities that were suspicious of new arrivals. Early conflicts broke out among "Yankees," "Micks," and "Dutchmen," followed by tensions among "Americans" and "foreigners" and "hillbillies." Akron became famous for its ethnic associations and secret societies.[13] This volatile social mix shaped Bliss. The Protestant-Catholic divide bedeviled him for most of his life, while ethnic differences and extremist groups were everyday realities in his profession. Bliss learned the value of building broad coalitions and respecting political differences.

It is small wonder, then, that President Nixon's offer of a diplomatic post abroad did not appeal to Ray Bliss: an ambassadorship was no match for the vitality of his native city. This lifelong connection began, of course, with his family.

Chapter 2

Family Matters

Raymond Charles Bliss was born on December 16, 1907, the first of three sons of Emil and Emilie Bliss and the only one to live into adulthood.[1]

Ray was close to his father's family. Emil was born in Muelheim, Germany, in 1883. He was the fourth of eight children of Johannes and Kathrina Bluess. The family immigrated to Akron in 1889 when Emil was six years old.[2] Their first and last names, like those of many other immigrants, were modified to fit their new country. By 1890 the last name was *Bliss*.

John and Catherine Bliss settled near the German community in south Akron. Two years after leaving Germany, John Bliss was working at the B. F. Goodrich "rubber works." He was prosperous enough to own a house in south Akron, but he also experienced the downside of the industrial economy: in 1909 he was out of work for nine weeks. John Bliss was a timekeeper at the rubber works when he retired in 1916 at the age of seventy-one.[3] Ray hardly knew his grandmother Catherine, who died of "exhaustion" in 1911 when he was just four years old. But his grandfather John lived to be ninety years old, passing away in 1936 when Ray was an adult.[4]

John Bliss's sons and daughters started work in the rubber shops, but as with many immigrants, they quickly moved up in the world. Emil was initially employed by B. F. Goodrich and the Miller Manufacturing Company. In 1903, he was hired by the Akron Electric Company, and he spent most of the rest of his life working with electricity, often being referred to as an "electrical engineer."[5]

Ray was even closer to his mother's family. His mother, Emilie, was born near Stuttgart, Germany, in 1884. She was the next to youngest of the six children of Gottfried and Kathrina Wieland. The three oldest Wieland children immigrated in 1895, first living with an uncle in Springfield, Illinois, and then moving to Akron in 1900. The rest of the family moved to Akron in 1901. Gottfried did not like his new surroundings and returned to Germany in 1910, but Kathrina stayed behind with her children. She passed away in 1920, when Bliss was thirteen years old. Like the Blisses, the Wieland children prospered in their new home.[6]

Emilie was about twenty when she arrived in Akron, where she met her future husband and became Emilie Bliss. The newlyweds had more in common than German ancestry. They were both Protestants: Emil grew up in the German Methodist Church and Emilie was a member of the Evangelical and Reformed Church.[7]

As an adult, Ray was not especially devout, but his parents' faith had a lifelong impact, said Madge Doerler. She called him a "Christian man."[8] "Ray was a compassionate person, helping out the other guy if he could. He believed that everyone should work for a living, and he cared deeply for someone who could not work. He felt an obligation to help the needy," Doerler remembered. Political scientist Arthur Peterson, who worked for Bliss, recalled discussions about the values young Bliss received from his family: "He [Bliss] would express what influence his mother had on him, as well as his father. That was part of the Protestant ethic. You worked hard.... If you worked hard, if you saved your money, if you worked harder than someone else, you were entitled to your gains and you had an obligation to do this."[9]

His family's economic success allowed Ray to grow up happy and secure. But his early years were also touched by family tragedies. Emil and Emilie Bliss moved to West Virginia after their second son, Calvin, was born in 1910. Less than a year later, the baby fell ill with marasmus, a wasting away of the body associated with inadequately assimilated food. The family drove back to Akron to seek treatment for their son, but to no avail. "He died in her [Emilie's] arms," said Rose Carlson, Bliss's cousin.[10]

Shortly after Calvin's death, the Blisses moved to California. Emil interrupted his work with electricity to manage an almond grove and a hotel. The family returned to Akron in 1917, and Emil went to work for the Imperial Electric Company, where he was employed for the rest of his life. He earned a good enough living to buy a home in south Akron.[11]

Ray worked in his uncles' grocery stores after school and during summers. These lessons left a lifelong mark on him, Doerler recalled. He never had a credit card and always paid cash. Although he was personally charitable toward the needy, he was skeptical of social welfare programs. "Ray believed in hard work, that people should take care of themselves," Doerler said. "This was how you should live your life."[12]

Family activities were at the center of Ray's adolescence. Among his favorite were excursions to Springfield Lake in Sawyerwood, south of Akron. "Ray loved to go to Sawyerwood. That was when we were kids. My uncle had the bathhouse. He'd pass out bathing suits and we'd go swimming…. They'd give us free ice cream cones. We thought that was big stuff," said Carlson.[13]

Outside the family, young Bliss could appear shy. He had weak eyes, including a detached retina suffered during a fishing trip on Lake Erie. "I don't think people warmed up to Ray a lot, probably as a child even…because of what his eyesight did to him," said Doerler.[14] Even at a young age he was known for becoming so engrossed in what he was doing that he would pass friends on the street without a word of recognition.

Ray wasn't a whiner, however. Doerler remembered a conversation with an Akron man who had known Bliss in school: "Ray was riding his bicycle when he fell off and broke his arm. He didn't whimper. He didn't cry. He didn't complain. He was just stoic. The man never forgot it and admired Bliss so much for it." Ray never outgrew shyness or stoicism. He preferred to work quietly, behind the scenes, avoiding, when possible, both the limelight and confrontation.

Ray attended Akron's public schools and graduated from South High School in 1925. A newspaper story looking back on his school days reported: "In high school, he was a rather inconspicuous student, studied hard, got good grades."[15] He also ran on the cross-country team. Ray was active in a Boy Scout troop sponsored by St. Paul Episcopal Church. He obtained the rank of Eagle Scout and served as a camp counselor in 1925. Bliss received a strongly positive evaluation at camp, forecasting his future diligence and a passion for detail.

In the following years, tragedy struck the family twice more. Ray's younger brother Norman, born in 1923, died from polio in 1927.[16] Ray's father died in 1932, after being injured in a spectacular explosion that tore apart the Ohio State Office Building, then under construction in Columbus. Ray's mother received a financial settlement of $6,500 from the accident, which he helped her invest in annuities.[17] These tragedies fostered an unusually strong bond between mother and son. "His mother was extremely proud of him," remembered Carlson. "She had lost a husband and two sons, which was kind of tough."[18]

Emilie Bliss gladly kept house for Ray as he pursued his political career. They seemed to enjoy their living arrangement. Emilie cooked and Ray did some of the shopping. "His favorite meal was corn on the cob and dandelion greens," Doerler recalled.

"He would go get these fresh, young dandelions. He might cut them himself. And his mother, being a German cook, she would make the dandelions in bacon grease."[19]

Mrs. Bliss also supported her son's career by participating in the Republican Party. She belonged to the Seventh Ward Women's Republican Club, the Akron Council of Republican Women, and the Ohio chapter of the Federation of Republican Women.[20] In turn, Ray was fiercely loyal to his mother, delaying marriage to his college sweetheart, Ellen Palmer, for almost three decades. Mother and son lived together in the family home until her death in 1956. "I still miss her," Bliss told an interviewer in 1981, a quarter century after her passing.[21]

Bliss's boyhood formed his values and character, but one of the few traits Bliss failed to inherit from his family was wanderlust: they moved constantly in search of opportunity, while he remained attached to one place all his life. Politics wasn't part of his family life either. Like many immigrants, Bliss's relatives were closely tied to where they had come from, including their churches and ethnic associations, rather than the civic life of their new community. "I don't think politics was ever mentioned in our family before Ray," said Carlson.[22]

This all changed when Ray Bliss enrolled at the University of Akron.

Chapter 3

The University of Akron

Ray Bliss never wrote a Top Ten list of the things that mattered most to him in life. But had he done so, his mother, Emilie, and his wife, Ellen, certainly would have shared the number one spot. Not far behind, even ahead of the Republican Party, would have been Bliss's beloved alma mater, the University of Akron. "It is the highlight of my life," Bliss wrote when the university awarded him an honorary doctorate of humane letters in December 1968—just weeks after he had helped Richard Nixon win the White House.[1]

By the time Bliss matriculated in 1925, "Akron U" had become a key institution in the city. It was founded in 1870 by the Ohio Universalist Convention. These Protestants believed that all mankind—even the vilest—would escape eternal damnation. Other Protestants were troubled by such "universalism."[2] But when the Universalists offered to locate their college in Akron if $60,000 could be found, civic boosters set aside theological disputes in favor of having a college in their city. Industrialist John R. Buchtel led the successful fund-raising campaign. The new institution was named Buchtel College after its chief benefactor.[3]

Akron puffed up with pride as construction of a five-story college building began on a hilltop just east of downtown. Horace Greeley came to Akron July 4, 1871, to give the address at the cornerstone laying. He was a Universalist, but also the editor of the *New York Tribune* and a founder of the Republican Party. The phrase Greeley popularized—"Go West, young man"—made him the perfect speaker for a city settled by people who had taken his advice.[4]

Students began arriving on campus in 1872, and the new college prospered until Buchtel's death in 1892. It then began experiencing financial difficulties, and in 1899 a fire destroyed the college buildings. Local business leaders came to the rescue, rebuilding the school's facilities.[5] In 1907—the year Bliss was born—Buchtel College cut its ties with the Universalists. The school had sought a grant from the Carnegie Foundation to build a state-of-the-art chemistry laboratory, but the foundation would not make grants to denominational schools. Buchtel College soon offered a course in rubber chemistry, the first in the nation.[6]

This link with the rubber industry did not, however, end the college's financial woes. So in 1913, President Park R. Kolbe proposed that the city take over the school and operate it as a municipal university, as other Ohio cities did. Later that year, Buchtel College became the Municipal University of Akron. A special tax of one-half mil was levied on property owners to provide a steady source of income for the school, and the mayor appointed a board of directors to manage it. In 1926, the name was shortened to the University of Akron.[7]

When Bliss started classes in September 1925, the university's enrollment was about 1,600 students, divided almost equally between men and women. Most students came from Akron.[8] Bliss took quickly to campus life—although he did not exactly qualify as a serious scholar. He majored in sociology with a minor in political science, having given up law school aspirations because of his poor eyesight. His attendance was spotty and his grades poor. Given his future career, it is ironic that Bliss received a D in American Government, Political Parties, and Political Theory courses.[9]

The hilltop campus introduced Bliss to a bigger world than his immigrant community. As civic boosters had hoped, the campus offered expanded opportunities for the children of the diverse, growing city. The fraternity system attracted Bliss. He pledged Sigma Beta Nu, a local fraternity that later became a chapter of the national fraternity Phi Kappa Tau. "It was a fair local on campus with some fine young men who appeared to provide a real opportunity for someone willing to join and help provide some leadership in building the fraternity on campus," Bliss said later. "It is my belief that I probably would not have achieved that which I have in the American political system without the training I had in my fraternity."[10] Bliss believed that fraternities "furnished a place where you learned to get along with other persons, learned to respect the deeply held convictions of others."[11] Many of Bliss's fraternity brothers became lifelong friends, business associates, and political allies.

In the Roaring Twenties, fraternities were a place where young men had fun. More than fifty years after he pledged in 1926, Bliss still fondly remembered the initiation rites that he endured.[12] He and his fraternity brothers took great pride in how they conducted themselves on campus and how others at the university viewed them. "Every pledge had to learn how to dance," Bliss recalled. "We made arrangements for some of the sorority girls to accompany our pledges to the East Market Gardens where they taught them how to dance. They couldn't be initiated until they learned.... There were a number of formal affairs by fraternities and sororities and some such affairs on campus, so we asked our pledges to have a tuxedo."[13]

The fraternity also emphasized involvement in campus activities, and in this regard, Bliss was a role model. His activity list was lengthy—an athletic letter in cross-country as a freshman, sophomore class treasurer, junior class vice president, Dramatic Club, reporter and editor on the campus newspaper (the *Buchtelite*), and contributor to the student directory. When Bliss became a fraternity leader, he put in long hours and paid close attention to details. "I was a perfectionist," Bliss later recalled. "I tried to make sure our [fraternity] rush was the best. I don't believe you should get involved in something unless you're going to do a topflight job."[14]

For Bliss, however, the most important opportunity on campus came in the person of another student, Ellen Palmer. Palmer actually was going out with another fellow the day that Bliss stopped by the alumni office where she was working. "He [Ray] came in and asked for Miss Fanning, who then taught French," she recalled. "Miss Fanning had classes so he introduced himself, sat down and talked to me for two hours." That first meeting stuck in their memories. "At that time the university was paying me 35 cents an hour," Ellen said. "Ever since Ray has made me contribute to the Alumni Fund because he says I still owe Akron U 70 cents for the time I wasted talking to him."[15]

Ellen Palmer was born September 16, 1909, in Akron. Her father owned a furniture store. Ellen was raised Catholic, the product of a mixed marriage. Both parents were native Ohioans: her mother, Ethel Walsh, was Irish Catholic, and her father, William Palmer, was an English Lutheran. The couple was married in a priest's house because in that era a Catholic and a non-Catholic could not be married in the church.[16] By the time Ray and Ellen were wed in 1959, such restrictions had eased. Yet the difference in religious upbringing was one reason their courtship lasted almost thirty years.

The differences between the couple went beyond their religious backgrounds. Ray was shy and had been raised as an only child after the early deaths of his younger brothers. Ellen was outgoing and the oldest of seven children, five daughters and two sons. While the Bliss family was reserved, the Palmer household overflowed with energy. "Ray wasn't really outwardly affectionate the way you are when you grow up in a big family. I think sometimes he was a little overwhelmed by all of us," said Louise Earley, one of Ellen's sisters. She couldn't put her finger on what attracted her sister and Ray to one another. "I don't know. What attracts you to someone? It can be someone the exact opposite. I think they probably were attracted to each other as persons first. And then maybe there were mutual interests."[17]

One mutual interest was the University of Akron. But in their senior year, campus life took a humiliating turn for Ray and Ellen.

Ray Bliss at five months, with parents Emil and Emilie Bliss, 1908. Emil and Emilie were both born in Germany. (From the Ray C. Bliss Papers. Courtesy of Archival Services, University Libraries, The University of Akron)

Ray Bliss in California, circa 1914. His family relocated in search of opportunity, returning to Akron in 1917. (From the Ray C. Bliss Papers. Courtesy of Archival Services, University Libraries, The University of Akron)

(*top left*) John Bliss Sr., 1921. Originally
Johannes Bluess, he emigrated with his
family from Germany in 1889. (From the
Ray C. Bliss Papers. Courtesy of Archival
Services, University Libraries, The
University of Akron)

(*top right*) Emilie Bliss (far left) and sisters,
circa 1921. Ray was very close to his mother
and her family his entire life. (From the Ray
C. Bliss Papers. Courtesy of Archival
Services, University Libraries, The
University of Akron)

(*bottom right*) Ray Bliss (second from left) and
cousins at Springfield Lake, 1923. Located at
Sawyerwood, a favorite place of Emilie
Bliss. (From the Ray C. Bliss Papers.
Courtesy of Archival Services, University
Libraries, The University of Akron)

Ray Bliss (center) at Boy Scout camp, circa 1924. Bliss was a camp counselor and an Eagle Scout. (From the Ray C. Bliss Papers. Courtesy of Archival Services, University Libraries, The University of Akron)

Ray Bliss (right) and high school friend. Bliss graduated from South High School in 1925. (From the Ray C. Bliss Papers. Courtesy of Archival Services, University Libraries, The University of Akron)

Ellen Palmer, high school yearbook photograph. The future Ellen Bliss graduated from St. Mary's Catholic School in 1925. (From the Ray C. Bliss Papers. Courtesy of Archival Services, University Libraries, The University of Akron)

Ray Bliss (top row, second from left) and his Sigma Beta Nu Fraternity brothers, University of Akron *Tel-Buch*, 1929. (Courtesy of Archival Services, University Libraries, The University of Akron)

Chapter 4

The May Queen Fiasco

When Ray Bliss started at the University of Akron, he had little interest in politics of any kind. But by the time he left, he was an accomplished political operative, adept at winning student elections. "At Akron University, he was quite a playboy, studied little and got poor grades because he found it a bore to attend classes," a newspaper story later said about student Bliss. "Although his scholastic rating was not high, he probably would have graduated cum laude if his record as a campus politician had been considered."[1]

To influence the social life of the University of Akron, the fraternities and sororities joined competing coalitions known as "combines." The combines pooled their resources in campus elections to back an agreed-upon candidate and then share whatever benefits victory brought. Bliss's fraternity, Sigma Beta Nu, and Ellen Palmer's sorority, Theta Phi Alpha, belonged to a combine known as the "Hilltop Party." The rival combine was the "Buktal Party."[2] The Hilltop Party was floundering when Bliss arrived on campus. "The fraternity I joined was, at that time, just a remnant of the political combine headed by Phi Delta Theta, one of the two nationals on campus. The Lone Star, a very old local fraternity, dominated the other political combine. The local I was in, Sigma Beta Nu, had been on campus awhile but wasn't in a power position. . . . We sort of floated along," said Bliss.[3] As he assumed a leadership role in his own fraternity, Bliss began to change the fortunes of the Hilltop Party. "During the time I participated in our political combine, I learned [that] it's organizing your vote, recognizing where it is, knowing who's going to vote that wins. Within a year or two, I was in charge of our political combine. We checked off our members after the campus elections and they were fined if they didn't vote," said Bliss.[4]

Bliss saw to it that the combine spread its influence among student organizations. If a campus club had no members from the Hilltop Party, Bliss ordered several fraternity members to join and try to take over the club. He asked his girlfriend, Ellen Palmer, to join the Democratic Club for just this purpose, even though she came from a Republican background. Interestingly, Bliss had been a member of the Democratic Club before he switched to the Republican Club, where he remained active until he left college.[5]

During his career, Bliss helped elect mayors, governors, and presidents. Yet campus politics stood out in his memory. "I've said to people since, campus politics was faster than downtown politics," said Bliss.[6]

By the spring of 1931, Bliss was a senior and scheduled to graduate. Unofficially, he already had won what amounted to highest honors in his real college major, political organizing. Three out of four class presidents at the university came from the Hilltop Party. There was one more contest Bliss hoped to win before finishing his college career, the election of the campus May Queen.[7]

The campaign for May Queen was more than a simple beauty contest. It was a key part of a major campus event that included elaborate floats and a big dance. "It was very serious, indeed," said University of Akron historian George W. Knepper. "That was really a big deal in those days. They played it straight."[8] The Hilltop Party's candidate was Ellen Palmer, one of four women nominated for the honor.

"Students to Vote Today in Title Race," blared the headline on the front page of the *Buchtelite* on the day of the balloting.[9] Bliss had been at work before Election Day. Not all students could cast their ballots in person. Co-op engineering students who worked off-campus were allowed to vote by mail. The Hilltop Party identified the co-op students eligible to vote and arranged for their ballots to be gathered up and delivered to the office of Professor Hezzelton E. Simmons, a member of a special election committee.

But things did not go as planned. Several days after the election, the Hilltop Party was accused of stuffing the ballot box in the May Queen voting. The *Buchtelite* reported on May 12 that a "Fraternity-Student Council" investigation found that ballots mailed to the co-op engineering students "had been tampered with; in several cases evidence of forged signatures and changed markings had been definitely proven."[10] As a result, Ellen Palmer was disqualified as a May Queen candidate. Bliss and another student, Agnes McGowan (a sorority sister of Ellen Palmer), were "disenfranchised from participating in student elections."

The worst was yet to come. "Early in the investigation, Bliss denied handling of the ballots, but did admit sponsoring the idea of gathering the engineering votes. Later, he admitted to looking at the ballots, but still denied his guilt in changing the markings of the ballots or addressing the envelopes to Professor Simmons. Bliss's handwriting was practically proved identical with that on many of the envelopes addressed to Professor Simmons," the *Buchtelite* reported.[11] The *Akron Beacon Journal* also covered the story on May 12. It quoted Bliss as saying that he would "assume all blame" and that he had explained the situation to university president George F. Zook. Bliss predicted the conversation would absolve the women of guilt.[12] This prediction did not come true.

"Bliss Is Suspended; Eight-Hour Penalty Given to Two Girls" was the front-page headline in the *Buchtelite* several days later.[13] The faculty committee that doled out the punishment made Bliss's suspension indefinite. This meant he would not graduate as scheduled that spring. Ellen Palmer still would be able to graduate because she had nine more credit hours than the 128 required for her education degree, compensating for her eight-hour penalty. Agnes McGowan was a sophomore, so she would have two more years to make up the penalty.

The decision reverberated across campus. Theta Phi Alpha sorority "lifted the pins" of Ellen Palmer and Agnes McGowan. Several Greek organizations withdrew from the Hilltop Party. But other students rallied in support of Palmer and McGowan, with some four hundred students—about a fourth of the student body—signing petitions to that effect. Bliss offered to turn in his fraternity pin to Sigma Beta Nu, but no action was taken.[14]

The suspension must have been a blow to Bliss's parents. His father, Emil, tried to help his son. The senior Bliss sought a meeting with President Zook to discuss the controversy. An attorney and fraternity brother, James Hinton, was retained to represent Bliss. "It is believed that the compromise attitude becoming apparent will result in settling the difficulty satisfactorily to all parties concerned and permit young Bliss to be reinstated so he can graduate next month," the *Akron Beacon Journal* reported.[15] No compromise was achieved, however. Dean Donfred Gardner expelled Bliss from school.

Bliss maintained a lifelong public silence on his personal role in the controversy. In 1981, half a century after the May Queen incident, Bliss still would say little. "Well, we had highly competitive 'combines,' as we called them in those days," Bliss told a reporter. "There was a problem with some absentee ballots we sent out. I was head of a combine, so I walked in and told them I set up the program and I accepted full responsibility for anything that had gone wrong—such as someone marking a ballot that shouldn't have been marked."[16]

Bliss's associates had differing views of his personal involvement in the matter. Alex Arshinkoff, Bliss's protégé, said that Bliss confided to him that other members of the Hilltop Party were responsible for whatever voter fraud occurred, and not Bliss himself: "Ray had nothing to do with this and was really teed off and was yelling at them [the responsible party members]....But Ray was the team captain. He was in charge. These other guys were going to get thrown out of school, so rather than that, Ray took the fall and never ratted on these guys."[17]

The perpetrators of the fraud deeply appreciated Bliss's loyalty and willingness to accept responsibility, traits that would become his trademarks. "He [Bliss] said those fellows were loyal to him all of his life. Many of them were Democrats and switched to Republicans, because Ray took the fall," reported Arshinkoff. One of Bliss's fraternity brothers, Charles Doerler, later confirmed this account to his sister-in-law Madge Doerler. "He said some of the fraternity brothers had forged ballots without Ray's knowledge."[18] An *Akron Beacon Journal* story on the controversy provides support for this view. Bliss told the newspaper "there is something deeper in this than has come out. It may never come out." The story noted that Bliss "smiles enigmatically behind his eye glasses and adds 'my fraternity brothers know what it is; that is why they are standing behind me to a man.'"[19] Many journalists later reported that Bliss privately insisted he was not to blame.[20]

Others had a different perspective. In 1940, a reporter wrote: "Today, though slightly sensitive when the affair is mentioned, Bliss is inclined to view it with considerable amusement. He swears he was not guilty of the charge for which he was expelled, but demurely admits sponsoring other activities along the same line."[21] Some of Bliss's associates had a similar view. Journalist Clyde Mann, a close friend of Bliss, believed Bliss played at least some role in the ballot irregularities. "He never denied it," said Mann. "But he learned from the situation. It had a big impact on Ray. Personal honesty became his touchstone."[22] Still another associate believed that Bliss had been overzealous on behalf of electing his girlfriend as May Queen.[23]

Even if Bliss was culpable, expulsion just as he was about to graduate was harsh punishment. It was in keeping, however, with the "tight ship" that Dean Gardner and other administrators ran at the university. They thought it was their job to enforce moral and ethical behavior as they saw it.[24] According to Arshinkoff, Bliss believed that there was more to his suspension than a stern lesson in ethics. The administrators, he felt, resented the success he had achieved as the campus political leader. By suspending him, the administrators sent a clear signal that they, and not any student, ran campus social life.[25]

Evidence of such resentment appears in the *Buchtelite* account of the controversy, where Bliss was referred to as the "dictator" of the Hilltop Party. The student council president hinted darkly, "This is a serious case. It is not just a petty case of trying to win an election. At least one of those involved has been guilty of such things before, and it is the council's duty to have a part in determining the punishment for those guilty."[26]

The May Queen fiasco brought Bliss's days as a campus politician to an unpleasant end. He was hanging around the fraternity house a few days after being thrown out of school when a friend suggested that he get involved in local Republican politics. His campus activities had not gone unnoticed in the community.[27] Bliss decided to give that idea a try.

Chapter 5

Ray C. Bliss Meets James A. Corey

When Ray Bliss became involved in local politics, he met James A. Corey, the long-serving chairman of the Republican Party, described as "one of the most powerful political figures in Summit County's history."[1]

"Jim Corey had a natural instinct for politics," Bliss remembered half a century later. "He took me under his wing."[2] Although they had different personalities—Corey outgoing and Bliss shy—a close bond developed between the "canny old war-horse" and the "budding young politico."[3] Corey, a cigar-smoking bachelor, taught Bliss the basics of politics the way fathers teach their sons how to play sports. "Corey viewed Ray as a son," said Madge Doerler. "He never raised his voice to Ray and gave him a great deal of freedom."[4]

Corey also provided a philosophy that would guide Bliss's career: good government wins elections; good government comes through good candidates; work ceaselessly to recruit and train good candidates. Most important of all, keep your word—never break a promise.[5] "Just remember one thing about politics," Bliss later told a reporter. "The only thing you have in politics is your word. When your word is not good, you've lost the bargaining power you have. I've never broken my word in my life, intentionally."[6] Bliss's commitment to keeping his word became legendary, to the extent that some journalists later described it as a "fetish." Another noted that such a principle was often problematic for Bliss: "A politician who concedes in advance that he won't squawk, no matter what the outcome, hands his opponents a massive advantage."[7] But long after his death, Bliss's associates remembered his honesty and integrity above all else.[8]

Corey was of Irish-German ancestry and was born in Massillon, Ohio, in 1877. After serving in the Spanish-American War, Corey arrived in Akron in 1902, and eventually found politics to be his calling. He was appointed a Summit County deputy sheriff in 1910, elected sheriff in 1914, and then reelected in 1916. Corey became chairman of the Summit County Republican Party in 1918 and served until his death in 1941.[9]

Corey got his political training on the job, drawing on a rich legacy of Republican politics in Ohio. Bliss became both an heir and a contributor to this legacy. Ohio Republicans dominated national politics between the Civil War and the Great Depression. Only two Democrats won the White House in this era, while seven presidents had Buckeye State roots.[10]

A watershed election occurred in 1896, when Republican William McKinley defeated William Jennings Bryan, the candidate of both the Democratic and the Populist parties.[11] This campaign was one of the "most fiery" in Akron's history, with "torchlight parades and tumultuous mass meetings" and "star spellbinding speakers" on both sides.[12] The Republicans won Summit County, in part because their message appealed to urban voters—like Bliss's family of immigrants. But there was also a strong local connection: McKinley was from nearby Canton; his campaign manager, Mark Hanna, was from Cleveland; and Hanna's right-hand man, Charles Dick, was from Akron.

As chairman of the Republican National Committee, businessman Mark Hanna applied business techniques to raising funds and running the campaign. His successors, including Bliss, built on this foundation,[13] although Bliss was never tied to any particular candidate, the way Hanna was to McKinley. As secretary of the Republican National Committee, attorney Charles Dick carried out Hanna's plans.[14] He was a master of the nuts and bolts of campaigns in his generation, much as Bliss was in his day.

With Hanna's and Dick's help, President McKinley was reelected in 1900. McKinley was not able to enjoy this achievement for long: he was assassinated on September 6, 1901. Hanna lived only a little longer, dying of typhoid fever in 1904, while serving in the US Senate. Dick served in the US House of Representatives and the Senate until 1911 and remained a respected party leader until his death in 1945.[15]

When Bliss was born in 1907, Republicans still controlled national politics. Vice President Theodore Roosevelt had succeeded McKinley in the White House, and another Ohio Republican, William Howard Taft, won the presidency in 1908. But in 1912, former president Roosevelt challenged President Taft for the GOP presidential nomination. When the challenge failed, Roosevelt launched the Bull Moose Party. The Roosevelt-Taft battle split the Republican vote, allowing Democrat Woodrow Wilson to capture the White House.[16]

It was against this backdrop that Jim Corey took over as chairman of the Summit County Republican Party in 1918. The local party was controlled behind the scenes by a triumvirate of leaders known as the "Knight-Sparks-Pardee machine."[17] C. L. Knight, publisher of the *Akron Beacon Journal*, promoted Republican politics with his hard-edged editorials, characterized as "concentrated thunder, with biblical overtones." C. Nelson Sparks was a former postmaster who organized veterans, a potent voting bloc. William E. Pardee, an appeals court judge, was the party's link to the legal community.

C. L. Knight sought out Corey to be local GOP chairman. "Knight told Corey to run the committee until he told him to quit," said the toastmaster at a 1940 dinner honoring Corey. "The years passed. C. L. died but Corey is still waiting."[18]

In Corey's day, newspaper publishers frequently combined journalism and politics. Mark Hanna had owned a newspaper in Cleveland, and Democrat James Cox, editor and publisher of the *Dayton Daily News*, served three terms as Ohio governor. In the only presidential election ever held between two Ohio newspapermen, Cox lost in a landslide to Republican Warren Harding, editor and publisher of the *Marion Star*, in 1920.[19]

C. L. Knight and Jim Corey, not surprisingly, had common enemies. One of them was the Ku Klux Klan. Beginning in 1921, Akron had become a center of Klan activity, like many industrial cities in the Midwest. This pernicious secret society was suspicious of "outsiders," including Catholics, Jews, foreigners, and blacks. They marched in full white-robed regalia on the streets of Akron and made unannounced appearances at schools and churches, presenting the principal or minister with a Bible and an American flag.[20] The Klan became a potent force in local politics. "Apparently a number of public officials or would-be public officials joined the Klan as a way of garnering votes," reported historian George Knepper. "They joined the Klan the same way they joined the Odd Fellows, Elks, or the Moose—if you wanted to be elected, you became a Klan member."[21]

Knight expressed his opposition to the Klan through newspaper editorials, but Corey had to be more creative. He wanted to take on the Klan without hurting the Republican Party. An idea came to him one night while playing pinochle at the Odd Fellows Temple.[22] The Odd Fellows was an example of a benign secret society. Like the Klan, it had a commanding presence in Akron's parades, with members wearing military-style uniforms with plumed hats and carrying swords. But unlike the Klan, the Odd Fellows were dedicated to charity. Their motto was "Friendship, Love, and Truth"; their name came from the fact that these values were uncommon—hence "odd."[23]

That night, another Odd Fellow surprised Corey by revealing that he was a Klansman and asked the party chief to join. Bliss later told Alex Arshinkoff what happened next. Corey agreed to join the Klan, and after being sworn in, attended a huge Klan rally at the fairgrounds in Akron. Corey had a big birthmark on his face that made him easily identifiable. Corey took his hood off and marched around so that the thousands gathered could get a good look at him. Corey then secretly gathered the Klansmen who had sworn him in behind the Odd Fellows Temple and told them: "This is the most disgusting thing I ever had to do in my life." He threw off his Klan robes, poured gasoline on them, and burned them. Corey had done what he set out to do: he had inoculated himself against attacks from Klan leaders. "What do you mean, get Corey? He's one of us," other members would say when Corey was criticized; "We saw him at the Klan rally."[24]

By the late 1920s, the Klan had faded in Akron as quickly as it had arisen. But some of the attitudes tapped by the Klan were still prevalent. Anti-Catholicism was part of the 1928 presidential campaign, when the Democrats nominated the first Catholic presidential candidate, Governor Al Smith of New York. Smith lost to Republican Herbert Hoover in Akron as well as nationally.[25]

When Bliss started working for the Republican Party, however, it was preoccupied with local politics.

Chapter 6

First Campaign Lessons

Ray Bliss's first real-world campaign experience was working with James Corey in the 1931 Akron mayoral election. "Corey was an astute politician," Bliss later recalled, "and he taught me much in that campaign."[1]

Beset with financial woes from the Great Depression, Akron's Democratic mayor, G. Lloyd Weil, decided not to seek reelection. The opening at City Hall divided the Knight-Sparks-Pardee machine. Sparks decided to run for mayor himself, with an endorsement from Knight's *Akron Beacon Journal*. Pardee, Corey, and the local GOP organization supported E. L. Marting, a city councilman.[2]

Bliss's first job was campaign gofer. He pitched in enthusiastically. Corey soon discovered that the former master of campus politics had more skills than most party veterans. Bliss ended up as assistant campaign manager.[3]

Marting narrowly defeated Sparks in a three-way nonpartisan primary, but did not get a majority. That put the two Republicans in a runoff election. But the Democrats were not completely left out: J. Earl Cox qualified for the general election ballot by petition, setting up a three-way contest. A former judge, Cox made a special appeal to an emerging force in Akron politics—organized labor.[4] The general election battle was intense. Sparks ran against Corey and the GOP "bosses." To counter Sparks's support among veterans and Cox's appeals to labor, Corey sought Democratic support for Marting. Sparks was elected mayor.[5]

Chairman Corey and Mayor Sparks were still at odds two years later. In the 1933 Akron mayoral race, it was two Democrats, J. Earl Cox and former mayor I. S. Myers, who qualified for the general election ballot by finishing one-two in the nonpartisan primary. After coming in third, Sparks failed to get on the ballot by petition.[6] The battle between Democrats Cox and Myers was as bitter as the previous contest between Republicans Marting and Sparks two years before. Corey and Bliss worked behind the scenes for Myers, who won a huge and unexpected victory. Perhaps in appreciation for this help, the new mayor appointed Corey's young assistant to the Akron zoning board.[7]

Bliss learned lifelong lessons in these campaigns, but the political world was changing dramatically. In 1932, Democrat Franklin Delano Roosevelt won the White House over President Herbert Hoover.[8] Locally, Judge Pardee was defeated for reelection in 1932, and, like former mayor Sparks, his political influence declined. The change in local Republican politics was complete with the death of C. L. Knight of cancer in 1933.[9]

John S. Knight succeeded his father as publisher and editor of the *Akron Beacon Journal*. At first, the younger Knight had his hands full with financial problems caused by the Great Depression, but he soon turned the *Akron Beacon Journal* into a profitable and respected publication. "Jack" Knight was on the leading edge of innovations in the newspaper business, paralleling the managerial revolution in industry.

Under the new editor, the *Akron Beacon Journal* was not enmeshed in Republican politics. Knight favored making independent judgments about news and opinion. This approach allowed the newspaper to be a trusted, nonpartisan source of information for voters. When it became the only Akron newspaper in 1938, Knight told his editors: "We are now solely responsible for printing and distributing information in this city, and that, gentlemen, is sobering."[10]

Years later, Knight would tell Alex Arshinkoff a story of how independent journalism and party politics did not easily mix. Knight had been appointed to his late father's seat on the Summit County Republican Executive Committee in 1933. As was his custom, Corey offered a resolution to endorse candidates in the primary. The *Akron Beacon Journal*'s new editor wanted to change things and asked for the floor. "Mr. Chairman, I'd like to speak out against endorsing. It stifles the government. You've got to have participation," Knight said in what others told him was an "eloquent speech." After he finished, Corey stood up.

"Mr. Knight, have you finished?" he asked.

"Yes, sir, Mr. Chairman," Knight replied.

"Is there anything else you would like to add?" Corey asked again.

"No, I think I've covered it thoroughly," said Knight.

Then Corey explained how things worked. "Young man, let's get one thing straight. You run the *Akron Beacon Journal*. I run the Republican Party. I move we endorse the candidates," said Corey. The motion to endorse carried. Although Knight retained his Republican sympathies and the affection of many Republicans, he soon resigned from party leadership.[11]

Young Bliss watched closely what was happening at the *Akron Beacon Journal*. He began developing his own approach for dealing with a politically independent press. "I knew Jack Knight and respected him. He respected me. I never got so close socially [to an editor] that I couldn't say 'no' and have him respect it," Bliss later told Arshinkoff.[12]

Bliss developed a similar approach with political reporters. He cultivated relationships with those he respected and would socialize with them on occasion. For Bliss, these contacts were a two-way street. He would help reporters with their stories, but seldom agreed to be quoted. In return, he wanted to know what they knew about politics. He was adept at getting his perspective across, but was also open to hearing other points of view. The key for Bliss was trust: he told reporters the truth, as he saw it, and he expected them to be accurate and fair in their stories. Bliss later told a political associate that "good ink is the lifeblood of politics."[13]

Chapter 7

Climbing the Political Ladder

Ray Bliss had a short apprenticeship in real-world campaigning. He fast became a trusted Republican operative and quickly climbed the local political ladder. Following the 1931 mayoral campaign, Bliss organized a Summit County Young Republican Club, and he ran its members for precinct committee posts in 1932. Twenty-five of his thirty-two candidates won, and Bliss was one of them, defeating an incumbent. He was also chosen as a delegate to the 1932 Ohio Republican Convention. These early successes became a foundation of Bliss's career: he served as a local precinct committeeman and was a regular participant in state conventions until he retired in 1978.[1]

In 1932, Bliss became chairman of the "David S. Ingalls for Governor First Voters Committee" in Summit County. Ingalls won the Republican primary against Clarence Brown Sr., a rising Republican star. Then in the fall campaign, Bliss served as an assistant to the campaign manager for the GOP ticket in Summit County. Although incumbent Democratic governor George White was reelected, Ingalls carried Summit County—no mean feat in a strong Democratic year.[2]

In 1933, Bliss was elected vice chairman of the Summit County Republican Central Committee (a large group made up of elected men and women from every precinct in the county). Later that year, Bliss was given a high-profile job: chairman of the annual summer GOP picnic. Equal parts social event, fundraiser, and campaign rally, the picnic attracted tens of thousands of participants.[3]

In 1934, Bliss managed his first campaign. A scandal involving the sheriff gave the Republicans a chance to take over county government. Bliss was assigned the tough job of running the campaign against incumbent Democratic auditor, J. C. Mung, who was untainted by the scandal. On election night, Republican James T. Flower led the ticket, winning the sheriff's office, and the GOP also won the prosecutor, county commissioner, clerk of courts, and coroner races—but not the auditor's. Bliss's close friends long kidded him about losing his maiden campaign.[4]

This defeat was not held against Bliss. Shortly afterward, he was recommended for a seat on the Summit County Board of Elections, a highly prized political post. Board members—two Democrats and two Republicans—were charged with insuring that elections were conducted honestly as well as protecting their parties' interests.

The recommendation of Bliss came from a sitting Republican board member, Wade DeWoody, who explained that the job took too much time away from his law practice. He noted that Bliss had "devoted great effort to Republican activities in recent years, with no remuneration, and felt he [Bliss] should be rewarded."[5] The notion that such a young man—Bliss was just twenty-six—was ready for such an important post was controversial among party officials, but Bliss got the job and began serving in 1935. It was his first paid political position, with a salary of $3,372 a year. He remained on the Summit County Board of Elections until he retired in 1978.

One reason for Bliss's quick rise was his intense attention to details in party operations. "He was kind of a stern person," remembered Madge Doerler, who got a job from Bliss at the board of elections in 1935.[6] Party dinners had to be run on time. He wanted to know how high the risers were at the head table—to make sure the speaker could be seen from the floor. He wanted to know how many almonds would be in the green beans. He wanted the servers to bring the cream with the coffee, not after the coffee had been served.

While Bliss was a stickler for details, there was a certain untidiness in his personal life that resulted from a habit he had picked up from Corey—cigar smoking. "Oh, God, he smoked those awful cigars....I was the first one in the office in the morning and I had to open that rolltop desk and here would be the ashtrays with these awful, awful cigar butts in there," Doerler reported. The cigar butts would accumulate as Bliss burned the midnight oil. He worked standing up, pacing back and forth across his office, and often dropping ashes on his clothes and the carpet. Bliss later switched to cigarettes. Doerler remembered a particularly tense election night when the chain-smoking Bliss had seven cigarettes lit at the same time.[7]

Bliss took some time off from politics to make some money to help his mother out. In 1933, during the same week that President Franklin Delano Roosevelt declared a national bank holiday and closed all the banks, Bliss bucked the economic tide and formed a debt collection agency with Kenneth Wells, a fraternity brother. Bliss got out of the debt collection business in 1937, partly because it was not very successful, and partly because he and Wells had different habits. "Ray got to work at 11 A.M. and he would work until 2 A.M. Well, Kenny wanted him in at 8 A.M. to work on the details of the business," reported Alex Arshinkoff.[8] A newspaper story of the era corroborated this account of Bliss's habits: "As a politician, Bliss lives a politician's life. His working hours are from 11 am to 11 pm.... His time at the board of elections is divided between board affairs and politics."[9]

In 1935, Bliss organized the Federation of Republican Clubs, an alliance of auxiliary groups across Summit County. This innovation was a source of volunteers for the local party—and of future Bliss supporters.[10] Bliss soon introduced another innovation: public opinion polling to gauge support for local candidates. Bliss began the practice in 1935, the same year George H. Gallup founded the Gallup Poll. Gallup had successfully used surveys on behalf of an Iowa Republican candidate in 1932.[11]

Bliss's polls were a variant of Gallup's approach.[12] After poring over results of a previous election, Bliss picked twelve precincts with voting patterns that appeared to be microcosms of the entire city or county. This was tedious work. He did the calculations by hand and they took hours to complete. When he had found his key precincts, Bliss drafted a mock ballot, using the same language the voters would see on election day. He then sent party workers (often fraternity brothers at the University of Akron) door to door in the key precincts with locked ballot boxes. Residents were asked to fill out the mock ballots and deposit them in the ballot boxes. Bliss didn't use the telephone. Too many people, particularly those of modest income, did not have telephones.

No one but Bliss knew the identity of all twelve precincts. He was the only person with keys to open the locked ballot boxes. When the workers returned from their door-to-door canvassing, he would unlock the ballot boxes, tabulate the results, and ponder what they meant for the candidates he was backing.

Bliss used polling to good effect in the 1935 Akron mayoral race. Eager to win back City Hall, the Republican organization backed businessman Lee D. Schroy. "Ten days before the primary election when everyone else was confident that Schroy was way ahead," Bliss later recounted, "I had a poll taken and it showed him losing by 2,000 or 3,000 votes. We redoubled our efforts. We called in the election workers and told them what the situation was and what additional work would have to be done."[13] Schroy won the primary by a narrow margin and then prevailed over the Democratic candidate in the general election.[14]

Bliss's political success brought him a measure of vindication from his alma mater. In September 1934, his fraternity at the University of Akron elected him president of its alumni group and feted him at a banquet. His fraternity brothers had not forgotten him after the May Queen fiasco.[15] Perhaps because of his growing prominence in local politics, the University of Akron quietly awarded Bliss his bachelor's degree in June 1935.[16]

In 1936, Bliss took another step up the political ladder. He was appointed secretary of the Summit County Republican Executive Committee (a small group that managed party operations). He also attended his first of many Republican National Conventions. The GOP met in Cleveland, Ohio, and nominated Governor Alfred Landon of Kansas for president.[17]

But the Democrats were on the move across the country. President Franklin Delano Roosevelt won a second term in the White House in 1936, burying Landon in a landslide.[18] Bliss anticipated the bad news before it arrived. Like the new Gallup Poll at the national level, his local survey results were more accurate than the well-known *Literary Digest* poll, which showed Landon carrying Summit County.

Madge Doerler worked with Bliss on the Landon campaign and remembers how badly she felt after the election loss. Bliss tried to cheer her up. "I wept and wept when we lost and he was so sympathetic. He said, 'Well, you know, we can't win them all,'" she recalled.[19]

Chapter 8

The Test Tube City

Being right about the 1936 election gave Ray Bliss little satisfaction. The Roosevelt landslide signaled that a new political era had begun, and Akron was at its center. After the election, labor unions flexed their muscles, seeking to extend economic gains into political victories. Akron already had emerged as a "test tube" city for innovations in labor-management relations. In the 1937 mayor's race, Akron became a test tube for innovations in union politics.[1]

By the mid-1930s, Akron had become one of the nation's most heavily unionized cities. The United Rubber Workers (URW) was an important part of this development. The three largest tire companies—Goodyear, Firestone, and B. F. Goodrich—employed more than 30,000 workers. By 1934, as the Great Depression deepened, 85 percent were URW members.[2] The URW was a new kind of union, affiliated with the Congress of Industrial Organizations (CIO). The CIO sought to represent unskilled and semiskilled workers who mined coal, forged steel, made tires, and assembled automobiles.

Previous efforts to organize such workers in Akron had been largely unsuccessful, but the situation changed when President Roosevelt signed the National Labor Relations Act in 1935. Soon Akron workers walked out of their plants, picketed factory gates, and staged "sit-down" strikes, demanding that management recognize the URW.[3] A pivotal strike occurred at Goodyear in 1936, "a turning point in the labor history in the 1930s."[4] The company announced plans to lay off three-quarters of its employees, cut wages, and require longer hours for the remaining workers. A fact-finding board appointed by Secretary of Labor Frances Perkins condemned the company's approach and recommended that it halt its plans. Goodyear went ahead with its plan and the URW went on strike.[5]

The strike attracted national attention. John L. Lewis, head of the CIO, came to rally the rubber workers, and five leading industrial union organizers were sent to Akron. At one point, 13,800 workers were idled at Goodyear and 500 pickets clustered at the plant gates.[6] The mood in Akron grew ugly. Former mayor C. Nelson Sparks went on the radio, denouncing "radicals and communists." He organized a "Law and Order League" and promised to lead armed citizens against the strike. The call for vigilante action was too much for John S. Knight of the *Akron Beacon Journal,* who rushed out a front-page editorial headlined "No Room for Vigilantes." It declared that Sparks's outburst was "an invitation to rioting and violence."[7]

Sheriff James Flower, a Republican, declined to break up the strike. He said that if he tried, "East Market Street [where Goodyear was located] will run red with blood."[8] The standoff ended after five weeks, on March 20, 1936. The URW did not get a written contract, but it got enough concessions to declare a major victory. Another strike occurred at Firestone on March 3, 1937, idling 10,600 workers. It ended quickly after the US Supreme Court ruled that the National Labor Relations Act was constitutional. The URW won a full contract with the company.[9]

In 1937, CIO leaders proposed a unified effort to win local elections across the country. It would be led by Labor's Non-Partisan League, the political arm of the CIO, which had helped reelect President Roosevelt in 1936.[10] A first step was to take over local Democratic parties. Labor activists blamed these organizations for failing to translate Roosevelt's popularity into local victories. Also, some local Democrats opposed the agenda of organized labor, while some union leaders dreamed of creating a separate "labor" party to replace the Democrats. Campaigns were launched in New York, Pittsburgh, and Detroit, but Akron was the top priority.[11] Besides Akron's local labor strength, there were reasons to believe that Akronites would welcome a change at City Hall. Under the Republican mayor, Lee Schroy, the city had been unimaginative about solving the problems of an industrial boomtown. Akron was among the most dilapidated cities in the country.[12]

Labor's first step was to recruit a mayoral candidate with the right credentials. The choice was Garnet L. Patterson, a local attorney for the URW. In 1935, Patterson had been appointed to the National Labor Relations Board by President Roosevelt.

When a vacancy arose for Akron municipal judge in 1936, union leaders bypassed the local Democratic Party and convinced Ohio's Democratic governor, Martin L. Davey, to appoint Patterson to the post. As a local judge, Patterson had more credibility to run for Akron mayor.[13]

The unions' effort bore fruit in the Democratic primary. Patterson defeated Summit County commissioner Henry Bixler for the mayoral nomination. During the primary, Patterson emphasized his ties to President Roosevelt and promised to bring "New Deal democracy" to City Hall. He called for better housing and expanded recreational facilities, a message with broad appeal.[14]

Akron's business leaders were not about to turn City Hall over to the unions without a fight. Despite labor's gains, they had some prospects for success. Akron's rubber workers embraced the economic gains that the URW had won for them, but most were not labor radicals. People who had come to Akron in search of opportunity were much more likely to be active church members than political activists.[15]

The campaign would demand energetic management. Business leaders turned to Bliss, who was not quite thirty. Alex Arshinkoff recalled Bliss's account of how it happened. The local business leaders met at the exclusive City Club in downtown Akron. Representatives of the four major rubber companies attended. They wanted to know what to expect in the upcoming mayoral campaign. Bliss bluntly told them: "Look, the rubber workers...if we don't stop them in this race, they are taking over city government...the Democratic Party would be dominated by the unions." Later the same day, the business leaders told Bliss they would buy as much broadcast time on Akron radio as the campaign needed. They had collected $75,000 among themselves to keep Mayor Schroy in office, an unheard of sum for an Akron mayoral race. "As long as you are responsible for the money, we'll give it to you," the business leaders said. "You've got to give us your word that you will be treasurer of the funds. We trust you."[16]

Chapter 9

The 1937 Akron Mayoral Campaign

Managing the 1937 mayoral campaign consumed Ray Bliss's life. He moved out of his mother's house in south Akron and into a suite of rooms at the Mayflower Hotel downtown. Bliss worked with Loren Poe, a public relations expert, to plan the campaign. Relying in part on Bliss's polling, they decided to draw a sharp distinction between Mayor Schroy and Judge Patterson. This would drive up turnout among Republican voters and split off conservative Democrats—even some union members—for their candidate.[1] The Republicans touted Mayor Schroy as the home-town candidate who wanted to save Akron citizens from a "carpetbagger," Democrat Patterson, who was allied with sinister outside forces. The basis for the "carpetbag-ger" charge was that Patterson had left Akron to serve on the National Labor Relations Board. The most sinister of the outside forces was communism.

There was a factual basis for the "red-baiting" charges against Patterson. In the 1930s, communist infiltration of labor unions was real, as prominent CIO leaders found help from communists essential to organizing efforts.[2] James Keller, a local Communist Party secretary, had endorsed Patterson—and Patterson had rejected the endorsement. The bigger question was whether Earl Browder, national secretary of the Communist Party, would endorse Patterson during an upcoming speech in Akron. Bliss had heard about the speech and arranged to have it broadcast over a local radio station.[3] Although Browder did not endorse Patterson in the speech, Bliss got what he wanted.

Browder told an interviewer: "On the whole we don't make it a policy to endorse individual candidates but we firmly stand behind the activities of Labor's Non-Partisan League."[4] Browder also praised John Lewis and the CIO, and endorsed Roosevelt's New Deal policies. Akron residents learned that a national Communist Party leader had allied himself with the allies of the Democratic candidate for mayor.

Bliss and the Republicans kept the Communist Party issue alive throughout the mayoral campaign. When the occasion arose, Schroy asked Patterson, "Why has your candidacy been endorsed by the Communist Party?" Patterson deflected the question, declaring that the Communists were "instruments of the Republican Party and the Republican Party contributed to the Communists to create false issues."[5]

Although he had campaigned on his close ties to the popular President Roosevelt in the Democratic primary, Patterson became cautious after winning the nomination. He was afraid of alienating voters not associated with labor. Union leaders assured him that votes from their members would be enough to elect him. Soon Patterson's speeches blasted the "closed," "undemocratic," and "big-business-controlled" Republican administration at City Hall. Labor leaders frequently appeared at Patterson rallies and on occasion even upstaged him. This made union power—not the Republican incumbent, Mayor Schroy—the principal issue in the campaign, thus playing into Bliss's hands.[6]

In contrast, Bliss deployed an aggressive multifront campaign on behalf of Schroy. The campaign sent direct mail to all Akron voters, canvassed door to door, put up yard signs, bought newspaper ads, and deployed billboards—450 at one time. The billboards made an easy target for vandals who splashed them with paint. Republican workers implored Bliss to clean the billboards up. Maybe, Bliss thought, it would be better to leave the signs the way they were. "Ray said, 'Let it go. Psychologically this will turn on them and show that they are dirty campaigners. Let it go. Let it go. People like fair play,'" reported Alex Arshinkoff.[7]

The Republicans even reached out directly to the rubber workers who were supposed to be backing Patterson. Union leaders were livid when an advertisement for Schroy, with the Republican candidate's picture, turned up in the program for the United Rubber Workers' convention in Akron. URW president Sherman H. Dalrymple explained that the ad had been solicited to pay for the entertainment. It was a taste of things to come.[8]

Splitting the Democratic vote was part of Bliss's strategy. Ohio's Democratic governor, Martin Davey, became an unlikely ally. After all, he had appointed Patterson as Akron municipal judge. But Davey was an anti–New Deal Democrat, fervently defending states' rights against federal programs. He had also infuriated labor when, in 1937, he sent the Ohio National Guard to break the "Little Steel" strike in Youngstown.

According to Arshinkoff, Loren Poe brought Bliss and Governor Davey together at the Ohio Statehouse in September 1937. "I want to help you," Davey told his visitor from Akron. "Well, governor," Bliss replied. "Get one thing clear. You are up for election next year and I'm going to support [the Republican]. I am out to defeat you…except we both don't want to see the unions take over the Democratic Party." Davey said he understood. They shook hands and the governor asked Bliss if he needed money for the campaign. When Bliss declined, Davey had another idea. "Well, let me spread the word among my people and I'll send a couple of my boys up to help you," he said. Bliss soon had a surprise introduction to the "helpers" Davey sent to Akron. Bliss was returning from dinner when he was approached by two men, who began to reach inside their coats. "Holy…. They are going to shoot us," Bliss thought. "They are going to kill us right here."

They were pulling out identification cards, not guns. They showed Bliss credentials identifying them as representatives of the state liquor department and other government agencies. They told Bliss they had been sent by Governor Davey to help with the campaign.

"What can we do for you?" they asked.

"What about your state jobs?" Bliss wanted to know.

"Helping you is our state job," they replied.

Bliss had an idea. Bars around the tire factories were plastered with Patterson signs. Bliss knew first-hand what happened to bar owners who refused to display signs promoting Patterson. Bliss frequented the LaFrance Bar near his neighborhood in south Akron. The owner wouldn't go along with the Patterson campaign and found his bar picketed by union members. Bliss asked Governor Davey's men if they could help with the signs in the bars. The two men began visiting Akron bars that featured signs promoting Patterson for mayor. The "inspectors" complained that the bars were dirty and threatened to close them. When the bar owners asked what they could do to prevent getting shut down, the inspectors told them to take down the Patterson signs.[9]

Patterson charged that the Schroy administration had persuaded Davey to send in eighteen liquor control agents to work for the mayor's reelection. "What are these men doing? Are they visiting liquor permit holders to see that they are obeying the law? They are not. They are visiting these permit holders and telling them, 'You vote for the reelection of this administration or else.' And then, if that is not clear enough, they explain that the 'or else' means the permit holder will be forced to close his business because if he doesn't play their dirty game, he won't get his permit back," Patterson said.[10]

In a speech to an Akron business group, Governor Davey assailed the CIO and the New Deal, in effect endorsing Republican Schroy. More forceful statements came from Democrat Henry Bixler, who had lost to Patterson in the primary. Bixler bitterly criticized the Non-Partisan League, lashing out at "political carpetbaggers who are hammering at Akron's doors" and "political weasels who seek to tear down our democratic form of government."[11] In response, Patterson charged that "hobgoblins" were trying to instigate a campaign of fear against him. He singled out Loren Poe and listed Bliss among the assistant hobgoblins "lurking behind the bushes flashing their jack-o-lanterns to scare the voters passing by."[12]

The 1937 mayoral race provided a test of John S. Knight's commitment to independent journalism at the *Akron Beacon Journal*. Overall, the news coverage of the campaign was factual and even-handed. An editorial endorsement of Republican Schroy was not guaranteed, and when the newspaper eventually backed Schroy for mayor, it was in a balanced editorial.[13] It had good words for Judge Patterson's record and was critical of Mayor Schroy's administration. But the editorial also worried about organized labor taking over Akron—the same fear raised by Bliss. It referred to Patterson as "John L. Lewis: Candidate for Mayor." "Our final judgment," the editorial said, "is that Lawyer Patterson has failed utterly to make a case and that the welfare of Akron will best be served by the reelection of Mayor Lee D. Schroy."

Even with the newspaper endorsement, Bliss took nothing for granted. According to Arshinkoff, Bliss had one more card to play before election day.[14] It was a variation on a strategy employed by Mark Hanna and Charles Dick in the 1896 presidential campaign, in which factory owners were asked to close their plants the day before the election and invite the workers to come in with their wives. The owners then told them that the factories would stay closed if the Democratic candidate won the election. The workers and wives got the message.

Bliss adapted this ploy to take advantage of the fact that every year the rubber factories shut down for a week or so for cleaning, usually in the summer. Bliss told the factory owners to close instead during the first week of November, when Akron would vote for mayor. On the Friday before the election, Bliss took Mayor Schroy to a road leading out of Akron to watch a long line of cars filled with rubber workers and their families leaving town to enjoy the week off. "This ought to just be the margin to get you elected," Bliss told Schroy.

On November 2, Akron experienced a "history-making election."[15] With a record-breaking turnout of more than 80,000 voters, the Republicans received 55 percent of the ballots for mayor and beat the labor-backed Democrats in nine of thirteen council races. "Organized labor has lost the fiercest battle it ever waged to become a political power in Akron," the *Akron Beacon Journal* reported.[16] Careful analysis of the election results found that Bliss had assembled a coalition of Republicans, conservative Democrats, and better-off workers, including homeowners. In contrast, Patterson won the support of staunch union members, the poor, and the unemployed.[17]

The numbers also revealed the effectiveness of the Republican organization. When Bliss first entered politics in 1931, the GOP could muster barely 15,000 voters for its favored mayoral candidate, and even in Mayor Schroy's 1935 victory, the party had polled fewer than 27,000 voters. In contrast, in 1937 the Republican received some 44,000 ballots, more than twice the 1931 total and 60 percent higher than in 1935. Patterson received about the same number of votes as he had in the 1937 Democratic primary—some 36,000.

Labor leaders learned a lesson. They could not win elections if voters believed that the Democratic Party represented only the interests of organized labor, particularly the more radical leaders. The dream of a "labor" party replacing the Democrats faded away.

The Republican victory elevated Bliss's status as a top operative among Republicans and the business community. "Ray made his bones in the 1937 campaign," said Arshinkoff.[18]

Chapter 10

A Quest for Party Unity

The 1937 Akron mayoral campaign was part of a broader improvement in Republican fortunes. The GOP made a comeback across the nation in the 1938 midterm elections. Ohio led the way, with John W. Bricker elected governor and Robert A. Taft, the son of President William Howard Taft, elected US senator.[1]

At home, Chairman Corey, now in his sixties, was gradually turning over responsibilities to his talented assistant. Bliss was getting a reputation as a man who could get things done. "He was the big wheel in the family," said Rose Carlson, Bliss's cousin.[2] This included helping family, friends, and University of Akron students find jobs in party and government offices. One contemporary writer noted: "Bliss probably knows more important politicians in Columbus than any other Akron man. While others may get credit for it, it is usually Bliss who arranges the appointments with the governor."[3]

Conflict over patronage jobs soon divided Summit County Republicans. While Corey deferred to elected Republicans on these matters, Bliss took a different approach. He wanted the party to be involved in patronage decisions so there would be loyalty to the organization and not to individual officeholders. Bliss wanted Republicans united to help all their candidates win. According to Madge Doerler, "Ray rewarded loyalty by getting his supporters jobs—and got loyalty in return."[4]

Bliss understood that cooperation and compromise were crucial to achieving unity. He preferred to settle all matters behind the scenes, avoiding open conflict and contentious public meetings. He worried about damaging the party's image with voters.

Bliss liked to please people, according to Doerler, but he also could be "thin-skinned, often taking criticism personally." He prized his independence and "liked saying to powerful people, 'you're wrong, do it right or I'll leave.'"[5] David Broder later described Bliss as "sensitive," having a "nervous manner, prickly personality, low boiling point and fear of public controversy" and often "too proud to fight" in intra-party conflicts.[6] But Bliss was willing to fight, when necessary, to build the party.

In 1938, the local Republicans split into two factions. The City Hall group led by Wade DeWoody, the city law director and also chairman of the party executive committee, included Mayor Schroy, other city officials, and allied officeholders; the Young Republicans group led by Bliss, secretary of the executive committee, included the young precinct officials Bliss had recruited, plus business leaders, lawyers, and judges. Occasionally, Chairman Corey sided with the Young Republicans.[7]

DeWoody and Bliss had worked together since the 1931 Akron mayoral campaign, but their relationship became increasingly tense. Bliss later recounted to Alex Arshinkoff how vicious the competition became between the factions. At one point, members of the City Hall faction threatened to embarrass Bliss by revealing that a Bliss ally had been having an extramarital affair. They had photos and even a statement. When they showed these materials to Bliss, he opened a safe in his office and pulled out evidence of his own, showing officials loyal to City Hall accepting financial kickbacks on contracts they had awarded. Bliss then told his opponents that a copy of his evidence was in the hands of an editor at the *Akron Beacon Journal*. He said he had not planned to use the evidence and still preferred not to, but he would take steps to keep them from using their material to attack him and his allies. "Upon my death, he [the editor] will open it up and he will not open it up until then," Bliss said. Neither side revealed its evidence of wrongdoing to the public.[8]

Bliss soon faced the challenge of uniting the factions to win the 1939 mayoral election. Mayor Schroy was seeking a third term, and the campaign looked like a repeat of the 1937 race, with the labor unions vowing to continue the fight. The prospect briefly brought together City Hall and the Young Republicans. However, the Democratic candidate, Wilford B. Bixler, was a young and inexperienced state legislator, and Schroy was easily reelected. One big surprise was that the Democrats took control of Akron City Council.[9]

These mixed election results renewed the Republican infighting. The dispute broke into the open in the spring of 1940, when the Young Republicans' candidate for state central committeewoman prevailed over City Hall's candidate in the primary. Then at the Summit County convention in the fall, the Young Republicans defeated City Hall's choice for a presidential elector. Wade DeWoody had had enough. In an outburst that shocked the convention into silence, he charged that the winning elector had been disloyal to the county and state GOP committees. After the meeting, he declared, "I'll get…Ray Bliss if it's the last thing I ever do."[10] Bliss was stunned by the public attack and sought to mend fences with DeWoody. Soon they were working together on the 1940 campaign.[11] It had a special twist: Senator Robert A. Taft of Ohio was running for the Republican presidential nomination and was supported by both factions.

The Republican National Convention in Philadelphia was contentious and dramatic. Taft represented the "conservative" wing of the GOP, and fellow Ohioan Clarence Brown Sr. managed his campaign at the convention. Although Brown and Bliss had tangled in the 1932 gubernatorial primary, the younger operative learned from a strong effort at the convention. One observer wrote, "Taft's campaign has been lavish and organized to a degree not seen since Mark Hanna, also of Ohio, used to take care of such things for William McKinley."[12] However, a dark horse from the "liberal" wing of the party, Wendell Willkie, won the nomination. Willkie had strong Akron connections, having worked for the Firestone Rubber Company in the 1920s.[13]

Although the 1940 general election was close, President Roosevelt won an unprecedented third term. But in Ohio, Governor Bricker was reelected and Harold Burton, Cleveland's Republican mayor, joined Taft in the US Senate.[14] These events contributed to a "peace pact" between City Hall and Young Republicans for the 1941 Akron mayoral campaign. All wanted an unprecedented fourth term for Mayor Schroy as well as to win back control of Akron City Council.

This time the Democratic mayoral candidate was state representative George J. Harter. He was an experienced legislator and a solid New Deal Democrat, but not strongly tied to the labor unions. Although most observers predicted a very close race, Harter defeated Schroy handily.[15] The unions finally had a Democratic mayor in Akron, albeit a different one than they had envisioned in 1937. But at the same time, the Republicans took back control of Akron City Council.

Local observers believed the public had grown weary of Mayor Schroy. But City Hall had a darker explanation: the Young Republicans had deliberately undermined the mayor. Corey and Bliss strongly denied this charge.[16] Despite Bliss's patient quest for unity, the Republican factions were poised for a showdown.

Chapter 11

Ray Bliss Becomes County Chairman

James Corey died December 14, 1941, at the age of sixty-four. Suddenly Ray Bliss was without the counsel of the man who had nurtured his career and become a second father. Serving as a pall bearer at Corey's funeral was one of the hardest duties Bliss had ever performed.[1]

The vacancies created by Corey's passing set off a brief but intense struggle between the local party factions. The Republican Central Committee quickly filled Chairman Corey's seat on the Summit County Board of Elections. Wade DeWoody, the leader of the City Hall faction, was passed over in favor of Bliss's handpicked candidate from the Young Republicans. This decision was a double blow to DeWoody: he had resigned from the board in favor of Bliss in 1935. Bliss soon took over as board chairman.[2]

In January 1942, the Republican Central Committee elected Bliss to serve out Corey's term as county chairman. He was then elected to a full term as chairman in August 1942. This meeting was the kind of stage-managed event for which Bliss was already known: "The Summit County Republican organization machine, containing many replacements and new parts, was rolling along in typical steam roller fashion today after a meeting last night which saw a purge of the ... 'City Hall' faction which leaves Ray Bliss in undisputed control," the *Akron Beacon Journal* reported.[3] Twenty-seven members of the Executive Committee, most of them loyal to City Hall, were replaced with loyalists from the Young Republicans group. Former mayor Schroy came to terms with the new chairman, seconding Bliss's candidate for chairman of the Executive Committee. The vote was unanimous. Bliss publicly asked Wade DeWoody to remain on the committee, but DeWoody resigned anyway.[4]

At thirty-four, Bliss was the youngest person to be party chairman in Summit County. However, the *Akron Beacon Journal* wondered if his victory might be a hollow one: "Whether Bliss' hard-swinging young cohort has captured an empty citadel will be determined by results of the next year's state election."[5]

Bliss immediately set out to answer the question. He set his sights on winning the Fourteenth District US House seat in 1942, a prize that had eluded the Republicans since 1932. He recruited Akron City Council president Ed Rowe to run against incumbent Democrat Dow W. Harter. Rowe won in a close race, 51 to 49 percent. It was part of a larger Republican gain of 45 seats in the US House of Representatives.[6]

Next Bliss got busy trying to win back the Akron mayor's office in 1943. Bliss recruited Charles Slusser, a school board member and former city council member, to run against the Democratic incumbent, George Harter. Bliss was able to run the kind of unified local campaign he favored. The Republicans won the mayor's office and maintained control of Akron City Council. The *Akron Beacon Journal* reported: "The mayor's stunning defeat came about chiefly because Republicans went to the polls in almost unprecedented numbers for a municipal election; the independent voters showed they favored Slusser, and the organized labor vote failed to turn out in numbers hoped for by Harter's backers."[7]

After the election, Bliss made sure there would be no mayoral faction squabbling with the party leadership. Bliss sprinkled allies in key city positions. Roy Browne, a classmate and fraternity brother at the University of Akron, was named law director—the post DeWoody had held in the previous GOP administration.

Bliss met every two weeks with the mayor and the Republican council majority to review city problems. Akron City Council meetings conformed to the Bliss model—scripted, short, and to the point, so that citizens got the impression that city government knew what it was doing. Bliss remembered Jim Corey's admonition that good government was good politics.[8]

Law Director Roy Browne performed another key function for Bliss at City Hall. Stopping gambling had become a personal crusade for *Akron Beacon Journal* editor John S. Knight. Bliss agreed and Browne ordered the police to crack down on gamblers. Then one night Bliss was having a drink at the LaFrance Bar (the same bar that figured prominently in the 1937 mayoral campaign), when a friend told him that the gamblers had started up again. Bliss said it couldn't be so, but the friend took Bliss across the street and showed him a casino in operation. "Ray almost grabbed his heart. He went completely red. I mean, the word was they thought he was going to die," said Alex Arshinkoff, who heard the story from Bliss and others. Bliss called Browne at home and said, "This is a personal affront to me." Browne quickly shut down the gambling joints. "Ray Bliss's rule was you keep your word unless you are released and Ray gave his word to Jack Knight," said Arshinkoff.[9] Bliss had not forgotten Jim Corey's rule about keeping promises.

Another aspect of good government was patronage appointments. Effective appointments could help at the ballot box, but incompetent or dishonest appointees could hurt. Besides, job seekers encouraged factionalism and conflict within the party—as Bliss knew from personal experience.

Bliss asked local GOP officeholders for a "60–40 patronage split," with 60 percent of the appointments made by the officeholder and 40 percent recommended by the party committee. He later introduced a system of applications at Republican headquarters for job seekers. It was a way to check the applicants' qualifications. In addition, Bliss decided that the party executive committee would make the recommendations—and that no members of the committee would "write separate letters of endorsement"—for key jobs, such as directors of the state Highway and Liquor Departments.[10] Summit County Republicans soon spoke with one voice on the sensitive issue of patronage.

Chapter 12

Strengthening the Local Party

Politics was Ray Bliss's full-time occupation. No day had enough hours to nurture the grassroots, recruit good candidates, and run good campaigns. His work was traditional in some ways and often ahead of its time in others. But Bliss was modest about his success. "Politically there is nothing much being done today that the Romans and Greeks were not doing," he frequently said. "It's just a case of dressing it up in a different package and trying to achieve perfection."[1]

Building the party at the grassroots was a top priority for Bliss. He strongly promoted Republican ward clubs in the neighborhoods, some of which he had helped organize back in the 1930s. He also backed clubs for veterans, college students, and young men. Bliss had a special regard for women's organizations. As a young woman, Madge Doerler was caught up in the enthusiasm Bliss brought to politics. "I couldn't even vote and I became president of the Young Women's Republican Club," she remembered.[2]

Bliss had an annual dinner to honor the ward clubs and other organizations, and recognized them at big party events, such as the Lincoln Day Dinner and party picnics. He was attentive to their needs, joys, and sorrows. "Ray always felt in debt to the party workers," said Doerler.[3] There was a practical side to this care. "If you don't produce in a corporation, you know what happens," Bliss later remarked. "If a volunteer doesn't produce, you just have to go out and recruit additional volunteers."[4]

The ward clubs became Bliss's talent scouts. That is how Bliss met Frances Rex in 1948. She was active in her club in the Ninth Ward in Akron and had gone door to door as a volunteer for a city councilman.[5] She wrote up a report about how many contacts she made and about issues that residents raised, such as problems with sidewalks. Bliss saw the report and liked her eye for detail. She went to work at party headquarters as what later would be called an "executive assistant." Back then it meant she did whatever Bliss told her to do. She soon became an integral part of the party operation.

Bliss took nothing for granted when he prepared for meetings and dinners, Rex recalled. One man who had been giving the invocation at party dinners repeatedly threw things off schedule. The designated prayer giver drank too much before the dinners and his prayers dragged on and on. "You get Rex to do that [pray] because Rex doesn't drink," ordered Bliss. Praying became one of her jobs. "He had categories for everybody," Rex said. "You fit in that category."[6] Organizing supporters was key for Bliss. "Success in politics...comes because thousands and thousands of people believe in what you're trying to do and support you," he told a reporter. "Without them you don't succeed."[7]

A foundation of party success, Bliss had learned from Jim Corey, was good candidates. According to Doerler, "Ray believed that the first task of party leaders was to put together a ticket that could win."[8] When it came to candidates, Bliss told Alex Arshinkoff: "Young man, let me give you two rules if you're going to stay in politics. Remember them the rest of your life. Number one, fill the ticket. If you don't fill the ticket, there's no reason for people to vote Republican. Number two, cut out the cancer before it spreads."[9]

To fill the ticket, Bliss was always on the lookout for good candidates. He later described such candidates this way: "I'm talking about a candidate who is qualified for the office he seeks, has a pleasing personality and appearance, and has the ability to express himself clearly and concisely on the issues. There are many different types, but normally you win with an energetic candidate who takes a constructive position on the issues of the day, sets them forth articulately, and exudes the type of leadership that draws people to him."[10]

Candidates had to fit local conditions. For Bliss, different kinds of candidates appealed to different kinds of voters. He promoted a "big tent" Republican Party decades before that term became popular. Bliss got to know potential candidates, introduced them to other party leaders, and offered advice on their careers. He didn't forget about them after they won an election for the first time. Bliss tried to "slot" candidates for a succession of local offices, helping them move up the ranks, expanding their appeal and increasing their name recognition.[11]

Once Bliss had identified a good candidate for an office, he worked to nominate him or her. But unlike Jim Corey, Bliss opposed formal party endorsements of candidates in primaries. One reason was that John S. Knight, editor of the *Akron Beacon Journal*, did not think parties should play that role, and Bliss wanted to avoid unnecessary fights with Akron's only daily newspaper. Another reason was to avoid conflict among party factions. If no party endorsement was made, it was easier to unite the party behind the eventual nominee.[12] "Bliss believed the nomination process had to be fair," Doerler said. "Everyone interested in an office needed a chance to compete."[13] Bliss was committed to backing any candidate who won the party endorsement before or during a primary election.

At the same time, Bliss wanted to minimize conflict. He told his friend Clyde Mann: "You can't just maul yourselves around and expect to put up a good showing against opposition that's fresh and well organized."[14] If two or more candidates wanted a Republican nomination, there were ways short of an endorsement to show support—a "nod and a wink," as Bliss put it. He later told a journalist that as chairman, "I always maneuvered."[15]

Sometimes rival candidates could be persuaded not to run. In 1943, former mayor Schroy considered running against Bliss's recruit, Charles Slusser, in the Akron mayoral primary. But a timely patronage appointment ended the challenge. Sometimes Bliss and his allies had to campaign behind the scenes to nominate the candidate they favored. Such moves did not always sit well with the losing candidates. In 1942, Ed Rowe's losing opponent in the Republican congressional primary, Joseph Sieber, was furious with Bliss. Sieber claimed there was "an improper action on the part of the chairman and calls for a purge of the party leadership so that it again becomes the party of the people."[16]

Every so often, a spot on the ticket was not filled. In one case, the shy Bliss ended up making the ultimate sacrifice—becoming a candidate himself. In 1945, Bliss ran for local constable and was edged out by his opponent three ballots to two.[17] This photo finish made a point that Bliss harped on: field a candidate for every office, from precinct committee races in wards with few Republicans to the top of the ballot in general elections. It's good discipline and, besides, if you don't have a candidate in the race, you can't complain about the outcome.

Bliss quickly mastered the care and handling of candidates of all sorts. But he found dealing with them frustrating. "Remember, if a candidate won, he and his private followers did it themselves, but if he loses, it's because the damned organization didn't do enough," Bliss said in 1974.[18] Ingratitude exasperated Bliss. "He'd say,

'You never can do enough for a candidate. And it isn't what you did for them yesterday. It's what you can do for them tomorrow. That's what they look at. You never get any credit from the candidates that you helped,'" said Doerler.[19] Bliss was blunter with political scientist Arthur Peterson: "'Punch them in the nose and send them down the road. They're temporary actors. The party is the entity of lasting importance.'...He [Bliss] always said it with a smile, but the meaning was clear," Peterson said. "There was a larger framework of more lasting importance than a particular race or a particular candidate." At the same time, Peterson said that Bliss was very tolerant of candidates during a campaign: "He figured they had to do what they had to do."[20]

There were times when Bliss had to cut out a candidate, even if it meant a setback for Republicans. "Sometimes you win by losing," Bliss told Arshinkoff, and illustrated the point with Representative Ed Rowe.[21] The freshman congressman spread the word around Akron that he had pretty much won the 1942 general election on his own, with little help from the party. As his reelection campaign started, Rowe came to see Bliss.

"Ray, the campaign's going on and I haven't heard from you. There are a lot of things that aren't getting done that you did two years ago," Rowe told the chairman.

"Congressman, is your name on the slate card?" Bliss asked, referring to the card with the names of Republican candidates distributed to voters. Rowe said it was. After Rowe answered "yes" to several other inquiries, Bliss said it appeared that the congressman was being treated like other Republican candidates. Then Rowe asked about special fund-raising efforts and other benefits he had received in the last campaign.

"What you're talking about is the 'extras,'" said Bliss. "You've been running around saying the Republican Party did nothing for you. If you win this time, I'll stand up and hold a press conference and say that you did it on your own. This time we're not doing any of the extras."

Rowe lost reelection in 1944.

Once nominations were settled, Bliss wanted to run a campaign on behalf of the entire Republican ticket—as he was able to do in 1942. He let candidates know that he would help them, but that he was in charge of the campaign. This was especially true when it came to raising and spending money. "Ray made it clear to the candidates that they were not to go out and do their own fund-raising," recalled Doerler. "He did the fund-raising and he, then, would allocate the dollars."[22] Bliss did not want donors, such as business leaders, to be confused by independent pleas for funds from Republican candidates. In return, the local party did not "assess" each candidate for his or her share of campaign costs, a common practice at that time.

Bliss dramatically expanded the local party's fund-raising. Between 1942 and 1944, party funds increased almost fourfold to $12,154. He used traditional methods, including revenue from patronage operations, such as the eight state automobile license bureaus in Summit County. The governor allowed local party committees to appoint the managers of the bureaus, who paid a portion of the license fees to the local party. But Bliss added a more systematic approach to soliciting contributions for party dinners and individual gifts. He developed extensive and detailed lists of potential donors, sought effective ways to cultivate their support, and then kept meticulous records of the results.[23]

Much of the campaign money was given in cash, as in the 1937 mayoral race. Bliss kept it in a safe at the Board of Elections at the county courthouse, said Doerler. He always worried about making sure it was safe. "That man would go home, go to bed and wonder if he had locked the safe at the elections board, where he had put the money. He would get up in the middle of the night and go back down and get into the Courthouse and go check that."[24]

Bliss soon appointed a permanent finance committee to raise money on a regular basis, not just at election time. This local committee paralleled efforts at the state level to revamp the Ohio Republican Finance Committee. The large urban counties became "divisions" of the state finance committee. The Summit County division had a contract with the state committee to meet a fund-raising goal, with some funds going to the county party and the rest to the state and national parties. In 1948, the Summit County goal was $175,000, with $55,000 for the county committee and $120,000 going to the state and national committees.[25] The finance committee insulated Bliss from pressure by individual donors because contributors gave to the party and not to Bliss personally. The rising costs of campaigns eventually forced Bliss to allow candidate fund-raising, but party campaign spending was always central to his approach.[26]

Bliss wanted to spend campaign money effectively. In 1943, he proposed a novel idea: a permanent headquarters for the local party, a rare thing at the time. Instead, Republican and Democratic leaders used donated space during campaigns, and between campaigns they used offices at the Summit County Board of Elections. These operations were called "mushrooms" because they appeared right before elections and then disappeared afterward—like mushrooms after a rainstorm. The Summit County Republican Party appropriated $2,000 to open a year-round office in a former doctor's office on the tenth floor of the Tower Building in downtown Akron. This was a large sum when compared to the executive committee's 1943 income of about $3,000. A year later, Bliss created a separate "Republican campaign committee" to be run by professional managers on behalf of the entire ticket. He soon experimented with salaried professional staff to "conduct publicity work at headquarters."[27]

Under Bliss, Summit County Republicans had a smoothly running operation.[28] Because the organization operated continuously, campaign preparations could begin early in each election year with the choice of candidates. After the spring primary, Bliss and his key allies met at party headquarters to lay out campaign plans, aided by Bliss's polling. The plans would be presented to the party executive and central committees, typically during the summer. Bliss lavished attention on these party meetings. He explained the strategy and also answered questions from committee members. There was often a good bit of give and take in these sessions and the plans were often amended. Bliss then sought formal agreement on the strategy with resolutions voted on by the committees. These plans often included a platform of sorts. In 1947, for example, the Akron mayoral candidate ran on a seventeen-point program.

The strategy was typically set by September. A first step was to raise money to fund the plans. The expenditures included literature and novelty items, yard signs and billboards, sound trucks, and newspaper and radio ads. The party also organized a wide variety of events. These included large rallies aimed at attracting big crowds as well as candidate speeches before local groups and coffees in each local ward. A final task was deploying precinct and ward workers at the grassroots level to campaign door to door. These efforts intensified as the campaign progressed, reaching a high point on election day, when the party mounted extensive get-out-the-vote drives.

The 1949 Akron mayoral race illustrates the scope of the Bliss operation. He raised and spent about $16,000. Some $7,000—about 44 percent of the total—went for direct advertising of various kinds to persuade voters. But nearly as much, $6,000—about 38 percent of the total—was spent on party workers, including men and women "ward captains," women "precinct captains," and "colored workers" (that is, African Americans). These workers harnessed the efforts of the party volunteers to get out the vote. More than $1,000 was allocated for "bonuses" for precinct workers who exceeded expectations in turnout. The remaining $3,000—18 percent—was spent on campaign events and administrative expenses.[29]

Republicans all across Ohio were taking notice of Bliss's success.

Chapter 13

Growing Recognition

In the spring of 1944, Ray Bliss was elected to the Ohio Republican Executive and Central Committee, a membership he would hold until 1974, shortly before his retirement. GOP state chairman Ed Schorr soon tapped him to lead an advisory committee on a platform for the 1944 general election campaign. Bliss solicited suggestions at half a dozen meetings around the state, and then chaired the subcommittee that proposed a party platform.[1] It was adopted at the state convention. Bliss liked the party platform: "Republicans have united for a harmony program in the state and there is a great deal of optimism in Columbus for the state ticket."[2]

The platform displayed the consensus-building skills Bliss had learned in Summit County politics. According to Madge Doerler, he was an able conciliator. "It was uncanny....I remarked about it to him many, many times. He just had a facility...he was a lightning rod, the flagpole...around which all these divergent forces could rally and they really did. I mean, he could get a consensus.... They could be really at odds and he could bring them together. It was a great gift." Bliss wasn't always conciliatory, Doerler reported. "He was tough and sometimes, boy, you hated him. The very idea that he could talk to you like that.... He could keep someone cooling their heels out there in the office [waiting room] as long as he wanted them to sit out there."[3]

Bliss knew that different issues mattered to different kinds of voters. The party's issue appeals had to be carefully crafted to win the most votes, whether it was in a mayor's race, gubernatorial campaign, or a presidential election. The candidates needed some flexibility on the stump, but at the same time the party needed an overall message.

Bliss was pragmatic, but he also believed in the larger purposes of party politics. The *Akron Beacon Journal* confirmed this perspective: "An ardent advocate of the party system of government, Bliss still holds to his early ideals that a party wins success by bringing forward able men as candidates for office with the result that the people get good government."[4] For this reason, Bliss wanted candidates and officeholders to be the voice of the Republican Party on issues. It was their job to persuade voters at election time and govern on behalf of the voters if elected. As a party leader, Bliss rarely expressed his own views publicly.[5] "If I wanted to make public policy," Bliss later said, "I would go out and run for office and make speeches."[6]

Although he often described himself as a "nuts-and-bolts technician," Bliss told a reporter in 1980: "Standing alone, [the label] distorts my interest in government. Here in Akron, the state and the nation, I always took an interest in issues....I participated actively in trying to solve problems. I recruited people who I felt were intelligent enough to come up with reasonable solutions."[7] Bliss was not an ideologue, however. Ideology could be a straitjacket that would hamper the ability of the Republican Party to win elections and govern effectively. He had learned that good government, not ideology, was good politics.

In pragmatic terms, Bliss did not like public speaking. He worried a lot about not being an "orator," Doerler recalled. David Broder later described Bliss's speaking in this way: "In private conversation, he can be funny, earthy, forceful and direct. Like most politicians, he loves to talk politics. But he is painfully ill at ease in public appearances; natural shyness, weak eyes, and a slight speech impediment made him self-conscious. With a skittish fear of public controversy, his formal discussions of politics soon dissolve into watery generalizations."[8]

In the summer of 1944, Bliss took the Summit County Republicans "on the road," setting up a headquarters at the state convention in Columbus and then at the Republican National Convention in Chicago. The Bliss organization had a visible presence at the state and national levels of the party.[9]

Bliss initially backed Senator Robert A. Taft of Ohio for the GOP presidential nomination in 1944 as he had done in 1940. But when Taft decided to seek reelection to the US Senate and endorsed Ohio governor John Bricker for the presidency, Bliss followed suit. Although Bliss opposed party endorsements in nomination contests, he asked the Summit County Republican Executive Committee to endorse Bricker's presidential bid.[10]

The Republican National Convention nominated New York governor Thomas Dewey for president, a representative of the "liberal" wing of the GOP. In a bid for party unity, Dewey chose "conservative" Bricker as his vice-presidential running mate. But it was to no avail. President Roosevelt won an unprecedented fourth term. Thanks to Bricker's presence on the ticket, Ohio voted Republican by a small margin. Taft was reelected to the US Senate in a close race.[11]

More high-level assignments followed for Bliss. In January 1945, Ohio secretary of state Edward J. Hummel appointed Bliss to a statewide committee to propose changes in voting laws.[12] Later in the year, Bliss was part of a six-person "fact-finding committee" established by the state party to propose improvements to party organization and campaigns.[13]

In October 1945, Ohio GOP chairman Ed Schorr resigned after fifteen years in the post—Bliss's entire political career. It was rumored that Schorr had taken an interest in the young Summit County chairman, just thirty-seven years old. Bliss was among those mentioned as a possible successor. "He's Ready," proclaimed the headline in the *Akron Beacon Journal.* "A good many people... believe Ray Bliss is about to leap from Summit County central committee chairman to the position of GOP state chairman.... If that happens, he will certainly be the youngest man to hold that position in the state's history.... Akron will be represented by one of the most powerful political figures since the late Charles Dick was helping Mark Hanna make presidents," the newspaper reported.[14]

But when the Republican state central committee met in Columbus to pick Schorr's replacement, Bliss refused to be considered. His noncandidacy cleared the way for the party to pick Fred Johnson of Zanesville, who had actively campaigned for the job. Bliss said little publicly about his decision, but reporters quoted insiders on an explanation: "Bliss never made a formal announcement that he sought the job but said that he would accept it if it were offered to him and proper arrangements could be made with respect to a salary."[15]

Bliss believed the state chairmanship should be a full-time, salaried position. The alternative was for the chairman to have another job. Indeed, retiring chairman Ed Schorr was a lawyer and a lobbyist, and the new chairman, Fred Johnson, was an insurance agent. Such employment could cause a conflict of interest between the chairman and the party, often resolved at the party's expense. According to Doerler, Bliss disliked leaders who profited personally from party office, but he also understood that leaders without salaries needed to make a living.[16]

Above all, Bliss believed that politics was an honorable profession. He felt that the key Republican constituencies, especially the business community, should treat party leaders with the same respect they accorded other professionals, like corporate managers, accountants, and lawyers. And like other professionals, party leaders ought to be paid a salary, allowed to do their jobs, and held accountable for the results. In return, Republicans of all kinds could expect technical competence, hard work, and honesty from party leaders.

Bliss could be very touchy about his social status and the image of his profession. On the first count, he joined prominent social organizations, including the Kiwanis Club, the Blue Coats, Omicron Delta Kappa, the Portage and Fairlawn Country Clubs (Akron), the Athletic Club (Columbus), and the Union Club (Cleveland); he was a thirty-second-degree Mason and a Shriner.

On the second count, Bliss wanted politicians to be treated with respect. Clyde Mann recalled: "Once Bliss ripped the political hide of his candidate for governor, who relentlessly attacked 'the politicians,' blaming them for all the problems of this nation. Bliss was furious and complained that blaming everything on politicians included him because he was proud to be one. He told the candidate: 'And what the hell are you—a politician like me.'"[16] In this vein, Bliss asked editor John S. Knight not to refer to him as "Boss Bliss" in the *Akron Beacon Journal*.[17] The term didn't fit with Bliss's professional image—nor the newspaper's judgment either: "Raymond Charles Bliss is a professional politician in what he hopes is the best sense of the phrase," the newspaper editorialized.[18]

Chapter 14

Ray Bliss Gets a Day Job

Ray Bliss had become concerned about his economic future. Nearly forty, he had earned very little money in his sixteen years in local politics. There was a practical side to Bliss's interest in a salaried position as state chairman. So Bliss listened with interest when he was approached by three Akron lawyers about going into the insurance business. As for the lawyers, "They admired Ray and wanted to help him continue his work with the party," said Madge Doerler.[1]

The result was Tower Agencies, Inc., incorporated in October 1947. The agency took its name from the location of its office—the National Tower Building in Akron, the same building that housed local Republican headquarters. Bliss, his mother, and his partners invested equal shares. The Bliss family portion came from settlement funds received from Bliss's father's accidental death in 1932. The agency began with "$500 in working capital" and "240 shares without value." Bliss was the president; one partner, Charles Sacks, was vice president; another partner, Herman Harris, was secretary; and the third, Hyman Subrin, acted as legal counsel. All the partners were associated with the agency in one way or another for the rest of their lives.[2]

Bliss's business partners were Jews who had formed their own law firm, Harris, Sacks, and Subrin in 1933. In those days, Jews were rarely asked to join "gentile" firms, so the partnership between Protestant Bliss and his Jewish associates was unusual.

But they had much in common: all came from humble origins, had achieved success in their professions, and were known for their probity.

The senior partner in the law firm, Herman B. Harris, was most like Bliss in background. He was born in Ohio in 1895, the son of a tailor and the grandson of German immigrants. Harris moved to Akron to practice law in 1920. He eventually served as president of the Akron Bar Association and founded the Legal Aid Society in Akron.[3]

Like Bliss, Charles Sacks was a Republican. He was born in Russia in 1898 to an electrician, who immigrated to the United States in 1907. In 1920, Sacks moved to Akron to partner in an electrical supply company. He attended the Akron Law School (which would later become part of the University of Akron) and began practicing law in 1926. Sacks served as a local Republican official in the 1930s and 1940s as well as an Akron municipal judge.[4]

Closest in age to Bliss, Hyman S. Subrin was a Democrat. He was born in 1907 in New York City, the son of a Russian furniture merchant who eventually settled in Akron. Like Bliss, Subrin graduated from South High School and enrolled at the University of Akron. In 1924, an uncle dared him to apply to Harvard University. "If you make it," the uncle said, "I'll pay your first year's tuition." Subrin was admitted to Harvard, earning bachelor's and law degrees. He returned to Akron to practice law in 1930.[5]

Affiliated with the Carter-Jenkins insurance firm, the Tower Agencies was chartered "to act for insurance corporations in soliciting and receiving applications for fire, casualty, plate glass, boiler, elevator, accident, health, burglary, rent, marine, credit, fidelity and life insurance" as well as to "conduct a general insurance agency and insurance brokerage business." The corporation was also chartered to engage in real estate transactions and other business enterprises, but insurance quickly became its dominant activity.[6] Bliss soon found there was a lot he didn't know about the insurance business. So he studied hard to learn about it, even taking night classes. The agency quickly became profitable, providing Bliss with a modest but comfortable lifestyle for the rest of his life.

A key factor in the success of the agency was Madge Doerler. The sister and wife of Bliss's fraternity brothers, she and Bliss had been active in local politics since 1933. She began working with the Tower Agencies in 1948 and took over its day-to-day management when Bliss was state and national GOP chairman. Although Bliss kept a hand in the business and worked on weekends when he was back in Akron, by 1969 he told friends that "the agency runs well without me."[7]

"I'm the person who made Ray Bliss's career possible," said Doerler. Bliss admired her. "A man cannot have very many friends, maybe just a few in his lifetime," he once told her. "Madge Doerler is my friend."[8] Doerler continued to be a trusted political ally, serving on the Summit County Republican Executive and Central committees and on the Ohio Republican Executive and Central Committee while Bliss was chairman.[9]

The insurance agency gave Bliss financial independence, said W. Richard Wright, allowing him to forge his own path in politics. "If things get difficult, I can always come back to Akron and sell insurance," Bliss told Wright.[10] Bliss protected this financial independence—and his commitment to professional ethics—by keeping his business and party work separate. He pledged not to sell insurance or have other business dealings with the local, state, or federal governments while serving as party chairman. According to Doerler, Bliss faithfully kept his pledge.[11]

Chapter 15

The Great Defeat of '48

President Franklin D. Roosevelt died in office on April 12, 1945. For the first time since 1932—almost all of Bliss's political career—Roosevelt would not lead the Democrats. Vice President Harry S. Truman succeeded Roosevelt. The Republicans took advantage of the altered political landscape in the 1946 congressional elections, winning control of both houses of Congress for the first time since 1933. In Ohio, John Bricker was elected to the US Senate, and the Republicans kept control of state government.[1]

Despite these gains, trouble awaited the Republicans. Bliss got an early indication of what might be in store in the 1947 Akron mayoral election. Mayor Slusser had been reelected in 1945 by a large margin[2] and was seeking a third term in City Hall. This time the unions had a new approach: they supported the popular incumbent mayor and concentrated instead on recruiting good city council candidates. Slusser handily won again, but the Democrats took ten of thirteen city council seats.

"Labor Scores," reported the *Akron Beacon Journal*. "Organized labor has for the first time shown that it can influence enough votes to be a decisive force in municipal elections."[3] Like the GOP, the Democrats and the unions were adjusting to the post-Roosevelt era.

In 1948, Senator Robert A. Taft sought the GOP presidential nomination again, with Clarence Brown Sr. again managing his campaign at the Republican National Convention in Philadelphia. But unlike in 1940, Brown was overmatched by the managers for the 1944 Republican nominee, Thomas Dewey. "The CIA were amateurs compared to the Dewey people," Bliss later remembered. "They knew where your bank loans were, who you did business with, who you slept with."[4] Dewey won the 1948 nomination and chose California governor Earl Warren as his vice-presidential running mate. The "liberal" wing of the GOP had once again prevailed over the "conservative" wing.

The Republicans had high hopes of winning the White House for the first time in sixteen years. The Democrats were divided, with President Truman facing twin revolts: Senator Strom Thurmond of South Carolina ran as a "Dixiecrat," and former vice president Henry Wallace was on the Progressive Party ticket. By September, Truman was so far behind Dewey that the pollsters and pundits declared that the election was over. But Truman campaigned vigorously, with blasts at the Republican-controlled "do-nothing Congress." Support for the embattled president grew, and "Give 'em Hell, Harry!" became the campaign's battle cry. The unions and other Democratic groups rallied to his cause.

Bliss was not much involved in the 1948 campaign, in part because he was learning the insurance business. In fact, he was thinking about leaving politics altogether. "My friends refused to believe it when I said I was through," Bliss later told a reporter. "But I got just as immersed in the insurance business as I had been in politics. I was ready to resign as county chairman."[5]

Bliss got a hometown dose of Truman's comeback in October, when President Truman came to Akron as part of a whistle-stop train tour of Ohio. About 60,000 people—roughly a quarter of the city's population—turned out for the campaign event.[6] Akron attorney Bernie Rosen, campaign manager for the Summit County Democratic Party that year, recalled the excitement: "We were kind of the turning point in that campaign."[7]

When all the votes were counted, Truman narrowly won Ohio—and the White House. Riding Truman's coattails, the Democrats took control of state government for the first time since 1938.[8] After the deflating defeat, many Ohio Republicans wanted a new state chairman.

Chapter 16

Ray Bliss Becomes State Chairman

On November 18, 1948, just fifteen days after election day, the Ohio Republican Executive and Central Committee met behind closed doors to regroup. Bliss was among those declining to give Fred Johnson, the state chairman, a vote of confidence. There was speculation that Johnson would be replaced by Ray Bliss when the central committee held its next meeting on February 9, 1949.[1] "A good many people have talked to me about it, but I am merely standing by," Bliss told reporters.[2] Bliss was genuinely ambivalent about taking the state chairmanship, according to Madge Doerler. "Ray believed it was a job he could do, but he also wanted to run the insurance agency and enjoy a quiet life in Akron."[3]

As the Republican meeting drew closer, Chairman Johnson refused to resign, setting up a confrontation between his supporters and critics, who traded anonymous accusations in the press.[4] Two accounts of the meeting survive. An official version, titled "Minutes of Meeting of The Republican State Executive and Central Committee," is perfunctory and antiseptic. A second, unofficial account reveals considerable friction.[5]

The official minutes recorded that 43 Republicans gathered at noon in Room 1212 of the Deshler-Wallick Hotel in downtown Columbus. Johnson called the meeting to order, but his control of the Republican Party ended quickly when a motion was made to declare the chairmanship vacant. The transcript reads: "Mr. Johnson then asked Mr. Marshall to pass and collect the ballots. The Committee voted.... The result was

27 votes for declaring the chairmanship vacant and 15 votes against. The chairmanship was declared vacant." Johnson thanked the committee for its cooperation.

The unofficial minutes reveal an emotional Johnson. He stepped down from the chair and asked Mrs. Florence Morris to take over while he addressed his critics. "The accusations made during the past several days are not true. I am not resigning as state chairman because I have no apology to make for the state campaign. Fred Johnson did not lose Ohio and you all know he did not. I am not saying it was a perfect campaign. Under the circumstances, we did the best we could."

Johnson then addressed specific ethical accusations:

"My father does not handle the coal buying for the state of Ohio and has not had any part of it."

"You do not have to come to see me to get contracts or pay me off on any other state business."

"I have not made a million dollars."

Johnson summed up his defense: "I have taken a physical beating and have been through mental anguish. I did not resign because I feel that a resignation is an admission of the things stated....Regardless of the outcome I shall continue to be a Republican and work for the candidates....I shall do everything in my power to unite the Republican Party."

The official minutes also handled the election of a new chairman in a clinical tone. Edward C. Stanton urged the committee to proceed with the nomination of a chairman and proposed Bliss. Mrs. Lila Black, from Bliss's own Fourteenth Congressional District, seconded the motion. "Mrs. Morris...asked for a vote on the election of Mr. Bliss as Chairman. The majority of the members having voted for Mr. Bliss, he was declared elected. Mr. Bliss then took the chair."

Bliss thanked the committee: "I deeply appreciate the honor that has been bestowed on me today. The job of being chairman of a state such as Ohio is a great responsibility. In order for a man to be a successful chairman he must have the cooperation of his committee. I ask you to give me a chance to do a job."

But in the unofficial account, Bliss also had a message for Johnson backers and other opponents. "A charge has been made here today without a foundation. I think we should face facts. The Party in Ohio cannot stand to have a factional split and mudslinging. It will be my purpose to be your chairman. I shall not be run by anyone. Anyone who is fair-minded can talk to individuals...who know me and they will tell you that no one owns Ray Bliss in Ohio. I hope that issue is closed." The new chairman pledged to keep his insurance business separate from his party job.

Bliss wanted the other Republicans to know that the new chairman did not agree with the former chairman's analysis of the 1948 election: "I disagree with Mr. Johnson about the loss of the last campaign. My course will be to cooperate with the women's organization, veterans' groups and young Republicans, many of whom have complained to me that they have not had proper cooperation. It is my intention to make this Committee an active cooperative committee. We expect to have an action policy committee of the state committee."

Both accounts ended on an upbeat note—the passage of a resolution to endorse Taft for the US Senate in 1950. However, the unofficial account has remarks by former chairman Schorr and about Senator Taft, both regarded as Bliss backers. Bliss later would say that Taft's fear of losing the 1950 election led to Bliss's taking over as state chairman.[6]

Outside the meeting room, Johnson had little to say: "Bliss is the next chairman." A newspaper account of the meeting said the voice vote for Bliss was not unanimous.[7]

In his new job, Bliss would work full-time and receive a salary. Although no details were reported at the time, in 1953 Bliss's salary was put at "about $12,000 a year." Bliss was said to be "the only paid GOP chairman in the country."[8]

His hometown newspaper was proud of Bliss: "Prophecies are risky in politics…, but the Republican state committee at least can count on intelligent and aggressive leadership from Chairman Bliss."[9] Bliss had no time to bask in such tributes.

John S. Knight (left) and Alfred M. Landon (right), 1936. The editor of the *Akron Beacon Journal* and the GOP presidential nominee at the Republican National Convention in Cleveland—the first convention attended by Ray Bliss. (Courtesy of the *Akron Beacon Journal*)

Ray Bliss (lower left) and James Corey (upper left) and political associates, 1939. Summit County GOP Chairman Corey was Bliss's mentor. (Courtesy of the *Akron Beacon Journal*)

Democrat Franklin Delano Roosevelt, 1940. FDR campaigning in Akron, Ohio. Roosevelt was president during Ray Bliss's early career, 1932 to 1945. (Courtesy of the *Akron Beacon Journal*)

Election recount, 1940. Ray Bliss (center) and colleagues at the Summit County Board of Elections. (Courtesy of the *Akron Beacon Journal*)

(Top) Summit County Republican Chairman Ray Bliss, 1944. (From the Ray C. Bliss Papers. Courtesy of Archival Services, University Libraries, The University of Akron)

(Bottom) Ellen Palmer and Ray Bliss, 1940s. College sweethearts, Palmer and Bliss were a couple until their marriage in 1959. (Courtesy of the *Akron Beacon Journal*)

Mayor Charles Slusser (left) and Ray Bliss, 1945. Bliss helped elect Republican Slusser to five terms in Akron City Hall. (Courtesy of the Summit County Republican Party)

Harry S. Truman, 1948. Campaigning in Akron, Ohio. After Truman's come-from-behind win, Bliss became Ohio Republican state chairman. From left, Truman, Congressman Walter B. Huber of Akron, and Stephen M. Young, Democratic candidate for congress-at-large of Cleveland. (Courtesy of the *Akron Beacon Journal*)

Chapter 17

Strengthening the State Party

Ray Bliss brought an immediate change to the Ohio Republican Party. Outgoing chairman Fred Johnson had worked just three days a week, but Bliss was in the office Monday through Friday and often on the weekends. "I'd drive him to Akron and he'd decide he wanted to come back to Columbus," said Frankie Avren, who worked for Bliss at state headquarters.[1]

Bliss's first task was to find out what had gone wrong in 1948. The results were alarming: Ohio Republicans didn't get out the vote.[2] A detailed breakdown of the election returns showed that 140,000 Republicans, mostly in rural areas, hadn't voted. Another 150,000 potential Republican voters weren't even registered. Back in Akron, a quarter of Chamber of Commerce members didn't go to the polls and one-sixth of Kiwanis Club members and their wives didn't vote either.[3] Meanwhile, Democrats had turned out in only slightly larger numbers in 1948 than in the past.[4]

One afternoon Bliss was discussing these results with Joe Neuger, the publisher of *Here in Ohio* magazine. "Joe wondered what would happen," Bliss later told a reporter, "if we polled some upper-crust organizations for their voting record.... After we had a second beer, the idea sounded even better. I went home and got things underway."[5]

Bliss sent out a "report card" of unregistered voters in triplicate—one copy to party headquarters, one copy to the unregistered voters themselves, and a third to the person's club or association. "Our work was done for us," said Bliss. "The pressure got so great that folks went to registration clerks in droves." Competition developed among the organizations—chambers of commerce, medical associations, auto dealers, grocers—to see who could register more members. According to Clyde Mann, Bliss "was convinced that any businessman not interested in politics was like a drowning man insisting he was not interested in water."[6]

These efforts were complemented by a traditional voter registration drive. Together the programs registered more than 250,000 potential Republican voters ahead of the 1950 election. Bliss also revamped the get-out-the-vote effort, holding campaign schools to increase the effectiveness of party workers. He instituted "achievement awards" for county parties that increased the Republican vote the most.[7]

Bliss developed a detailed program to revive the party, drawing on his success in Summit County. He later described six problems facing the GOP in 1950:[8]

1. We needed to prove to the Republican organization workers that there were enough Republicans and independent voters to elect a Republican ticket in Ohio if we effectively organized and properly presented our campaign.
2. We needed a closer working relationship with Republican county committees.
3. We needed a campaign program that would develop a high degree of team spirit between national, state, and local Republican candidates.
4. We needed an all-out drive to get every possible potential Republican voter in registration areas registered and eligible to vote.
5. We needed to aggressively sell our Republican candidates to the voters.
6. We needed a well-organized and effective organization in each of the counties in the state for the purpose of getting our potential Republican vote to the polls at the November election.

Bliss paid special attention to state party headquarters. The usually reserved Bliss sounded almost like a man holding an open house: "I want state headquarters to be a place where every interested person will be welcomed and feels welcome."[9] Bliss revamped the units at headquarters, including the Speakers, Legislative and Research, Publicity, Mailing and Shipping, Filing and Reference divisions. These operations provided a wider range of services to local party leaders and candidates, and even space for candidates who needed it. As a consequence, the staff grew from thirty to fifty-seven, a figure about half the size of the Republican National Committee staff at that time. Bliss made a point of hiring young staff—at forty-two he was the oldest person at headquarters.[10]

Bliss reorganized the forty-four-member state central committee and formed eight subcommittees—Audit, Finance, Speakers, Policy, Political Research and

Development, Publications, Campaign Literature, and Committees (a subcommittee on committees). Applying his inclusive approach to party politics, Bliss established an advisory committee "made up of members of the party whose viewpoints are now not adequately represented on the state committee." This new committee, said Bliss, would include representatives of "labor, war veterans, farmers, young voters, colored groups, nationality groups and others."[11] With expanded outreach in mind, Bliss revitalized the Ohio Federation of Republican Women and created a women's division within the party, headed by a vice chairman. Bliss also strengthened the League of Young Republican Clubs of Ohio, the War Veterans Republican Clubs of Ohio, and the "Negro Division" of the state party.

The new chairman quickly put his own stamp on party finances and budgeting. The party needed money as well as revamping, he discovered soon after taking over. "The first package that came in here after I became chairman arrived C.O.D.," Bliss later would recall. "They were going to take out the phones unless I guaranteed the bills myself."[12] The Ohio Republican Finance Committee soon was moved out of the building that housed state party operations to a new location. As in Summit County, the new chairman wanted there to be no question that fund-raising and party policy were separate operations. "He didn't want anybody making contributions to the finance office to think they were buying Republican state headquarters," said Avren.[13]

In return, Bliss was careful with the funds. Twice a year, an auditor checked the records for income tax and Social Security purposes; staffers had to keep detailed expense account records. Because he was a full-time chairman with a salary, there was little danger that he would use the campaign funds for personal benefit.[14]

It would be a morale buster, Bliss thought, to propose a huge budget that would have to be cut if contributions lagged. So he actually used three budgets—one for minimum needs, a second for intermediate needs, and a kind of deluxe budget for maximum needs. As the money came in, he spent it first on essentials and gradually build up to luxuries, such as sending a special Farm Edition of the *Ohio Republican News* to all rural post office box holders in the state if there was enough extra money.[15]

Bliss brought his Summit County approach to state party meetings. No detail was left unattended. Bliss wanted to know what would happen at meetings of the Ohio party before the meetings were held. He picked the members of the subcommittees that prepared reports for the party meetings and knew what the reports would say ahead of time. No outsiders were allowed at the sessions. "I feel the trick of having a successful political meeting is to have people there who know and trust each other implicitly. Then they will have confidence in the situation and let their hair down.

But if there is even one outsider there, any inward doubts they have will not be spoken of, and thus go unresolved."[16]

Bliss also held regular round-table discussions with local leaders in each congressional district. County chairmen complained that in 1948 the state party had tried to run everything, assigning little responsibility to the leaders closest to the voters. Bliss addressed this complaint in two ways. First, he provided each county chairman with a packet of basic information about the county and the campaign, so they could do their job well. Second, he hired state-party "field staff," whose job was to provide ongoing contact between the state and local party committees, with a special focus on voter registration and get-out-the-vote efforts.

Bliss later explained why the local party committees were so important: "In a state like Ohio—a big agricultural state, a big industrial state, and a lot of other things besides—you simply can't set up a state-wide campaign that is going to be suitable everywhere. You can't reach down into all the crevices. This is what the local chairmen must do for you. You can tell them on a broad general level what your campaign effort is going to be, but they must modify it so it will be locally applicable."[17] Local chairmen trusted Bliss in part because he was still the chairman of the Summit County Republican Party. He saw local politics as the foundation of state and national success. Bliss urged the local parties to "put on hard drives" in the 1949 municipal elections to prepare for the 1950 campaign.

Bliss did his part back in Akron. Before he accepted the state chairman's job, Bliss secured a promise from Mayor Charles Slusser to run for a fourth term in 1949. The Democrats united behind Richard Tobin, a member of Akron City Council.[18] Fearing embarrassment if the Democrats succeeded in Akron, Bliss made the mayoral race a "must" win. The *Akron Beacon Journal* reported strong interest in the mayoral campaign: "The Republicans act as though they were seeking some sort of revenge for what happened to them last fall [1948]. And the Democrats are acting as if they feel—'we won't let you do it.'"[19] The results were something of a draw: Slusser won an unprecedented fourth term in City Hall, but the Democrats remained in control of Akron City Council.

Despite his focus on Akron, the new chairman did not ignore Ohio's Republican members of Congress. They were worried about the 1950 campaign. He traveled to Washington in June to assure them that he would wage an intensive congressional campaign. "I think you'll find the most united and aggressive Republican campaign in Ohio's history in 1950," Bliss told reporters.[20]

Chapter 18

Taft and TV

In 1950, Ray Bliss's top priority was getting Senator Robert A. Taft reelected. Known around the country as "Mr. Republican," Taft was facing a tough race. Bliss had supported Taft in his previous senatorial and presidential bids, and the senator had confidence in the "quiet, effective political organizer from Akron."[1]

Bliss revealed his gifts as a strategist and innovator in crafting the Taft campaign. "Well, in politics, if you are living with it and want to be a success, you have to develop an instinct and I have had an instinct for politics," Bliss said years later. Although Bliss believed in polls and election statistics, his decisions weren't based on facts alone. "I'll get a hunch and move with the hunch. Whenever I have moved against a hunch and went with facts, I have always been wrong. So, I look at the facts and then get a feel for it and move," said Bliss.[2]

A key "hunch" came to Bliss in the fall of 1949 when he was taking a train from New York to Philadelphia for the Army-Navy football game. The train whizzed by rows of apartment houses where large numbers of working-class and middle-class voters lived. "I'm looking out the window and I'm seeing all these aerials, one after the other," said Bliss. The aerials were for televisions. Bliss had a hunch that television was a coming thing in politics.[3]

Television had been used sparingly in 1948 by the Republican presidential nominee, Thomas Dewey. He had staged a few events for the cameras with mixed reviews. Advertising experts warned Bliss that there were too few television viewers at home to make a difference in elections.[4] Bliss then tested his hunch with one of his favorite sources of information, bartenders. They told him that people were crowding into their establishments to watch television—whatever was on the tube. Many people didn't have televisions at home but gathered at corner taverns to take part in what was becoming a national pastime. "The beer joints were filled to the gills," Bliss recalled.[5]

Bliss regularly relied on his "tavern keeper's poll." He would stop at bars for a beer and a talk with bartenders—Bliss was a big tipper, so they were always happy to see him. "If politicians ever learn about bartenders," Bliss told a journalist, "Mr. Gallup will go out of business. . . . It's there that you can hear the sidewalk vote of America talking."[6]

It took a little persuasion by Bliss, but Taft and his handlers agreed that the new medium of television would help the campaign. Taft was hardly a made-for-television candidate. He was scholarly, aloof, and sometimes abrupt with people. He lacked the personal charm and conversational style that would characterize future candidates adept at televised politics.[7]

Bliss used television in two ways in the 1950 Taft campaign. One was to arrange for live television coverage of speeches, adding TV footage to regular reporting. The other was more innovative. Reporters were invited to take part in panel discussions with Taft, which were later broadcast as paid advertisements. They ran for fifteen minutes or half an hour, said Bliss's aide Frankie Avren, who helped produce them. As was his style, Bliss carefully reviewed them before they were aired. "He went over those so g-ddammed much it would drive us crazy," said Avren. Television programming was sparse in those days, so sometimes the panel discussion with Taft was one of the few offerings available. "If you watched television at night, the only thing you got was us," said Avren.[8]

These events gave reporters access to Taft. They asked him tough questions, with "no holds barred." Bliss found that Taft did better if he was challenged by a reporter. "I'd always try to get to one reporter to get Taft angry," Bliss recalled later.[9]

The state party presented more than thirty television shows in every major city with a television station. After the election, it was regarded as the most successful use of television in any election to date. "The same pattern won't work every year," Bliss remarked. "This is a Barnum & Bailey business. You've got to steam up the voters with new gimmicks."[10]

As he had done in Summit County, Bliss deployed an array of tactics to help Taft and the Republican ticket. In addition to TV, the party bought extensive radio spots, displayed approximately 1,400 billboards, and ran two ads listing the entire GOP ticket in most of the newspapers in the state. The party also mailed 400,000 copies of the *Ohio Republican News* to potential voters and distributed another 540,000 copies at county fairs and other venues. The GOP passed out over a million pamphlets about the entire Republican ticket.[11]

Television was not the only innovation Bliss brought to the Taft campaign. Taft was strongly opposed by labor unions because of his sponsorship of the Taft-Hartley Labor Management Act of 1947. He needed to show his connection with regular folks. Bliss organized a series of special campaign committees, such as Teachers for Taft, to appeal to Democratic and independent voters. This effort targeted school superintendents, school boards, teachers, and parents' organizations. In addition, he sought out the membership of ethnic, religious, farmer, business, and professional associations. Liquor permit holders—tavern owners—were a special target.[12]

Bliss worked closely with the general chairman of the Taft campaign to knit these volunteer activities together with Taft's personal campaign and Republican Party efforts.[13] These efforts focused on getting out the vote in all precincts with a 60 percent or greater Republican presidential vote in 1948. Less extensive efforts were waged in other precincts. State party field staff coordinated the effort, drawing on the extensive voter registration efforts Bliss had put in place.[14]

Bliss was involved in races up and down the ticket in 1950. At the congressional level, he showed his knack for matching candidates with constituencies. Bliss always had his talent scouts on the lookout for a good candidate in the Akron congressional district. They discovered William "Bill" Ayres, a veteran and a furnace salesman who had made a name for himself by winning a confrontation with the East Ohio Gas Company. He had persuaded the Public Utilities Commission to rule against the company's attempt to prohibit independent contractors from converting older homes to gas heat.

News of Ayres reached Bliss and he wanted to take a personal look. Ayres came to Columbus and Frankie Avren picked him up at the airport. Avren started grilling Ayres right away, saying the word was that Ayres was "not much of a Republican," Ayres recalled. "He was a tough little guy. I liked him right off the bat because he's boom, boom, boom. And I said 'I've never voted in a primary but I've voted in every general election.'" Ayres reminded Avren of his successful struggle with the gas company and asserted that it had been a "free enterprise issue." Avren told him that Bliss had heard that he was a good speaker. "I said, 'Well, that's not for me to judge. I've had a little experience, did a lot of debating in college and high school, for that matter,'" Ayres said. Eventually Ayres met with Bliss. "It was very enlightening to me....Not once did he ask me where I stood on certain issues. It was, 'Can you raise money? Are you willing to devote full-time to the job of running or is this going to be just something to promote your business?' The general gist of it was just getting acquainted," said Ayres.[15]

Although he did not know it at the time, Ayres had undergone a typical Bliss candidate screening. Bliss always wanted to get the opinions of others as well as his own before making a decision, said Avren.[16]

Ultimately, Bliss settled on Ayres as the best candidate to oppose incumbent Democratic congressman Walter Huber. But he did not want Ayres to face a contested Republican primary. So in typical fashion, Bliss went to work behind the scenes and Ayres was unopposed for the nomination. "I might have won the primary, but I wouldn't have won the [general] election," said Ayres.[17]

As election day neared, Bliss did his best to fire up the Republican troops with public speeches—an uncharacteristic activity on his part. He warned that Taft's reelection "is not in the bag."[18]

The Ohio Republicans won big on election day—up and down the ticket. Although Bliss rarely engaged in self-promotion, he later highlighted the stark differences between the 1948 defeat and the 1950 victory:

> In 1948, with eight state-wide offices in contest, we elected only one Republican candidate. Forty-four counties gave the GOP candidates a majority in these races. In 1950, with seven state-wide offices in contest, we elected five Republican candidates. 63 counties gave the GOP candidates a majority in all seven of the races.
>
> In 1948, the Republicans won eleven of the 23 congressional seats in Ohio. In 1950, the Republicans won fifteen out of 23 congressional seats in Ohio.
>
> In 1948, Republicans won only 14 seats in the state senate. In 1950, they won 27 seats.
>
> In 1948, Republicans won 65 seats in the lower house of the state legislature. In 1950, they won 98.

Bliss's summary was directed in part at fellow Republicans who doubted his approach. He concluded: "The results in Ohio conclusively prove that we waged a campaign on behalf of the entire ticket."[19] The biggest prize was Senator Taft's reelection. Taft won with a comfortable 58 percent of the vote. Bill Ayres won a very close election in the Akron-area congressional district—49 percent in a three-way race.[20]

The biggest disappointment was that Democrat Frank Lausche was elected governor. Lausche would vex Bliss for years to come.

Chapter 19

Mr. Republican Loses White House Bid

"Bliss Star Rises with Taft Victory" was a headline in the *Akron Beacon Journal* after the 1950 election. The story went on to say that a spokesman from the Republican National Committee said privately that the Ohio GOP organization was the best in the country. The newspaper warned: "Bliss, new in the chairmanship and responsible for a campaign which the whole nation was watching, displayed remarkable finesse. He's liable to become Republican National Chairman someday if he doesn't watch out."[1]

Bliss's name would be regularly mentioned for national chairman as his career advanced. As became evident during his selection as state chairman, Bliss had a characteristic approach to such discussions, playing his cards very close to his vest. Bliss's friend W. Richard Wright described how Bliss operated. "He let the flow come to him," said Wright.[2]

Bliss knew that in politics the appearance often becomes reality. If it appeared that the flow was coming to him, not that he was avidly seeking the chairman's job, most people would get the impression that the job was indeed coming to him. This appearance, however, masked an important Bliss trait. According to former Akron congressman Bill Ayres, Bliss sought the top party job "an hour after he became state chairman." Bliss did not want to be an officeholder who could aspire to be governor, senator, or even president. Instead, he wanted to be a party leader, so the national chairmanship was "the place for him to go," said Ayres.[3]

In 1951, Bliss became a featured speaker at Republican gatherings across the country.[4] He soon had a chance to prove he could win close elections as well as landslides. Back in Akron, Mayor Charles Slusser was reelected to an unprecedented fifth term in City Hall in a rematch of the 1949 race. The contest was extraordinarily close: Slusser prevailed by just 511 votes out of more than 75,000 cast. The contest was not settled until the last two precincts reported at 3:30 A.M. Bliss was on hand in his capacity as Summit County chairman to tell reporters that the mayor would not concede until all the votes were counted—or recounted if necessary. "The election proved there were deep undercurrents of feeling and a tremendous amount of campaign work done that did not appear on the surface," the *Akron Beacon Journal* reported.[5]

Back at the national level, Chairman Bliss appeared before the US Senate Committee on Rules and Administration on January 7, 1952.[6] The Senate was considering changes to the campaign finance laws and wanted to know about the 1950 Ohio senatorial race. More than two dozen Ohioans from both political parties testified along with Bliss.

Bliss's testimony was detailed, precise, and forthright. The senators learned that each party ran its campaign differently. All told, $276,000 had been spent on behalf of Democratic senatorial candidate Joe Ferguson, with $230,000 coming from labor union committees, supplementing union activists at the grassroots. In contrast, $467,000 was spent on behalf of Senator Taft. But what made the difference were the activities of the state Republican Party. The GOP spent $1.2 million on behalf of the entire ticket, including its sophisticated party headquarters and extensive grassroots operations.

When asked about this campaign for the entire Republican ticket, Bliss said: "I am an organizational man in my belief, and I believe in the fundamental theory that we should have a ticket operation."[7]

Later that year, when Taft announced that he would seek the Republican presidential nomination for a third time, Bliss was expected to play a major role.[8] Things did not work out well for either "Mr. Republican" or the "organizational man."

Bliss managed Taft's primary campaign in Ohio, delivering all the delegates for the senator. One of these delegates was Bliss himself. Although he had attended previous Republican national conventions, it would be Bliss's first trip in an official capacity. He would serve as a delegate to every Republican national convention until 1976, just before his retirement in 1978.

Once the campaign moved to the national convention in Chicago, Bliss was sidelined by Congressman Clarence Brown Sr., a longtime Taft ally and strategist, who had managed his convention efforts in 1940 and 1948. Bad feelings between Bliss and Brown dated from 1932, when Bliss opposed Brown's nomination for governor. Bliss had only two assignments at the convention, both of which he accomplished: to hold Ohio's delegation in line for Taft and to deliver the support of his fellow state chairmen (all but one stuck with Taft).[9]

The 1952 GOP convention was "one of the most bitterly contested struggles for a nomination in American history."[10] It was a showdown between Taft's "real Republicanism" and the "modern Republicanism" of General Dwight D. Eisenhower. Eisenhower had been Supreme Commander of the Allied Forces in Europe in World War II and was drafted for the presidential nomination.

The two candidates were closely matched in terms of delegates, so strategy at the convention was crucial to winning the nomination. Brown was again ineffective. Critics claimed the Taft managers showed the "least possible understanding of people and publicity" and were nicknamed "the stumbling board" by Ohioans at the convention.[11] Eisenhower won the nomination on the first ballot and picked Senator Richard Nixon of California as his vice-presidential running mate.

After winning the nomination, Eisenhower showed unusual deference to Taft. He reversed the tradition of the vanquished candidate calling upon the victorious candidate. Instead, he sought out Taft, saying he "came over to pay a call of friendship on a great American."

"I want to congratulate General Eisenhower," Taft replied. "I shall do everything possible in the campaign to secure his election and to help in his administration."[12] Bliss found this appeal to party unity encouraging.

The Democrats drafted Illinois governor Adlai Stevenson II as their presidential nominee. An eloquent speaker with an intellectual bent, Stevenson chose Senator John Sparkman of Alabama as his running mate.[13] A hard-fought general election campaign was expected.

Chapter 20

Ohio Likes Ike

Ray Bliss emerged from the 1952 convention with his status enhanced within the Republican Party. The convention changed the membership of the Republican National Committee. It had been made up of one national committeeman and one national committeewoman from each state, but a new rule added party chairmen from states that had recorded Republican victories. Bliss's success in Ohio meant that as state chairman he qualified to be a member of the national committee.[1]

Bliss quickly involved himself in the presidential campaign. The Republican convention ended July 11, and Bliss invited Eisenhower to speak to the Ohio State Republican Convention in Columbus on July 31.[2] The GOP nominee declined and instead sent his running mate Richard Nixon. Bliss responded by inviting Arthur E. Summerfield, Eisenhower's choice as chairman of the Republican National Committee, to attend as well. "We extend this invitation to you because we want Ohio to take the lead in launching the 1952 campaign to elect Gen. Eisenhower president and Sen. Nixon vice president next November," Bliss wired. Summerfield was equally pleased and wired back: "Out of such a cooperative spirit we shall forge a glorious victory in November."

Summerfield was not on good terms with either of the other two Ohioans on the national committee, Clarence Brown Sr. or Katherine Kennedy Brown (unrelated to each other). He needed another contact in Ohio. On September 6, Summerfield announced that Bliss had been named to the Republican Party's fifteen-member national executive committee, the prestigious group assigned to implement party strategy in the campaign.[3] Bliss's appointment sent a message: Eisenhower and his supporters wanted to heal any Ohio wounds left by the bitter nomination struggle with Taft, and Bliss was the person who would do the healing.

Overall, Bliss and the Eisenhower campaign worked well together. Bliss's devotion to detail appealed to Eisenhower, who had spent nearly his entire adult life in the army and appreciated order. "He wanted things to happen 1-2-3 and so on," Bliss said later.[4] That was not the way things had been going for Eisenhower before the general's campaign rolled into Ohio. "He had just come in out of another state where the train he was on was just a damn mess. They had room for 50 [people] and they couldn't kick anybody off once they were on and I guess they wound up by the time they got to the other side of the state, you couldn't even walk through cars," Bliss said.

"The first time he came into Ohio, I took charge of him and had everything organized and didn't have everybody running around pulling at his coattails....I was lucky....It went off just right....He appreciated orderliness," Bliss said. Bliss carefully choreographed Eisenhower's September 23 nine-stop whistle-stop tour in Ohio. The original plans called for the campaign train to leave Cincinnati at 8:15 A.M. and arrive at its final destination, Cleveland, at 6:15 P.M., 10 hours and 239 miles later. In between, stops were scheduled at Middletown, Dayton, Springfield, Columbus, Delaware, Galion, and Wellington.[5]

Bliss took absolutely nothing for granted. A few days before the scheduled tour, Bliss got word that Eisenhower's handlers planned to eliminate the stops at Wellington and another one at Delaware. Bliss did not agree and wired the campaign. "I strongly protest proposed change in 15-minute scheduled stop Delaware Ohio. Chamber of Commerce has arranged for stores to close, schools to close, Ohio Wesleyan [a college located in Delaware] to let out classes. Caravans are coming from many adjacent Republican counties. This is a strong Republican area and any change in plans at this late date will be extremely harmful," the telegram read.[6] Bliss got his way—this time, but not always.

Bliss's influence with the presidential campaign did not mean that he ignored his primary constituents, the men and women working for the Republican cause across Ohio. Martin Coyle, the Republican chairman in Butler County, which includes Middletown, was displeased with part of Eisenhower's whistle-stop tour. He sent Bliss a telegram reporting that the nominee had failed to meet with the local press and had not acknowledged city and county political leaders on the rear platform of the train. Bliss wrote back to Coyle on September 26 to let him know that his criticism had been received. Even while negotiating with the handlers of the nation's top Republican, Bliss knew that his strength came from people like Coyle at the grassroots. They were his eyes and ears all over Ohio, and he would do all he could to keep them happy and retain their loyalty.[7]

Political scientist Arthur Peterson said that the chairman developed categories for campaign tours. One category was "statewide" or "permanent party" tours, which included prominent elected Republicans, party officials, and other dignitaries. Another category was "district" tours, which included district elected officials and dignitaries. Two other categories were "regional" tours, limited to finance committee members, and "county" tours, which included county elected officials and dignitaries. "Insofar as possible," wrote Peterson, "the person in each category accompanied the permanent party only within the categorical jurisdiction, thus allowing for maximum exposure of the presidential candidate with local and state party leaders and office holders."[8]

All the hard work paid off for Republicans in Ohio. Eisenhower carried the state with nearly 57 percent of the votes. In addition, the GOP held all its statewide offices, all its congressional seats, and control of the state legislature—but failed to dislodge Governor Frank Lausche.[9]

Chapter 21

The Organizational Man in Action

The 1952 election put a Republican in the White House for the first time in twenty years—and for the first time in Ray Bliss's political career. Ohio's organizational man wanted to make sure that the party faithful, who had worked so hard for Eisenhower's election, would be well taken care of at the celebration that followed. Elaborate plans were made for the Ohio Hospitality Suite at the Raleigh Hotel in Washington, DC, for those attending the inauguration on January 20, 1953.

A memo to Bliss from aide Florence Morris contained the kind of attention to detail for which Bliss was famous: There would be "Yummy Treat" syrup for making punch, 2 alphabetized registration books (one for Ohioans, the second for out-of-state guests), 4 scratch pads, 100 plain envelopes, 1,000 silk badges with pins attached, 1,000 paper cups, 6 ball-point pens, 12 lead pencils and, in case they needed sharpening, 3 pencil sharpeners (five and dime store variety).[1] "Politics," Bliss told Madge Doerler "is a thousand little favors."[2]

In the nation's capital, the usually cautious Bliss sounded almost cocky when he talked to a reporter about his success in Ohio. "I'm the kind of a guy that likes to do things that people say can't be done," Bliss said. "I did not want to be state chairman in 1949, but the Taft campaign presented so big a challenge that I couldn't turn it down. My friends told me we didn't have a chance of reelecting Taft to the Senate, that Ferguson couldn't be beaten....Almost everybody in the country knows how that one came out."[3]

A few weeks earlier, Bliss's peers had recognized his accomplishments by choosing him chairman of the twenty-one-state Midwest and Rocky Mountain Republican State Chairmen's Association.[4] Organized in the late 1940s, one of its goals was to influence presidential politics. But another goal was professional: the chairmen wanted to learn how to run better campaigns. Thanks to a 1952 rule change, state chairmen who won elections became members of the Republican National Committee. Bliss was a model state chairman on all counts.

As with polling and television advertising, Bliss did not invent the chairmen's association, but he used it in an innovative fashion. The association linked the state and national Republican organizations. This linkage was so productive that Bliss was reelected as chairman of the association until 1962. Then the group "metamorphosed" into the national Republican State Chairmen's Association, with Bliss as its leader, absorbing the other regional associations. In 1968, all state chairmen became official members of the national committee, along with the national committeeman and committeewoman for each state.[5]

In March 1953, Republican national chairman C. Wesley Roberts abruptly resigned due to a controversy in his home state of Kansas. Ray Bliss was one of several possible candidates mentioned in a story in the *Akron Beacon Journal*. Another name on the list, former congressman Leonard W. Hall of New York, eventually became national chairman. But Bliss had positioned himself as acceptable to—even admired by—Eisenhower and his allies. "Although Bliss is an ardent supporter of Senator Taft, he was said Saturday to be acceptable to former National Chairman Arthur Summerfield because of his diligent campaign last fall for the Eisenhower-Nixon ticket. Bliss is rated high among Republicans as an organizer," his hometown paper reported.[6]

Bliss said he didn't want the job. "I am honored that some of my friends feel the way they do about me, but I would decline the chairmanship of the national party if it were offered." William "Bill" Saxbe, the Republican Speaker of the Ohio House of Representatives, was relieved: "Our whole legislative program would probably collapse if Bliss moved to Washington."[7]

Throughout 1952, Saxbe had waged a campaign to become Speaker. But the underlying contest was between Bliss and former GOP state chairman Ed Schorr. Schorr had supported Bliss for state chairman in 1949. But when Schorr had stepped down as state chairman in 1945, he did not return home to Cincinnati. He stayed in Columbus and became a full-time lobbyist. Schorr saw the state legislature as a source of personal income, while Bliss saw it as a source of public policy that could attract votes for Republican officeholders and candidates.[8]

After the Republicans took control of the Ohio legislature in 1950, a Schorr ally and relative by marriage, Gordon Renner, became Speaker of the Ohio House of Representatives. Renner worked hard on Schorr's agenda but was indifferent to other matters and careless in managing the chamber. This ineffective legislative leadership allowed Governor Lausche to gain an upper hand, even though the GOP controlled the legislature.[9]

Anticipating that the Republicans would retain control of the Ohio House in the 1952 election, Saxbe decided to seek the speakership. "Bliss was chairman and he wanted me to beat Renner," said Saxbe, noting that Bliss "played his cards close to his belly" and operated behind the scenes.[10]

The first part of Saxbe's campaign coincided with military duty, when he was called back to service in the US Army during the Korean War in January 1952. He wrote letters to Ohio legislators asking them for support in the upcoming leadership battle. When he returned from service in the fall of 1952, he put his campaign into high gear. "I got an old car and I started traveling Ohio. I visited every Republican legislator," said Saxbe.[11]

Saxbe won the contest by about a two-to-one vote in the Republican caucus.[12] Schorr's influence as a lobbyist began to wane once he had lost his connection to the Speaker's office. Bliss filled the vacuum. He began meeting regularly with the legislative leadership. The sessions were similar to those he had held in Akron with the mayor and city council. Saxbe recalled, "It wasn't what was discussed there. It was the fact that we were working together and we had a good relationship. . . . It was so casual that nobody presided." If a businessman with a problem came to Bliss, he would set up a meeting with the lawmaker but would not tell the legislator what to do. "Ray was very smart in handling legislative matters. He did not interject himself into lobbying like Schorr had done," said Saxbe.[13]

Not everyone viewed Bliss's legislative efforts as gentle. Clyde Mann teased the chairman about his autocratic style. Mann would call him the "little Prussian" and "dictator." The terms irritated Bliss, but under Speaker Saxbe's leadership, he got the kind of "good government" he needed to win statewide elections.[14]

Bliss's interest in public policy went beyond elections. For example, in 1953, Bliss helped create the Ohio Legislative Service Commission to assist legislators in developing good policy proposals. Bliss believed this work should not be done at party headquarters because legislators from both parties needed such assistance.[15] Bliss was also an advocate for increased public spending on highways. According to Mann, Bliss strongly backed a state ballot issue to improve highways—against opposition from the Republican legislature and the Democratic governor. Eventually, the issue was put on the ballot, where it won handily.[16]

Having an ally in charge of the Ohio House of Representatives and a Republican in the White House were positive developments for Bliss. But he also got some bad news in 1953. In the Akron mayoral race, the long-serving Republican mayor, Charles Slusser, was not on the ballot; Bliss had helped him become the Federal Housing Administrator in the Eisenhower administration. Longtime Republican leader J. P. Riddle faced off against Democratic city council member Leo Berg, who won a decisive victory. For the first time in ten years—since Bliss had become Summit County chairman—the Democrats controlled Akron city government.[17]

Then on July 31, 1953, Senator Robert A. Taft died. "The passing of Robert A. Taft is a tragic loss to America," said President Eisenhower. "The American people have lost a truly great citizen and I have lost a wise counselor and valued friend."[18]

Bliss, years later, used similar words to describe Taft's death. "It was a tragic loss to this nation in critical times when he died," said Bliss. "He had the ultimate respect, even the liberals respected him and that's unusual in Congress." One of the pillars of Bliss's professional life had fallen. "I have a great fondness for him. I think he was a great man," Bliss said. "He was the most knowledgeable man in national politics on governmental affairs that I have ever known. He had a mind like an encyclopedia."[19]

Taft's death presented Chairman Bliss with a thorny political problem back in Ohio.

Chapter 22

George Bender and a Judas Goat

Governor Frank Lausche appointed fellow Democrat Thomas Burke, mayor of Cleveland, to fill the US Senate seat left vacant by Robert A. Taft's death. Ray Bliss's goal was for Republicans to pick a candidate who could oust Burke in a November 1954 special election and then serve out the last two years of Taft's term.

Bliss normally would have worked behind the scenes to find a consensus candidate to challenge Burke without a formal party endorsement. As he had done in Summit County, Bliss wanted to develop candidates in lower offices and then move them up. "We've got to have a 'farm system' like they have in baseball. We must develop honest, aggressive and intelligent candidates,'" said Bliss.[1]

But this time Bliss did not get his way. While on a trip out West, he came down with hepatitis and was hospitalized for nearly two months, said Madge Doerler.[2] The hospitalization loosened Bliss's control over the state party.

US Representative George Bender, the chairman of the Cuyahoga County Republican Party, wanted the state party's endorsement in the senatorial primary. This was contrary to Bliss's policy, but Bender obtained it on a voice vote when the Ohio Republican Executive and Central Committee met in Bliss's absence on January 7, 1954.[3]

In a letter to a disgruntled Republican, Bliss later explained his initial thoughts about the 1954 senatorial nomination: "I, as chairman of the state committee, was interested in securing either Bob Taft Jr. or C. William O'Neill to run for that office."

But Bliss continued, "business people and various party leaders who I am sure honestly thought that Bender would be the strongest candidate, inasmuch as he had successfully run for Congressman at large and his name was well-known to the voters of Ohio,...convinced a majority of our party leaders that such was the case and they decided to support him."[4]

Bliss tried to take defiance of his position in stride. He said he did not "oppose or endorse any endorsement. It has always been my policy to endorse only incumbents. However, a majority insisted on making endorsements and took action accordingly."[5]

The state party's endorsement of Bender, however, must have been particularly hard for Bliss to take.[6] Bender had become a regular and vociferous Bliss critic. Back in 1950, Bender had accused Bliss of lacking the "intestinal fortitude" to have the party endorse state treasurer and Akron native Don Ebright for governor. Bender's discontent grew, and by the time of the 1952 Republican state convention, he vowed to get Bliss "thrown out as state chairman." When Eisenhower campaigned in Cleveland in September 1952, Bender felt slighted and lashed out. "Bliss is stupid," he ranted to reporters. "What can you expect from a stupid state chairman....Bliss has a bunch of stupid men around him."[7]

As was his custom, Bliss did not respond publicly to such attacks with attacks of his own, although he sometimes explained his position. But privately he could be tough: "I have worked day and night, both as county and state chairman and have no apologies to make to you or anyone else for my record," Bliss wrote to a critic. "All I challenge you to do is show me a better one. Ask any Washington newspaperman, any White House aide, any ranking staff member of the Republican National Committee, any Republican state chairman in the 21-state Midwest and Rocky Mountain State Chairmen's Association, which state organization they consider as being the finest and doing the best job."[8]

Bliss was resigned to supporting Bender for the US Senate nomination, but Bliss ally and Ohio House Speaker Bill Saxbe was not. Saxbe thought someone else would get into the race against Bender, but a formidable opponent failed to materialize. As Saxbe recalled in his memoirs, at breakfast with his wife Dolly one morning he said, "This is ridiculous. This guy is a clown and an insult to the Republican party." If he felt that way, why didn't he get into the race himself? Mrs. Saxbe asked him.[9] According to John S. Andrews, who served as state chairman after Bliss, Mrs. Saxbe was not the only person encouraging him to get into the race. Republican members of the Ohio legislature also urged him to run. Andrews remembered having a "couple of beers" with Saxbe in Columbus when the Speaker told him that he was going to run against Bender. Andrews reported back to Bliss before Bliss heard from Saxbe. "He was stunned," said Andrews.[10]

Saxbe tried to explain himself to Bliss. "I believe in the open primary and I am convinced Mr. Bender should have opposition because he and I represent two different kinds of political theories," said Saxbe. If Bender won, Saxbe said he would support him. "I hope Bender will support me if I am nominated," he added.[11]

Saxbe announced his candidacy for the Senate nomination on January 13, 1954, a week after the state party's endorsement of Bender. Once in the race, Saxbe lost no time taking after his opponent. "I think Bender typifies the old style ward heeler and petty politician that we have tried to get away from in Ohio," Saxbe said.[12]

Bliss reacted quickly to Saxbe's public announcement: "In view of the endorsement of the Republican state committee and in the interest of party harmony in Ohio, I strongly urged him not to be a candidate. I also told him the Republican committee would wage a vigorous and aggressive campaign to nominate its endorsees, and they include George Bender."[13] Despite their friendship, Saxbe made Bliss a campaign issue in the primary. "I have no quarrel with Bliss, despite the latter's support of Bender. Bliss is a victim of circumstance," Saxbe said, and then added, "It is common talk that Bliss' days are numbered if Bender wins."[14]

Bender suddenly became a strong Bliss defender. The candidate and the chairman staged a show of "mutual esteem" at a breakfast press conference in Columbus on April 1. The party's reputation was on the line. "I am for Ray for state chairman now and in the future, too. There's no question where I stand," said Bender.[15] Bliss said that the central committee had reaffirmed its endorsement of Bender.

A turning point in the campaign came April 14 when Saxbe was in Washington, DC, trying to drum up support for his candidacy among Ohio Republicans in Congress. He discarded any effort at flattery and went after Bliss with a slaughterhouse metaphor.

Bliss, Saxbe said, was a "Judas goat leading the state party to slaughter in November."[16]

In other words, by backing Bender, Bliss would lead all Republicans to defeat. That criticism energized Bliss, said Andrews. Bliss began calling the Republican chairmen in Ohio's urban counties and asking them to make sure Bender won. Bliss's message was clear: "By criticizing me, he [Saxbe] was taking on the whole party organization. You can't have some guy out there that's going to beat us. We've endorsed. We need your help."[17]

In his autobiography, Saxbe wrote that the Judas goat reference doomed his campaign.[18] Bender won a convincing victory in the May 4 primary, getting 57 percent of the vote. Saxbe telegraphed congratulations to both Bender and Bliss. He offered his services to Bender in the general election campaign and said keeping Bliss as state chairman was a must for the party.[19]

"Ray didn't like to get into fights," said Alex Arshinkoff. "Now, if one came along, he didn't run away from it." Arshinkoff said Bliss gave him this lesson on how to use power: "Power is the reputation of power. It is the illusion of power. To use power is to lose power. And, in all cases, negotiate and compromise, but, if a fight comes, and it is inevitable and unavoidable, use your power so strongly and so tough and so vicious and so... with all the strength you have.... When you use it, you lose it. So, if you use it, use it for every nickel's worth."[20]

Bliss emerged a winner from the Bender-Saxbe battle, but he had used some of his power and there was a price to be paid in the future.

Chapter 23

Success and Sorrow

After the bitter senatorial primary contest, Ray Bliss made every effort to win the 1954 general election. There had been a challenge to his authority, but no change in the way he approached his job. The key was work, work, and more work, up to fifteen hours a day. Bliss, said employees at state headquarters, didn't know what a clock was for.[1]

The results were a success for Ohio Republicans: George Bender won the race for the US Senate by one of the smallest margins ever: 2,970 votes out of 2.5 million cast. The GOP also picked up a congressional seat, reelected all its statewide office-holders, and retained control of the state legislature.

The *Akron Beacon Journal* reported that Bliss "is credited with having pulled the political miracle of the year.... State chairmen from most states have been showering him with congratulations."[2] Bliss said the election was a tribute to Eisenhower and hard-working Ohio Republicans. He didn't mention himself.[3] He later said that the key to the campaign was a focus on the popular state legislative program enacted under Speaker Bill Saxbe's leadership.

Whatever the reason, Ohio bucked the national trend. Despite Eisenhower's personal popularity, the Republicans lost both houses of Congress in the 1954 midterm elections. The GOP would not regain control of Congress during Bliss's lifetime.

Bliss set his sights on winning the one office that had so far eluded the GOP under his chairmanship, the Ohio governorship. In 1954, Democrat Frank Lausche won a fifth two-year term. Bliss wanted good policies and a good candidate to run against Lausche in 1956.

First, however, Bliss's approach was put to a test in July 1955. Legislation on workers' compensation and unemployment benefits was stalled in the Republican-controlled legislature. Because of his experiences with labor unions in Akron, Bliss was especially sensitive to such matters. Many blue-collar workers and even union members would vote Republican if the party had good positions on these issues.

Republicans, Democrats, industry, and labor were all squabbling over details. The arguments became so heated that Senate President Pro Tem C. Stanley Mechem sent the workers' compensation bill back to committee to die. In the House, Speaker Roger Cloud refused to act on the unemployment compensation bill until the Senate passed the workers' compensation legislation.[4]

Bliss tried to bring industry's lobbyists in line. They could not get all they wanted, Bliss told them. They balked at first. Fine, said Bliss, there would be no legislation, but that would not end the controversy. He predicted that there would be a labor-initiated ballot issue on unemployment compensation and the state GOP would do nothing to oppose it. Bliss also sent a message to the union lobbyists: there would be no increases in either workers' compensation or unemployment compensation benefits if they held out for their demands. In the end, compromise legislation was passed. The Republicans had good policies with which to appeal to blue-collar voters—and such workers had received needed assistance.

Meanwhile, Bliss had to find a strong gubernatorial candidate. Because of the GOP victories in Ohio, there were many options. But the candidate to watch was C. William "Billy" O'Neill, the Ohio attorney general. O'Neill was just thirty-nine years old, but he always seemed to be moving up in Ohio politics. O'Neill had begun campaigning for a seat in the Ohio House of Representatives in 1938 before graduating from his hometown school, Marietta College. He won and at twenty-two became the youngest member. After serving six consecutive terms in the House and working his way through law school at Ohio State University, he became Speaker of the Ohio House of Representatives in 1947. At thirty, O'Neill was the youngest Speaker ever, and at thirty-four he became the youngest attorney general when he won the post in 1950. After six years in that office, O'Neill was ready to move up to governor in 1956.[5]

There was potential friction between Bliss and O'Neill. O'Neill had arrived in Columbus before Bliss took over as state GOP chairman and during his eighteen years of public service had built up his own extensive political organization, largely independent of the state party. Bliss's model for running a statewide campaign recognized the value of independent committees for the candidates, but these "supplementary" organizations were to perform different tasks than the state party. At the time, Bliss thought that the Republican organization should be able to give the Republican candidate about a million votes, approximately the same as for the Democratic Party. The supplementary organizations, in Bliss's view, should appeal to independents and Democrats, where another million votes were up for grabs. Bliss would ask for a liaison from the supplemental organization at state party headquarters.[6]

Years later, Bliss explained how he tried to make this system work: "My pattern has always been to run strong party organizations at the local, state and national levels. That means never get so involved with a single candidate that you get all wrapped up in him to the exclusion of strengthening the party and building its base for all candidates to run on." The approach had its downside: "There aren't too many who believe in that philosophy, you know. I made it work, and it paid dividends. But with that philosophy you don't usually get into the innermost sanctum of thinking of any particular candidates. If you do, you get too wrapped up with that candidate and ignore the interests of other candidates on the ticket, and I always found that undesirable."[7]

There were rumors in the press that O'Neill, if elected governor, would oust Bliss as state Republican chairman.[8] Bliss arranged a meeting with O'Neill and told him that if the attorney general was elected governor, Bliss would step down as state chairman. "Bill, you and I are not going to see eye to eye and I am not going to be going through two years of your governorship where I am constantly in a battle having to worry about my position. So, I am going to step down and not run for chairman in 1956 and you can have your man. I just don't need it. I am going back to my insurance business," Bliss later told Alex Arshinkoff.

O'Neill did not want Bliss to leave. "Ray, we can't have that. Who is going to raise the money? These industrial boys, they like you. They trust you. You can't quit," said O'Neill.

"Well, Bill, you know, I am not going to be a coat check guy. If I am the chairman, I am the chairman," Bliss responded.

"Ray, you be the chairman. I'll be the governor," said O'Neill. O'Neill said they wouldn't have problems.[9] "But of course we did have problems," Bliss later told a reporter.[10]

Bliss soon faced a serious personal problem: his mother, Emilie Bliss, died January 8, 1956, after a three-year illness. She was seventy-one.[11]

Although Bliss worked in Columbus as state chairman, he still lived in the family home in south Akron. Bliss was building a new house in the Fairlawn Heights section of Akron, but his mother resisted moving there, preferring to stay in the old neighborhood.[12] Bliss was forty-eight and had lived his whole life with his mother. He eventually moved to the new house, but a small part of him stayed behind.

"Ray just idolized that lady," recalled Madge Doerler. "He used to say to me, when my mom got sick, he says, 'Madge, take care of her. There's nobody who loves you like your mother loves you.'"[13]

Chapter 24

A Republican Governor — At Last

As Ray Bliss mourned his mother's passing, another health issue troubled him. In August 1955, President Eisenhower suffered a heart attack while vacationing in Denver, Colorado. At sixty-four, he was about the same age as Robert A. Taft had been when he died in 1953.[1]

Some Republican leaders could barely contemplate political life without Ike. While Bliss was concerned about the president's health, he was more hopeful about politics. He told a state Republican meeting in November that even without the popular ex-general leading the ticket, Republicans could win in 1956. "The Republican party is in better shape than it realizes and needs only an effective selling campaign to win in 1956, whether or not Mr. Eisenhower is the candidate," said Bliss.[2]

President Eisenhower recovered and on Leap Day 1956 declared he would seek reelection. As a popular incumbent, he faced no formal opposition in the GOP primaries. But a key question remained: did he want Vice President Nixon on the ticket again?

Eisenhower was urged to pick a less controversial Republican running mate. He was also intrigued by the possibility of Ohio's Democratic governor, Frank Lausche. An Eisenhower-Lausche ticket, the president thought, would attract millions of Democrats, move the Republicans toward the political center, and make the GOP the nation's majority party. Lausche's success in Ohio, his fiscal conservatism, and his ethnic background could bring strength to the ticket. "I'd love to run with a Catholic, if only to test it out," Eisenhower said.[3]

Vice President Nixon would not go quietly and did not volunteer to leave the ticket for a high-ranking cabinet post. At Eisenhower's direction, two of the president's political operatives, Leonard Hall and Robert Humphreys, presented the Lausche idea to Nixon. Hall later said that he "never saw a scowl come so fast over a man's face."[4] Nixon was popular with rank-and-file Republicans, in part due to his tireless campaigning for GOP candidates across the country. Bliss advised Eisenhower to keep Nixon on the ticket.

Meanwhile, Lausche had decided to run for the US Senate seat held by Republican George Bender. In June, Lausche hinted that if elected he might vote with Republicans to choose the Senate leaders. This was too much for Bliss. He let Lausche have it: "His statement concerning whether he would vote with us to organize the US Senate is a typical double-meaning Lausche statement. He doesn't say he will and he doesn't say he won't. He has used the same technique before." Voters should consult Lausche's record, not his rhetoric, Bliss urged. Lausche's actions proved he was a Democrat. Bliss added, "Now, by a statement full of innuendo, Lausche is frantically attempting to grab onto Eisenhower's coattail."[5]

The 1956 Republican National Convention in San Francisco had the feel of a coronation. President Eisenhower's name was to be placed in nomination by the Indiana delegation. As every other state passed up the opportunity to offer an alternative, Bliss provided a moment of levity when he said Ohio has no candidate "for the first time in twenty years," a reference to Taft's and Bricker's presidential campaigns.[6]

Back in Ohio, Billy O'Neill had won the Republican gubernatorial nomination over incumbent lieutenant governor John W. Brown with 73 percent of the vote. Brown complained about the "well-heeled and well-oiled machine of my opposition" and compared it to New York's Tammany Hall.[7] After the primary, Bliss was elected to a fourth two-year term as state chairman.[8]

By 1956, Bliss had developed a process for organizing general election campaigns at the state level. The process started with a combined meeting of the Ohio Republican Executive and Central Committee two weeks after the primary. At this meeting, Bliss shared his plans and deployed the committee members, plus the headquarters staff, to carry out the plans. Although Bliss asked for a formal endorsement of his plans, there was typically little opposition. Bliss provided the state committees, and later the county committees, with detailed information on the party nominees as well as campaign literature and materials.

The nominees had three opportunities to speak to the party leaders: a meeting of county chairmen in June, the state convention in September, and a fall meeting of the Ohio Federation of Republican Women. Candidates received financial support if they agreed to be part of an integrated fund-raising effort. They could take a lump sum or send bills to state headquarters. Bliss expected candidates to run their own campaigns. But he kept close tabs on their progress, and was always available to give advice. The keys to this strategy were thorough preparation, cautious decision making, and avoiding controversy.

Political scientist John Kessel wrote that "the fundamental difference between the Ohio Republican Party and other state parties is that the Bliss organization was a living presence in Ohio precincts. It was not a paper institution."[9] In 1956, the state-wide Republican campaign, including the governor's race, worked the way Bliss said such campaigns should—or as Kessel put it, as the "most thoroughly organized campaign Ohio has seen in modern times."[10]

For starters, the GOP centralized fund-raising was very successful. The state committee—with Bliss having a big role—decided how much of the state money individual statewide candidates were to receive. O'Neill got $150,000, and there were also fifteen separate "O'Neill for Governor" committees. These "supplemental" organizations raised and spent another $85,000. In total, O'Neill benefited from some $235,000, more than the roughly $82,000 spent by the Democratic nominee Mike DiSalle. O'Neill had a three-to-one advantage over his opponent in the new, hot advertising medium—TV. Here Bliss built on his pioneering use of TV in 1950. The television "air war" came of age in the 1956 campaign.[11]

Following the Bliss script, the Republican committees focused on getting out the base GOP vote, while the O'Neill committees went after independent and Democratic voters. The campaign featured tent meetings in July in nonmetropolitan areas, a campaign caravan through rural areas in August, and events in the big cities in September and October.[12]

On election day, the Eisenhower-Nixon ticket overwhelmed Democrat Adlai Stevenson II and his new running mate, Senator Estes Kefauver of Tennessee. Nationally, the Republican nominees got 57 percent of the popular vote, up from 55 percent in 1952. They did better in Ohio at 61 percent, up from 57 percent four years earlier.[13]

In the Ohio governor's race, O'Neill won with 56 percent of the vote. Republicans carried all the other statewide executive offices, held all their congressional seats, and retained control of the state legislature.

Democrat Frank Lausche won again, this time for the US Senate, ending the senatorial career of George Bender. Lausche's continued success did not dim Bliss's growing reputation with his fellow Republicans. The voting was barely over before

reports again surfaced that he was in the running to be national Republican chairman. Leonard Hall, chairman for the previous four years, was planning to leave the
job. The early frontrunner for the position, Fred C. Scribner Jr. of Maine, was named
an assistant Treasury secretary. Bliss and Meade Alcorn Jr. of Connecticut were
touted as the new favorites.[14]

For some Republicans, Bliss's past ties to the late Senator Robert A. Taft and the
"old guard" were troubling. Alcorn, in contrast, was said to be a "triple-threat man,"
a friend of top White House assistant Sherman Adams, former New York governor
Thomas Dewey, and Attorney General Herbert Brownell. Other Republicans saw
Bliss, who had a power base outside Ohio, as the only candidate capable of winning
a fight against Alcorn and the "eastern establishment." Bliss quickly took himself out
of the running, and Alcorn was chosen national chairman.[15]

Bliss was in no mood for a fight: there was trouble enough back in Ohio.

Chapter 25

A Rocky Start and a Showdown

When Billy O'Neill was sworn in as governor on January 14, 1957, he was the first Republican governor since 1948. It was a proud moment for Ray Bliss, but the good feelings did not last long. Governor O'Neill got off to a rocky start. Suddenly nothing seemed to go right for a politician whose career had been one success after another. He even fouled things up when attending Eisenhower's second inauguration in Washington, DC. When the car carrying O'Neill in the inaugural parade came to the viewing stand where Eisenhower was sitting, O'Neill mistakenly turned his back on the president to acknowledge cheering in the crowd.[1]

Back in Columbus, O'Neill seemed to turn his back on common sense. First, the governor recommended salary increases for state government department heads and board and commission members. He wanted higher salaries to attract top people to key cabinet posts, such as highways and mental health, but his inexperienced advisers told him it would be inconsistent to raise only some salaries. The legislature reacted strongly to the idea. "Wow," exclaimed one Republican lawmaker when the bill was introduced. "The $6,000-a-year raise itself is more than my school principal back home gets in a year." And "Heavens," said another Republican legislator, "increasing the salary $6,000 a year is unprecedented. Why that's more money than 95 percent of my constituents make in a year."[2]

By April, O'Neill asked the legislature to rescind the raises. The flip-flop left O'Neill's Republican friends confused, frustrated, and even "shocked." "I was surprised that they were so shocked," O'Neill responded.[3]

Soon O'Neill was in a fight over the failure of three cabinet appointments to meet Ohio's residency rules for appointees. Charlie Noble, the governor's choice for highway director, lived in New Jersey, not Ohio. Eventually Noble had to be hired as a consultant for a year before he fulfilled the state residency requirement.[4]

"O'Neill just had one disaster after another," said Keith McNamara, a Republican who later served in the legislature and who liked O'Neill. "Nothing worked out the way for him as it had been planned."[5]

Around Columbus, there seemed to be agreement on one thing—"that the Governor should take more advantage of the consistently reliable political thinking of State Chairman Ray C. Bliss whom he has virtually ignored since he took over the state executive post," wrote the *Akron Beacon Journal*'s Clyde Mann.[6]

Bliss had his own problems with O'Neill. Before the 1956 campaign, O'Neill and Bliss had come to an agreement about their respective roles if O'Neill was elected governor. But Alvin I. "Buddy" Krenzler of Cleveland, O'Neill's campaign manager and chief political adviser, had not signed on to that understanding. He wanted to replace Bliss as state chairman. "The state chairmanship had been on his mind," the *Akron Beacon Journal* reported, "ever since he became the big wheel in O'Neill's political machine. He had hoped to make his move to take over GOP headquarters in Columbus after the successful O'Neill campaign."[7]

According to Alex Arshinkoff, Krenzler was O'Neill's "hatchet man." He was part of a "bunch of young kids around him [O'Neill] and they all wore bow ties and had crew cuts."[8] Bill Saxbe, who was elected Ohio attorney general in 1956, said O'Neill's advisers were not the only ones who believed the governor should be the key figure in the state party: "It was just that O'Neill thought he was the key to the Republican Party in Ohio. No state chairman was going to take his place."[9]

Krenzler decided to pursue an indirect strategy for seizing control of the party. His plan was to unite the Republican organizations in Ohio's three largest and most powerful counties—Hamilton (Cincinnati), Franklin (Columbus), and Cuyahoga (Cleveland) against Bliss.[10] The plan failed.[11]

Krenzler's effort was hurt by O'Neill's poor relations with local party leaders. After the Republicans had been out of the governor's office for eight years, the new governor was giving preference to his own people and not the party faithful. Some opportunities were lucrative, such as running state liquor stores and motor vehicle license bureaus. In fact, Krenzler held an appointment as deputy registrar for motor vehicles in Cuyahoga County that earned him $30,000 to $45,000 a year.[12]

Bliss years later recounted what he considered O'Neill's misadventures to Arshinkoff: "For the first six months [of the O'Neill administration], none of the patronage decisions had gone through the party. They had all been decided by Bill O'Neill and his boys."[13] Bliss had a skeptical view of patronage. He once told a reporter that a "party organization built on patronage is built on quicksand."[14] And he understood from personal experience the problems it could cause. "Give a man a job," Bliss once told Madge Doerler "and you create nine enemies and an ingrate."[15]

Bliss also knew that patronage was part of the glue that held party organizations together. Every two years—and sometimes every year if municipal elections were included—party chairmen asked local activists to work hard, register voters, raise money, and get out the vote. To keep their loyalty to the party, instead of to individual candidates, the party leaders would help them win patronage appointments. Arshinkoff remembered Bliss's personal view of patronage requests when he was state chairman: "'I don't care about it. I don't like it. But when I want something, I expect it to be done in a day. That's how rare I call you [an officeholder], but if I do call you, handle it.'"[16] Just like the City Hall faction Bliss had faced in Akron, O'Neill was building loyalty to himself, not the party.

According to Arshinkoff, Bliss waited until June to call the governor and set up a meeting for that same day.

"Governor, this is Ray Bliss," he said.

"Hi, Ray. How are you?" the governor asked.

"What are you doing for lunch today?" Bliss responded.

"What do you mean?" inquired O'Neill.

"I want to have lunch with you," said Bliss.

"Well, I have a lunch, Ray," said the governor.

"Where are you having it?" wondered Bliss.

"Over at the Athletic Club," said O'Neill.

"What time is your lunch?" asked the chairman.

"Noon," said the governor.

"Governor, I don't need a lunch. All I need is a few minutes, so if you are going to have lunch at noon, I'll meet you there at 11:30. It's ahead of your lunch. It's going to take about 10 minutes for what I have to say to you. Will you meet with me?" asked Bliss. O'Neill agreed.[17]

"The place was packed for lunch," Bliss later told a reporter. "You could hear them buzzing when O'Neill and I walked in. I said, 'Bill, obviously you think there ought to be another state chairman. I gave you that opportunity. You urged me to stay on.... Well, I'm here. I never ran from a fight in my life, and remember, I never lost one in my life, and I don't intend to start now.'"[18]

Arshinkoff said the opening of the Bliss-O'Neill showdown was even more brutally candid. "Bill, you don't like me and I don't like you," Bliss reportedly said.

Bliss reminded O'Neill that during the campaign "you worked with me and I raised your money and you are in there and now you invited three of 46 state committee members and eight of 88 county chairmen [to inaugural activities]. And you don't give anybody else the time of day. Now that makes me look bad. I mean, I don't care about patronage, but the boys do in the county organizations."

Then Bliss told—he didn't ask—O'Neill what the options were. "You and I are going to talk over this whole situation, and if we aren't in agreement when we leave here, I'll call a meeting of the state committee.... If you want, I'll let you say all the reasons why I shouldn't be state chairman. We will take a secret ballot, and, after you count your two or three votes [out of 46], I will then propose the name of a man to run for governor. He will be drafted to run against you at the next primary. I will raise the money," said Bliss.

O'Neill said that wouldn't be necessary. "Ray, we can work this out," said the governor. The man he was supposed to have lunch with arrived, but O'Neill canceled the appointment. Instead, he and Bliss started negotiating, writing down their proposals on paper napkins.

The end result: no one could be hired or promoted in a state agency without the endorsement of that person's county chairman. The system was similar to the one Bliss put in place in Summit County back in the 1940s. Arshinkoff said the statewide system still was in effect when he became GOP Summit County chairman in 1978.[19]

After their showdown, Bliss and O'Neill "got along on a strained basis from then on," Bliss later told a reporter. Years later, before O'Neill died in 1978, they became close personal friends.[20]

But before this friendship blossomed, a political disaster struck Ohio Republicans.

Chapter 26

Business Defies Bliss

While Ray Bliss frequently had difficulties with fellow Republicans, he had come to terms with labor unions. The official party position was: "The Republican Party has for a long time been the friend of the working man and we will continue this policy of helping the working man all along the line. Our main purpose will be steady, increasing employment at good wages."[1]

By 1957, about one third of Ohio workers were union members—an all-time high—but pro-business Republicans dominated state and federal elected offices. The only Democrat elected statewide was Senator Frank Lausche, who frequently disagreed with organized labor.[2]

Ohio business leaders were not satisfied, however. Like their counterparts across the country, they were concerned by the success of the labor movement. "Big labor" had replaced communism as a prime domestic concern of conservatives.[3] A popular response was to seek state "right-to-work" laws. Such laws prohibited "union shops," where all workers in a unionized company were required to pay dues, whether they joined the union or not. Right-to-work laws were permitted by the Taft-Hartley Act, enacted in 1947 over the veto of President Harry Truman. One of the authors of the law was the late Ohio senator, Republican Robert A. Taft. The other author of the law, Congressman Fred A. Hartley (R-NJ), helped found the National Right to Work Committee in 1955. Its goal was to expand the number of right-to-work states beyond the existing eighteen.[4]

By 1957, the Ohio Chamber of Commerce was developing a right-to-work proposal. At the group's annual meeting, Herschel C. Atkinson, chamber executive vice president, outlined the proposal. The best approach was to amend the Ohio Constitution so that it would be difficult to change. A constitutional amendment required approval of Ohio voters, and there were two ways to get it onto the ballot. One was by an act of the legislature. However, five right-to-work proposals had previously been introduced in the legislature and each one had failed, due to lobbying by labor. The other way was through a petition drive. To get the issue on the November ballot, signatures of 354,210 registered voters would have to be gathered by August 6, 1958.[5]

Atkinson warned members that if they tried and failed, there would be negative consequences. The chamber members, by a voice vote, approved a resolution to launch the right-to-work petition drive and related campaign. The Ohio Chamber of Commerce wasn't alone in pushing the right-to-work proposal. The Ohio Manufacturers' Association, the Ohio Council of Retail Merchants, and the businesses they represented joined the effort. They were confident they would succeed.

"I feel it is one of the greatest things the state of Ohio has ever undertaken. The nation has her eyes on Ohio, and if Ohio is successful it will be a help in other states," said Calvin Verity, the Ohio chamber's vice president and state finance chairman of Ohioans for Right to Work, Inc., an umbrella group formed to promote the issue.[6] The right-to-work campaign quickly became a crusade for business—and generated a strong negative reaction from organized labor.

Ray Bliss was deeply troubled by the right-to-work proposal. He knew the campaign would not be conducted in a vacuum. If, as Bliss feared, the right-to-work campaign aroused union members, other Democrats, and Democratic-leaning independents to vote in big numbers, it would hurt the entire Republican ticket. Alex Arshinkoff described Bliss's views: "Ray's rule was when all things are equal, we're for business. But, g-ddamit, it better be equal. Right-to-work was a problem because it revved up the workers. You don't rev them up when they are coming in to vote. You want them so happy they are staying home so we can elect a few people. He [Bliss] understood that there was a fine line between being fair and hurting people."[7]

John Mahaney, later president of the Ohio Council of Retail Merchants, was just twenty-six in 1958 and the spokesman for the right-to-work campaign. At that time, many Ohio businesses were owned by families. The leaders of these companies were used to doing what they wanted, deferring to no one. Unlike Bliss, they saw the issue in terms of personal freedom and the marketplace. "I don't think they thought about it in a political context. They thought about it in the context of their own corporate interests," said Mahaney.[8]

As usual, Bliss had polling data to back up his views.[9] A mail poll conducted for the state Republican Party found that Senator John Bricker, who was up for reelection in 1958, had only a narrow lead over his likely Democratic opponent, Cleveland attorney Stephen Young (52 to 48 percent). Both candidates led among their own partisans, but Young was ahead among independents (47 to 41 percent). These numbers were not good for a governor or a senator seeking reelection.

The prospect of such losses frightened Bliss because a change in the Ohio Constitution was about to take effect. In 1954, voters had approved lengthening the term for the governor from two to four years. So a loss in 1958 would mean the GOP would be out of the governor's office for twice as long as in the past.

Bliss relied on more than polling data to gauge prospects for the election—he had a listening post in the labor community. Michael Pavick had been appointed to the Ohio Industrial Commission by Governor O'Neill, representing labor. Bliss had helped Pavick land the commission post.[10]

Pavick was an unlikely candidate to be labor's representative. He did not belong to a union and never had. He came from south Akron, Bliss's part of town, but he was born into much humbler circumstances. His parents, like Bliss's, were immigrants: his mother Mary was Slovenian and German and his dad Steve was "pure Croat." They arrived in 1910.

Disaster began striking the family in 1929. Pavick, then five, was hit by a drunk driver. Doctors wanted to amputate his right leg—they feared gangrene—but his father wouldn't let them. He underwent seven major surgeries and spent the next three years in and out of Akron Children's Hospital. In 1930, Pavick's father lost his job at B. F. Goodrich, and soon afterward his mother died of tuberculosis. Taking care of the family became too much for his father, so Pavick, a brother, and a sister were sent to orphanages. Eventually Pavick returned home, finished school, and attended Ohio State University for his undergraduate and law degrees.

Pavick had trouble finding a job with an Akron law firm. "I covered all the law firms. They didn't take foreigners," recalled Pavick, who was born in the United States but had a "foreign" name. "They were so g-d prejudiced. One of the guys [in a law firm] wanted me. His partner said 'we don't want any foreigners.'... Unless you were a white Anglo-Saxon you didn't get a job." He worked on a few cases for B. F. Goodrich and did pro bono work for the Akron Chamber of Commerce.

In 1950, Pavick volunteered for Billy O'Neill's campaign for attorney general. After O'Neill won, Pavick was recommended for a job as an assistant attorney general. But before he got the appointment, he had to see the chairman of the state and Summit County Republican parties. He met Bliss at the chairman's office in

Akron. "Ray looked me in the eye, with a big smile. You know, Ray wore kind of thick lenses. Sometimes his eyes looked a little crossed," Pavick remembered. Pavick thought maybe he had done something wrong.

"The first words out of his [Bliss's] mouth—'Are you a Republican or a Democrat?'" recalled Pavick. He said he really didn't know. "We'll find out," said Bliss, who picked up the phone and called the Summit County Board of Elections. Pavick had not voted in any primaries and therefore was considered an independent. Bliss said that would have to change. "He looked at me, pointed his finger at me and said 'you're a Republican now,'" said Pavick, who accepted his new party affiliation.

Pavick developed a close relationship with Bliss. "I idolized the man," Pavick said.

When O'Neill was elected governor, Bliss urged him to appoint Pavick to the Industrial Commission but O'Neill had another candidate—"a Teamsters' guy," as Pavick recalled. "I remember being in a car, coming from an Ohio State football game. Bill [O'Neill] and Ray [Bliss] got into an argument about the commission job," said Pavick. Bliss went to work drumming up support for Pavick with the building trades unions and used these contacts to win support for Pavick. When Pavick got the job, Bliss called him to his office in Columbus.

"He sat me down alone. He gave me the rules of conduct. 'When you go on that commission, Mike, you're only 34 years old. There are going to be people who are going to try to swing your vote...to give you money. You take nothing from anybody. I don't want to hear of it.'" Bliss told him to look after the interests of both employers and labor, although he officially was labor's representative. "I want you to be fair to everybody," Bliss said. Pavick followed Bliss's advice and developed a good rapport with union leaders.

When the right-to-work campaign began, a group of about ten labor leaders went to see Pavick. They had a proposal for O'Neill. "Go see Billy O'Neill and you tell him you talked to us and that all he has to do is not say he is for or against. All he has to say around the state on right-to-work is that 'everybody should vote their own conscience as I will vote mine.'" Otherwise, the labor leaders said, they would oppose the issue by sending sound trucks all over the state. They would tell housewives going into grocery stores to be sure to buy all the groceries they could because if right-to-work passed they wouldn't have the money to buy any more.

Pavick went to see Bliss. Now Bliss knew just how angry the union leaders were about the issue. Bliss told Pavick to tell O'Neill about the meeting with the labor leaders. Pavick didn't have much luck when he talked to the governor. O'Neill's response was: "They [unions] can't do anything about this. This is the right time for right-to-work. They can't hurt us."

In July 1958, Charles R. Hook, chairman of the ARMCO Steel Company in Middletown and a leader of the right-to-work campaign, called a luncheon meeting in Cincinnati to update supporters and Republican leaders on the campaign.[11] The list of attendees was like a Who's Who of Ohio industry and business. Governor O'Neill was invited, but it is unclear if he actually attended. To add to his many political problems, he had suffered a heart attack earlier in the year.[12]

Bliss and Senator Bricker attended the meeting. Bliss warned the group that if the issue was on the November 1958 ballot the Republican Party could lose everything in Ohio. Bricker spelled out the specifics of Bliss's doomsday prophecy. He told the enthusiastic businessmen that if they put the right-to-work issue on the ballot, Republicans might lose the legislature, the governor's office, and some seats in the US House—and Bricker himself might lose.[13] Bricker and Bliss make a last-ditch argument to postpone the issue until 1959, when there would be no elections for state or federal offices.

Some attendees openly laughed at Bricker's gloomy predictions. Others said Bricker was "gutless" and concerned only with "saving his own skin." Bricker walked out of the meeting.

"When I left the meeting," Bricker later told a friend, "nobody said 'goodbye,' 'good luck,' or even 'to Hell with you,' but I thought the latter was on the minds of most of those there. It is very hard to take from those who should have been my friends."[14]

Whether Governor O'Neill was in attendance or not, he was not willing to challenge the business leaders. Charles Kurfess, then a young Republican member of the state legislature and later Speaker of the Ohio House, said O'Neill always seemed eager to do what the business leaders wanted. Kurfess remembered a meeting he and another legislator had at the governor's mansion with O'Neill. A call came in for the governor and at first O'Neill said he would take it later. Then the aide said the call was from John W. Galbreath, a major business leader. "Bill O'Neill jumped up to take that call when he knew who it was," said Kurfess.[15]

Joseph Alsop, a nationally syndicated political columnist, concluded: "As a weak and unpopular Governor, poor O'Neill was the only Republican candidate who was then in danger of defeat.... Therefore, he melted rather more easily than usual, obediently announcing that he was for the Right-to-Work law and that Right-to-Work was the campaign's big issue."[16]

The right-to-work campaign met the August deadline with enough signatures to get the issue on the 1958 ballot. Now the outcome would be up to the voters.

Chapter 27

The Right-to-Work Disaster

Governor O'Neill had told the business leaders of the right-to-work campaign that he would back the issue, but it was not until September that he issued a written statement explaining that "personally, as a citizen of Ohio, I am going to vote for the right-to-work amendment." O'Neill based his support for the issue on "the growing cancer of corruption" in the labor movement: "Given the freedom, I am convinced that the working man would take things into his own hands and throw out the racketeers."[1]

The governor had enjoyed some labor support in the 1956 governor's race, but his public support for right-to-work guaranteed strong opposition. And opposition to the ballot measure was evident among Republicans as well.

J. C. Marion of Akron, Bliss's hometown, wrote to O'Neill and declared that he and his wife "have been lifelong Republicans.... But after listening to your political harangue of low blows and falsehoods and deceit we have come to the conclusion that our future would not be safe under such a demagogue as you and your kind—that no Republican is fit to hold an office of public trust.... We're switching. We're voting Democratic all the way," Marion wrote.[2]

Meanwhile, Senator Bricker tried for as long as possible to avoid taking a stand on the issue. He finally endorsed it on October 14 and, like O'Neill, couched his support as a stand against corruption in the labor movement.[3]

As state Republican chairman, Bliss did all he could to avoid formally tying the state party to the issue, but it was hard to do when the major GOP candidates, O'Neill and Bricker, endorsed the initiative. The usually calm Bliss was reported to be "madder than a blue jay" as election day approached.[4]

The right-to-work campaign did what Bliss feared. It energized both Ohio labor unions and the Democratic Party.

Even before the Ohio Chamber of Commerce formally launched the right-to-work campaign in 1957, the unions, aware of what was happening in other states, were preparing for battle. By November, labor forces came together to form "United Organized Labor of Ohio," representing 1,250,000 union members. Voter registration was a primary goal. The unions then worked hard to get out the vote and sound the alarms over the perils in store for working men and women if the issue passed.[5]

The timing was right for close cooperation between labor and the Democrats. Frank Lausche's election to the US Senate cleared the way for unity. Lausche had been a one-man show as Democratic governor and was not particularly close to labor. Union leaders and other anti-Lausche Democrats charged that Eugene H. Hanhart, who had become Democratic state chairman in 1948, served only Lausche.[6]

In 1956, Michael DiSalle of Toledo, the Democratic candidate for governor, picked a new state Democratic chairman, William L. Coleman, a lawyer from Union County in central Ohio. Under Coleman's leadership, the state Democratic Party made defeating the right-to-work issue part of its platform. Also, the Democratic candidates in the two highest-profile races—governor and US senator—made opposition to right-to-work key parts of their campaigns. DiSalle was running for governor against O'Neill again in 1958. Even before the right-to-work issue arose, O'Neill's problems in his first year in office made DiSalle a formidable challenger.[7]

However, taking on Republican Senator Bricker was more difficult. It fell to Stephen M. Young of Cleveland. Dubbed a "longtime political warhorse," he won the nomination to take on Bricker "by default" after potentially stronger Democrats stayed out of the race. Young was sixty-nine years old in 1958, and had served in the state legislature and the US House of Representatives. He had failed in campaigns for Ohio attorney general and governor. Young was opinionated, sometimes cranky, and like the late Robert A. Taft, certainly not made for television.[8]

Howard Metzenbaum, then a Cleveland lawyer and businessman and later a three-term US senator from Ohio, agreed to be Young's campaign manager. Metzenbaum knew that the right-to-work issue struck a raw nerve with workers. "Right-to-work legislation was known for what it really was, that is a way of breaking unions.

The union shop was a way to get all members of an employer to share the obligations and the expenses of the union. When you didn't have a union shop, it meant that a lesser percentage would be supporting the union although [everyone] would be getting the benefits of the union activities," he said.[9]

The Democrats and the unions had other allies in the campaign, an ecumenical combination of religious leaders. On March 24, 1958, the state's six Roman Catholic bishops announced their opposition. Seven days later, Rabbi Abba H. Silver of Cleveland, a widely known Jewish leader in the state, launched what one researcher called a "blistering attack" against it. The Ohio Council of Churches, representing Protestant denominations, also joined the opposition.[10]

Bliss returned to Akron for election night and ran into D. E. "Gene" Waddell, an Akron lawyer working for the Summit County Republican Party. "I said, 'Well, we really think we are going to win this governor's race,'" Waddell remembered. "Don't count on it," Bliss responded.[11]

Bliss was right. The results were a disaster both for the right-to-work advocates and the Republicans. The right-to-work issue got just 37 percent of the vote. It was the largest margin of defeat for a ballot issue in Ohio history. There were more votes against the issue—2,001,512—than votes for any of the winning candidates.[12]

Governor O'Neill was defeated by the largest margin ever for an incumbent governor. DiSalle won with 57 percent of the vote. The US Senate race was closer, but Young was the clear winner over Bricker with 52 percent of the vote. Democrats won every statewide race except secretary of state, took control of the state legislature, and added three congressional seats.[13]

What Bliss feared had come to pass. Voter turnout had exploded. More than 3.2 million Ohioans cast ballots, far in excess of previous nonpresidential election years. Political scientist John F. Fenton took an in-depth look at the returns and reached a conclusion that would not have surprised Bliss.[14] "The most interesting aspect of Ohio's 'right-to-work' vote was its well-nigh universal unpopularity," Fenton concluded. Middle-income voters joined members of the working class in voting "no." It seemed that clerks and foremen sensed that their wage increases followed those won by union workers, and many middle managers were not as antiunion as the Chamber of Commerce.

It was a grim night for Bliss.

Chapter 28

Ray Bliss Rebuilds — Again

As 1959 began, the Ohio Republican Party was back where it had been in 1949 when Ray Bliss became state chairman. Democrats controlled almost everything. President Eisenhower could not run again in 1960, being the first president limited to two terms in the White House. Even in Bliss's home base of Akron, the GOP was losing.

It was the kind of challenge Bliss had thrived on since 1937, the year he masterminded the winning campaign for Akron mayor.

Bliss pinned the blame for the Republican rout where he thought it belonged: "The defeat of many of our Republican candidates is directly attributable to the placement of the Right-To-Work-Issue on the Ohio ballot this year. The proposed amendment provided a live issue through which the labor leaders were able to turn out a huge off-year labor-Democrat vote.... During the past year, I repeatedly warned the proponents of this issue that this defeat would be the possible consequence. They chose to ignore my warnings," he thundered.[1]

Bliss got some pushback. Some Republicans believed Bliss was too quick to blame others for the 1958 election results. An anonymous critic opined: "Bliss had better stop heaping ashes on his head and wallowing in his own misery and get back to the job of winning elections."[2] However, Bliss had leverage: either the culprits would change their ways or he would resign as chairman.

Soon after the election, Bliss demanded a meeting with 25 chief executive officers of the top businesses in the state. Some 130 executives showed up for the session at developer John Galbreath's 4,300-acre Darby Dan farm about 25 minutes west of downtown Columbus. The executives flew directly to the farm, landing on Galbreath's private airstrip.[3]

Galbreath, one of the masters of ceremony for the postelection seminar, was a self-made millionaire. From humble circumstances, he made a fortune in real estate development and other businesses. He was a winner in sports, too: his horses twice won the Kentucky Derby, and he was part-owner of the Pittsburgh Pirates. Galbreath had the ear of fellow businessmen as well as public officials, such as the just-defeated governor O'Neill. For all his business success, Galbreath realized he was out of his league when it came to politics.[4]

At the seminar, Bliss said he was willing to continue as Republican state chairman, but on his terms, according to John Andrews, who later became Republican state chairman and attended the meeting. "You know, I don't need this job," said Bliss. "It's a headache, but I love it. And I'm willing to continue to do it, but we are going to do it my way. . . . I'll stick around as long as I call the shots."[5]

The business leaders had to promise to raise $1 million—a hefty sum in those days—for the next campaign. What became known as the "Ohio Republican Finance Quota Program" came out of the meeting. The amount of money to be contributed was based on factors such as the industrial strength of each community and the size of executive salaries.[6]

The businesses would also need to find jobs for Republicans who lost their jobs as a result of the right-to-work disaster. Furthermore, business lobbyists, Bliss told them, were not to interfere with his business—politics. He would concentrate on registering voters, raising money, finding candidates, and winning elections. The executives should stick to their businesses, and Bliss wouldn't bother them.

To make sure they got the message, Bliss came to the meeting with slides, charts, and graphs that detailed their bungling and what would have to be done to correct it. Andrews remembered the scene in the theater at Galbreath's estate. "The screen came down [from] the projection booth hidden in the wall up there . . . all the slides were shown from the projection booth." Bliss, as always, had numbers. He would identify a precinct in Dayton, tell the executives what a normal Democratic voter turnout was and then tell them how much higher the turnout had been in 1958. "It was clear and there was no argument about it. And then various people in the audience got up and said, 'Well, we were wrong,'" recalled Andrews.[7]

The executives agreed to do as Bliss had asked. They got back in their planes and flew home, leaving Darby Dan and the right-to-work fiasco behind them.

Bliss had learned some lessons as well—from the labor unions. The unions had grassroots representatives in communities large and small all across the state who worked together with labor leaders to defeat the right-to-work issue. "We had working against us last year the biggest organization in history. We couldn't compete with the Democratic forces and COPE [the AFL-CIO's Committee on Political Education]. They got their people registered and to the polls in greater numbers than we did because they outmanned us by a tremendous total of paid workers," Bliss said in January 1959.[8]

"Labor was doing all of this...get out the vote, registration, but it just happened to be for the benefit of the Democratic Party. That's what Bliss wanted to counteract," said Andrews. Bliss had been thinking about increasing and upgrading the state party's "field staff" to "field men" for a decade. In addition, he wanted to install political professionals as full-time executive directors in Republican county headquarters. Unlike Bliss, who had been a full-time chairman in Summit County, many other county chairmen were part-time, often lawyers who practiced politics on the side—and, in some cases, to the benefit of their law practices. Only a few large county parties had full-time staffs, but "most of the other counties simply had an office with a girl," Andrews said.[9]

After the 1954 election, Bliss persuaded Andrews's boss at Owens-Corning Fiberglas in Toledo to raise some extra money to pay the salary of a full-time director for the Lucas County Republican Party. Andrews eventually became the full-time chairman of the Lucas County Republican Party.

In 1959, Bliss decided that Andrews was a good candidate to assemble field man operations. Andrews knew, as did Bliss, that local political leaders resented outsiders telling them how to do their jobs. Field men were to be professional resources for local party leaders, not rivals. At a June meeting of county chairmen in 1960, once Andrews had the program ready to go, Bliss told the local leaders that they could use or reject the help as local conditions indicated. He told the field men that they were to "supplement," not "supplant," the county chairmen. The field men's detailed manual emphasized their balancing act. They worked with the county chairmen but worked for Andrews and Bliss.

The manual Bliss gave the field men showed sensitivity to the local autonomy that county party leaders guarded so closely: "Because each county and district is autonomous in relation to the State Committee, the relationship between them is purely voluntary. No field men will organize, direct or otherwise become involved in any county or district political activity without the knowledge and consent of the local leadership. It is intended that the field men develop and maintain a harmonious spirit of cooperation with the local leadership. Field men suggest programs and activities recommended by Headquarters, anticipating that local leadership will accept those which have reasonable opportunity for success in the area involved."[10]

Political scientist Frederick M. Wirt, a Democrat who served as a polling consultant for Bliss and the Ohio Republican Party, regularly reviewed the reports from the field men. The field men both provided services and became Bliss's early warning system for problems. "Let a local chairman complain of delays in literature ordered, and the field man got on the telephone to Andrews; he quickly looked up the snag and immediately got back to the local chairman about headquarters' response. This procedure gave the sense locally that Headquarters was not only aware of special problems, but was doing something about them; it also gave locals…a sense of participating in a campaign which reached outside their borders," wrote Wirt.[11]

By the time of the 1960 general election, ten full-time field men were deployed in congressional districts in Ohio's nonmetropolitan areas.

Bliss also needed to do some rebuilding back in Summit County, where he was still the Republican chairman. The *Akron Beacon Journal* reported that "if the GOP in Akron muffs this city election as it has the last three, the organization will suffer further loss of prestige and will go into the presidential election year [1960] under a serious handicap."[12] The story noted the devastating effect of the right-to-work issue on the local GOP, but the problems predated 1958. Akron had not had a Republican mayor since 1953. In the 1955 and 1957 elections for the thirteen-member Akron City Council, there were only two Republican winners. One reason was the growing clout of the local unions, but another reason was a popular and effective Democratic mayor, Leo Berg. After three Republican defeats in a row, it was time to innovate.

As the 1959 mayoral race approached, Summit County Republican Party executive director D. E. "Gene" Waddell had a plan to revive Republican fortunes. Bliss had appointed Waddell to the job after Clyde Mann said that Waddell had potential. Waddell had run for and lost a ward council seat in 1957, but in 1959 he was working full-time in politics while going to law school.

"I was real active in the Jaycees and that's where I got a lot of young guys to run for office," Waddell said. Waddell persuaded a political newcomer, Ed Garrigan, to run for mayor. Garrigan beat a more experienced Republican in the primary—Bliss's old foe Ed Rowe—and faced the popular Mayor Berg in the general election. But Garrigan needed an issue to run on, and Waddell wanted him to run against a city income tax, which was on the November ballot. The Akron Chamber of Commerce, which backed the tax, called Bliss in Columbus to protest. Bliss called Waddell to his office and told him, "You know, I'm getting a lot of heat on this income tax." "'Mr. Bliss, that's the only shot we've got to win.... We've got to have an issue and that's one that people are talking about,'" Waddell remembers telling Bliss, who reluctantly agreed.[13]

The campaign was an uphill battle. Besides the Chamber of Commerce, the *Akron Beacon Journal* backed the income tax as a way to pay for city capital improvements. In the end, Mayor Berg prevailed by about 100 votes; the income tax also won narrowly.[14] Bliss, however, was pleased with the Republican effort. "Bliss did not usually compliment too many people to their face, but some of his guys that would work in Columbus with him let me know that he was really complimentary toward me and toward the efforts we made in that race," Waddell remembered.[15]

Although Bliss wanted better Republican results in Summit County, he wanted the improvement to come honestly. His reputation for fair play was boosted by his treatment of Democrat Oliver Ocasek in 1958. Ocasek was running for a state senate seat against a Republican incumbent, Fred W. Danner. Unofficial results showed Ocasek losing by about 1,400 votes, but he noticed that there were more votes tallied from an Akron suburb than the total votes cast. The Democrats on the county board of elections showed little interest in pursuing this discrepancy, but Ocasek persisted, and a tabulating error showed that Danner had been credited with 2,000 more votes than he actually had received. Ocasek was pronounced the winner and went on to become president of the Ohio Senate.

"I have always given Ray Bliss a large part of the credit for looking into that matter and correcting it," Ocasek later told a reporter. "He's a Republican, but that doesn't interfere with his sense of justice and fair play."[16] When asked about the incident in 1981, Bliss seemed surprised that anyone would think it was unusual that he had done the right thing.[17]

Chapter 29

Wedding Bells

In 1959, Ray Bliss was fifty-two and hardly looked the part of a romantic. But there was another side to Bliss. He had been involved romantically for nearly three decades with Ellen Palmer, then fifty. They started dating at the University of Akron and suffered together through the May Queen fiasco and Bliss's expulsion from college. Ellen graduated on time in 1931 and Bliss received his degree in 1935.

For a while, Ellen had other suitors besides Bliss, but eventually they became regular companions. Ellen's parents approved of Ray, and Bliss's mother was fond of Ellen, but it was not a foregone conclusion they would wed. According to Alex Arshinkoff, Bliss's mother "did not want him to marry a Catholic."[1] Louise Earley, one of Ellen's sisters, agreed: "I do think that [difference in religions] might have had something to do with it [the long courtship].... After twelve years in the Catholic schools, you know the nuns...stay away from those non-Catholic boys." Once in a while someone would ask why the couple didn't get married. "We would say they're both too busy," said Earley.[2] Clyde Mann agreed: "Ray was really too busy with politics to get around to getting married."[3]

Ellen continued to live at home with her parents. But she didn't sit by idly, waiting for a proposal from Bliss. She taught sixth and seventh grades for twenty-nine years. "She really was a wonderful teacher," remembered Earley. "Ellen and I might be downtown and someone would come up to her and say, 'Miss Palmer, I'm so and so and you had me in the sixth grade.' They were so delighted to see her and many times thanked her for inspiring them."[4]

For her, teaching meant more than an eight-hour day. She sponsored the Junior Red Cross, brought clothes to school for a needy student during the Depression, and served as a delegate to the National Education Association convention. "Ellen was such a fine teacher that at one point they [school administrators] wanted to make her a principal. At that time to be a principal you had to have a master's degree.... They offered to skip that if she would agree to be a principal," said Earley.

When she wasn't at school, Ellen kept busy in alumni activities at the University of Akron and at her church, St. Vincent. She also was involved in Republican politics as a precinct captain and was a member of the Summit County Republican Central Committee and Ohio Council of Republican Women.[5]

Ray and Ellen frequently had dinner with Clyde and Della Mann, and sometimes Congressman Bill Ayres and his wife, Mary Helen, would join them. Dining out was one of Bliss's few relaxations. Ayres recalled Bliss's fondness for steak: "I can hear him now saying, 'medium rare and tender, please.'"[6]

Ellen, while not unhappy, sometimes would tease Bliss about the prospect of marriage, Della Mann said. "She'd say, 'Ray, I'm available' when we were out enjoying ourselves." Ellen also accompanied Ray to social events in Akron and out of town and sometimes this became awkward because they weren't married. Occasionally, the couple would be announced as "Mr. and Mrs. Ray Bliss." Della Mann recalled, "Ellen told us, 'Ray doesn't think about it, but it's an embarrassment.'"[7]

By 1957, the couple was clearly a team. When Bliss had a dispute with the contractor building his new home in Fairlawn Heights, Bliss gave the contractor Ellen's phone number to contact about the needed work. However, when the work still hadn't been done, Bliss wrote to the contractor: "I have checked with Miss Ellen Palmer whom I told you to call...if the contractors needed access to the house. She reports that you have never called her."[8]

When Bliss's mother became ill and he was in Columbus serving as state party chairman, Ellen and her mother, Ethel Palmer, would make sure that Mrs. Bliss got to the doctor and hospital, said Earley.[9]

In January 1956, Ellen attended the funeral service for Bliss's mother, said Della Mann: "If he hadn't had Ellen, I don't think he would have made it. She was right there with him."[10]

Emilie Bliss's passing removed the religious roadblock to marriage. But there was no immediate proposal from Bliss. Some friends thought Bliss was already married to his work, but others thought that Bliss was inherently shy and, despite his professional success, a bit insecure. It's possible that the prospect of marriage—and he would take seriously the commitments involved—unsettled him. Clyde Mann put it bluntly. "I think he didn't have the guts."[11]

"Once Ray said to me," Mann recalled, "'I think I'm going to ask Ellen to get married this weekend' and I said, 'Ray, that is great. But I'll bet you a bottle of Scotch you don't do it.' The next Monday I saw him, and he didn't say anything, just smiled and handed me a bottle of Scotch."

When the couple decided to get married, the announcement caught Clyde and Della Mann by surprise. They were on vacation when Bliss called them. The Manns had begun to wonder if it would ever happen. "This [plans to marry] had happened three times," reported Della Mann. "He told Clyde, 'This time I'm going to do it.'"[12]

"Clyde had razzed him," said Della Mann.

It would be a Catholic wedding at Ellen's church, St. Vincent. The wedding date, Thanksgiving, November 26, 1959, would be a special one for Ellen's family. It also would mark the fifty-first wedding anniversary of her parents, William and Ethel Palmer.

The wedding was a small one, with just twenty-two people present, most of them from Ellen's large family. Her father gave away the bride, sister Jean Wade was Ellen's only attendant, and Jean's husband, Jason "Jake" Wade, was Bliss's best man.[13]

Della Mann said she and Clyde appeared to be the only people on Ray's side of the church. From their seats they could see him before the service, pacing back and forth in the room where the groom waited, puffing one of the cigarettes that always seemed to be in his mouth.[14]

According to Earley, it was a nice wedding. "It was very brief because there was no Mass because Ray was not a Catholic. But they did have to get a dispensation of some sort so that they could be married in the church." A family dinner followed the wedding at Akron's Portage Country Club. "We had an orchestra and lots of champagne," said Earley.[15]

The newlyweds planned a honeymoon on the East Coast, where they would attend the Army-Navy football game in Philadelphia. While the wedding was small, "congratulatory messages began to arrive before Ellen and Ray left for the East," reported the *Akron Beacon Journal* story.[16]

After the wedding, the new Mrs. Bliss had a special thanks for the man who finally had become her husband.

"Ray, I'm so glad you came," she said.[17]

Ohio Republican Chairman Ray Bliss, 1949. (From the Ray C. Bliss Papers. Courtesy of Archival Services, University Libraries, The University of Akron)

Hugh Scott (left), Ray Bliss (center), and Robert Taft (right), 1950. Republican National Chairman Hugh Scott and Ohio GOP chairman Bliss helped re-elect Senator Taft to the US Senate. (From the Ray C. Bliss Papers. Courtesy of Archival Services, University Libraries, The University of Akron)

Dwight Eisenhower (center) and Ray Bliss (right), 1952. Although Bliss backed Robert A. Taft for the GOP presidential nomination, he worked closely to elect Eisenhower to the White House. (From the Ray C. Bliss Papers. Courtesy of Archival Services, University Libraries, The University of Akron)

Democrat Frank Lausche and Republican Dwight Eisenhower, 1953. Ray Bliss was never able to defeat Frank Lausche, who served as governor of Ohio and in the US Senate. Eisenhower considered Lausche for his running mate in 1956. (Left to right) Defiance Mayor Elmer Rost, President Eisenhower, Gov. Frank J. Lausche, Republican Sen. John Bricker, and Defiance College President Kevin McCann. (Courtesy of Defiance College Archives)

George Bender (third from left) and Ray Bliss (second from left), 1954. Bliss helped Republican Bender win the 1954 US Senate race, despite a tense relationship. Also pictured are Paul Weick (far left, a Bliss political ally) and Charles Sacks (far right, one of Bliss's business partners). (Courtesy of the *Akron Beacon Journal*)

Ray Bliss (second from left) meeting with reporters, 1950s. Bliss had a good relationship with reporters, but he preferred off the record conversations. (Courtesy of the Ohio History Connection [P391])

Ray Bliss (center left) and C. William "Billy" O'Neill (center right), 1956. Bliss helped elect O'Neill Ohio governor in 1956, but had a difficult relationship after the election. (Courtesy of the Ohio History Connection [P391])

Mr. and Mrs. Ray Bliss (left) with the parents of the bride, Mr. and Mrs. W. J. Palmer (right), 1959. (Courtesy of the *Akron Beacon Journal*)

Chapter 30

Politics Writer

James M. Cannon, assistant national affairs editor of *Newsweek*, wanted to put together a nonpartisan book on practical politics in anticipation of the 1960 election. The book would focus not on "who-done-it" but on "how-to-do-it." He explained himself to Ray Bliss in a January 26, 1959, letter: "This book will be a collection of articles by professional politicians, each writing about a political technique in which he excels.... One contributor I would very much like to include in this book is you." Cannon suggested that Bliss write on "The Role of the State Chairman," stating, "My friends in both political parties tell me that no state chairman in the nation is more highly regarded than you, and it is for this reason that I would like to have you write about it."[1] Bliss agreed to participate.

The list of contributors showed the elite company Bliss was keeping in American politics. Among the twenty-three writers in *Politics U.S.A.: A Practical Guide to the Winning of Public Office* were Vice President Richard Nixon and Senator John F. Kennedy, Democrat of Massachusetts, likely rivals for the presidency in 1960; Leonard Hall and James A. Farley, former chairmen of the Republican and Democratic national committees, respectively; CBS News president Sig Mickelson; labor leader Gus Tyler; campaign consultant Murray Chotiner; and a host of elected officials.[2]

Drawing on his own experience, Bliss got right to the point in his chapter: "In modern American politics, the primary role of a state chairman, whether he be

Republican or Democrat, is to build a party organization dedicated to good government and victory at the polls."[3] He compared the kind of organization that a chairman must build to the kind of factory a successful car manufacturer must put together. The organizational men who had made American factories the envy of the world appealed to Bliss. In his own field—politics—he wanted to be like them.

> If an automobile manufacturer doesn't score a hit with one year's model, he doesn't shut down his plant—he comes along next year with another model. The same philosophy applies to politics. If a party suffers a severe defeat, or if one of its key leaders becomes incapacitated, it should be geared to move ahead. A political organization must be a continuous thing. It must always be an alive, alert and aggressive operation.

Bliss had experienced both the highs of political victory and the lows of defeat. And he knew something about rebuilding, as he had done after 1948 and 1958 in Ohio.

Parties exist to elect candidates, and Bliss named the five basic factors in any campaign—an effective organization, the right candidates, adequate financing, the right issues, and the right party image.

Organization was not listed first by accident. It had been the key to Bliss's political successes over more than twenty years. In a nuts and bolts way, Bliss waxed poetic about what, to him, was the essence of politics.

> Organization is a major key to success in politics on any level—county, state or nation. It is the driving force which gives politics mobility, the bridge which spans the gap between the candidates and the voters, the source of motivation which binds together all phases of a campaign, the nourishment which keeps the party alive and healthy.

These were the kinds of organizations Bliss had built in Summit County and the state of Ohio.

The state chairman, said Bliss, is like the hub of a wheel with six spokes—headquarters services; auxiliaries such as women's clubs and Young Republicans; financing; general campaign programs; candidates; and supplemental organizations.

Bliss was in the vanguard of providing campaign services from headquarters, nurturing political clubs, and integrating candidate organizations (like Citizens for Eisenhower in 1952) and supplemental organizations (like Teachers for Taft in 1950) into the general campaign program.

While he listed candidates as only one of the spokes, the organizational man conceded that without them nothing else meant much. He drew on the automobile industry again as an example: "A state chairman can work endless days and nights in building a fine organization, but all his effort goes for naught if he fails to make provision for a constant flow of good candidate material. A party without competent, appealing candidates is pretty much like a large automobile agency without cars to sell."

Developing competent candidates, he noted, was often a contentious process—such as with Senator George Bender in 1954 and Governor Billy O'Neill in 1956. "But it is better to have friction...than no candidates at all."

Bliss reminded his readers that candidates, like cars in the showroom, run on their own special fuel—money. The party needs a separate state finance committee "comprised of prominent and respected individuals" to raise money, but the committee and the chairman must work together.

> Since I have been state chairman, the state committee has provided some funds, within its budget, which are distributed to the nominees for state-wide office for use in their individual campaigns. Likewise, some funds are provided in our budget to assist our congressional nominees in their respective personal campaigns. However, the bulk of state committee funds are used in an overall campaign for the entire ticket.

Such party-centered campaigns in Ohio—in 1950, 1952, and 1956—had become famous across the country.

Bliss emphasized that party finances must be above reproach because "nothing destroys public confidence in a party organization more quickly than failure to meet its financial obligations."

Bliss identified different approaches to the job: "There are two types of chairmen—the office chairman, managing the party affairs from headquarters, and the speaking chairman, traveling the state and making public appearances....I have chosen to be primarily an office chairman."

Bliss listed the characteristics a chairman needed: a reputation for fairness to help mediate disputes; being understanding but firm with leadership ability; desire and drive; and the energy needed to inspire members and candidates. He must be a common denominator—a link between the state party and the national and county party organizations. Bliss noted, wryly, that "a state chairman needs the patience of Job, the wisdom of Solomon and the hide of a rhinoceros." The chairman must also have an instinct for making the right decision. Ray Bliss did this when he put Senator Robert A. Taft on television in 1950.

Image and issues, Bliss told his readers, are closely related. The positions that the party and its candidates take on issues determine the images, he wrote. Bliss noted that there was a growing bloc of independent voters and blamed this on party organizations that "have failed to create an appealing image."

Bliss became clinical when describing how the party should decide which issues to emphasize. Surveys must be done periodically to test the voters' mood, and followed up to see if the party and the candidate were making a good impression. For example, a 1954 survey indicated that voters were pleased with the Republican-controlled state legislature in Ohio but not so favorably inclined to the Republican Party nationally. Bliss organized the campaign around the legislative program.

Bliss reminded readers that parties and candidates ignored surveys at their own risk, but that polls are "a tool, not a guarantee of victory." Even the best-laid plans can go awry if an emotional issue damages a party's image. The right-to-work campaign in 1958 was a good example.

A state party chairman can derive great satisfaction by enacting programs and helping elect candidates dedicated to good government, wrote Bliss. But party chairmen also paid a price: "They are on call twenty-four hours a day, seven days a week, and 365 days a year. They are likely to have little home or family life." Surely Bliss was thinking of his long courtship of his wife Ellen.

Bliss concluded with a warning: "It is my observation that when a state chairman begins breaking his word, pondering the lateness of the hour or the length of the road ahead, he is all through in politics."

Although Bliss had been tempted to quit several times, he was not through with politics yet.

Chapter 31

Presidential Politicking

The right-to-work disaster in 1958 had not diminished Ray Bliss's stature as a top party leader. A few years later, David Broder wrote that the Ohio Republican organization had become "a national force comparable in influence to Wall Street, organized labor, or a major religious denomination."[1]

Fellow Republicans shared Broder's high regard for Bliss. As a member of the national committee, Bliss had been chosen to lead the committee to select the site for the 1960 Republican National Convention. Shortly thereafter, Meade Alcorn announced his resignation as Republican national chairman, and Bliss's hometown paper, the *Akron Beacon Journal*, reported that Bliss had the "inside track" to succeed Alcorn.[2]

The Ohio chairman shot down his candidacy the next day in a story by Clyde Mann. Bliss said he had too much to do rebuilding the party in Ohio: "I just couldn't leave that job undone at this time."[3] Mann reported that Bliss had been in Washington, DC, to talk with Alcorn, "presumably about the chairmanship," and Alcorn had raised the possibility with President Eisenhower. But Bliss said he would be happy to cooperate with anybody who got the job. The "best bet" to succeed Alcorn, wrote Mann, was Senator Thruston B. Morton of Kentucky.

At the next meeting of the national committee, Morton got the job and Bliss recommended that the 1960 national convention be held in Chicago. Always a stickler for fairness, Bliss argued that the Windy City would be a "neutral area" as far as potential presidential candidates were concerned. Among the competing cities, Los

Angeles and San Francisco were out because Vice President Richard Nixon was from California; New York City was out because it was the home state of Governor Nelson A. Rockefeller. Besides, Bliss explained, Chicago had offered $400,000 cash, plus a free hall and other benefits for the convention.[4]

Vice President Richard Nixon quickly became the front runner for the 1960 GOP presidential nomination. Bliss and Nixon were not personally close, but the vice president looked like he could unify the GOP. When Republican precinct commit-teemen from Summit County gathered at the Sheraton Hotel in Akron on May 16, Bliss was positive: "I want you to know that I feel that Richard Nixon is the only vice president in the history of this country who has trained for the presidency and I think he's done a fine job," Bliss told the grassroots Republicans on whom he would count to deliver the state for the Republican nominee.[5]

Bliss was personally close to Nelson Rockefeller, but very skeptical of the gov-ernor's offer to be drafted at the GOP convention, in part because it threatened party unity. "It would take some major upheaval, something that can't be foreseen, for Nixon to lose the nomination," Bliss said on the eve of a private luncheon he was hosting in Washington, DC, for the vice president and thirty-six state chairmen from the Midwest and Rocky Mountain State Chairmen's Association. According to polls, Rockefeller would be no stronger than Nixon against Senator John F. Kennedy of Massachusetts, a likely Democratic nominee, Bliss reported.[6]

Bliss was doing his part for Nixon in Ohio. But these efforts encountered a momentary roadblock in the form of George Bender. Bender had lost his US Senate seat to Democrat Frank Lausche in 1956 and was itching to get back into the lime-light. Ohio Republicans were to pick ten at-large delegates to the national convention in their May primary. Eleven candidates were running for the ten spots, and ten of the eleven, at Bliss's urging, were pledged to Nixon for the presidential nomination. The eleventh—Bender—wanted to go to the convention pledged to himself as the first choice for president, a variation on the "favorite son" candidate common in Ohio.

Bender's efforts were an affront to Bliss. "It would be most helpful if you would urge...the Republicans throughout your county to vote for all 10 of the Nixon-pledged delegates-at-large," Bliss wrote Republican county chairmen and state central committee members.[7] Many of these leaders had listened to Bliss when he backed Bender over Bill Saxbe for the 1954 US Senate nomination. Most listened to Bliss again and Bender was not chosen. Bliss called it a "tremendous victory for Vice Pres-ident Nixon"—but it was also a victory for Chairman Bliss.[8]

As Republicans prepared to open their 1960 convention on July 25, a fight for the nomination between Nixon and Rockefeller seemed likely. In fact, Rockefeller had already agreed to withdraw, leaving Nixon unopposed for the nomination. On the weekend before the convention, the two candidates had met in Rockefeller's Fifth Avenue apartment in New York City and come to an agreement about the party platform. Known later as the "Treaty of Fifth Avenue," the fourteen-point agreement called for increased defense spending on US nuclear capability, establishing "a flexible response force" to deal with armed conflicts, and government measures to stimulate economic growth, fund education, and end racial segregation.[9]

To some ardent Eisenhower supporters, the pact appeared to repudiate the president's national leadership, while conservative party leaders were strongly opposed. But it was the price Nixon was willing to pay to avoid a convention fight. According to political scientist Arthur Peterson, who worked for Bliss, the agreement stunned all of Nixon's advisers. The platform drafting process was thrown into chaos. Bliss and other leaders worked behind the scenes to avoid a public showdown on the convention floor. "The constructive roles played by these men," Peterson wrote, "known only to a few people were indeed crucial."[10]

Once the platform debate was resolved, the convention followed Nixon's script. On July 27, his name was placed in nomination for president. There was token opposition, however, which foreshadowed the growing influence of conservatives within the party. The Louisiana delegation nominated Senator Barry Goldwater of Arizona, and on a final roll call, the delegate tally was 1,321 for Nixon and 10 for Goldwater. Goldwater said that conservatives had made a "splendid showing" and predicted that they soon would be able to "take this party back." United Nations Ambassador Henry Cabot Lodge of Massachusetts was Nixon's choice for vice president.[11]

Bliss took good care of the Ohio delegation at the convention. The delegation office was in a good location and there was a full-time bellhop to carry their luggage. That didn't mean they all left Chicago happy, however. Lodge's selection as vice president had displeased some of them. Bliss finessed his way out of the dilemma. No vote was taken, but Lodge was endorsed by acclamation.[12]

Some of the grumbling was directed at Bliss personally. Nixon asked Bliss to keep in touch with Midwest GOP chairmen, a job that often kept him away from his own delegation. Some leaders were "embarrassed because their delegates kept contacting them for word on what was happening and they had to admit they didn't know."[13]

One key Ohioan left the convention particularly displeased with Bliss. Representative Clarence J. Brown Sr. was removed as a vice chairman of the Republican National Committee and replaced by Bliss. Clyde Mann reported, "Brown probably feels it was bad enough to lose out as vice chairman of the national committee, but to be replaced by Ray Bliss? Ouch!"[14]

Chapter 32

Ray Bliss's Masterpiece

The 1960 presidential campaign would be different from the 1952 and 1956 races. The Democratic nominee was Senator John F. Kennedy of Massachusetts, a young, handsome, and charismatic war hero. From a wealthy political family, he had his own version of Ray Bliss in John Bailey, a long-serving chairman of the Connecticut Democratic Party.[1]

One potential liability was Kennedy's religion: he was the second Roman Catholic to be nominated for the presidency. The first, New York governor Al Smith, had been soundly defeated in 1928, while Bliss was still in college.

As state chairman and a Nixon backer, Bliss expected to direct the presidential campaign in Ohio. Nixon aides, many from California, had a different idea. A staffer who worked for Bliss at Ohio Republican headquarters recalled a showdown between Bliss and the Nixon operatives. Two Nixon advance men came to see Bliss during the 1960 campaign. They told Bliss how the Ohio campaign would be run, the staffer recalled. Bliss listened and then told them that in Ohio he ran things. Next Bliss called Robert Finch, a longtime Nixon friend and campaign adviser who also knew Bliss, using a speaker phone. Finch told the two advance men that Bliss was right— Bliss, not the Nixon people, would run the campaign in Ohio. As it turned out, Ohio was the only state where Nixon turned over complete control of campaign operations to the state party.[2]

Once the question of who ran Ohio was settled, Bliss had a good relationship with the Nixon campaign. However, it was not a two-way street. Outside of the Buckeye state, the national campaign often ignored Bliss's advice, such as his recommendation not to debate Kennedy, especially on television.[3]

In contrast, Bliss followed general directives from the national campaign. On September 6, employees at state headquarters in Columbus received a note from Bliss: all staffers were to strictly comply with the attached document, which began by quoting Nixon.

> Religion will be in this campaign to the extent that the candidates of either side talk about it. I shall never talk about it and we'll start right now...
>
> From these statements the following guidelines are essential:
>
> 1. No person or organization conditioning their support on religious grounds will be recognized in this campaign.
> 2. There should be no discussion of the "religious issue" in any literature prepared by a volunteer group or party organization supporting the Vice President, and no literature of this kind from any source should be made available at campaign headquarters or otherwise distributed.
> 3. Staff and volunteer workers should avoid discussing the "religious issue" either informally or casually since this might be construed as some kind of deliberate campaign.[4]

From personal experience, Bliss was aware of how divisive religion could be. There is no evidence that Bliss violated the campaign directive on religion. But there was latent anti-Catholic sentiment in Ohio that didn't need to be addressed directly by the campaign, said Eugene P. (Peter) O'Grady, a Democrat active in Kennedy's campaign and later Ohio Democratic state chairman. "I think the thing that made Ray really outstanding was he called the shots in the Ohio campaign against John Kennedy.... Ray knew enough about the state of Ohio. He knew about the hard-shell Baptists south of Route 40. He knew they would not be sold a Catholic for president."[5]

After the 1958 right-to-work disaster, business leaders had pledged to raise $1 million for the next campaign, and in 1960, they doubled the goal, raising $2 million. About 40 percent of these funds went to the county organizations; 30 percent was spent directly by the state Republican Party; 25 percent went to national and congressional campaign committees, and the final 5 percent was spent directly on Ohio congressional races.[6]

This ample funding helped Bliss find ways for the state party and the local parties to work together for their mutual benefit—electing Republicans at all levels. A good example of such cooperation was Ohio Volunteers for Nixon-Lodge.[7] It was patterned on a group used in Eisenhower's campaigns, Citizens for Eisenhower, formed to back Eisenhower for the presidential nomination against Senator Robert A. Taft of Ohio, the favorite of Bliss and the state party. When Bliss became an Eisenhower supporter, the volunteer group began cooperating with the state party. The group was continued in 1956.

Some of the volunteers who had served on the original Eisenhower committee were among the eighteen Ohio civic leaders who made up the board of a new volunteer effort for Nixon and Lodge in 1960. Bliss made Volunteers for Nixon-Lodge part of the broader statewide campaign effort. He ultimately believed the volunteers in 1960 worked harder than the 1956 volunteers because Nixon, unlike Eisenhower, was not a sure winner.[8]

Volunteer groups were organized in 141 separate communities in 82 of Ohio's 88 counties. Forty of the groups had their own headquarters, and an estimated 150,000 volunteer membership cards were generated. The volunteer operation had a middle-class orientation. A key goal was mobilizing support from professional groups. From the rosters of professional organizations, an executive board member of the Nixon-Lodge volunteers would recruit a member in each county to recruit others in his field. The professionals organized included doctors, lawyers, optometrists, dentists, veterans, farmers, and educators. Blacks and labor leaders also were approached.[9]

The biggest responsibility of the Nixon-Lodge volunteer organization was to provide local groups with materials and ideas. A national manual on voter mobilization was modified for Ohio and provided to the counties. Volunteers received kits that helped them recruit twenty-seven other volunteers who, in turn, would get out voters.

County leaders of the Nixon-Lodge volunteers got requests for Nixon's biography, statements on civil rights, a rental copy of a film on Nixon's travels abroad, and other materials. Altogether, the volunteer effort cost slightly less than $80,000. Of the total, a third went to salaries of party staff and expenses. Another third went for publicity, including campaign supplies. The statewide organization bought and distributed $18,000 worth of campaign supplies. The potpourri included 25,000 yardsticks— "Measure Up with Nixon and Lodge"—to pass out at county fairs, bumper stickers, buttons, literature, and hats. Less than a fifth went outright to county affiliates, while 13 percent went to maintenance and the remaining 4 percent for a statewide meeting.

Bliss did not rely solely on volunteers. The field man program he had developed a year earlier was in full swing. Under the leadership of John Andrews, the field men provided a link between state headquarters and county Republican parties. They sent requests for help from the counties to Columbus and also tried to persuade local party leaders to use the campaign technology available at state headquarters to get out the Republican vote.

The volunteers and field men made winning Ohio for Nixon their top goal, but they also helped with congressional races. Bliss used the money set aside for congressional races selectively. He focused on the four races that appeared to be competitive.[10]

One was in the Sixth District that sprawled across nine counties in southern Ohio. The Democratic incumbent recently had died, so the seat was open. The field man in the area worked with the Republican candidate, William Harsha, to develop a Harsha for Congress Citizens' Committee. The head of the special committee was picked from names submitted by county chairmen. Committee workers were placed in every precinct possible to register voters and get out the vote on election day, except in precincts that party headquarters research showed to be heavily Democratic. A poll conducted in 1959 helped provide Harsha with an issue: voters were dissatisfied with the Democratic-controlled state legislature and Governor DiSalle, so the Democratic governor became a prominent issue.[11]

The field men also provided Bliss with first-hand intelligence on the Kennedy campaign. Field man Bob McAllister filed a report on October 6 with Andrews about a Kennedy visit to Cincinnati. Andrews passed the detail-filled assessment on to Bliss.[12] "Kennedy visited…the public square in Cincinnati and had a dinner in the hotel. There was also a small airport reception last night when he arrived. The latter was 'disappointing.'" The report gave Bliss figures to digest, analyze, and put into the context of the whole campaign. "Crowd size: Airport—small, several hundred if that; Covington—8,000—fairly crowded along the route. Kennedy visited some private homes and spent quite a bit of time in them because they had some national TV program set up to cover them; Cincinnati Square—press estimate, 20,000, McAllister estimate—12–15,000, bus service was cut off from downtown at 5 p.m. so they had a captive crowd; dinner—Mac talked to the cook and learned that there were 510 meals served." "Impact: Nothing extraordinary. About what you would expect with a national candidate, but the enthusiasm was not outstanding except among the young people who hollered and screamed etc. Kennedy attitude—about the same as elsewhere."

Bliss used the field reports alongside his statewide polls. He later described how he used polling data: "For a poll to be any good to a working party chairman, you've got to read the thing ten, 15 times so it becomes part of you," Bliss said later. "And what happens when situations arise, you have this plugged into your mind and you get a mental reaction right like that, what you ought to do, because you have all this stuff assembled in your upper storage."[13]

About October 1, Bliss's polls picked up something that was missing from the coverage of the campaign by newspapers, radio, and television. The reports focused on the enthusiastic crowds at Kennedy's campaign rallies, but Bliss concluded that the intensity of support for Kennedy was slipping. "The greatest slippage was those that said they felt moderately strong about him, down to where they were fairly strong. Well, when they slip into fairly strong, that gets down to how you manage your campaign to swing them over. When I caught that, we set up a massive TV program, a massive newspaper ad program the last ten days of the campaign," said Bliss.[14]

Bliss saw an opening and acted. The Republican National Committee had prepared a report on Kennedy, entitled "'Where's Johnny?' Profile of an Empty Chair." The research showed that as of July 5, Kennedy had been absent for 129 of 171 roll-call votes. Kennedy had missed 32 votes on civil rights, 4 votes on the debt limit and tax extension, and 20 votes on mutual security. Kennedy had not attended meetings of the Senate committees and subcommittees to which he was assigned, including subjects that were highlighted in Kennedy's "New Frontier" platform.[15]

The tough advertising campaign that Bliss unleashed featured the empty chair from which Kennedy too often had been absent. Bliss modified the research to raise further doubts about the Democratic candidate: "I took Kennedy's record, like where he said he was going to do things for the Colored people. Well, he sat, for instance, on the committee that dealt with the African relations. Well, in the examination of the record, he had never, ever attended the committee meetings."[16]

No one in Ohio in 1960 was more popular than W. W. "Woody" Hayes, football coach at Ohio State University. Bliss asked Coach Hayes to do a radio ad endorsing Nixon, and the coach agreed. Years later, Nixon's 1960 national campaign chairman Robert Finch told the writer Tom Wicker that the Hayes commercial had been effective.[17]

As the campaign neared its end, Bliss was aboard a Nixon campaign train as it pulled into Toledo. Herb Klein, a Nixon aide, asked the Ohio chairman to brief the reporters. Bliss later recalled the meeting.[18] "All the Nixon people, they usually wound up fighting with the press by the end of the campaign," said Bliss. "They were mostly press I had never seen before and they asked me, 'What's going to happen in Ohio?' I said, 'Nixon is going to carry it.' Well, you could have heard a pin drop. They said, 'What did you say?' I said, 'Nixon is going to carry Ohio.'"

The national reporters pressed Bliss. How could he know this? They had seen the adoring crowds that greeted Kennedy. "On an analysis I have made of the state" said Bliss. Bliss, who normally did not complain much in public, said the reporters started harassing him, particularly those who seemed pro-Kennedy. "I don't give a damn what you print tomorrow. I've answered your question, you can print anything you want," Bliss said in disgust. "Well, a few of the papers, like the *St. Louis Dispatch,* grabbed it and made it front page and was one of the few papers that did and they bragged about it ever after."[19]

Bliss was right. Nixon defeated Kennedy decisively in Ohio, getting 53 percent of the vote. But even Bliss was surprised by the size of the win—a margin of 273,363 votes.

"Trends tend to accelerate over that last weekend," Bliss said in 1974. "People who know each other get into talking about how they are going to vote and people start shifting. Not all of them, but enough of them to accelerate what I call trends.... What happened in the Kennedy race was Nixon started gaining momentum that last ten days and over the last weekend."[20]

But Ohio was not enough for Nixon to extend Republican control of the White House. In one of the closest presidential elections ever, Kennedy won the popular vote 49.7 to 49.6—a difference of 112,881 votes, out of nearly 69 million cast.[21] The vote in the Electoral College was not as close, 303–219.

A postelection analysis of the Ohio campaign by the respected journal *Congressional Quarterly* concluded: "The victory turned out to be not only a Nixon victory, but a victory for the Republican party. Republicans ousted Democrats from control of both houses of the state legislature, won all statewide races and captured two Democratic Congressional seats."[22] One of the latter was William Harsha in the Sixth District.

"The mainstays of the Republican victory appeared to be organizational skill, ample finances and enthusiastic volunteer aid," the analysis continued. "The Republican state organization operated smoothly under Ray C. Bliss, its chairman for 11 years." It noted that the 1960 campaign had not been a one-time thing, but part of Bliss's continuing effort to maintain Republican strength in a battleground state.

Despite silence on religion in the Ohio campaign, the analysis found that faith was a factor at the ballot box. In Ohio's eight most Catholic counties, Kennedy got 55 percent of the vote, but in the 27 least Catholic counties, Kennedy got 36 percent of the vote.

Author Theodore White called Nixon's win in Ohio the "greatest upset of the election."[23] Kennedy was shocked at losing Ohio. On election night, he momentarily lost his cool, according to White: "His right hand, by the end of the campaign, had swollen with the handshaking of the months to grossly disproportionate size and he displayed it now—calloused, red, the scratches reaching as far as his elbow. He held up the inflamed hand, bare to the elbow, and said, 'Ohio did that to me—they did it there.'"[24]

Nixon thanked Bliss for his work in Ohio right after the election, but then nearly a month later wrote a longer, more reflective letter.

"Dear Ray, Now that my office staff has been able to dig its way out from under the mass of mail that has come to us in the days since November 8, I want to take this opportunity to tell you how much I appreciated all that you did on our behalf during the campaign," Nixon wrote. The defeat was hard to bear, said Nixon. "Losing the closest election in history was naturally a keen disappointment to Pat and to me....But we shall never forget the devoted and selfless work that you and other party leaders did for our cause....Carrying Ohio in the face of overwhelming odds was a tremendous achievement and I know this would not have been possible except for your outstanding leadership in the state."

Nixon urged Bliss not to be dismayed. "I think we can all agree that this is not the time for defeatism or discouragement as far as the Republican party is concerned."[25]

Chapter 33

A Big City Assignment

The Republican win in Ohio brought Ray Bliss renewed national attention. The *Akron Beacon Journal* portrayed Bliss as a conquering hero when the shy Ohioan attended a postelection meeting of the Republican National Committee in Washington, DC. "Ohio GOP Chairman Ray Bliss is like the most popular girl at the ball—everyone wants him to lead the march," the story reported. "In town for four days of top-level Republican meetings, the man who carried Ohio for Vice President Nixon is constantly being congratulated, milled around, and acknowledged as the one elephant in the herd with reason to trumpet."[1]

There was yet another spate of rumors that Bliss was a candidate for national chairman. Chairman Thruston Morton was up for reelection to the US Senate in 1962 and was expected to step down as top party leader. "Throughout the drama, Bliss continued to behave like the wise beauty at the ball, greeting such suggestions with the enigmatic smile and the attitude that 'there are so many others more qualified,'" the newspaper reported.[2]

But Bliss did seem to be opening the door just a sliver to the possibility that someday, under the right circumstances, he might take the national chairman's job. "Once I said I'd never become state chairman, and yet I did," Bliss told his hometown newspaper. "So I don't like to say that I'd never become national chairman. Circumstances might be such, someday, that I would."[3]

This shift in position reflected Bliss's interest in the job. But there were two stick-ing points. As in Ohio, Bliss wanted to be a full-time, salaried chairman. Recent GOP chairmen had been part-time and unpaid, like Thruston Morton. The always cautious Bliss wanted up-front support from all the major leaders of the GOP. He had the backing of Eisenhower and Nixon, and Barry Goldwater asked him to take the job. But when Bliss solicited Nelson Rockefeller's views, the governor told him if he wanted to be chairman, he should simply announce his interest. Bliss felt the comment implied that he was acting out of personal ambition and withdrew from consideration.[4]

Ray Sutcliff of Bliss's hometown newspaper, the *Akron Beacon Journal*, described Bliss's views on the chairmanship: "The fact is he [Bliss] undoubtedly would agree to become Republican chairman if he could get national party leaders to subscribe to a program that would give him the power and the freedom to operate on the national scale in the same way he does in Ohio GOP circles." Sutcliff concluded: "Until such an agreement is worked out to the satisfaction of Bliss, he is not likely to give any encouragement to those who are talking him up for the national chair-manship. It took him more than a year to convince Ohio's Republican leadership that he would not become state chairman except on his own terms and his friends feel he will continue to take the same attitude toward the national job."[5]

Ultimately Morton was replaced as national chairman by William Miller, a congress-man from New York, in June 1961. But before leaving, Morton gave Bliss a new assignment: to head a blue-ribbon committee to investigate how the Republicans lost the election.

Within a few weeks, Bliss had a postelection analysis: "The Republican party lost the 1960 presidential election in the big cities of this nation. If we had done a better job in some of these big cities, we could have carried eight more states with 173 electoral votes."[6] Bliss was credible on this point because of his success in the big cities of Ohio. In 1960, Kennedy had won just 51 percent of the metropolitan vote—not enough to overcome the GOP margin elsewhere in the state.[7]

The group Bliss chaired, soon dubbed the "Big City Politics" committee, took a year to finish its work. Bliss didn't sugarcoat its findings when he reported to the Republican National Committee on January 12, 1962, in Oklahoma City: "As we have long suspected, the Republican organizations in many big cities do not have ample resources either in funds or manpower to compete with the well-financed and heav-ily-manned ward and precinct organizations available to Democratic voters through Labor's operations and local political patronage."[8]

A survey done for the report showed that in heavily Republican precincts in several large cities where the party lost, an average of 100 or more Republican-minded persons were not registered or did not vote in 1960. Those votes could have made the difference because of Republican strength outside the cities. "I would like to stress that it is not necessary for us to carry the big cities," said Bliss. "We just need to reduce the Democratic margin in the big cities; then our out-state and suburban strength, under normal conditions, should enable us to carry the state."[9]

In Michigan, for example, Nixon carried 70 of the 83 counties and outside the Detroit city limits had a majority of 244,880. "In Detroit, however, Kennedy piled up a plurality of 311,721, which was enough to wipe out the Republican out-state lead and deliver the state to the Democrats by some 66,000 votes. This cost Nixon 20 electoral votes." A similar pattern held for other big cities, including Chicago, Philadelphia, and New York City.

Representative Glenard P. Lipscomb of California, chairman of the subcommittee on party organization and candidate recruitment, acknowledged, "We must face the fact that there is no shadow army of Republicans sitting around in the big cities waiting to be mobilized instantly with a bugle call." Lipscomb took his argument to the precinct level. In 11 states with 55,000 voting precincts, the study showed that the Republicans did not even have one worker in 5,000 of those precincts. "Political power flows upward from the precincts; it does not seep down from higher levels," Lipscomb said. "It sends cold chills up your spine to think of the thousands of big city precincts that regularly have not a single Republican precinct worker, either year-round or on election day."[10]

Senator Gordon Allott of Colorado, who chaired the subcommittee on labor, business, professional, and independent groups, wanted to dispel two myths—that all labor automatically belonged to the Democrats and that the business world is solidly for Republicans. "Neither could be further from the truth," Allott said. Thirty-five percent of union voters picked Nixon, not Kennedy, in 1960; and four years earlier, 43 percent of the union vote had gone to Dwight Eisenhower. Union members even worked for the Republican Party. Allott then gave the members of the national committee a detailed and, without exactly saying so, complimentary description of the AFL-CIO's Committee on Political Education (COPE) program. At the same time, Allott was highly critical of business and professional organizations for their lack of political involvement. Republicans needed to educate them on the importance of partisan politics. "We found no magic wand to wave over our problems: We found little new. We found only that there is no substitute for hard work, based on common sense and dedication to a common cause of American freedom and opportunity," he said.[11]

Representative Edward Derwinski of Illinois chaired the subcommittee on ethnic and minority voters. "Our record and principles entitle us to great support among

ethnic groups and Negro groups," Derwinski said. Too often, however, the Republicans had ignored these potential voters. He identified 18 states where 19 million
people of ethnic heritage resided, most of them in big cities. After warning that there
was no quick fix, Derwinski had some good news. There were ways to reach these
voters. The foreign-language press and radio and television programs directed to
ethnic groups provided the access that the party needed; much the same was true for
black newspapers and media. "We must develop the permanent organization which
has the staff and talents to promote Republican material through all these media,"
said Derwinski. He recommended welcoming new immigrants, reaching out to young
people, and sending speakers to ethnic and minority organizations.[12]

New York GOP state chairman L. Judson "Jud" Morehouse chaired the subcommittee on public relations, surveys, and educational methods, including television. The 1960 presidential election had taught the Republicans a painful lesson about
the growing power of television: the message could be less powerful than the medium.
Morehouse pointed to the broadcast debate between Kennedy and Nixon. More
people heard the debate on radio than on TV, and most listeners thought the well-
informed Nixon won. But on TV, Nixon appeared haggard and ill at ease, and most
viewers thought he had lost.

Morehouse told the members of the national committee that if they wanted their
party to survive and win they had to adjust to the new medium. To win elections in
these changing times, politicians had to understand what was troubling the voters
and then communicate solutions with "the utmost clarity and detail." Morehouse
brought along experts who made individual presentations on television, surveys,
public relations, and educational methods.[13]

The presentations and the accompanying document, "Report of the Committee
on Big City Politics," offered nineteen specific recommendations. It preached the
political gospel that Ray Bliss had practiced his entire career. And in keeping with
the report's recommendations, Bliss soon appointed a committee to improve GOP
operations in Akron, his hometown.[14]

Although generally well received, the Big City report received some political
pushback. To conservative followers of Barry Goldwater, the recommendations
sounded biased toward the liberal Republicanism of New York's Nelson Rockefeller.
They wanted less emphasis on metropolitan, ethnic, and minority voters, and more
focus on winning in the South.[15]

For Bliss, it was time to get back to work in Ohio.

Chapter 34

Ray C. Bliss and James A. Rhodes

Republicans had an opportunity to regain the Ohio governorship in 1962. Governor Michael DiSalle, the Democratic incumbent, was unpopular for backing a large tax increase and opposing the death penalty. He also was feuding with other Democrats and was likely to face a strong primary challenger. On the day after the 1960 election, Governor DiSalle said, "We have to find a scapegoat and it might as well be me."[1]

All the GOP needed was a good slate of candidates, and the favorite for governor was State Auditor James A. Rhodes. In some respects, Rhodes resembled C. William O'Neill, whom Bliss helped elect governor in 1956. Like O'Neill, Rhodes came into politics before Bliss became state chairman and had developed his own following.

Rhodes had a singular long-term focus: "When I got into politics, I decided that I would become governor of Ohio one day," Rhodes said. "So I picked a path."[2]

Rhodes was elected to the Columbus school board and also city auditor before he won the mayor's office in 1943, at thirty-four the youngest person to hold that post. Rhodes was reelected mayor in 1947 and 1951. In 1950, he took his first shot at the governorship, losing the Republican primary. Democrat Frank Lausche then won the general election. Rhodes took his own crack at Governor Lausche in 1954 and lost as well. In 1952, Rhodes was elected state auditor and was reelected in 1956 and 1960. Rhodes called the auditor's office "the catbird's seat." He used the office to acquire a statewide reputation, investigating Democratic officeholders and building a personal political organization.[3]

Bliss and Rhodes were similar in some respects. About the same age, they began politicking in college, where they were poor students, and then worked their way up the political ladder in urban areas. In his vocation, Rhodes was arguably as successful as Bliss was in his, eventually becoming the only person to be elected to four four-year terms as Ohio governor (1963–71 and 1975–83).[4]

But Bliss and Rhodes had strikingly different styles. Bliss was shy, a perfectionist, and self-conscious about his professionalism. Rhodes, from Jackson County in southern Ohio, was outgoing and earthy and never lost "his southern Ohio twang." His favorite joke involved an off-color tale about an oversexed coonhound called "Old Blue."[5]

Bliss was suspicious of Rhodes because he had his own organization separate from the Republican Party. Bliss had seen this kind of candidate damage the party, both by dragging the party down at the polls and by weakening the organization if elected. Rhodes, meanwhile, was jealous of Bliss's power and the way he had made the party organization more important than any single candidate.

Part of the problem was regional—Rhodes's base of power was in central Ohio, whereas Bliss was from northeast Ohio. Rhodes was backed by Preston Wolfe, whose family controlled the *Columbus Dispatch*, the major newspaper in the state capital, while Bliss's journalistic allegiance was to John S. Knight and the *Akron Beacon Journal*.[6]

The Knights and the Wolfes often did not see eye to eye, said Alex Arshinkoff.[7] The divide went back a long way. The Wolfes and the *Dispatch* had supported a rival candidate when Knight's father, C. L. Knight, unsuccessfully had sought the Republican nomination for governor in 1922. Then when Bliss became state Republican chairman in 1949, John S. Knight wanted to host the reception in Columbus honoring Bliss. But the Wolfes considered Columbus their town and believed it was their right to honor the new state chairman. Bliss went along with Knight.

After that, Bliss believed that he did not receive fair coverage in the *Dispatch*, despite its conservative editorial policy. When Gene Jordan, then *Dispatch*'s Public Affairs editor, called Bliss to arrange an interview for a profile of Bliss in 1980, Bliss at first refused. He relented only after Jordan persuaded Bliss that "things had changed, that he would be treated fairly," said Arshinkoff.

In early 1962, there were rumors that if Rhodes were elected governor he would remove Bliss as state chairman. There was so much talk that Rhodes was moved to declare that he was considering no such thing. "Ray Bliss is devoted to the cause of Republicans and is one of the outstanding leaders of our party," Rhodes said. "He has served the Republican party of Ohio selflessly and has been of great assistance to all Republicans in Ohio. As far as I'm concerned personally, Ray Bliss can remain as long as he wishes as state chairman. I hope that he will continue. I don't want any doubt in anyone's mind on this."[8]

Bliss wanted his own assurances and met with Rhodes, just as he had met with C. William O'Neill before the 1956 election. Bliss offered to step aside as chairman if Rhodes won. Bliss later related the conversation to Arshinkoff: "Look, Ray. You've got to stay on [as chairman]. Those industrial boys don't like me. I'm good with the working guys. I'm good with the black churches. I can have the 'amening' and you get those industrial guys and bring in the dough.... We will be a great team," said Rhodes.[9]

"Now, Jim, you don't want me to resign?" Bliss said.

"No, I want you to stay on," said Rhodes.

"O.K.," said Bliss.

Rhodes later denied that there had been friction in their relationship. He explained the relationship between himself and Bliss this way: "I don't want to be state chairman and Ray Bliss...never wanted to be governor." Rhodes professed respect for Bliss and Bliss's ability: "He always treated me fair and always went along with what we were doing," said Rhodes. "He never did anything but be professional....He brought to politics a lot of innovations....He was guided a great deal by surveys. For the most part, he was found out to be right....He'd stay on the job 12 hours a day."[10]

Bliss once expressed his frustration about Rhodes's style while having dinner at a Columbus restaurant. Rhodes, said Bliss, had to be watched all the time. What Bliss didn't know was that Rhodes was sitting in the next booth with Roy Martin, his longtime aide. As Bliss recalled the incident to Arshinkoff, the plastic flowers separating Bliss's booth from Rhodes parted and Rhodes popped up behind them.[11]

Rhodes later brushed off the incident. "I called him the next day," said Rhodes. Bliss, he said, was talking about Rhodes's driving ability. The state chairman had had a couple of beers before making the remarks, Rhodes continued. "You always told me 'don't be playing politics with beer on your breath.'"

Rhodes said he always had to approach Bliss through one of his assistants, not directly. "You had to see two or three people associated with him before you talked to Bliss. They would feel everything out," said Rhodes. Bliss kept up with what Rhodes was doing and occasionally called with advice, said Rhodes. "Someone would call him [Bliss] and say 'Rhodes is doing this.' He [Bliss] would say 'he'll come out all right.' He [Bliss] would say to Flanagan [a Bliss assistant], 'Call him [Rhodes] and see what he's doing.' He'd get me on the telephone and straighten me out," Rhodes recalled.[12]

In May 1962, Bliss was reelected as state chairman to a seventh, two-year term, with a salary of $18,000. He declared that Republicans must wage a "first class, aggressive campaign" to win in November. The road ahead would be tough, he said. The Kennedy administration had targeted Ohio for attention and the AFL-CIO planned an "intensified" effort on behalf of Democrats and Governor DiSalle.[13]

Bliss and Rhodes already had the theme for the campaign against DiSalle. Bliss was given credit for the nickname that stuck with DiSalle: "Tax-Hike Mike."[14] Rhodes, with Bliss's encouragement, chose to emphasize economic themes. Bliss's polling helped Rhodes develop his trademark phrase "Jobs and Progress."[15] Creating jobs required low taxes and fiscal responsibility, Rhodes argued, saying "profit is not a dirty word in Ohio."

Governor DiSalle struck hard at Rhodes on personal finances. In 1958, the Internal Revenue Service had charged that Rhodes "borrowed" $36,000 from his campaign committee. The IRS required him to pay back taxes on the loans or repay them. Rhodes chose to repay the loans in July and August of 1958.[16]

DiSalle then opened a second line of attack on Rhodes, involving alleged irregularities in the state auditor's office. Local governments had been charged for the rental of auditor inspectors' adding machines under a lease-purchase agreement when the machines actually had been paid for by the state. DiSalle told of how the machine rentals were collected in cash, crammed into "plain white envelopes."[17]

These attacks had a personal impact on Rhodes, who had projected an image as a swashbuckling, down-home tough guy. But the charges from the Democrats rocked him, Bliss told Arshinkoff years later. Rhodes came to see Bliss with tears in his eyes.[18] Rhodes later recalled the advice Bliss gave him this way: "Bliss called me. He said, 'get in the ditch. Get in the weeds. Stay out of it.... If he [an opponent] can't get you to answer, he's firing blanks.'"[19]

Heeding Bliss's advice, Rhodes conducted a "low-key" campaign, holding few press conferences, making relatively few stump speeches, and saying little about the Democratic charges. DiSalle, in contrast, seemed to be everywhere. He visited all of Ohio's 88 counties and 130 towns he never had been in before, trying to get Rhodes into a face-to-face showdown. Campaigning against Rhodes was "like trying to play ping-pong on a pogo stick," DiSalle told reporters.[20] The two candidates finally met up at the traditional Cleveland City Club debate the weekend before the election. They agreed that it had been "the most vicious campaign for the Ohio governorship."[21]

Meanwhile, Bliss had been active in other races. He made a special effort to promote Robert Taft Jr., son of the late Senator Robert A. Taft and the grandson of

President William Howard Taft. The younger Taft was running for a new at-large congressional seat created after the 1960 US Census. It would give Taft statewide name recognition and prepare him to run for the US Senate in 1964 and win back the seat lost to Democrat Stephen Young in 1958. Winning an at-large district in 1950 had helped George Bender in his 1954 race for the US Senate—although Bliss, while helping the legislature with redistricting, decided to abolish the seat after the 1950 US Census to help Republicans elsewhere in Ohio.

Bliss paid special attention to congressional redistricting, said Charles Kurfess, a former state legislator and Speaker of the Ohio House of Representatives. "He sat at the table with us every time we did it," said Kurfess. "I was involved three times, twice as Speaker and once as chairman of the [elections] committee."[22] The redistricting strategy paid off when Taft won the at-large seat as part of a big GOP victory.

At the top of the ticket, Rhodes scored an overwhelming victory, beating DiSalle with 59 percent of the vote. The Republicans won all other statewide offices, retained control of the state legislature, and picked up a second congressional seat. In a continuing disappointment for Bliss, Democrat Frank Lausche was reelected to the US Senate.[23]

As in 1960, Ohio Republicans outperformed the national trend. Overall, the GOP gained just one seat in the US House of Representatives and lost three seats in the US Senate. Among other casualties was Richard Nixon, who ran for governor of his native California—against the advice of party leaders, including Bliss—and lost a close contest.[24]

After the election, the power arrangements between the new Republican governor and the long-serving state chairman were still to be settled. According to Arshinkoff, Bliss won the first scrimmage.[25] On the day Rhodes was inaugurated, the new governor's secretary called state headquarters and talked to Bliss's secretary.

"The governor would like to see the state chairman," said the governor's secretary.

"Well, it's a busy day, but tell the governor to come over here at 3 o'clock," replied Bliss's secretary.

That was not what Rhodes had in mind.

"The governor expects him to come here," said Rhodes's secretary.

"I have a card from Mr. Bliss. Let me read it to you. He thought this might happen. 'The governor is first among equals.' He can come over and see the state chairman at 3 o'clock." Rhodes came to Bliss's office.

The chairman and the governor were not finished jockeying for position.

Chapter 35

Recruitment Matters

Ray Bliss was constantly looking for prospective Republican candidates. In 1963, there was no more appealing prospect than John H. Glenn. As the first American to orbit the earth in 1962, Glenn was a national hero. A retired Marine colonel from the small Ohio town of New Concord, he and his wife Annie, his sweetheart since they met as toddlers, were the All-American couple. Like General Dwight Eisenhower in 1952, astronaut Glenn was sought after by Democrats and Republicans.[1]

J. Willard "Bill" Marriott Sr., national motel and restaurant operator and active Republican, helped arrange a meeting between Glenn and Bliss in October 1963. Afterward, Bliss sounded optimistic about bringing the space hero into the GOP: "Just a note to thank you for setting up the luncheon meeting with John Glenn last Monday which I hope will ultimately result in his becoming affiliated with the Republican Party. I was very much impressed with him and aside from the glamour attached to him as an astronaut I think he is a very solid and sound individual who would be an asset to any political party."[2]

According to Alex Arshinkoff, Glenn said he wanted to run for the US Senate in 1964. Bliss responded that the party was committed to Congressman Robert Taft Jr. for that post. Instead, Bliss suggested that Glenn run for the US House of Representatives. "Look, young man. You are an astronaut, a pilot...this is great. But we are talking about government here and you need to get a little experience. Look, I'll carve you out a congressional district," Arshinkoff recalled Bliss saying.[3]

An account of the Republican courtship of Glenn appeared in the *Akron Beacon Journal* a few months later, reporting two meetings between Glenn and Bliss.[4] The article reported that Bliss tried to interest Glenn in running in a specific congressional district, the Fifteenth US House District in central Ohio, against the Democratic incumbent Robert T. Secrest. "It would be more logical, Glenn was told, to get some congressional experience under his belt. This would serve him in good stead when Democrat Frank Lausche's senate term expired in 1968."[5]

Whatever happened between Glenn and Bliss in their private meetings, Bliss miscalculated if he believed that he could talk Glenn into running for another office. "I wanted to run for the Senate," Glenn said years later.[6] And he did so in 1964—as a Democrat. "His decision did not surprise me too much," Bliss wrote to a colleague, "in view of the fact that his mother and father are Democrats, his close friendship with Jack and Bob Kennedy, etc., and his views concerning the positions some of our potential Republican candidates for president have taken. However, I feel that it was worth the effort I made. At least I tried."[7]

Glenn had to withdraw from the 1964 race due to an injury suffered in a fall. He was eventually elected to the US Senate in 1974 and became the only Ohioan to win four consecutive Senate terms (1975–99). According to Arshinkoff, Senator Bob Dole was in Summit County for a Republican Party event years later and commented on Glenn's vote-getting ability in Ohio. "Ray, you know this John Glenn is looking tough," said Dole. "How did you ever let this guy get away?"

"You know," said Bliss. "I may have made a mistake."[8]

Bliss was always looking for new ideas that could be used to win elections, whatever the source. In 1962, he began recruiting college professors for an "Arts and Sciences Division" of the Ohio Republican Party. "These men are thought leaders in their communities," Bliss said. "They have special talents with which they can be helpful."[9]

Political scientist Arthur Peterson headed the new group. Although intellectuals were more frequently associated with the Democratic Party, Peterson explained why many were drawn to Bliss: he cared about their ideas, their notions of how parties should be organized to help win elections, and how they could best serve the need of providing citizens with a responsive government. Peterson first met Bliss after the 1960 elections and found that the organizational man could hold his own with a professor. Having served in the state legislature in Wisconsin and then lost a close congressional race, Peterson won a national competition among political scientists to be the adviser to Thruston Morton, the Republican national chairman. Morton sent Peterson to Ohio to make a speech, and after the speech he recognized Bliss in the hotel bar and introduced himself. They began talking. "We didn't quit until 4:30 in the morning," said Peterson.

Peterson had a low opinion of the state party organization in Wisconsin. "I had taken on the [Republican] party when I had first run for office at the age of 23 and defeated the party. And I thought, 'Well, the party's a paper tiger, easy to beat them and I did,'" he said. Bliss told Peterson that the party operated differently in Ohio than it apparently did in Wisconsin. "You ought to come out and understand and study our party," Bliss told Peterson. "Well, I got sort of intrigued with the guy, again with the intellectual force of mind," Peterson recalled. Petersen ended up working for Bliss in Columbus and later in Washington, DC.[10]

Bliss also recruited talent at home: he asked his wife, Ellen, to monitor turnout in the precinct where they lived in Akron. She kept meticulous records of all the contacts the Republicans had with the voters—mail, telephone calls, door-to-door visits—and then matched the contacts to turnout in local, state, and federal elections. Ray reviewed her work and listened to her suggestions. "Ray wanted to know what could be done to increase the vote," Mrs. Bliss recalled. "This was how he worked, he was methodical and open-minded."[11]

In 1963, Bliss found himself on the other end of a recruitment effort. New York governor Nelson Rockefeller wanted Bliss to run his 1964 presidential campaign. In a "personal and confidential" memo to Governor Rockefeller on December 14, 1962, aide George L. Hinman argued that "Ray Bliss is the man and we should start right away with the effort to bring him into our organization.... He should be ostensibly in charge of our preconvention effort.... Actually, as we have said many times," continued Hinman, "our preconvention effort should be part and parcel of the 1964 election campaign."[12]

Hinman and Bliss served together on the Republican National Committee and regularly consulted each other. Bliss liked Rockefeller personally and the governor might well have been Bliss's own choice for the nomination.[13] Hinman wrote: "I think it is important that you and I spend a leisurely evening with Ray at the earliest opportunity." But he warned: "Ray is still carrying some hurts from his interview in your office when he wanted to be National Chairman and an early session with him is awfully important."[14]

According to Arshinkoff, Bliss met with Rockefeller and his advisers. Bliss was offered a job with the Rockefeller campaign and a substantial salary. It was implied that if Rockefeller won the GOP nomination, Bliss would be named chairman of the Republican National Committee. Bliss said he would have to talk with his wife Ellen.

"Ray was very flattered by the offer," Arshinkoff remembered, "and the money was very attractive. But Ray wanted to be his own man. He never wanted to be beholden to a candidate—he was always for the party."[5]

There may have been a pragmatic reason for this refusal as well. Bliss's stock was already rising as a future candidate for national chairman. *Time* magazine did a profile on Bliss after the 1962 elections and concluded, "Bliss is an obvious possibility to succeed [William] Miller as national chairman someday." Bliss did not rule out the possibility: "I have not been interested in being national chairman up to now....I reserve the right to change my mind."[6]

Chapter 36

Trouble in San Francisco

As the 1964 presidential election approached, Ray Bliss was worried: infighting among prospective candidates threatened Republican chances of defeating President Kennedy. Besides Governor Nelson Rockefeller of New York, other governors from the liberal wing of the party—William Scranton of Pennsylvania and George Romney of Michigan—were interested in the nomination. From the 1960 presidential ticket, Richard Nixon and Henry Cabot Lodge II were possible moderate candidates. Arizona Senator Barry Goldwater was another option, a leading voice of party conservatives. In 1961, Goldwater supporters began a "draft Goldwater committee."[1]

Goldwater backers in Ohio often took an "us-against-the-world" approach—and even Bliss was suspect. Representative John Ashbrook of Johnstown, a founder of the draft Goldwater committee, began spreading the word that Bliss was not friendly toward the Arizona senator. Bliss's hometown newspaper, the *Akron Beacon Journal,* came to the state chairman's defense. "Bliss IS NOT Hostile to Goldwater Candidacy," blared a headline on September 19, 1963. "The chairman's very success as a master behind-the-scenes organizer is based on his canny ability to remain 'neutral' in a matter of this kind," the story reported.[2]

Indeed, there was no public hostility between Bliss and Goldwater. In early 1962, during a dinner speech in Cleveland, Goldwater singled Bliss out as "the outstanding politician in the Republican party." Not much in Republican politics in Ohio went on without Bliss's approval, and there was no doubt that Goldwater had come to Cleveland with the state chairman's blessing. As usual, Bliss had made a wise decision: Goldwater appealed to the conservative element of the party and helped the GOP raise funds.[3]

Ashbrook was at least partially right, however. Bliss was not sure that Goldwater would win the Republican presidential nomination. Enthusiasm was fine with Bliss as long as it united the party—but he wanted no part of enthusiasm that divided Republicans. He feared that would happen if Ohio became a battleground for the Republican nomination in the primaries and caucuses leading to the 1964 Republican National Convention in San Francisco.

Bliss quietly negotiated with the campaigns of all the GOP presidential candidates and persuaded them to campaign against each other outside Ohio, according to Alex Arshinkoff. "Ray saw what happened in '52. In '52 there was the Eisenhower cat fight [against Robert A. Taft] and he did not like that," recalled Arshinkoff. "He was so respected that…he got all the presidential candidates together and said, 'Look, Ohio's key to winning. I carried for Nixon in '60 even against the national trend. Let me put the Republican organization on hold at the convention. We'll stay neutral— that's the best chance we have to carry the state. That's the only way you are going to do it in this tough, industrial state.'…So, everybody agreed to it."[4]

Bliss's tactic was for Ohio's fifty-eight convention delegates to be committed to a "favorite son candidate." This would facilitate negotiations at the convention.[5]

Meanwhile, events dramatically changed the campaign. On November 22, 1963, the nation was stunned by the assassination of President Kennedy. Chairman Bliss immediately issued a statement on behalf of the Ohio Republican Party:

> The assassination of our President is a shock that saddens all of us.
>
> Despite the assassinations that have been perpetuated in other lands, it seems unbelievable that such a crime could be committed on the streets of an American city.
>
> I join all Americans in extending my deepest sympathy to the President's family.[6]

While the nation mourned the loss of the president, the candidates had to adjust their political strategies. The Republicans would now be running against the man who succeeded Kennedy, Vice President Lyndon Johnson of Texas.

Once the 1964 nomination campaign began in earnest, no clear GOP frontrunner emerged in the early primaries. But Goldwater did well in the South, beginning with Texas, and then narrowly defeated Nelson Rockefeller in the California primary. Rockefeller then withdrew from the race.[7]

Meanwhile, Bliss had troubles of his own in the May 5 Ohio primary. The "favorite son" strategy was not popular with everyone. Ed Rowe, a Bliss foe, decided to take advantage of party divisions by running against Bliss for state central committeeman. If Rowe had defeated Bliss for the seat on the central committee, Bliss would have been humiliated in his own backyard and his power as state chairman would have suffered.

Bliss tapped D. E. "Gene" Waddell, the executive director of the Summit County Republican Party, to run his campaign against Rowe. "Number one, I had to raise separate money for that, get a committee lined up and make a mailing. I mean it was like running a regular election, because you had to win that thing," Waddell later recalled. Waddell also did his best to minimize publicity on the challenge to Bliss. "Robert Feldkamp was the political writer [at the *Akron Beacon Journal*]. I knew Ed Rowe wanted publicity and we didn't want any publicity....So, I said to Bob, 'Bob, you don't put anything in the paper about this race. Just forget it exists and I will get you a private, personal interview with Bliss,'" Waddell said.[8]

Bliss won the contest easily, trouncing Rowe by a margin of nearly 4–1. "The vote was regarded as a mandate from the home district for the man who is the guiding force in State GOP policy," the *Akron Beacon Journal* reported. Feldkamp remembered the deal he made with Waddell. He didn't ignore Rowe's challenge to Bliss altogether, but he didn't make a big deal out of it, either. "I used to call it the 'Ed Rowe card,'" Feldkamp said in 1997. "I would sort of hold it over Gene's head."[9]

While Bliss was struggling to keep the battle for the Republican presidential nomination outside Ohio, he also attacked a less worldly but more down-to-earth problem back at state headquarters in Columbus.

Some male staffers failed to flush the toilets. In a memo to "All males," Bliss addressed the problem. "Failure to flush the men's room commodes, from time to time, indicates that we have one or more males who are used to the old-fashioned outhouse and unfamiliar with modern toilet facilities," Bliss wrote. The detail man provided do-it-yourself details for using the commode.

> For the benefit of that person or persons, please be informed that back of the commode seat is a water tank which holds the water which flushes the modern toilet. As you face the commode you can see on the left a small handle protruding from the water closet.
>
> After you use the commode you press the protruding handle firmly until the flushing of the commode begins and then release. That's all—it only takes a second of your valuable time.[10]

Never one to leave anything to chance, Bliss assigned a staff member who was not too busy with the regular business of organizing meetings and getting out the vote to provide some extra help.

"If the outhouse group members do not understand the above instructions as to the use of modern facilities, then see Charles Crowder. It will take him only a minute or two to instruct you," the chairman said.

While the memo was meant in good humor, Bliss, of course, expected the males to pay attention. Seven signatures from male staffers at the bottom indicated that they had read Bliss's instructions.

In the summer of 1964, moderate Republicans began to organize a "stop Goldwater" campaign. Ohio's Governor Rhodes played a major role in the effort. He and a dozen other anti-Goldwater governors met in Cleveland on June 9. Rhodes personally arranged for Richard Nixon to attend the meeting. The talks did not get very far because of political rivalries among the participants, and the party's divisions were showcased. Ultimately, Governor Scranton of Pennsylvania emerged as a stand-in for the stop-Goldwater effort.[11]

Bliss was reluctant to be identified with the stop-Goldwater effort, but he was not entirely silent. At a party meeting in Akron, Bliss sent a public signal that Goldwater at the top of the ticket might mean trouble. "In my book, the best kind of candidate for this state is the kind who goes down the middle of the road," he said.[12]

According to W. Richard Wright, "Ray didn't disagree with Goldwater on most issues, but his polls showed that Goldwater couldn't win in Ohio." Bliss was later reported to have the same grim assessment of Goldwater's national chances, predicting that the GOP "won't carry a state north of the Mason-Dixon line," and adding, "Then we'll have to put this party back together."[13]

When the Ohio delegation to the Republican National Convention met June 22 in Columbus, the "favorite son" strategy was followed: on the first ballot at the national conventions, Ohio's fifty-eight votes would go to Governor Rhodes. Even the Goldwater supporters in the delegation agreed.[14] Behind the scenes, however, Bliss and Rhodes were jockeying for position as the state's top Republican in the presidential sweepstakes.

Rhodes pulled the rug out from under Bliss's carefully crafted neutrality strategy on Thursday, July 9, just before the San Francisco convention, by issuing a vague but explosive statement: "During the [Ohio delegation] caucus next Monday morning, those delegates who may wish to support their choice will be welcome to express their beliefs and persuade their colleagues.... I am confident that every delegate will exercise individually that fine judgment which is characteristic of this splendid group of public officials and private citizens."[15]

Rhodes's statement all but doomed the favorite son strategy as well as any hope of preventing Goldwater's nomination at the convention. Although Rhodes had participated in the stop-Goldwater efforts with other governors, he also had been keeping in touch with the Goldwater campaign, according to Arshinkoff. Bliss knew of these contacts because Goldwater staffers kept him informed. "Ray knew the entire time. He did not know when Rhodes was going to do this," Arshinkoff said.[16]

Robert Feldkamp, the *Akron Beacon Journal* political writer, later explained Rhodes's reasoning: "A canny politician himself, Rhodes also sensed the possibility of a sizeable first-ballot bolt by the Ohio Goldwater block, 'favorite son' candidacy or no. ...Rhodes realized this could have resulted in considerable embarrassment to him personally, and to his so-far unblemished image both in and out of Ohio. ...So, discussing it only with some of his cronies, Rhodes decided to try and get himself off the hook."[17]

While Bliss may have known what Rhodes planned, the announcement still embarrassed him. He had given his word not just to Goldwater but to Scranton, Romney, Rockefeller, and all the other possible contenders for the Republican nomination. "The news hit San Francisco like a thunderbolt," reported the *Akron Beacon Journal.* "'What happened?' was what everyone wanted to know. Bliss didn't have an answer."[18] He was at a loss to explain Rhodes's behavior. "Jim Rhodes has always honored previous understandings," said Bliss. "And I can't explain why he ran out on me this time."[19]

Rhodes and Bliss made a show of patching things up. They released a brief statement: "It was agreed that they would jointly recommend to the Ohio delegation at its Monday, July 13 breakfast caucus that each delegate vote for the man of his choice on the first ballot."[20]

Rhodes sought to discourage any talk that he and Bliss were at odds at another meeting of the Ohio delegation. "I have been asked whether this event is a going away party for Ray and Ellen Bliss," said the governor. "Far from it. This is just an occasion when the elected state officials attending this Republican national convention give deserving recognition to Ray Bliss for the magnificently effective leadership he has given Ohio Republicans for more than 15 years."[21]

Goldwater won the Republican presidential nomination on the first ballot, with 57 of 58 ballots from Ohio. But the San Francisco convention was a public relations disaster for Goldwater and the Republicans. Bitter infighting among the Republican delegates was broadcast on television coast to coast. Goldwater contributed to the divisive message in his acceptance speech: "I would remind you that extremism in the defense of liberty is no vice! And let me remind you that moderation in the pursuit of justice is no virtue."[22]

Goldwater chose Congressman William Miller of New York as his vice-presidential running mate. Miller resigned as chairman of the Republican National Committee, so the top party job had to be filled.[23]

Goldwater's advisers recommended three candidates: Clifton White, a leader of the draft Goldwater committee; Dean Burch, a Goldwater campaign aide; and Ray Bliss. The advisers unanimously believed that Bliss was the best choice because he could unite the party. They knew that Bliss was interested. But the confusion surrounding the "favorite son" strategy had convinced Goldwater that Bliss was against him and for Nelson Rockefeller. Goldwater recommended Burch as national chairman instead.[24] When Bliss was asked about the national chairmanship, he said: "I doubt very much I'd take it if it were offered."[25]

Bliss did achieve one victory at the San Francisco convention: he replaced Congressman Clarence Brown Sr. as one of Ohio's two permanent representatives on the Republican National Committee. Brown had been Ohio's national committeeman since 1944, holding the slot reserved for a man, with the other one going to a woman. Bliss had joined the national committee in 1952 because he had a strong record of electing Republicans. He would have lost his spot on the committee if he was no longer state chairman or if the Republicans were less successful at the ballot box. So Bliss wanted the permanent spot as Ohio's national committeeman. The change revealed Bliss's interest in being national chairman. "I would not consider serving as national chairman," Bliss told a reporter, "unless I was a duly elected member of the national committee."[26]

Brown and Bliss had a long rivalry, dating back to the gubernatorial primary in 1932. "They hated each other," said former Akron congressman Bill Ayres.[27] Brown did not take his ouster gracefully, seeing a connection between the national committeeman vote and the national chairmanship: "The way was greased, I think, so Bliss could be national chairman."[28]

Bliss saw the situation differently. In a private letter to a Brown supporter, Bliss explained the history of his recent conflict with Brown. As the 1956 election approached, Bliss had expressed an interest in becoming the national committeeman, and told Brown so, proposing a secret ballot election at the national convention. Brown, Senator John Bricker, and others urged Bliss to stay on as state chairman for the 1956 campaign—with the understanding that Brown would not seek reelection to the national committee post in 1960. Bliss agreed. But when 1960 came, Brown claimed to have misunderstood the arrangement. Once again, Ohio party leaders prevailed upon Bliss to stay on as state chairman, this time for the 1960 campaign—

once again with the understanding that Brown would not seek reelection to the post in 1964. Bliss went along again.

When 1964 arrived, however, Brown again failed to step aside, telling Bliss that he did not recall the 1960 agreement. This was too much for Bliss. Bliss told Brown that he expected him to keep his promise. Bliss would challenge him for the national committee post, and if Brown chose to run, Bliss would "request a secret ballot so as not to embarrass anybody and would graciously accept the results whatever they might be." His letter continued: "I have a deep conviction that once a man gives his word in politics, he should keep it. He [Brown] chose to give his word in 1960 which he now says he cannot recall, despite the fact that a number of responsible persons recall in detail his 1960 commitment and said so to him in my presence. In spite of the foregoing he chose to make a contest of it and, therefore, any ill feeling created is his responsibility, not mine."[29]

Chapter 37

The Goldwater Debacle

The 1964 Republican National Convention was a low point in Ray Bliss's political career. Ohio conservatives believed that their state chairman had not done enough to back Goldwater, while moderates were alienated by the party's presidential nominee. Bliss was at odds with Governor Rhodes and his fight to replace Clarence Brown Sr. on the Republican National Committee added to the strain.

Bliss's friend W. Richard Wright saw Bliss when he returned to Akron from the convention. "I remember when Ray came home," said Wright. "He was in no hurry to get back to Columbus because he was devastated by it."[1]

Bliss supporters feared that he would quit as state chairman and rallied to support him. Congressman Robert Taft Jr., the 1964 Republican nominee for the US Senate, wrote to Bliss on July 20, just four days after the convention ended: "Before we get further into the campaign I wanted to write to assure you of my hope that you will continue as State Chairman, despite any rumors to the contrary. I know that the fine work you have done over many years has been of great value to the party, the state, and the individual candidates, including myself. I am certain that you, better than anyone, can direct the campaign for the state in the vital coming election."[2]

The Goldwater supporters did not own all the political passion in Ohio. Mrs. Roy C. Ahern of Cincinnati was still seething over the convention's outcome when she wrote Bliss on July 23: "I am still in a state of shock over the Republican Convention at the Cow Palace in San Francisco. When the votes were being polled, I held my rosary and prayed—then when I heard 'Ohio casts [its] votes for Goldwater,' I cried," she wrote. "Mr. Bliss, please stay with us in Ohio—remember I am a 'Bliss Republican'—and we cannot survive without you!"[3]

Clyde Mann, now an official with the Ohio Savings and Loan League in Columbus, used his skill as a former newspaper reporter to sum things up concisely in his July 20 letter to Bliss: "I don't know what it's all about but this is the time when all good friends should rally around you.... You can depend on me."[4]

Bliss gratefully wrote back to all his admirers that he was staying on as state chairman and promised to do all he could to win the election.[5]

An early indication of the abiding respect national Republican leaders had for Bliss came from Richard Nixon, who was willing to campaign for the Republican ticket. Remembering the 1960 campaign, Nixon wrote to Bliss on August 24: "Incidentally, when I come to Ohio I would like to ask you and your fine State organization to handle all of the arrangements. Since I am not the candidate I shall not have the usual advance men available. In some states this will be a problem. But, in Ohio, as I have learned from past experience, the State organization knows my operation so well and handles it so expertly that I need no one to advance appearances there for me!"[6]

Goldwater supporters in Ohio were not as generous with praise of Bliss, but they still expected Bliss to work for Goldwater. Representative John Ashbrook explained why Goldwater backers now deferred to Bliss: "At this point, Barry needs Ohio more than Ohio needs Barry."[7]

Dr. N. B. Livingston, a Columbus physician who headed Ohioans for Goldwater, which operated independently of the state party, made clear that Bliss's leadership was needed and expected. "We'll probably continue working for Goldwater as an independent group," said Livingston. "But everything we do will be coordinated through state headquarters. I see our role as one of assisting the regular organization."[8]

The Goldwater campaign also reached out to Bliss for help. After the convention, Goldwater named Bliss to a national steering committee to map out strategy for the national campaign. Bliss appeared at a surprise news conference in Goldwater's Senate office in Washington, DC, for the announcement. "I feel that we have a great cause and a great American running for the presidency," said Bliss. Goldwater, he said, "can and will win."[9] Goldwater promised that he and his vice-presidential running mate, Congressman William Miller, would follow the committee's recommendations "to the letter."[10] That turned out to be a hollow promise. Neither he nor Miller attended any of the meetings.[11]

In fact, Goldwater and Miller paid little attention to their own national chairman, Dean Burch. In a fashion reminiscent of Bliss, "Burch turned out to be a superb manager who transformed the old headquarters of the Republican National Committee into a model of modern communications and organization," wrote Lee Edwards, a Goldwater biographer.[12]

Although Goldwater apparently paid little attention to nuts-and-bolts advice, he made an effort to mend political fences, meeting with rival leaders in Hershey, Pennsylvania, on August 12. However, the effort flopped. According to author Theodore White, "All the dissident governors made their points, left Hershey and then ran their own campaigns, avoiding appearances with Goldwater as if he were cursed with political halitosis."[13]

Bliss never gave up on Goldwater publicly, but a campaign event in Akron suggested that Bliss did not want to get too close to the candidate. According to former congressman Bill Ayres of Akron, Bliss handled the situation delicately when Goldwater made a campaign stop. "Bliss had a way of staying above the fray," said Ayres. "Normally, when the big name at the top of the ticket came for a big rally or something, Ray was the one who would, you know, introduce him. So when Goldwater came to Akron, Ray said, 'You know, I think Barry would appreciate your introducing him.'" Ayres made the introduction, but he did not predict a Goldwater victory in the general election. Instead he spoke of his son, who was serving in the navy in Vietnam, in introducing Goldwater. "I said I have a son serving in Vietnam and I would be glad to have Senator Goldwater as commander-in-chief. I got away with it," said Ayres.[14]

Goldwater's stridently conservative rhetoric on domestic and foreign policy alienated many voters. Then he reinforced his image as a reactionary by voting against the landmark 1964 Civil Rights Act. He made no attempt to hide how much he detested moderate and liberal Republicans. "Sometimes I think this country would be better off if we could just saw off the Eastern Seaboard and let it float out to sea."[15]

By the end of September, Bliss despaired over the course of the campaign. "As things stand right now, we face another 1936," he told a journalist friend, referring to the year Franklin D. Roosevelt won his first reelection in a landslide. "And any goddam fool that doesn't believe it had better. I don't know what there is now that can save this thing except maybe an act of God, and you know those things don't come along too often in a lifetime."[16]

An act of God did not occur. On November 3, Lyndon Johnson won the election in a landslide, with 61 percent nationally. Goldwater won just six states: his own state of Arizona and five Southern states. Republicans were hurt down ticket, losing thirty-six seats in the US House of Representatives and two in the US Senate.[17] In Ohio, a must-win state for any Republican presidential candidate, the results were as devastating as the national figures, with Johnson winning 63 percent of the vote. Bliss had hoped that Robert Taft Jr. would recapture the US Senate seat from Democrat Stephen Young. But even the Taft name was not enough to overcome the downward pull Goldwater imposed on the whole ticket. Young squeaked by Taft, winning reelection by just 17,000 votes. The Ohio GOP was strong enough, however, to retain control of the state legislature.

The pundits put Goldwater and the GOP in a political coffin and started to close the lid.[18]

Walter Lippmann, perhaps the mostly widely respected columnist of the era, wrote that "the returns prove the falsity of the claim…that there is a great silent latent majority of 'conservative' Republicans who will emerge as soon as the Republican party turns its back on 'me-tooism' and offers them a 'choice.' The Johnson majority is indisputable proof that the voters are in the center."

The *Wall Street Journal*, Goldwater's friend editorially, had trouble finding a silver lining in the outcome of the election and joined the doomsday chorus—"conservatism has been given a black eye it will be a long time recovering from."

Political scientists Nelson W. Polsby and Aaron B. Wildavsky warned that the party put itself in peril by nominating candidates like Goldwater. If this tendency persisted, "we can expect an end to a competitive two-party-system."

Bliss took no joy in the Goldwater debacle. However, he had thrived on this kind of situation: rebuilding the party from the ruins of a lost election, against odds that seemed to heavily favor the other side. Now the national Republican Party needed rebuilding.

Chapter 38

Plotting for Bliss

To many Republican leaders, the 1964 debacle indicated the need for a change in direction for the party. National chairman Dean Burch immediately became a target. Plotting to remove Burch began just a few days after the 1964 election. The plotters wanted to be ready to act at the next meeting of the Republican National Committee in Chicago on January 22, 1965.[1]

An initial private meeting occurred on November 26, 1964, at the Sheraton-O'Hare Motel near O'Hare Airport in suburban Chicago. Donald R. Ross, the national committeeman from Nebraska, emerged as leader of the plot.[2] Ross was a classic Republican insider. Described as "a man who can make himself inconspicuous in a crowd of three" and "tough in the clinches" who "knew how to get what he wanted,"[3] he had been a Goldwater supporter but "felt the party needed drastic surgery."[4] Early in the plotting, Bliss's name came up as a possible replacement for Burch.[5] The plotting was soon reported in the press and was followed by a call for new party leadership from Republican governors meeting in Denver on December 3, 1964.[6]

Goldwater reacted slowly to the anti-Burch sentiment. A few days before Christmas 1964 he met with Burch and his vice-presidential running mate, William Miller. Goldwater came out strongly for Burch. "They want us to compromise," Goldwater reportedly said, "but they want Burch to get out and that's no compromise."[7] Burch was supported by conservatives, who wanted to extend their grip on the national party organization. Later, Goldwater himself said that the 1964 campaign really had not been primarily about winning the presidency—although he certainly would have accepted the prize—but about remaking the Republican Party: "We knew exactly where we were going—to defeat at the polls and victory in the party."[8]

Goldwater's candidacy did mark the beginning of a sea change in Republican politics. The tide was high in 1980 when Ronald Reagan was elected president and still higher in 1994 when Republicans took control of both houses of Congress.[9] But in 1964, many Republicans were more concerned about winning the next election than the long-term future of the party.

At Miller's suggestion, Goldwater decided to write members of the Republican National Committee in support of Burch. Bliss received one of the letters, dated December 26, 1964. "As chairman of the Senatorial Campaign Committee," Goldwater wrote, "I spoke on behalf of and raised money for many candidates with whom I often disagreed on the Senate floor, and the national ticket in 1960 had my whole-hearted support." Goldwater said he had not changed. "I am still for unity. Even today if I felt the resignation of Dean Burch would serve to unify our party, I would be glad to recommend such action. It has never been my nature to reject compromise, nor have I rejected any proposed compromise out of hand in the current situation." He urged "fair play" for Burch and said that if Burch succeeded in staying on, the party would be stronger because "the sacrificial blood-letting now being discussed will have been avoided."[10]

The letter did not stop the anti-Burch bandwagon and probably strengthened it. "That letter killed him," a powerful East Coast Republican leader said. "He [Goldwater] said, in effect, 'Dean is my boy' and those Midwesterners didn't want anybody who was anybody's boy."[11]

By early January, Ross had enough votes on the national committee to oust Burch, and better yet, he had support for Bliss as Burch's replacement. Characteristically, Bliss said little publicly about the behind-the-scenes maneuvering. Ross and Bliss flew to Washington, DC, on January 5, 1965. Bliss met with Goldwater that evening. "Goldwater tried to talk Bliss into announcing his support for Burch," it was reported, "but Bliss replied that he intended to stay neutral."[12] If the chairmanship became vacant, Bliss told Goldwater, he would allow himself to be nominated—he had given Ross his word.[13]

The next day Ross met with Goldwater. "It came as a complete surprise when Ross, a little-known Omaha lawyer, calmly announced that the group he was leading had 70 solid votes lined up against Burch," journalists James McCartney and William

McGaffin reported. "Ross handed Goldwater a piece of paper containing the 70 names. Among them were some Burch thought were committed to him."[14] Ross had a clear majority of the 132 members of the national committee.

Negotiations began between Burch's backers and those who wanted Bliss to replace him. Burch's friends did not give up easily. They argued that the plotters were bluffing and did not have as much strength as they claimed. Burch's backers charged that the plotters were really "fronting" for New York governor Nelson Rockefeller and other Goldwater foes—and even brought up Bliss's deposing of Clarence Brown Sr. as Ohio's national committeeman.[15]

Burch floated a possible compromise. He told reporters that his continuation as national chairman was not negotiable, but his critics could have a role in picking a new executive director and executive committee for the national committee.[16] Burch also made an effort to show he understood his opponents. In a speech at the National Press Club in Washington, DC, Burch said: "I seek to remain as chairman because this nation needs a two-party system." He spoke up for party unity and against "the dictates of radicalism in any form."[17]

But Ross kept the pressure on, showing that 21 out of 31 committeemen from 12 midwestern states opposed keeping Burch. When Goldwater and Burch learned that the midwestern Republicans wanted a new chairman, they knew a change was inevitable.[18] By Friday, January 8, Goldwater and Burch tentatively agreed that Burch would resign and that Bliss would replace him.

Several bases still had to be touched. Goldwater met with former president Dwight Eisenhower and former vice president Richard Nixon in New York City at the Waldorf Towers Hotel. "With Burch left waiting outside the door, the three men agreed that if Burch could not achieve a 'broad base of support within the party' before the national committee meeting on January 22, he should step aside as chairman," reported Goldwater biographer Lee Edwards. Eisenhower then suggested that the leadership crisis could be resolved by selecting Ray Bliss of Ohio as national chairman. This push from Eisenhower, with Nixon's apparent support, ended Goldwater's resistance.[19]

Eisenhower may well have been active in recruiting Bliss for the chairmanship. Louise Earley, Ellen Bliss's sister, remembers a visit by the Blisses to the Earley home in Atlanta, Georgia, during which "Ray called Eisenhower from this phone. We always used to say, put a big bow on [the phone]." Eisenhower was in Augusta, Georgia, at the time, said Earley. "That's when Eisenhower was really working on Ray to become national chairman. Ray did not want to become national chairman."[20]

But at Eisenhower's request, Bliss flew to Augusta. On November 10, 1964, Bliss met with Eisenhower and staffers Clifford Roberts and Barry Leithead. The topic was "Republican re-organization."[21] Given the plotting underway, it is likely that the chairmanship was discussed. Bliss later said that the fact that Eisenhower wanted him to take the job was crucial.[22]

By Monday, January 11, the deal was so far along that the usually reticent Bliss needed to comment publicly. In coordination with Burch, the Ohio chairman issued a statement at 6:30 P.M. but labeled for "Tuesday Morning Release": "Because of the fact that my name has been so frequently mentioned in speculation concerning the chairmanship of the Republican National Committee, I feel it is imperative to express my views on this matter." Bliss said he was "strongly hopeful" that the GOP would avoid "bloodletting over this issue," and in any event, he would not participate in such conflict. The statement continued: "I would not accept the chairmanship under any circumstances until such time as an actual vacancy occurred and I were asked to do so by Senator Goldwater and had his full support."[23]

This position may have been window dressing to protect Burch's and Goldwater's feelings. Bliss wanted Republicans to appear united, even if they were not. It would never do for Bliss and his allies to appear to be wrestling control of the national committee from Goldwater and his supporters. Bliss would need the support of Goldwater's backers to rebuild the GOP.

To help orchestrate an orderly transition, Bliss flew to Arizona on January 12, 1965, and went to Goldwater's home in Phoenix.[24] Goldwater presided. He made it clear that as leader of the party he had invited Miller, Burch, and Bliss to his house for a discussion about the chairmanship of the national committee. But he also wanted to send a signal of broad support for his actions. "Let me also assure every Republican that within the past few hours I have discussed my position with General Eisenhower and with my good friend, Dick Nixon, and each of them has concluded it as being in the best interests of our party and our country," Goldwater said.[25]

Goldwater reported that he and Chairman Burch had been in contact with the membership of the Republican National Committee. The two of them had concluded that Burch could have been reelected in Chicago, but the chairman would not have a "clear working mandate." With this reality in mind, Burch decided to offer his resignation. "Burch deserved the party's thanks for a job well done," Goldwater said.[26]

Now Goldwater turned to Bliss. The Ohio chairman was more than all right, he said. After all, Bliss had announced his opposition to any kind of resolution of no confidence aimed at getting rid of Burch. Now that Burch was stepping aside, Goldwater threw his support to Bliss—a signal that his followers should do the same. He had been a Bliss man for a long time, Goldwater said, perhaps longer than many of his followers knew. "I pledge my complete support of him just as I did over six years ago when I first asked him to be National Chairman and as I have done twice since on similar occasions," Goldwater said.[27]

Miller then joined Goldwater in praising both Burch and Bliss and stressing the need for unity. Miller looked to the immediate future: "the 1966 Republican campaign will begin in Chicago on the 22nd and 23rd of January, and the Democrats had better take note, because Republicans won't be kicking themselves around anymore—we will be out to win elections."[28]

Burch had the toughest role to play—gracefully bowing out of the job he desperately wanted to keep while maintaining his self-respect. He announced his resignation as chairman, effective April 1. Then he urged members of the national committee to accept his resignation and to choose Bliss to take his place. He praised Bliss and especially Goldwater, before noting that the party was more important than any one person: "As I have said repeatedly since the election, the issue before us now is not Dean Burch—the issue is how to build our Party for the victories we can and should win in 1966 and 1968."[29]

Now it was Bliss's turn to speak—something he never enjoyed doing. Bliss said he would serve as chairman if the national committee wanted him to and if Goldwater supported him in "building a strong organization capable of winning Republican victories." Bliss paid homage to Goldwater and Burch, but without commenting on whether Burch would have been reelected as chairman in Chicago. Bliss always searched for what unified Republicans, not what divided them. That was what he would do as chairman, he said:

> If by serving as Chairman I can in any way help to strengthen the bonds which unite all of us as Republicans, I will feel the confidence Senator Goldwater and others have expressed in me to be earned....I offer my assurance that if I am selected to succeed Mr. Burch, I will give myself as wholeheartedly to the national interests of our Party as I have over the past sixteen years to the Republican party of Ohio.[30]

Other Republican leaders responded positively to the news from Arizona. Former President Eisenhower said Bliss was "an amicable solution." The Republican leader in the US Senate, Everett Dirksen of Illinois, remarked, "The rule of reason always comes to its own." New York governor Nelson Rockefeller stated, "This is a wise move in the best interest of the party."[31]

As the news spread, it caught at least one politician by surprise. In Columbus, Governor James Rhodes was among the last to know that Bliss had left town for the Phoenix meeting, according to Robert Feldkamp of the *Akron Beacon Journal*.[32]

"Newsmen called the governor's office that morning wondering if Rhodes had any comment on the report Bliss was in Arizona.

"'What's he doing in Arizona?' the governor was quoted."

Feldkamp believed that he knew why Bliss had gone west without informing Ohio's chief executive and Bliss's fellow Republican.

"Remember the GOP convention in San Francisco last July? Ray Bliss on the coast and Jim Rhodes back in Ohio releasing the Buckeye delegation? Who was among the last to find out? Ray Bliss, of course. It wasn't a secret then or now that the chairman was rankled. We predicted the canny Bliss would have the last word," wrote Feldkamp. "He did."

Chapter 39

Ray Bliss Becomes National Chairman

The public endorsements of Ray Bliss to become Republican national chairman did not mean the deal was done. Not all conservatives were ready to follow Barry Goldwater's lead and replace Chairman Burch.

Just three days after the Phoenix meeting, members of the Republican National Committee received an anonymous letter attacking Bliss. It said that Bliss was "no miracle worker" and that he had a negative record as chairman in Ohio.[1] Kent Courtney, a conservative from New Orleans, caused a stir when he said that Goldwater favored the idea of a "third" party for conservatives.[2] Although Goldwater rejected the notion, saying, "The Republican party is the place for conservatives," he soon seemed to have forgotten all about party unity. Goldwater lashed out at the Ripon Society, a group of moderate to liberal Republicans, comparing the group to the secretive John Birch Society. The moderates quickly rose to the bait.[3]

In contrast, the Bliss endorsement drew praise from many Republican elected officials, including the governors who had called for a change in leadership back in December 1964. Editorial opinion was generally positive. For example, *Newsweek* wrote: "In a Republican age of ideology, Ray Bliss is a mechanic. He has all the charisma of an Akron insurance agent (which he is), but as Ohio's veteran GOP state chairman, he enjoyed an unrivaled nationwide reputation as the rarest of Republican wizards: a winner. If any carpenter can mend the fractious GOP house, Bliss is the man for the job."[4]

Bliss's hometown newspaper, the *Akron Beacon Journal,* proclaimed Bliss as "The Ideal Choice" for national chairman. The editorial offered lavish praise: "As for the party, it is fortunate indeed to have Bliss available for the massive rebuilding job that must be done if anything like political balance is to be restored.... When it comes to party organization and financing, he is a master craftsman. Prominent Republicans everywhere respect his ability and judgment. They know him as a man of unquestioned integrity."

The editorial continued: "Philosophically, Bliss probably is more moderate than Barry Goldwater, more conservative than Nelson Rockefeller, but we shall be surprised if he attempts as national chairman to exert an ideological influence on the party one way or the other. Instead, we expect him to concentrate on two goals: reducing factionalism and strengthening the party's organizational structure."[5]

But others believed that rebuilding the shattered GOP was too much even for Bliss. *New York Times* columnist Tom Wicker detailed the divisions in the party and concluded: "For that reason, an effective compromise at the top, temporarily settling the leadership of the Republican National Committee, could have little if any effect on the separate factional and personal rivalries." Wicker continued, "Seldom if ever in American politics, however, has the reverse proposition been so graphically demonstrated; that is, that one major failure to effect the compromise and accommodation that alone holds a party together can shatter that party down to the precinct level, and dim its election prospects for many years."[6]

This volatile political mix was made worse by the publication of a detailed account of the plot to oust Burch on January 13, just a day after the Phoenix meeting, by journalists James McCartney and William McGaffin.[7] An argument followed about the details of the story between the plot's leader, Don Ross, and the journalists and their editors. The next day, a short article revealed Ross's motivation for the squabble: he did not want to embarrass Goldwater and Burch.[8]

It is unclear what role, if any, Bliss played in Ross's complaints. Bliss did not regularly quibble with reporters. "Never argue with anyone who buys ink by the barrel," he counseled politicians. But Bliss was also wary of stories that laid bare Republican infighting: "It isn't that I fear the press, but frequently there are things that you ask questions about that if you answer you'd rather not have published and this turns up a furor and offends somebody's feelings."[9]

In 1974, Bliss made clear that he had been well aware of the straits the national party was in ten years before: "So, we had a philosophical difference there. It was wide. It was deep.... That was a problem of bringing together divergent parts of the party and don't misunderstand me, they knew we were on the brink of disaster." He also argued that the Republicans' problems provided him with circumstances tailor-made for a strong-willed chairman to reshape the party: "So, the elements were there for me as chairman to call the shots.... Because they figured if I failed or resigned or quit that that might be the end of the Republican Party."[10]

Some of Bliss's friends worried about him taking the job. "Ray is too much of a perfectionist for his own good," a Bliss backer told journalist David Broder. "I am afraid his enemies will just nibble him to death with petty criticism. They'll make him a nervous wreck."[11]

Despite all this friction, the January 22 meeting of the Republican National Committee went smoothly. It was Bliss's kind of meeting. Even behind closed doors, Republicans were getting along. At a two-hour meeting of the executive committee, "nothing of a blood-letting nature" came up, a party spokesman said.[12]

Bliss certainly wanted no blood-letting. The day before the full committee meeting, he had presided over a gathering of state chairmen and refused to talk about the upcoming change in party leadership. This drew complaints from some reporters. Jack Bell of the Associated Press tried to persuade Bliss that he would have to change his style. "Ray, you're going to have to open up more than this when you get to Washington," Bell said. Bliss, according to Robert Feldkamp of the *Akron Beacon Journal*, "just looked at Bell and smiled."[13]

At the public meeting of the full national committee, Dean Burch submitted his letter resigning as chairman shortly before noon on January 22, effective April 1, 1965. Samuel Mellinger, the national committeeman from Kansas, part of Bliss's midwestern base, nominated Bliss for chairman. Mellinger's motion was seconded by Katherine Kennedy Brown, Ohio's national committeewoman. There were no other nominations and Bliss won the job by apparent unanimous approval of the 132-member committee.[14]

Bliss was making history, and he knew it. The moment called for a speech. Briefly, he savored and marveled at the significance of what had happened to him.

"Chairman Burch, members of the Republican National Committee, distinguished guests: It is an honor indeed for a man who 32 years ago started as a precinct committeeman, to have bestowed upon him the highest office his Party can bestow upon anyone," Bliss told the group. Always a realist, Bliss put the honor in perspective: "I have taken due note, of course, of Dean Burch's statement that there have been 18 national chairmen in 28 years. So well I understand this is not a lifetime selection. It is well recognized I am assuming an awesome responsibility."[15]

The Ohioan also wanted members of the committee to know that the attention he had been receiving had not swelled his head. "Contrary to all the stories you read…I am no modern miracle man." This comment was in part a response to his conservative critics, but it was offered in good humor. "The other night I was sitting with my wife in a restaurant, prior to coming over here and she was discussing some of the stories she read and she said, 'Ray, I have read so many of those even I am beginning to believe them,'" said Bliss, as Ellen stood a few feet away during his speech.

Bliss promised: "I will work hard and try to do a good job for you."[16]

Applause shook the room as Bliss sat down.

"To most of the 132 members of the Republican National Committee, the man they chose for the $30,000-a-year job is neither a Moses who will lead them to the promised land nor an incompetent who will lead them to perdition," wrote David Broder. "He is the same stocky, florid-faced political professional they have known for years, a man who is content to stay in the background and let the candidates do the talking."[17]

Not everyone was happy. Kent Courtney from Louisiana, who advocated a conservative third party, said: "Bliss was an April Fool present for the Republican party."[18]

Bliss would not become chairman until April 1, but it was clear at a luncheon shortly after his speech that he was now the party's leader. At the head table, Bliss was flanked by former vice president Richard Nixon and Congressman Gerald R. Ford of Michigan, the newly elected Republican leader in the House of Representatives. A few feet away, no longer at the center of things, sat Goldwater, still the party's "titular head," with William Miller, his running mate.

Goldwater passed the torch of leadership to Bliss, reminding everyone that he had asked Bliss to take the job, adding, "This was the third time I went to that man on bended knee to take the chairmanship."[19]

The third time turned out to be the charm.

Ray Bliss (center left) and Republican Vice President Richard Nixon (center right), 1960. Bliss supported Nixon in the 1960 presidential election. Nixon won Ohio to the surprise of many analysts, but narrowly lost the White House to John F. Kennedy. (From the Ray C. Bliss Papers. Courtesy of Archival Services, University Libraries, The University of Akron)

Ohio Governor Mike DiSalle (left) and John F. Kennedy (right), 1960. Democrats DiSalle and JFK campaigned together in Ohio, but the Republicans carried the state. DiSalle was elected in 1958, in large part due to an unpopular right-to-work ballot measure that Bliss opposed. (Courtesy of the Ohio History Connection [P90])

John F. Kennedy (upper left) and astronaut John Glenn (center), 1962. Ray Bliss made a strong effort to recruit Glenn to run as a Republican. Instead, Glenn was successful as a Democratic US Senator from Ohio. (Courtesy of NASA)

Ray Bliss (right) and James Rhodes (left), 1962. Bliss helped Republican Rhodes win the 1962 gubernatorial election over Democrat "Tax Hike" Mike DiSalle. Bliss and Rhodes had a rocky relationship. (From the Ray C. Bliss Papers. Courtesy of Archival Services, University Libraries, The University of Akron)

Ohio Chairman Ray Bliss, 1963. Bliss drafting a press release in response to the assassination of President Kennedy. (From the Ray C. Bliss Papers. Courtesy of Archival Services, University Libraries, The University of Akron)

Ray Bliss with Republican state chairmen, 1963. The support of Republican state chairmen was a foundation of Bliss's success. Bliss is in the front row, fifth from the left. (Courtesy of the Ohio History Connection [P391])

Ray Bliss (second from left) and Nelson Rockefeller (center), 1960s. From the liberal wing of the GOP, New York Governor Nelson Rockefeller and Bliss were friends, but Bliss did not back him for the 1964 or 1968 presidential nominations. (Courtesy of the Ohio History Connection [P391])

Democratic President Lyndon Johnson (right) campaigning in Akron, 1964. President Johnson won a landslide victory in the 1964 election, and as a consequence, Bliss became GOP national chairman. (Courtesy of the *Akron Beacon Journal*)

Chapter 40

Good-Bye Columbus

Ohio Republicans were pleased that Ray Bliss was becoming national chairman, but they weren't happy to see him step down as state chairman. Bliss met with members of the Republican state committee in Columbus on January 20, 1965, two days before he was to be nominated for the national chairmanship in Chicago. He told the committee that his new job would demand all his time and energy.

"I just think it's not in the party's interest that I hold these two posts," Bliss said at a press conference following the meeting.[1] Although he had remained chairman of the Summit County party while being state chairman, he would leave both the state and county posts to be national chairman. D. E. "Gene" Waddell would replace Bliss as chairman in Summit County. Earlier Bliss had announced that the national chairmanship would be an interval in his life and that his home would continue to be in Akron, as it had been during his years as state chairman. He said he was not planning on making a career out of the national chairmanship.[2]

Despite Democratic success nationally in 1964, Bliss forecast good things ahead for Ohio Republicans: "We're the only large industrial state with a majority of our party in the Congressional delegation, with a Republican House in the state legislature and at least a tie in the [state] Senate."[3]

At least five persons were mentioned as possible successors to Bliss as state chairman, but Bliss's choice prevailed: John Andrews of Toledo, who had worked closely with

Bliss at state headquarters.[4] The *Akron Beacon Journal* paid Andrews the ultimate compliment: "A 'Bliss-type' politician. That's what they call John Andrews."[5] And when a reporter asked Andrews if he considered himself a "middle-of-the-road" Republican, he gave an answer worthy of Bliss: "It's unfair to attach any label to me. My field is the managerial side of politics. I'm more concerned with campaigns and candidates."[6]

With his successors chosen, there was little left for Bliss to do but say good-bye to the men and women he had worked with for sixteen years at state headquarters. The farewell came March 17, 1965, at the Fort Hayes Hotel in Columbus, where Bliss, for the last time as state chairman, presided over the Republican legislative dinner.

By 1965, the Republican legislative dinners had become a Columbus ritual, carried off with the same precision and devotion to detail that Bliss demanded of every special occasion. Bliss began by recalling the chilly reception he received the first time he tried to get legislative leaders to have dinner together. Bliss then directed the legislators to the commitment they owed to the Ohio Republican Party and demands of their elected offices.

"Many of you have received assistance from state headquarters in the way of financial aid or other types of aid in your recent campaign.... Are there commitments because of that aid? No, the only commitment you have, and the only commitment I have ever made as state chairman... is that those who are elected such as you will do a job for the citizens of Ohio and the citizens only," said Bliss.[7]

Republicans, he emphasized, had to stick together: "My only hope is that you'll do that which you've always done—do a job for Ohio by supporting your Republican platform and supporting the Republican governor in the program which he advocates. Only by a united process such as that can we hope to maintain a united and effective Republican party in this state."

John Andrews, the incoming state chairman, then spoke and sounded a humble note.

"Following you in this job is not easy, of course. You have set very high standards, and I'm going to have some difficulty, I'm sure, in measuring up to them," said Andrews.

The next two speakers knew first-hand about the way Bliss had worked and worked to delicately craft cooperation among Republican elected officials, Senate Republican Leader Theodore "Ted" M. Gray from Miami County north of Dayton and House Speaker Roger Cloud from Logan County in rural west central Ohio.

Bliss had turned weaknesses into strengths to build a party broad enough to accommodate farmers, factory workers and industrial leaders, and still regularly win elections. Few in Columbus appreciated this more than Cloud, who arrived in Columbus to serve in the legislature in 1949—the same year Bliss came to the capital to try to jump start a stalled state Republican Party.

Cloud presented Bliss with a resolution from the House that had received the backing of both the Republicans and Democrats, reflecting the respect Bliss had on both sides of the aisle. The "Whereas" clauses of the resolution succinctly captured Bliss's devotion to not only the Republican Party but to the American two-party system. The resolution commended Bliss for his work and wished him and his wife Ellen well in their upcoming adventure in Washington, DC.

The last speaker, Governor James Rhodes, had a politically convenient memory for just the good times he and Bliss had shared. As Rhodes recalled history, he had helped Bliss win the state chairman's job back in 1949 when Rhodes was mayor of Columbus. "I got a couple votes for Ray Bliss back in 1949," said Rhodes. "When I was mayor of this capital city, I campaigned for him because I believed in him and I never regretted the fact that I was a 'Ray Bliss' man in 1949."

Rhodes gushed with admiration at the departing chairman's never-ending effort to keep the party together. "Ray, over these 16 years, you've given nothing more than loyalty and great fidelity to our party and to the members," said Rhodes.

Rhodes soon had Bliss zooming past the national chairmanship and headed for the White House. "There's only one step up after you become national chairman and that's to run for president," said Rhodes. "And I know, in the past, that you'd have been a better choice and I say that from experience, because I think that you have the human touch and also know what's in the hearts and minds of Republicans."

Bliss had the last word and didn't mention the friction with Rhodes. Bliss ended his remarks by saying: "The greatest gift you can give me as your new national chairman, those of you who are my friends, is to continue to do the fine job you have done in Ohio and redouble your efforts to give us a smashing Republican victory in 1966."

Bliss was already building a team to revive the national Republican Party, and he wanted Ohioans on the front lines. "Our party has been sliding downhill for 24 years," Bliss told David Broder, "and for anyone to think we are going to reverse it in one, two or three is unrealistic. What I am hoping for is an improvement, but it's going to be no picnic."[8]

Chapter 41

Mr. Bliss Goes to Washington

April 1, 1965, was Ray Bliss's first day on the job as Republican national chairman. Breaking a lifelong habit of sleeping in late, he was up at 8 A.M. to meet with special visitors from Akron: Summit County Republican chairman D. E. "Gene" Waddell and Robert Feldkamp, the politics reporter from the *Akron Beacon Journal*.

Feldkamp's early morning presence in the Blisses' Washington, DC, apartment was no accident. Waddell had arranged for what amounted to a daylong interview with Bliss, who was keeping a promise made to Feldkamp in the 1964 Ohio GOP primary. The result was a nearly an hour-by-hour account of Bliss's busy first day.[1]

The master of political details was caught with an almost bare cupboard. Mrs. Bliss had to provide sugar for the morning coffee from small complimentary packets that had come off an airplane. Bliss gave his wife a gentle ribbing: "You know, Ellen, this is the first time we've had a visitor and you didn't even have sugar." "Breakfast for Bliss consisted of a tall glass of tomato juice, coffee and a cigarette," wrote Feldkamp.

Soon Bliss was driven to the Sheraton Hotel for a speech to the thirteenth annual Republican Women's Conference. He already had begun to notice the pressure of the new job. "It's amazing, just amazing, how many people want to see you. Why, just meeting with the press would set me back a week," Bliss said.[2]

At the hotel, Chairman and Mrs. Bliss were escorted to a small receiving room across from the main ballroom where he was to speak. Republican House Minority

Leader Gerald Ford and other dignitaries greeted Bliss, and, before long, former vice president Richard Nixon stopped by to check on his speaking role.

"Whatever you want to do is fine with me," Nixon told Bliss. "Where will we meet later?"

"I'll be on the platform," Bliss responded. "We can leave together."

It was the right audience for Bliss. From his days as a local party leader in Akron through his successful years as state chairman, Bliss had always worked closely with women's groups. "I worked all day Wednesday on this," Bliss told Feldkamp. "I don't like to read a speech. But I want this to be perfect."

Political scientist Arthur Peterson, who worked for Bliss, also labored hard on the speech. In fact, Peterson's youngest daughter was born on the night Peterson was writing the first draft. Bliss became godfather to Ingrid Bliss Peterson. "I kept wanting to finish it and he [Bliss] kept telling me, 'Go home, Art. Connie [Peterson's wife] needs you. Go home, go home,'" said Peterson. "But I stayed, almost until Ingrid Bliss was born. But we got the speech written and it was pretty good, if I do say so myself."[3]

Bliss provided the two thousand participants at the women's conference with a clear declaration of what he wanted the Republican Party to become and what he did not want to see happen. "We must transmit a sense of sound responsibility to all our citizens—young and old, rich and poor, black and white, employer and employee, city dweller and farmer," said Bliss. Republicans had to show the country that the party had an open door policy and a room big enough to accommodate all who wanted to fit in. "We must expand this sense of purpose to build a party which offers a broad appeal to all citizens of the United States," Bliss said. "Mud-slinging and negative thinking will win neither supporters or elections, and, even if they did, I'll have no part of them."[4]

Bliss went on to say: "As important as issues are, they cannot be brought forcefully to the attention of the people without alert, knowledgeable and attractive candidates. . . . We Republicans must be more tolerant of the deeply held views of potentially good candidates." But the new chairman did not want to be misunderstood: "On some issues and on some candidates, we should not and we will not compromise. A party that seeks to win at any cost, that sacrifices fundamental principles for temporary victory is worse than no party at all." The answer was party unity on "fundamental principles" rather than on every detail on every issue and controversy.

Bliss had timed the speech beforehand at fifteen minutes. He stuck to his text and the audience responded with frequent applause. Consequently, it was twenty-two minutes before the other speakers, including Nixon, had their turns.

"We don't need a new image," Nixon said of Republicans. "We need to let people know our true image." As Bliss had before him, Nixon urged Republicans to move ahead together and to put personal ambition aside: "Ray Bliss will unify the party behind all the nominees."[5]

Bliss didn't let Feldkamp in on everything. After the speeches and lunch, Bliss took Nixon to the airport and they talked privately, while Mrs. Bliss and Feldkamp followed in a second car. From the airport, Bliss went to national Republican headquarters.

"It was 3:30 p.m. when Bliss walked through the second floor doorway at 1625 I Street NW—the office he officially took over," wrote Feldkamp.

The chairman's office was decorated with congratulatory telegrams and floral arrangements sent by well-wishers. There was hardly time for the staffers, most of them holdovers from the Burch-Goldwater days, to size up their new boss. Feldkamp later described the operation on Bliss's first day as "vast disorder, confusion, inactivity. . . . Morale was terrible."[6]

Soon it was on to a reception for Republican women from all fifty states back at the Sheraton Park Hotel. The receiving line seemed to grow longer, and as it did, Bliss nervously glanced at his watch. The last event of the day was with women from Summit County at the Marriott Twin Bridges Motor Hotel. It was several miles away and scheduled for 7 P.M. Bliss had a passion for punctuality and did not want to be late for an event with local backers who embodied the Bliss style of politics. He whispered to his wife that it was time to leave and the couple left, after shaking hands and chatting for ten more minutes.

"At the Marriott, the new chairman seemed to relax completely for the first time all day," Feldkamp wrote.[7] Representative Bill Ayres from Akron had seen to it that the women from his district felt welcome. Bliss spotted Ayres, motioned him to come over, and then threw his arm around the gregarious congressman.

"You know, Bill, I needle you a lot. But I wish I had 100 like you. Then we'd take back the Congress," said Bliss. About 8:45 P.M. Bliss went to a small rostrum and began speaking to his old friends, joking at first, then turning serious with the people who meant the most to him in politics. "You people here have known me for a long time," he said. "I wouldn't be here without many of you. . . . I'll continue to need your help as I always have. Thanks for coming," he said. A weary Bliss chatted with many of the guests as they filed out and then turned to his wife: "Ellen, let's go home."[8]

Bliss was soon back home—in Ohio—for a set of concurrent dinners in eight cities on June 9, 1965. "A Salute to Ray Bliss" was designed to lift party spirits and raise funds. Bliss was willing for once to draw attention to himself, something rare in his long political career.⁹

Using then cutting-edge technology, Bliss hooked all the dinner venues together through closed-circuit television. Each event showcased a Republican leader—some well-known and some rising stars. Each spoke on his special expertise, covering a wide range of issues and different perspectives within the party. "The program also was typical of Bliss in that it offered a wide range of party philosophy, from conservative to liberal," Feldkamp wrote in the *Akron Beacon Journal*, "and the formal portion was over in one hour."¹⁰

Cleveland was the site of an anchor dinner featuring Bliss, former president Dwight Eisenhower, and Michigan governor George Romney. Drawn from the liberal wing of the party, Romney talked about equal rights. Party centrists included former vice president Richard Nixon, who held center stage in Columbus and talked on foreign policy. From the conservative wing, Ronald Reagan was in Cincinnati to speak on free enterprise. Reagan was considering running for governor of California in 1966.

The only nationally prominent Republicans missing from the program were New York governor Nelson Rockefeller and 1964 presidential nominee Barry Goldwater. Their absence was no accident. Bliss wanted a love feast, not a banquet of conflict.

Bliss offered his own thoughts on the importance of the two-party system—widely viewed as endangered by the 1964 debacle. "Make no mistake about it," Bliss lectured the audiences gathered across Ohio. "Under the American system of government, with its checks and balances, with its specific administrative and legislative responsibilities, if either of the two parties ever becomes so weak that the other is unchallenged and unrestrained, we then shall have ceased to be a Republic."¹¹

Bliss, known for understatement rather than hyperbole, later described a sense of desperation. "There was a genuine fear, even among the press, that the weakness of the GOP would result in one party and ultimately result in dictatorship," Bliss said. Reporters were friendly to him because "they felt there was going to be a total cave-in of the two-party system in this country."¹² Bliss's support of the two-party system was more than a platitude. He believed the Democrats needed Republicans to keep them on their toes and Republicans needed Democrats to make sure they didn't become sloppy and corrupt.

When asked by a reporter in 1965, "Why did you finally take the National Chairman's job after turning it down several times?" Bliss replied: "The last thing I ever wanted was to be National Chairman, because I knew the trials and tribulations of the job. But I felt strongly that something had to be done to strengthen the Republican Party in order to maintain a vigorous two-party system in this country."[13] Political scientist Arthur Peterson recalled Bliss saying that if the Democrats appeared headed for extinction he would go to work to save the Democrats.[14] "I still think that this country needs a two-party system to field two slates of candidates to give the citizens of the nation a choice as to which leader they prefer to serve them in various offices," Bliss said in 1974, just as the Republican Party was going through another crisis, the Watergate scandal.[15]

More than twelve thousand Republicans turned out for the "Salute to Ray Bliss" dinners, which netted $1 million. In typical Bliss fashion, reported Feldkamp, the proceeds were divided "50 percent to county GOP organizations in Ohio, 30 percent to operate Ohio Republican headquarters and 20 percent into the national party treasury."[16]

Chapter 42

Fixing the Finances

The "Salute to Ray Bliss" dinners provided Ray Bliss with a welcome infusion of cash. The Republican National Committee was almost broke. One account said that as of April 1, 1965, the national party had just $300,000 on hand. With expenses of $145,000 a month, there was only enough money to pay expenses for a little more than two months.[1] "When I became national chairman, the treasury was down to darn near nothing," Bliss told a seminar in 1974. "The treasury had a few hundred thousand dollars, which some people mistakenly thought was a lot of money.... That's a pittance ... we had to generate some money."[2]

Bliss had been national chairman little more than a week when a financial controversy arose. Citing an anonymous source, syndicated columnists Robert S. Allen and Paul J. Scott claimed that Bliss received a record salary, double the size of his predecessor's—$60,000 a year. "At Bliss' insistence," the column continued, "the National Executive Committee deposited two years' pay ($120,000) to his account in a Washington bank, where he can draw on it as he sees fit."[3]

A response came quickly from the Republican National Committee. An April 23 letter repudiated all the points in the column: Bliss received a salary of $30,000 a year, which was the same as his predecessor's, and no money was held in escrow. "This is important to us in the Republican Party because, not only would it set the record straight, but information of this sort, when not accurate, can have a negative effect on the important fund-raising program that lies ahead," the letter said.[4]

Allen and Scott were convinced and issued a "Correction" in a May 5 column.[5] Bliss wanted to create the same kind of financial system at the national level that Republicans had in Ohio, with a fund-raising committee separate from the party divisions that spent money. After an extensive search, he asked Lucius D. Clay to head the National Republican Finance Committee. A retired four-star army general, hero of the Berlin Airlift, former corporate CEO and senior partner in the investment firm Lehman Brothers, Clay was literally an "Eisenhower" Republican—having worked with the general and president throughout his career.[6] At a June 20 press conference, Bliss said he was "proud, happy and pleased" to have someone of Clay's stature to approach potential donors, many of whom had been alienated by the 1964 campaign.[7]

A potential competitor for funds, however, had appeared just three days before. On June 17, Barry Goldwater had announced the formation of the Free Society Association, of which he would be the honorary chairman. It would be a "nonpartisan" group, more "academic" than "political." It would perform no organizational tasks, back no candidates, and only raise funds to educate the public on "freedom, our Constitution and our system of enterprise." Goldwater said it would welcome almost anyone as a member, including those in the right-wing John Birch Society—but not the Ku Klux Klan.[8]

Bliss was asked about the Free Society Association at the press conference with Clay. "If you believe in a free society," Bliss said, "the best way is to work through the regular two-party system. Only a novice would think that splinter groups don't drain off funds." Clay joined in denouncing the new group. He said that he had been asked to be a trustee of Goldwater's new group but declined: "I didn't want to be identified with any one segment of the party." Clay also would try to reclaim money left over from Goldwater's presidential campaign—about $600,000 he believed should go into the national party's treasury. Bliss, who lived by the maxim that a man's word is his bond, felt betrayed by Goldwater. "I had a commitment from party leaders that they would unite behind me and help build a strong Republican Party," said Bliss. "I am hopeful that Barry Goldwater will continue to support the party."[9]

General Clay had an unusual effect on Bliss, who was comfortable around national leaders such as Eisenhower and Nixon, business leaders, and wealthy donors. "Clay was one of the few people, I think, that intimidated him," said political scientist John Bibby, who worked for Bliss at the Republican National Committee. "Bliss was not a particularly neat and tidy guy in terms of his desk," recalled Bibby. "When Lucius D. Clay was coming in to see him, he'd be throwing papers and stuff in drawers, so that when Clay arrived there was nothing on his desk. . . . Clay was a successful man in a whole range of activities. He was a distinguished person."[10]

Bliss and Clay were soon hard at work raising funds. In August 1965, Bliss put together a get-acquainted picnic for Clay and the "financial shock troops" of the party—past $1,000 donors. They gathered under striped tents on Eisenhower's Gettysburg farm. "The problem before the canvas-covered gathering was one of supply: How to coax money out of the pockets of Republicans and into the party's national coffers," reporter Philip E. Meyer wrote in the *Akron Beacon Journal*.[11]

Bliss wanted those attending the picnic to feel good about the GOP. He told them they wouldn't be asked to empty their bank accounts at the get-together. He and Clay wanted their ideas, not their money, at least this time. Some guests were skeptical. Sam Marting Sr. of Washington Court House in Ohio said he was "one of those dummies who helped finance it." Reporter Meyer wrote that Marting "snorted" when asked if he believed that nobody would put the arm on him for some campaign contributions: "What do you think?"[12]

When the eating and drinking ended, the guests were taken to a nearby motel. Clay and the other hosts let them know what the party planned to do to come up with the dollars it needed to get back in the political ring. In honor of Eisenhower's seventy-fifth birthday on October 14, Clay told the guests, he planned to hold fifty birthday parties in fifty cities around the country. Like the "Salute to Ray Bliss" dinners held earlier in Ohio, the "Ike" birthday parties would convince donors that the Grand Old Party was on the way back and worth investing in. The goal was to help raise the $3.2 million that the party still needed to fill out a $5 million budget for 1965. Next year, Clay promised the contributors, the party would "streamline" fundraising and try to cut down on the number of times each donor was asked to give.[13]

In fact, another of Bliss's goals was to unify the fund-raising operations of the national party, combining the separate committees that raised money for Republican candidates for the US House and the US Senate with the national committee. However, Bliss and Clay were unable to persuade the congressional leadership to go along with a united fund-raising effort and a centralized disbursement of funds. The best Bliss could do was to ensure more cooperation among the Republican fundraising operations. One of Clay's top aides worked out of Bliss's office to help the other committees. In this fashion, Bliss and Clay were able to help the newly formed Congressional Boosters Club raise money for the 1966 election.[14]

While bringing back big contributors was important, the party under Bliss also raised small contributions. Former chairman William Miller had revived the party's "sustaining membership program" in 1962. Donations, which averaged $10, were mostly raised by mail. The program expanded under former chairman Dean Burch due to a surge of contributions from Goldwater supporters.[15]

Bliss worked diligently to expand the sustaining membership program, saying that he would rather have a $10 donor than a $1,000 donor. "Our highly successful 1965 broad-based $10 Sustaining Program, which even in a non-presidential year enlisted roughly 145,000 members, indicates the level of potential financial support the Republican Party has," he said.[16]

Overall, the Bliss-Clay team was successful in raising money. In 1965, the party raised $4.2 million, of which $1.7 million was from sustaining membership contributions. These were all record amounts for the Republicans in a year without a federal election.[17]

Not everything went smoothly, however, as Bliss took over as national chairman.

Chapter 43

Bliss Survives a Scandal

When Ray Bliss started work at the national committee offices, he was astonished at how the staff operated. Everybody cleared out of the office early and headed for home, Bliss recalled to Alex Arshinkoff.[1] "It looked like a grade school," Bliss said. "The doors fly open and the people came running out." Bliss called a staff meeting.

"What time do we close around here?" Bliss asked at the meeting.

"Well, 4:30," the staffers said.

"Does anyone know what time it is in California when it's 4:30 here?" asked Bliss.

"Well, it is 1:30," they said.

"Now, let's figure this thing out," said Bliss. "Let's say that there's a Republican that works in downtown Los Angeles or downtown San Francisco. Now, that's a big town, not a small town. And, in Los Angeles, if I am not mistaken, it could take you an hour to get home. So, let's say this is a normal, hard-working executive and he works until about 7 o'clock. Then he grabs a bite to eat. It's 8 o'clock, maybe 8:30. It takes him an hour to get home. It's 9:30. He looks at the mail, maybe thinks about a few things…10:30, he may want to make a call to the National Committee….So, let me see, what time is it when it's 10 o'clock in California?"

"One o'clock," they said.

Even taskmaster Bliss didn't require staffers to stick around until 1 A.M., waiting for phone calls, but he came close.

"Midnight. We leave our phones open until midnight," said Bliss.

Not everybody stayed every night until midnight, but staffers kept the office open later than before on a rotating basis. Telephone lines were kept open for calls from California. Bliss, of course, regularly stayed at the office until after midnight. He liked to work late at night and he also wanted to set an example.

"A good leader is a pace horse," Bliss told Arshinkoff. "People will work as hard as the leader works. If the leader works light, people work light. If the leader puts in 200 percent, the people put in 100 percent to 150 percent. But a leader cannot ask people to do things he is not willing to do himself."

Not everybody welcomed the new pace horse, said Arthur Peterson. "It had always been loose as a goose, you know. And suddenly he was going to change this and he did. And it was tough."[2] Some staffers quit, but most adapted as best they could to Bliss's style.

There was soon friction between some of Bliss's new staff from Ohio and the veteran operatives at party headquarters. Josephine Good had worked for the national committee since the 1950s and was used to know-it-all newcomers—from Ohio and Arizona. "They came in with the idea that they were going to remake the Republican Party and distrusted anybody who had been around. I was there in '56 and I was involved in '52. But if you weren't an original Goldwater operative, ringing the bells for him, they distrusted you," said Good, referring to staffers who had come in with the Arizonan.[3]

Bliss himself contributed to the tense atmosphere when he arrived at his new job, Good recalled. Bliss knew her and the work she had done over the years for the party, but at first was reluctant to rely on her. Instead, he looked to James Baker, one of the aides who had followed him from Columbus.

"He [Bliss] wanted everything to be just so. I had an office," Good said. "Then there was an open space and Jim Baker was over here. He [Bliss] usually talked to Jim Baker instead of me, you know....I liked Jim Baker pretty well. When he [Baker] began to intrude on my territory, there were really sparks flying. I thought, 'This is what I'm doing. What I'm supposed to do and I don't need any assistance, you know,'" Good recalled.

As she always did before national committee meetings, Good prepared a detailed script for the chairman. She stayed late at the office the night before the meeting putting the finishing touches on Bliss's script. "I had written everything out for the chairman for the meeting and I stayed, it must have been 1 o'clock [in the morning] before I went home," Good said. She left the script on her desk, but when she came in the next morning, a woman assistant who had come to Washington, DC, from Ohio had interfered.

"She goes in and looks on my desk and sees this [the script] and proceeds to take it to Mr. Bliss. When I came in and it was gone, I was petrified," Good said. Good had had enough. "We had open offices, kind of semi-private.... You could hear anything. I threw my coat on the floor and I said 'I want you [the Ohio woman] to mind your own goddam business.' I said it in a voice so loud that everybody heard me. Nobody came near me," said Good. Her outbreak cleared the air.

Bliss liked the script for the national committee meeting, recalled Good: "He thought, well, I did it almost as well as Jim Baker."

Bliss brought more to Washington than his work ethic and detailed focus. He maintained his untidy habits. "Because of the gout he would often go in his stocking feet, you know, when he was around the office," said Good. As the usually formal detail man padded around the office in stocking feet, he constantly puffed on unfiltered cigarettes. "He smoked constantly," recalled Good. But it really wasn't smoking. Bliss was too impatient to inhale, particularly at times as tense as preparing for his first national committee meeting. "He would puff and shake the ashes," Good said. Bliss had a big desk and his chair sat behind it, atop a big vinyl platform. "At the end of the day, it would be gray with ashes. He never bothered to use an ash tray."

Another Ohio staffer, William Cody Kelly, almost caused Bliss's undoing as national chairman. Kelly was the new chairman's top aide and came into conflict with the remaining Goldwater backers on the staff. Ironically, Kelly had been chairman of Goldwater's campaign in Ohio in 1964.

The conflict came to a head on the night of June 18, 1965—the same day Bliss announced his opposition to Goldwater's new Free Society Association. Suspecting that Frank J. Kovac, the outgoing national party finance director and former finance director of the draft Goldwater movement, might join Goldwater's new group, Kelly broke into Kovac's desk at party headquarters looking for incriminating information.[4]

Peterson was one of the first to learn about Kelly's actions. Kelly showed up about 11 P.M. on June 18 at Peterson's apartment. "You've got to help me out," Kelly told Peterson. "I've got myself in a little trouble.... You know those damned Goldwater people.... I was trying to find some things in Kovac's office." Peterson wanted nothing to do with the break-in, telling Kelly he would not help him. Peterson said that Kelly lit a fire in a big trash container outside the apartment after Peterson sent him away.[5]

Kovac protested the intrusion. He took his complaint to Bliss in person and through a letter, accusing Kelly and others of "forcible entry into my locked desk....This affront to my constitutional rights was perpetrated at about 9:30 to 11 p.m. Friday night, June 18," wrote Kovac. "My desk was rifled and evidence of witnesses indicate that correspondence, personal and committee, was pilfered and read by these individuals." He didn't blame Bliss, telling a reporter, "This was a fishing expedition....Just what they were looking for I don't think they knew themselves."[6]

Bliss and Kovac had already parted ways after Bliss discovered that Kovac was selling the party's mailing lists to raise much-needed cash for the party—including to right-wing groups. Kovac's resignation as party finance director was effective July 1.[7]

When Bliss found out what Kelly had done, he knew what he had to do. There had been just one previous blemish on his record—the May Queen fiasco at the University of Akron in 1931. Without delay, Bliss fired Kelly on June 23, 1965. Bliss announced his decision in a Republican National Committee news release headlined "Bliss Asks Resignation of Administrative Aide."

> I have today asked for and received, effective immediately, the resignation of my Administrative Assistant, Mr. William Cody Kelly.
>
> I have taken this action following a complaint from Mr. Frank Kovac, executive director of the Republican Finance Committee, relating to an incident regarding Mr. Kovac's desk. I had no knowledge of this incident until it was brought to my attention by Mr. Kovac.
>
> Mr. Kelly has been a long and devoted friend. I regret that in his enthusiasm to serve he has taken action which is contrary to standards which I have established for my staff. There can be no deviation from these standards.[8]

Kelly did not go quietly. He sent telegrams to all members of the Republican National Committee with his own version of what happened. Kelly said he broke into Kovac's desk because he suspected Kovac of spying for Goldwater. It was part of a "systematic search" of party headquarters for a missing list of $1,000 party contributors as well as Goldwater campaign films. Kelly claimed he promptly reported what he had come up with to the chairman. "He [Bliss] professed satisfaction with my work and the locating of the list and of the film copies," said Kelly.

Then Kelly denied that he had been fired. "When the adverse publicity started to flow, the chairman weakened in his support of me and it was apparent that I was to be sacrificed," said Kelly. "I submitted my resignation. A few minutes later, the chairman issued a statement saying in effect that I had been fired." He took a parting shot at the party Bliss was trying to rebuild: "I must confess that my short stay in politics in Washington has proven that a position with the Republican National Committee is more dangerous than that encountered in my time as a liaison pilot in World War II, and as much as I regret the entire situation, I am happy to be out of it."[9]

The Republican National Committee became the capital's laughingstock, the butt of Democratic jokes. "I checked out my desk tonight before I left and I'm sure it's locked and no one is going to get into it," President Lyndon Johnson said at a Democratic fundraiser. Vice President Hubert H. Humphrey joined the fun: "I've heard of crime in the streets, but I never heard of rifling desks in the suites."[10]

The joke was on Bliss and he was not amused. The timing was awful. It came just as Bliss was preparing for his first meeting of the Republican National Committee as chairman. He was devastated. "It hurt Ray so much that he got an attack of the gout," Peterson said. Peterson had never seen Bliss look worse. "He was just like a sick puppy. He just was sick. . . . It was the saddest I have ever seen, just like at a funeral. He was just sad." Bliss lived by trust and couldn't believe what had happened to him at the hands of one of his closest associates. "He was just full of shock and sorrow and . . . betrayed. He couldn't believe that anybody would do this to him," Peterson said.[11]

"Bliss himself was deeply hurt," Feldkamp of the *Akron Beacon Journal* wrote of the incident a year later. "Worse, from his standpoint, his time now was taken up for most of the rest of 1965 healing new rifts that the incident sparked."[12]

According to Peterson, Bliss called an old friend and party employee from Ohio, Jack Flanagan, and asked him to come to Washington, DC, to discuss the problems at the Republican National Committee. Bliss, Flanagan, and Peterson repaired to the 1520 Club, a bar near party headquarters at 1625 I Street. The basement bar had a saying on the wall that had been popular during World War II—"Loose Lips Sink Ships"—a slogan that seemed fitting for Bliss's troubles. The Republican Party resembled a sinking ship, and the new captain wasn't sure he wanted to go down with it. "Ray was thinking of resigning," said Peterson.[13]

It turned into a long night of drinking and talking. Slowly, Bliss began to change his mind about leaving the job. He was not a quitter, Bliss decided. Matters were resolved about midnight: Bliss would stay on and Peterson would take Kelly's job as the top assistant with the title chief of staff.

The decision to stay on as chairman meant Bliss had to get ready for the national committee meeting—just two days away. Bliss told Peterson to put together the agenda, a welcome invitation for a young political scientist eager to try out all his ideas. When Peterson came in with the program for the meeting, Bliss was taken aback by its ambitious scope.

"What have you done to me?" he asked Peterson.

Chapter 44

A Single Voice

On June 28, 1965, Ray Bliss presented a battle plan for reviving the Republican Party to the men and women who had hired him in January. At his first national committee meeting as chairman, he gave the committee members enough material to keep them from dwelling on the firing of his top aide.[1]

Some proposals echoed Bliss's Ohio experience. The new chairman wanted the party to put its scattered campaign operations under one roof. He suggested that the national committee buy a site near the Capitol to house the chairman's office as well as staffs of the campaign committees for the US Senate and US House candidates. Bliss announced he would be holding seminars and workshops for party leaders: state chairmen, county chairmen, big city chairmen, down to the grassroots of the party. He would make a special effort to train campaign managers, researchers, and public relations staff. Bliss planned new programs to assist state and local parties.[2]

Other proposals came from the Big City Politics Task Force that Bliss had chaired in 1962. Republicans needed to provide professional staffs at party headquarters in big city and suburban areas, Bliss told committee members. He wanted more of the big city vote, including the votes of "Negroes." Young voters also would be courted. To lure young voters, Bliss planned to hire a Republican professor to lead an "arts and science program" at the national committee. Older voters did not escape Bliss's attention. They had been exiting the Republican Party, too, Bliss said, and a special effort would be made to woo them back.[3]

Bliss put reforming the national nominating conventions on the agenda. The 1964 convention in San Francisco had been a public relations disaster. The whole nation learned from watching television that Republicans apparently hated each other. Former president Eisenhower, one of Bliss's strongest backers, told committee members that conventions were marked by "confusion, noise, impossible deportment."[4]

The most important proposal was to start up the Republican Coordinating Committee. The national committee had agreed to this organization at the same January 1965 meeting at which Bliss was elected chairman. Originally proposed by Representative Melvin Laird of Wisconsin, the coordinating committee's membership included former president Eisenhower; four former presidential candidates (Alf Landon, Thomas E. Dewey, Richard Nixon, and Barry Goldwater); five governors; five senators; seven members of the US House of Representatives; five members of the Republican National Committee; and the president of the Republican State Legislators' Association. Bliss was the "presiding officer," and the national committee provided funds and staff, including two of Bliss's top aides, Arthur Peterson to manage research and James Baker to handle logistics.[5]

The Republican Coordinating Committee was the vehicle for Republicans to speak with a single voice. For Bliss, it was an answer to the question he had raised in his initial speech to the Republican women's conference: "Then how do we develop the party's fundamental positions on issues?"[6]

The need was urgent. In 1965, the party sounded like a political Tower of Babel. Republicans talked past each other with competing ideas. More than twenty groups operated outside the formal GOP organization, ranging from Goldwater's Free Society Association to the liberal Ripon Society. The public had stopped listening to the discordant Republicans.[7]

Although the leaders of all party factions had pledged to support him, Bliss knew that opposition remained. "It's worse, far worse than I dreamed it would be," Bliss confided to friends, according to columnists Rowland Evans and Robert Novak. To illustrate the depth of the division within the party, they recounted that one apprehensive conservative called another and asked: "What are we going to do about Bliss?"

"Wait five months," was the answer, "and let nature take its course."

"And what if nature doesn't take its course?"

"In that case, we will have to *help* nature take its course."

Meanwhile, a spokesman for moderate Republicans was just as demanding. "If elected party officials won't set the ideological tone," he said, referring to Bliss, "who the hell will?"[8]

Bliss refused to take sides and advised his fellow Republicans to "stop worrying about the ideological position, collect a lot of money, put up as many attractive new faces as you can find, advise them all to adapt themselves…to the conditions of the local electorates, and run like hell, shouting 'me too' if necessary. That way the Republicans might win enough offices to make a position mean something."[9]

The Republican Coordinating Committee fit perfectly with Bliss's view of his responsibility as national chairman. He wanted a party that was diverse and inclusive, but also unified behind a persuasive message. Bliss described this mix of diversity and unity in 1974: "I feel the party should be able to live with a Jake Javits [a liberal Republican senator from New York], as I did successfully, and a Barry Goldwater. It doesn't hurt to have divergent points of views. The thing to do is to keep it congealed enough so that you move forward and you field candidates and you get a platform," said Bliss. The chairman had a clear role to play, according to Bliss: "I feel the chairman of the party should be a congealant."[10]

It was a big task to be a congealant on such a committee. The personalities on the committee were huge and often volatile. Many zealously protected the prerogatives of their offices. Most had their own ambitions, and there were sharp policy differences among them. As Bliss explained the process, "you don't say anything nasty, at least not publicly, about someone you are going to have dinner with tonight."[11] Peterson was more direct: "But there are very few men in American political life with Bliss's skill at resolving conflict."[12]

Bliss received help from Eisenhower in organizing and managing the committee. Bliss and the former president had developed a close relationship since the 1952 convention, when Bliss had backed Ohio's Robert A. Taft for the nomination. When asked years later which man he admired more, Bliss said: "It would be a draw between them."[13]

Eisenhower blamed himself for the state of the GOP and wanted to make amends. "One of his great regrets was that he hadn't given more attention while he was president to the political side of the presidency," Bliss later recalled. "He said that was his mistake. He should have given more attention and built up the party and that's the reason he got so intensely interested in my accepting the chairmanship."

Eisenhower became Bliss's enforcer, both on the coordinating committee and in other party business. "He backed me up with deep intensity in the early days of my chairmanship," said Bliss. "I mean, one thing he had, he had the respect of all factions. They were scared to death of him."

Bliss was playing in the political big leagues now and had to respond to the national press corps, where Bliss's detractors had plenty of outlets to criticize him. Eisenhower did not let the critics go unanswered when Bliss was their target. "If somebody got on my back in the papers, he [Ike] would call them up and tell them off," Bliss remembered.

Eisenhower came to the coordinating committee meetings, too, and took after Bliss's critics in person. "Well, he would show up and he would take them on," said Bliss. When Eisenhower could not attend the meetings, he made himself available to help Bliss. This proved particularly important as Bliss's relationship with former vice president Nixon grew more complicated with the 1968 election coming up.

Eisenhower uncannily predicted just how Nixon would react to specific situations, Bliss told Alex Arshinkoff. "The only guy who is going to give you any trouble is Dick Nixon," Eisenhower told Bliss ahead of time. Arshinkoff noted, "One thing that always impressed Nixon was money."

Eisenhower told Bliss how they would arrange the meeting. The strategy called for Nixon to speak last, after the financial and political leaders all had voiced their strong support for Bliss. The former president then predicted what Nixon would say and how he would say it, Bliss told Arshinkoff. "Oh, I'm for Ray. Oh, I'm for Ray.... And we've got to rebuild the party and this is so good. I couldn't think of anybody else who could do this like Ray Bliss." The meeting turned out almost exactly that way.

Once the Republican Coordinating Committee got started, Nixon sometimes missed meetings, Bliss told Arshinkoff. "Bliss had a special phone put in to Ike's office ... where all Bliss had to do was pick up the phone and it rang [in Eisenhower's office].... He used it very rarely, but he would call him and he says, 'Mr. President, we are in real trouble here and Dick's not coming.... Obviously, he is trying to sabotage this damn deal [coordinating committee]'.... He [Eisenhower] says, 'I'll handle it.' Ike calls Dick Nixon. He's there at the next meeting. And so Ike was really important, a very important force for Ray Bliss," said Arshinkoff.[14]

Former New York governor Dewey, the Republican presidential candidate in 1944 and 1948, also helped discourage bickering on the coordinating committee. Neither Dewey nor Eisenhower suffered fools gladly, according to political scientist John F. Bibby, who worked for Bliss and attended the meetings.[15]

Dewey must have felt some hostility toward one member of the coordinating committee, US Senate Minority Leader Everett Dirksen of Illinois, who had attacked him publicly at the contentious 1952 Republican convention, blaming Dewey for losing the 1944 and 1948 presidential elections. Josephine Good, a top aide at the national committee, remembered that some of the potential drama of the first coordinating committee meeting focused on what might happen between Dewey and Dirksen. To Bliss's obvious delight, they let bygones be bygones. Dewey, in fact, turned out to be a star at the meetings, said Good. The two-time presidential candidate had a knack for redrafting resolutions and reports so that they satisfied everyone.[16]

Peterson had been prepared to dislike Dewey, who had a reputation for being stuffy and arrogant. But Peterson came to admire him. He, Bliss, and Dewey frequently would go out to dinner after coordinating committee meetings. "He was funny and bright.…It was sort of a post-game evaluation," Peterson said.[17]

Bliss structured the committee meetings to cut down on acrimony. All members had an opportunity before the meetings started to suggest revisions to the papers being discussed. Still, that didn't guarantee agreement. There was some rough going, especially in the beginning.

The Republican governors found Bliss to be their advocate. In the past, they had felt crowded out of the party spotlight by Republican congressional leaders. Bliss sometimes ate dinner separately with the governors on the coordinating committee on the evening before a meeting as well as at other times. New York governor Nelson Rockefeller frequently hosted such dinners at a family home in Washington, DC.[18]

Republican congressional leaders joined the governors in supporting how Bliss wanted to use the coordinating committee. By making the party a "big umbrella," the congressional leaders hoped that a wide variety of viewpoints could be accommodated and that splinter groups would more closely align with the national party. In addition to chairing the coordinating committee, Bliss was the presiding officer of the Republican Joint Leadership of Congress Committee—in much the same way that he had played parallel roles with the Akron City Council and the Ohio legislature.[19]

Instead of battling with each other in the newspapers or on radio and television programs, the top Republican leaders could use the coordinating committee as a place to thrash out their differences in an organized, behind-the-scenes process. It helped "bank the fires of ideology that almost consumed the Republican Party in 1964."[20]

The coordinating committee did more than mute Republican squabbling. It produced eighteen substantive position papers and sponsored eight task forces composed of business executives, academic experts, and political leaders. Together these activities provided Republican alternatives to Democratic President Lyndon Johnson's "Great Society" on topics including fighting poverty, housing, education, civil rights, and problems facing cities. The committee called for fewer prescriptions dictated by the federal government and more choices for state and local governments closer to the people.

When Richard Nixon became president after the 1968 election, he used the coordinating committee's proposal for revenue sharing—sending blocks of federal money back to states and cities to use as they chose, rather than for prescribed programs.[21]

For Bliss, good policy was good politics.

Chapter 45

Denouncing Extremism

The Republican Coordinating Committee gave Ray Bliss a tool to rally the divided Republicans around policy proposals. However, the process would take time. Meanwhile, the GOP's image was in tatters. The party suffered from a taint of "extremism." Barry Goldwater's 1964 rhetoric was one source, but so were right-wing groups that advocated extreme issue positions and tactics.

The most vocal and active group was the John Birch Society (JBS). Founded in 1958 by Robert Welch, a retired candy manufacturer from Massachusetts, it was named after an American army captain and Baptist missionary killed by Chinese Communists shortly after the end of World War II.[1] The JBS had militantly conservative views on most issues, but what set it apart was its secretive behavior and conspiratorial view of politics. Welch and his followers saw a wide range of groups as plotting to collectivize American society. Communism was a chief culprit, but the alleged conspirators included liberals, unions, Democrats, businessmen, bankers, and Republicans. Among the latter were US Supreme Court Chief Justice Earl Warren— a former Republican governor of California and the 1948 vice-presidential nominee— and former president Eisenhower.[2]

Liberal and conservative Republicans criticized the JBS in return. Some strongly urged Bliss to denounce it, but others urged caution, lest he alienate conservatives who were not "Birchers."[3]

Bliss decided to act. "We've got to get this [the Republican Party] in the middle of the road," Bliss told Arthur Peterson. Peterson remembered the night Bliss told him the time had come to take on the society. "I've got a gut feeling we have got to do this," said Bliss. "Eisenhower and his people have taken enough."[4] Bliss decided to publicly divorce the Republican Party from its association with the group on November 5. The denunciation would come in Albuquerque, New Mexico, at a meeting of the Western Republican Leadership Conference.

Just by making the statement, Bliss slipped out of the role as an "office chairman" working behind the scenes and became a "speaking chairman," the face and voice of the Republican Party on an important issue. Bliss consulted with both Barry Goldwater and Richard Nixon, the two most recent Republican presidential nominees, and with Peterson's help carefully framed a measured statement that rejected extremists at both ends of the political spectrum:[5]

> When we talk about extremism, we should look both to the radical left and radical right....
>
> It is quite obvious to me that the radical left is attempting to throw a smoke-screen around its own activities by slanderously charging all conservatives with extremist views.
>
> While the Republican Party has been exhorted to repudiate radicals who do not speak for and who do not lead or influence the Party, the Democratic National Committee has helped finance and promote the Group Research, Inc.[6] smear list which includes such noted Americans as former President Dwight D. Eisenhower.

Bliss did not identify the John Birch Society by name, but singled out Robert Welch:

> One of my major concerns in the matter of extremism of the radical right is that honest, patriotic and conscientious conservatives may be misjudged because of irresponsible radicals such as Robert Welch, who has accused General Eisenhower of being "a dedicated, conscious agent of the Communist conspiracy."

Bliss made clear where he stood.

> Therefore, I ask all Republicans to reject absolutely and without reservation any resort to slanderous irresponsibility.
>
> I ask all Republicans to reject membership in any radical organization which attempts to use the Republican Party for its own ends, or in any organization which seeks to undermine the basic principles of American freedom and constitutional government.
>
> I also call upon all Republicans to reject absolutely and without reservation organizations which condone violence and violation of the law, whatever their motives.

Our country will be well served if the Democratic Party takes the same position toward <u>ALL</u> extremists.[7]

On December 13, a little more than a month later, the Republican Coordinating Committee backed Bliss up with a statement of its own, offered jointly by Senate Minority Leader Everett M. Dirksen of Illinois and House Minority Leader Gerald Ford of Michigan and approved unanimously by the committee: "The Republican Coordinating Committee endorses the position of Republican National Committee Chairman Ray C. Bliss that all Republicans reject membership in any radical or extremist organization including any which attempts to use the Republican Party for its own ends or any which seeks to undermine the basic principles of American freedom and constitutional government."[8]

Bliss's statement was criticized by Republicans—on both sides of the issue. David C. Attridge scorched Bliss with a letter on December 29, 1965:

You recently asked all Republicans to get out of the strongest and most effective anti-Communist organizations in the United States and the world. I question your motives.

Every man has to stand on his record of the past. If Welch lied in his long book about President Eisenhower it should be simple to point out where Welch was wrong and settle the whole matter. Calling Mr. Welch names settles nothing. Mr. Welch takes full responsibility for the book, he can be found any time you want him, he can be taken to court or all his money taken from him providing your charges against him are true.

Attridge called Bliss "sneaky" and noted, not approvingly, that Bliss had not named the society:

All these charges are false and I am sure you know it yourself which leads me to wonder why? The State of California Committee investigated the Society for two years and found everyone [sic] of these charges to be untrue. I know you did not come out honestly and name the Society but anyone would be very stupid to not know who you were shooting at.

To Attridge, a "radical" was someone to be praised, not condemned:

I was surprised to find out there is no evil meaning to this word. It appears that radicals are fine folks according to my dictionary. It appears that a radical "is one that does not stop at the surface, but reaches down to the very root, and is entire, thorough, total, since the majority find superficial treatment of any matter the easiest and most comfortable, radical measures which strike at the root of evil or need, are apt to be looked upon as extreme." Now read what the dictionary says about moderates who are the opposite of radical "INADEQUATE, INCOMPLETE, MODERATE, PALLITIVE, PARTIAL, SUPERFICIAL."[9]

Bliss also heard from people who did not think his statement went far enough. J. H. Blitzer Jr., president of Integrated Ceilings, Inc., in Los Angeles, California, was one. "As I read the statement, it disowns radical right and radical left extremism, but stops short of identifying specific right-wing groups, particularly the John Birch Society. I do not believe the Republican Party can be the strong and worthy opponent which we need to continue our two-party system until it has the courage to name names. Until that time I am afraid it cannot receive my support," Blitzer wrote in a November 29, 1965, letter.[10]

Overall, the statement on extremism had some success. Peterson concluded that "it gave us a lot of standing with the moderates who had wondered when we were going to stand up for something." Bliss did not second-guess himself. "He made the decision and that was it. No turning back. But it was something that he was waiting for and you never knew when he was going to get that feeling," said Peterson.[11]

As it turned out, Bliss was unable to immediately gauge reaction to his statement. A few minutes after delivering the speech, he suffered chest pain and was taken to Presbyterian Hospital in Albuquerque. Doctors ruled out a heart attack, with the eventual diagnosis of a "muscle spasm." Bliss returned to Akron on November 12 for a few days of rest before resuming his duties.[12]

It had been a busy year for Ray Bliss.

Chapter 46

A Hometown Win

In 1965, Ray Bliss needed to win elections. He couldn't wait for congressional and state races in 1966. So he focused on big city mayors, reflecting his strong commitment—and past success—in winning a larger share of the urban vote. "He wanted to show his ability to win some big city races early," said Arthur Peterson. "He just wanted the psychological impact badly.... The Big City Report was out. He sort of was on the line.... He had his bet out there."[1]

Akron, Ohio—Bliss's hometown—presented a special opportunity. Although the Democrats had controlled City Hall since 1953, they faced big problems. Mayor Edward O. Erickson, a Democrat first elected in 1961, was unpopular.[2] Bliss's handpicked successor as Summit County chairman, D. E. "Gene" Waddell, sensed that the time was ripe for a Republican comeback. "Of course it was important that we win in his hometown the first year as national chairman," Waddell said.[3]

The Republicans needed a good candidate. The best prospect was attorney John S. Ballard. Born in Akron, he attended the University of Akron, served in World War II, and earned a law degree from the University of Michigan. In 1955 Ballard worked on a successful court-ordered investigation of gambling. Based in part on this success, he was elected Summit County prosecutor in 1956 and reelected in 1960.[4]

When the political bug led Ballard to seek statewide office in 1962, he found that Bliss was opposed. Ballard wanted to run against the hugely popular Democratic

Senator Frank Lausche. But Bliss already had a candidate, John Marshall Briley of Toledo, who could finance his own campaign, leaving party funds for other races.[5]

Bliss's close associate Roy Browne tried to talk Ballard out of running for the Senate. "I guess I was hardheaded," said Ballard, who stayed in the race. "I, of course, was defeated," said Ballard. "I'm glad I ran. It was a college education for me. I realized I had no interest in [statewide] politics."[6] In 1964, Ballard decided he lacked interest in local politics as well. He resigned early as county prosecutor so the Republicans could appoint a successor—who promptly lost the election as part of the Goldwater debacle.[7]

Around Akron, the forty-two-year-old Ballard struck what he himself called a "low silhouette," a lack of flamboyance that masked self-confidence and political independence. He had a good record, citywide name recognition, and popularity among local Republicans. The problem was that he did not want to run for mayor.

At first Waddell appealed to Ballard's sense of civic pride and duty to his hometown. "I did not want to run," Ballard later recalled. "I told them that I had no interest.... Waddell was the guy really pressing me."[8] Waddell wouldn't take no for an answer. "'Do whatever you have to do to get him in and keep after him,'" Waddell recalled Bliss telling him. With the candidate filing deadline looming, Waddell called Ballard and asked for the courtesy of a face-to-face conversation. Ballard agreed to have dinner with Waddell.

Waddell got to the Tangier, a popular Akron restaurant, before Ballard and put a plan into action. "I told the waitress, 'Now when Ballard is drinking you give him regular Martinis, but when I am drinking you give me something that looks like alcohol but is not,'" said Waddell. "It cost me $100 that night, I know. And booze was not expensive back then. So, anyway, finally, he says, 'Yes,'" Waddell said. Waddell didn't want to take the chance that Ballard would change his mind the next day. Earlier he had alerted Bliss in Washington, DC, that he would be wooing Ballard. Bliss stood by to take a call in case Ballard could be persuaded.

"So I get Bliss on the phone and I said, 'John Ballard has decided to run for mayor. Here, I want you to talk to him.' So I had John talk to Bliss and say, 'Yes, I am going to run and Waddell talked me into it,'" said Waddell. Bliss hung up but Waddell wasn't finished. He contacted Ben Maidenburg, executive editor of the *Akron Beacon Journal*. "Now wait, John, one more call," Waddell told Ballard. "And I called Maidenburg and I said, 'Ballard has decided to run. Here I want him to tell you.' I gave it [the phone] to Ballard and he told him, 'Yes, I am going to run' and so forth."[9]

Ballard remembered talking to Maidenburg that night but not to Bliss. Of course, he hadn't been in the greatest shape, Ballard recalled. "I guess he [Waddell] got me about half looped," said Ballard. "I thought he was drinking with me."[10]

Waddell expected to hear from Ballard the next morning and he did. "The next morning Ballard calls and has changed his mind," Waddell said. "John, you can't," he told his candidate for mayor. "You committed with Ray Bliss and Ben Maidenburg. Once you give your word in this business, it's gold."[11]

On May 22, Ballard entered the Republican primary for mayor. But he insisted that party politics had nothing to do with his candidacy. "I'm not getting into this as a partisan," he said. "I do not intend to be a political mayor."[12] Ballard said he had been courted by supporters who promised him bipartisan backing. He did not mention dinner and drinks at the Tangier.

The stage seemed set for a showdown between Ballard and Mayor Erickson. "Race for Mayor Narrows to Two," blared the headline in the *Akron Beacon Journal*.[13] But ten days later Erickson decided not to seek reelection, blaming Ballard and the Republicans for the city's financial woes. Erickson's decision set the Democrats to fighting among themselves. In the September 7 primary, Ray Sheppard, law director in the Erickson administration, squeaked by city councilman Victor Herbert for the Democratic nomination. Ballard had no opposition for the Republican nomination.[14]

Even before Ballard knew who his Democratic opponent would be, the Republicans were off and running. Waddell and Bliss did all they could to fuel Ballard's enthusiasm. When Dwight Eisenhower came to Cleveland in June for a Republican Party fundraiser to celebrate Bliss's birthday, Bliss got the former president together with Ballard. Suddenly Ballard found himself talking with a former commander-in-chief and Ballard's own military leader during World War II. "I'd never met him before," Ballard said of Eisenhower. "This amazed me."[15]

Back in Akron, the Republicans framed the Ballard campaign as an above-the-fray crusade. "Let's Put Akron First" was the campaign theme. "Our theme means exactly what it says and much more," Ballard told two thousand Republicans gathered at Sandy Beach Park in August as part of the largest crowd ever to attend the annual Summit County Republican picnic. "It also carries with it other meanings, personal meanings to you. It means we will put you, the citizens, first. It means we will put responsibility for your tax dollars first.... And by returning City Hall to proper responsible hands, you may be confident the new administration will have the integrity, honesty, and management capability to return Akron to the first class calling the citizens of this community deserve," Ballard said.[16]

The Republicans figured that organized labor would officially back the Democratic candidate, and the Akron Labor Council did. "It's true that I wasn't invited to appear before the Labor Council but I won't criticize its decision. That's their prerogative," said Ballard. He had his own way of appealing for labor votes. "I'm getting into local union meetings, despite anything the hierarchy may be doing to keep me out.... And I've seen a lot of evidence of support at these meetings." Some union leaders came out publicly for Ballard. W. A. "Big Bill" Nelson, a longtime official of the United Rubber Workers, was named chairman of the "Democrats for Ballard Committee."[17]

Ballard did not concede the minority vote to the Democrats, either. A photo in the *Beacon Journal* with the caption "They Dial for Votes" showed a playful Ballard holding two telephone receivers while posing with two volunteers, both African American women.[18]

A seventeen-year-old African American high school student, Thaddeus A. Garrett Jr., got his start in Ballard's 1965 mayoral race, leading the youth groups committee in the campaign. This brought him to Bliss's attention, Garrett remembered years later. "I went to a candidates' forum one night.... I think the word got back to him [Bliss] and I stood up. It was at Lane Elementary School. I stood up and made a speech or something for Ballard," Garrett said.[19] Thanks in part to Bliss's help, Garrett went on to have a career in politics, eventually serving as an assistant to Vice President George H. W. Bush.

While Ballard seemed to be doing all the right things, the Democrats had trouble even getting their campaign started. Sheppard resigned from his job as city law director and kicked off the general election campaign against Ballard in a most unorthodox way—by blasting his old boss, Mayor Erickson.[20]

On November 2, 1965, Ballard won a landslide victory. With 62 percent of the vote, it was one of the largest victories for mayor of Akron. In a dramatic shift from previous elections, Ballard did well in blue-collar and minority wards. Ballard's appeal was not contagious, however. Democrats kept control of city council, 10–3, the same margin they had going into the election. While Ballard might have preferred a council majority of his own party, Republicans had targeted their resources on the mayor's race and had succeeded beyond their dreams.[21]

Bliss was in Akron on election night because he still served on the Summit County Board of Elections. The win had proved what he had been trying to tell Republicans all along. Ballard's victory, he said, was a "prime example of what can happen in big cities when good candidates run."[22]

Bliss got more good news that night.

Chapter 47

New York, New York, A Republican Town

Akron was not the only city that Ray Bliss targeted for Republican attention in 1965. New York was the nation's largest city and a national center for finance and the news media. Winning the mayoral election there would draw national attention to the Republican revival that Bliss was trying to create.

It was also a test case for Bliss's approach to recruiting candidates to match local conditions. According to David Broder, "Bliss told friends that he would not intervene to pick candidates in local situations, but would use the leverage of his office to provide personal encouragement and financial and political support to the men local Republicans judge their strongest candidates."[1]

There was no guarantee, of course, that the Bliss method would work outside Ohio. New York City was even more Democratic than Bliss's hometown of Akron. Democrats outnumbered Republicans and the city had not had a Republican mayor for twenty years. But in 1965, Bliss sensed a potential opening.

First, New York City Democrats were feuding with each other. Three-term mayor Robert Wagner was at odds with "Tammany Hall," the Democratic machine, and it was unclear if he would seek a fourth term. Second, New York had a unique multiparty system—Democrats and Republicans, plus minor parties, such as the Liberals and Conservatives. In 1961, the Liberal Party had endorsed Democratic Mayor Wagner and its endorsement would be available if Wagner did not run again.[2]

A good prospect for the Republicans was Congressman John V. Lindsay.[3] He was born in New York City to a wealthy family, attended prestigious private schools, and served in the navy in World War II. Lindsay earned undergraduate and law degrees from Yale University and in 1949 began practicing law in New York City. In the 1950s, he became active in politics, becoming the president of the local Young Republican Club and joining the US Justice Department during the Eisenhower administration. In 1958, Lindsay was elected to the US House of Representatives from the affluent "Silk Stocking" district on Manhattan's Upper East Side.

In Congress, Lindsay was a fervent supporter of civil rights and civil liberties, compiling a voting record more like his northern Democratic opponents than his Republican colleagues. Lindsay won his district in 1964 despite—or perhaps because of—his refusal to support Republican presidential nominee Barry Goldwater. However, on Capitol Hill, Lindsay showed party loyalty, voting for Republican leaders that were far more conservative than he was. The major obstacle was that he announced on March 1 that he would not run for mayor. Like John Ballard in Akron, John Lindsay needed to be persuaded.[4]

Bliss may have met Lindsay during the Eisenhower administration, but the congressman was certainly on Bliss's political radar after he became national chairman. Alex Arshinkoff later heard Bliss's account of recruiting Lindsay. In early 1965, Bliss was in New York on business and several people mentioned to him that Lindsay would make a good Republican candidate for mayor. At the end of the visit, Bliss was taking a cab to the airport when the driver started telling him about Lindsay. The cabdriver said: "'You ought to be looking at that Lindsay. At least he's honest,'" Bliss told Arshinkoff. On the spur of the moment, Bliss told the cabdriver to take him to the congressman's office. Lindsay happened to be in and the two men talked about a Lindsay candidacy.

"Alex, sometimes you just get the feeling," Bliss said.[5]

On May 8, Bliss and Lindsay attended the radio-television correspondents' dinner in Washington, DC, where they had an opportunity to talk. Bliss stressed that fielding the "strongest possible candidate in New York City was important in the effort to rebuild party strength all across the country." Lindsay was interested, but he knew what it would take to win in New York—back-breaking campaigning and plenty of money. Bliss said he thought he could help with the money and added that good candidates usually attract good organizational and financial support.[6]

On May 13, Lindsay took the plunge, reversing his earlier decision not to run.[7] Two days later the *New York Times* put Bliss's purported role in headlines on the front page: "Bliss Pledges Aid to Lindsay's Race," with the subtitle "Chairman Urged Candidate to Run for Mayor—Won Assurances of Funds."[8]

True to form, the story did not quote Bliss directly. In fact, the information for the story came from Ray Price, who had managed Lindsay's first congressional campaign in 1958 and Governor Nelson Rockefeller's Oregon presidential primary campaign in 1964—the only one Rockefeller won.

Price had been working on a possible Lindsay mayoral campaign since January 1965.[9] "I began preparing without Lindsay knowing," Price said in a 1997 interview. "It was just my arrogance." Price and Lindsay had a political marriage with clearly defined roles: "I was the politician. He was the statesman." By the time Lindsay and Bliss talked at the May 8 dinner in Washington, Price had put together most of the pieces for a campaign. When Lindsay jumped into the mayoral race days later, Price got a call from a man who identified himself as Ray Bliss. "I didn't know if Bliss was calling to want us out [of the mayor's race] or to help," said Price. He thought Bliss might have wanted Lindsay to step aside to help William Buckley, the conservative editor of *National Review* magazine who had announced his candidacy for mayor as the Conservative Party's candidate.

"You did a hell of a job for Rockefeller in Oregon," Bliss told Price. "What can I do to help [Lindsay]?" Price was shocked, having considered Bliss an ideological conservative who didn't see eye to eye on the issues with Lindsay. Maybe the caller wasn't really Ray Bliss but a prankster or somebody trying to embarrass Lindsay and Bliss. "I was surprised to hear from the national chairman," said Price, just thirty-two. Needing time to figure out what to do, he asked for the caller's phone number. Price didn't want to take any chances. "I wanted to call back and make sure it was Ray Bliss," he said. Price called back and it was indeed Bliss who had called him.

"Who can I tell that you offered to help?" asked Price, who was warming up to the idea of having the Republican national chairman on board. "You can tell anybody," said Bliss. At Bliss's request, Price arranged a meeting in New York with Price and Lindsay. Bliss's major contribution was agreeing to call Republican contributors around the country and urging them to supply Lindsay with campaign contributions. "He probably made about twenty phone calls for me to major Republicans contributors around the country," said Price. "Bliss got everyone we wanted."[10]

The *Akron Beacon Journal* understood what Bliss was up to. "Ray Bliss already has injected new life in the Republican party.... Six weeks after taking office as national chairman, the Akron political wise man scored this accomplishment," the paper editorialized. "He persuaded the personable, popular and able Rep. John Lindsay to run for Mayor of New York.... Here we see Mr. Bliss using his oldest and most reliable political tool—getting a quality candidate."[11]

Bliss was not worried about a backlash from conservatives. "You know, the Goldwater people had already given us a hard time," said Peterson. "I think at this point, his [Bliss's] feathers were ruffled a little. He was ready to fight."[12]

Back in New York, Lindsay was both burnishing his Republican credentials and trying to expand his support. At a May 27 gathering at the Hotel St. George, more than 1,200 local party leaders endorsed Lindsay for mayor by voice vote. After the crowd shouted "aye," the presiding officer did not bother to ask for "no" votes.[13]

On June 10, Mayor Wagner announced he would not seek reelection, setting off a struggle for the Democratic and Liberal Party nominations. On June 28, the Liberal Party endorsed Lindsay for mayor at the Astor Hotel.[14] The endorsement intensified the Democratic infighting. In the September 15 primary, the Democrats choose City Controller Abraham D. Beame as their mayoral candidate.

On November 2, Lindsay won with a plurality of the vote—45 percent—with Democrat Beame receiving 41 percent and Conservative Party candidate William F. Buckley getting 13 percent. Lindsay got some 280,000 votes cast for the Liberal Party, while Buckley got about 340,000 ballots cast for the Conservative Party. Both these figures were greater than Lindsay's margin over Beame.[15]

"The Republican Party has a new national hero in John Lindsay today," one reporter wrote, "and just in the nick of time."[16]

Characteristically, Bliss took no credit for the 1965 mayoral victories. "I was just an innocent bystander," he told reporters. "These campaigns were run locally and that's the way it should be."[17]

Chapter 48

The Elements of Victory

Right after the successes of the 1965 election, Bliss told *U.S. News & World Report*: "Well, I was pleased with the gains we made in some of the bigger cities in the country where we have been weak in the past. The point has been proven that, with the right candidates and the right issues and the right management, you can win."[1]

Bliss proposed a model for good campaigning at the January 1966 meeting of the Republican National Committee. Central to the presentation was a thirty-nine-page guide for how to win elections entitled *Elements of Victory*. It was a summary of the professionalism Bliss had learned and practiced throughout his career.[2]

Political scientist John Bibby, who worked for Bliss in Washington, DC, recalled the genesis of *Elements of Victory*: "It was originally a slide show presentation that I helped develop with Art Peterson—under Ray's supervision and with his input." Bliss needed visual aids when he was making presentations to party groups, Bibby said. "As the resident political scientist, my job in this project was to find relevant political science data for the presentation. Bliss seemed pleased with what I came up with and, of course, he and Art Peterson added additional material for slides."[3]

After the national committee presentation, Bibby reported, "We used it whenever there was a major party meeting—e.g., a Women's Federation luncheon in Washington in the spring of 1966, and a series of meetings around the country for party leaders. Because Ray did not enjoy public speaking, he would introduce me to present the slides as a part of his presentation. Bill Fischell, the staff artist, did the slides and prepared the booklet. He was a happy-go-lucky guy, who always called me 'Charts' after we got started on the project.... It was then published as a booklet."

In the booklet, Bliss got right to the point in his back-to-the-basics introduction. "Let me emphasize that there is nothing basically new or revolutionary about these points. They involve the basic building blocks which have always been necessary for a political victory in depth," Bliss wrote. "I am a win-oriented Chairman, and win-oriented political leaders must deal with the nuts and bolts of Party Activity."[4]

The booklet listed eleven points:

1. Recruit Qualified Candidates
2. Idea Councils
3. Statewide Workshops
4. Strengthen Women's Organizations
5. Broaden Financial Base
6. Enlist Young Voters
7. Arts and Sciences Divisions
8. Expand Supplemental Groups (Young Republicans, Senior Citizens, Ethnic, Minorities, etc.)
9. Voter Registration
10. Vote Quotas
11. Utilize Elected Officials

The first five points, Bliss wrote in the pamphlet, "involve the four basic corner-stones of any stable political structure—recruitment of attractive candidates, devel-opment of constructive positions on the issues of the day, strengthening and extend-ing our Republican organization, and providing adequate financial support for both short-range campaign activity and long-range organization building."

"Points 6 to 11," Bliss added, "set forth specific programs which our Party orga-nization at all levels must initiate and/or enlarge in the weeks ahead. November 1966 is already just around the corner."

He cautioned members of the committee that the program did not include every-thing they needed to succeed in politics: "Obviously, points 6 to 11 related to only some of the areas in which we must move ahead. Established service fields, such as research and public relations, have been omitted from my discussion."

The program was practical, not hypothetical. Bliss told committee members he had the evidence to show that the eleven points really worked. He referred to a "story of a recent Governor's race—a race which many people felt already had been won by the Republican candidate in June because of a seemingly unpopular Democratic incumbent." In the governor's race, polling showed that the Republican candidate actually trailed the Democratic incumbent, Bliss wrote. Further polling also showed the high importance that voters attached to three issues—job opportunities through industrial development, education, and state welfare services.

"*The question was:* How could responsible Republican positions be developed to attract voters to the Republican candidate to overcome his deficit problem?

"*The answer was:* The development of idea groups which embraced top specialists in these fields for each of these issues—and the effective dissemination of the resulting Republican answers to these deeply-felt concerns among the voters."

When Bliss became national chairman, he told a reporter, "I don't have a fixation that I have all the answers—everything is a compromise."[5]

Political scientist Joel Marshall Fisher concluded that Bliss "felt that the prescription for victory was not in finding someone with the answer, but rather, finding somebody who *was the answer.*"[6]

In the booklet, Bliss said the election results proved he had found the right answers: "It is interesting to note that, largely as a result of this procedure, the greatest Republican sweep in 34 years was accomplished in this particular state.... This indicates that idea groups or idea councils can be used to great effect if seriously called upon."[7]

Bliss did not identify the state or the candidates for governor. However, a few months later, O. F. Knippenburg, a correspondent in the Ohio Scripps-Howard Bureau in Columbus, reported that according to "sources close to national [Republican] headquarters," Bliss was referring to the 1962 Ohio race in which Republican challenger James Rhodes unseated Democratic incumbent Michael V. DiSalle.[8]

In the pamphlet, Bliss used the results of polling to show members of the national committee how to increase fund-raising. National polls in 1962 and 1964 found that 13 percent of all Republicans would contribute to the party if asked, he wrote. "The point I really want to make here is that, with an effective, broad-based financial effort, conducted at all Party levels, nearly all of the 3.5 million Republicans who say they contribute *will indeed respond affirmatively.*"[9]

Bliss used more statistics to show the significance of what he was trying to accomplish. One chart showed that support for the Republican candidate in presidential elections among young voters—ages 21–29—had plummeted from 57 percent in 1956 to 36 percent in 1964. "It is absolutely imperative that we arrest this decline through new approaches to young people and through the actual involvement of young people in meaningful Party activities. By Party activities, I mean within the framework of the Party organization," he wrote.

Bliss cited an example from "some years" before of a Young Republican Club with 300 members that signed up 3,700 new members and issued membership cards on a non-dues-paying basis. Bliss did not say where the example came from, but it sounded similar to his own experience in Summit County, Ohio. "What were the results? It was discovered that 70 to 80 percent of the new members were not registered. The club also found that about 40 to 50 percent of the new members came from Democratic families. It then waged a registration drive and pushed the vote in the primaries. As a result of this effort, about 80 percent of the new club members became registered Republicans. They were attracted to the Party because of their membership in the Young Republicans," he wrote.

It was important to get to young people before the Democrats did, Bliss suggested: "The point here is that you will find once a person commits himself to a party, it is hard to make him switch to the other party. We must get to them first."

Bliss used still more data to show that Republicans could get help from academics, generally thought to be friends of the Democrats. This apparently was related to Bliss's call for the creation of an Arts and Sciences Division within the party.

> I know that many of you have the impression, as I did once, that most college professors are Democrats, and this is true in the social science fields. It is not always true, however, of professors and teachers in general. A thorough analysis of all registered professors in Ohio in 1962, for example, revealed the following Party registration figures.
>
> 1.   Twenty-eight percent of 8,877 professors, whose voting records were individually checked, did not vote in either of Ohio's primary or general elections in 1962.
> 2.   Twenty-two percent could be classified as Independents based upon their voting record.
> 3.   Of the remaining 4,425 professors, 62 percent were registered as Republicans and 38 percent as Democrats.

Bliss wrote that the Republicans' "academic friends" could be helpful in winning the allegiance of young people. That was because teachers are among those who influence a young person in retaining or rejecting his or her initial party loyalty.

Bliss got back to nuts and bolts when he discussed voter registration and vote quotas. His data showed that among groups "who often vocally differ most markedly with Democratic politicians, from one-fourth to one-third were not even registered." He used an example of an industrial state in the 1964 presidential election in which 1,655,000 citizens of voting age did not vote.

Registering voters was not enough, Bliss wrote. He told the committee members that they should create competition aimed at getting more voters to the polls: "In this connection," he wrote, "I have urged that each State be analyzed precinct by precinct so realistic vote quotas can be established to encourage competition among precincts and counties of each State, with certificates of recognition awarded to those meeting the quotas."

Besides discussing specifics of his plan, Bliss showed what a "concerted organizational effort" could accomplish in a close campaign. The example cited was Republican Richard Nixon's surprise victory in Ohio over Democrat John F. Kennedy in the 1960 presidential race.

While Bliss used the pamphlet to provide his eleven points for winning victories, he also wanted the members of the national committee to know what he and his staff already had accomplished. He was no braggart, but he had been hired to do a job and it was time for a progress report.

The inside cover of the pamphlet listed "Eleven Firsts" for the national committee:

- The weekly meetings of our Public Relations staff with the Congressional Committees' Public Relations staff and the daily conferences for the purpose of coordinating their activities IS A FIRST.
- Early production of extensive campaign materials produced by the Republican National Committee IS A FIRST.
- The weekly meetings of our Research Directors with the Republican Research personnel on Capitol Hill to discuss and coordinate research efforts and eliminate duplication IS A FIRST.
- The series of National Committee-supported meetings of the Coordinating Committee IS AN HISTORIC FIRST.
- The series of training schools for Republican Campaign Managers, co-sponsored by the National Committee and the two Congressional Committees, IS A FIRST.
- A series of National Committee conferences for Republican state research directors IS A FIRST.
- The series of National Committee-sponsored meetings of Big City Chairmen IS A FIRST.
- Activation of a Committee to seriously consider a permanent Republican Headquarters building IS A FIRST.
- The establishment of a Committee to explore the feasibility of more effective use of electronic data processing equipment at all Party levels IS A FIRST.
- The appointment of a Committee to consider national convention reforms IS A FIRST.

- The utilization of more than 70 college libraries across the nation as depositories for major documents prepared by the Republican National Committee IS A FIRST.

Bliss wanted his fellow Republicans to learn from the booklet. But Bliss could not keep his materials away from his rivals. Knippenburg, who moved from the Ohio Scripps-Howard Bureau to the *Dayton Daily News*, reported in 1967 that Ohio Democratic chairman Peter O'Grady "acquired a copy of 'Elements of Victory,' had it duplicated and distributed statewide to party officials." There was no doubt that O'Grady was following Bliss's recipe, Knippenburg reported:

> That he [O'Grady] is following it faithfully is evidenced by the party's most recent newsletter in which O'Grady spells out the Democratic intent. He says he wants to set up a full-time, year-round Democratic state finance committee, to set up a year-round problems, issues, and research program, to organize a full-time communications section, to utilize able organizational leaders in all aspects of party recruitment, to build a 150,000 dues-paying membership at $10 a head, to organize a 1,000-member Century Club at $100 per member per year, and a Capital Democratic Club, 100 members strong, each paying $1,000 a year.[10]

In 1970, O'Grady used Bliss's program to help elect Democrat John J. Gilligan as Ohio governor.[11]

This turnabout was fair play: Bliss had learned from the tactics of organized labor in Ohio, and as national chairman, he sent copies of their political action manuals to Republican officials. In 1968, one observer commented that the AFL-CIO had been "bliss-krieged."[12]

Chapter 49

A Tiger in the Tank

In February 1966, Robert Feldkamp of the *Akron Beacon Journal* paid a return visit to Washington, DC, following up on his chronicle of Ray Bliss's installation as chairman the previous April. Feldkamp found an upbeat chairman. "For the first time since becoming Republican national chairman, Ray C. Bliss of Akron is talking as if his party has a tiger in its tank," Feldkamp wrote, drawing on a popular advertising slogan.[1]

"I think it's really starting to come now. It's starting to move," Bliss told Feldkamp. Bliss didn't ladle on the optimism too thickly. That would have been out of character. He was naturally cautious, but he also had a habit of underestimating his strength and overestimating the enemy's. If Bliss's side won, this made the victory seem more impressive. "We've got a long way to go and it's taking the work of tens of thousands of people but..." Bliss said to Feldkamp, a slight smile crossing his usually unexpressive face.

After eleven months on the job, Bliss had the national headquarters working efficiently. "Outside, in dozens of glass-topped cubicles where 108 National Committee employees are working at tasks such as fiscal research, poring over foreign relations reports, preparing campaign materials, compiling election figures and projections and much more, headquarters fairly hums.... The air is one of intense activity, perhaps excitement," Feldkamp reported.

Things had gone so well at the recent meeting of the Republican National Committee that even the usually taciturn Bliss couldn't hide his excitement. "I saw a degree of enthusiasm at that meeting that leads me to believe the party is forgetting the past and finally is ready to pull together," said Bliss.

Bliss didn't gloss over the rough start he'd had as party chairman. "As a result, Bliss said recently, he is at a point today where he wanted to be last fall," wrote Feldkamp.

Bliss had worked hard to professionalize the Republican Party organization, and he listed for Feldkamp the "Eleven Firsts" from *Elements of Victory*. "These are the things that must be done to rebuild confidence both in the party and in the committee," Bliss told the Akron reporter.

The meetings and conferences that Bliss organized did more than educate the participants. They helped Republicans from around the country get to know each other so they could work together to win elections.

D. E. "Gene" Waddell of Summit County, Bliss's home county in Ohio, and Carl F. Wise of neighboring Stark County, which includes Canton, were among the county chairmen called to Washington, DC, for a series of three meetings for the chairmen representing the nation's seventy-five largest cities. These sessions reinforced Bliss's commitment to winning more Republican votes in urban centers and cutting down on the huge Democratic majorities that helped the Democrats in statewide elections. "Due to the importance of the big-city drive to the future of the Republican Party, I have called in some of the most knowledgeable persons available for the benefit of the chairmen," Bliss said to the group.[2]

David Broder wrote that Bliss rebuilt the party "in the dullest, most prosaic way possible, the only way that could possibly work, by holding workshops.... It was obvious, 'nuts and bolts' (Bliss' favorite expression). Yet suddenly—after years of part-time, speechifying chairmen; after years of nothing but ideological bickering—Ray Bliss' hackneyed phrases were becoming the basis for a fresh stream of action."[3]

All told, Bliss spoke at some 150 meetings of various kinds around the country during his four years as national chairman—an average of one every ten days.[4] His theme never varied: "There are no pushbutton methods for victory.... The Republican party is out-manned, out-organized, out-spent and outworked.... We need to realize on all levels that politics is a full-time job and not a three-month fling."[5]

In Washington, Bliss soon settled into a routine familiar from his days in Columbus and Akron. A driver from the national committee staff would pick Bliss up at his apartment and deliver him to the office by 9 or 9:30 A.M. Bliss's top aide, Arthur Peterson, described the daily routine in a 1995 interview. He had an office right behind

Bliss's, and the chairman would stop by. "What's up today?" Bliss would ask. Bliss would review the agenda and then look through his mail and make phone calls.

Many calls went to members of Bliss's political network, including Republican state chairmen scattered across the country. They were Bliss's power base. He wanted to know what was going on in California, Massachusetts, and every other state. Had the Republican victories in the mayoral races spurred interest in the party? Had contributions picked up? Bliss knew that the future of the party depended at least as much on what was going on in the county courthouses and state capitals around the country as it did on what Republican members of Congress were doing. Bliss dialed most of the calls himself and kept the door shut during many of the conversations.

"Ray Bliss was a guy who believed that he had to know everything about everything and he would only share what he wanted to share," said Peterson.[6] David Broder described this aspect of the chairman's character: "The penchant for secrecy and the willingness to keep his word, no matter what the cost, are the qualities that make Bliss a favorite with other organization men."[7]

The chairman also read each morning. About forty newspapers arrived at headquarters each day, and staffers clipped stories for Bliss and his top aides. "He wanted to read the clips," said Peterson. He would spend half an hour or even an hour poring through stories from the *Washington Post*, the *New York Times*, the *Wall Street Journal*, his hometown *Akron Beacon Journal*, and newspapers from Dallas, Los Angeles, San Francisco, and other cities around the country.

By 1 P.M., Bliss would be ready for lunch. Sometimes he and Peterson would eat at a little sandwich shop in the building that housed Republican headquarters. "We would get a sandwich and sit down at a bar stool and talk for a little bit," Peterson said.

After lunch, he and Peterson would return to the office. By 5:30 P.M., Bliss was ready to talk politics. It was his way of unwinding, but the daily chats were more than relaxation. Bliss believed that he could develop ideas and plans by talking through the issues, rehashing ideas, and sometimes just arguing—as long as the opponent was worth arguing with. He loved to bait the academic-oriented Peterson, accusing him of harboring naive, pie-in-the-sky political notions that were out of touch with reality.

Peterson could be as stubborn as Bliss when it came to sticking to a position. "He'd get mad at me....He'd say, 'damn you,'" Peterson recalled. Peterson almost cherished the outbursts. "He was a fun guy to work with, fun in the sense that it was wonderful to work with his mind. He had a great mind," said Peterson.

Political debate aside, Bliss occasionally lost his temper with the hyperenergetic Peterson. "Sometimes in the day he would rap on the door or open the door and scream at me or throw books at me," Peterson recalled.

Bliss demanded not only a strong work ethic but a tight ship. He wanted to control the flow of information from the committee, which Peterson learned the hard way. Once Peterson gave David Broder a briefing on Republican plans, the details of which appeared in the newspaper along with a quote from Peterson. "Oh boy. I got chewed out," Peterson recalled. The information he gave Broder in one interview could at least have been rationed out to provide four good stories for the Republicans, said Bliss.

By 7:30 P.M., Bliss was ready to go to dinner. A driver from the staff always drove Bliss and his dinner companions back and forth. Bliss savored the dinner hour for the conversation as much as for the food, accompanied by a drink or two. When Peterson ate with him, he tried to get the chairman's mind off business back at head-quarters. "We would get into fields that ordinarily you wouldn't get into with other people.... What I purposely tried to do was to get him to relax and forget politics," said Peterson.[8]

Dinnertime brought out a different side of Bliss, always formal in the office. Josephine Good from the national committee staff was sometimes invited. "A lot of the women called him Ray.... I never called him Ray. I always called him 'Mr. Chairman.' I never called any of the chairmen by their first names. I thought it was very disrespectful," said Good, who worked for thirteen national chairmen during her career. The formality seemed to evaporate at dinner, particularly when they'd go to a German restaurant, which served food like Bliss's mother had cooked. "He loved German food. He loved beer. There was this place on 15th Street.... We'd just walk up there from the national committee [headquarters]," said Good. "When you were out with him, he would relax. He could tell jokes. I smoked then. He was always lighting my cigarette. I never smoked in the office. With a drink I would smoke," said Good. "He finally got so used to me sometimes I think he forgot I was there. He used some pretty salty language."[9]

Bliss worried about using salty language when working with women. Elly Peterson of Michigan, the first female Republican state "chairman," remembered an embarrassed Bliss saying "Excuse me" to her every time he swore during private sessions of the Republican National Committee. She eventually said: "Ray, let's knock it off. My husband is in the Army. I know probably more words than you do."[10] The formal Bliss tried to behave like a gentleman and expected the same from women. "He really liked women who were not too aggressive and were real ladies. He appreciated real ladies," said Good.[11]

Dinner sometimes lasted two hours, but by 10 P.M. Bliss usually had returned to the office. "Then we would work until about 2 A.M.," said Peterson. There didn't seem to be enough hours in the day to get what Bliss wanted done. He was determined to rebuild the Republican Party and he was obsessed with every detail of how the job would get done. Bliss wanted to know what Peterson was doing to shape the party's agenda. He wanted to know what public relations man Fred Morrison was doing. How was research going? Most of the staff had gone home, Peterson recalled. "I would have to go around and get their stuff and he would sit in there [his office] and just go over it.... He was totally conversant with everything that went on."

Sometimes Bliss and Peterson would walk over to the 1520 Club for a nightcap or two before finally going home for the day. "We would have a few beers and talk some more," said Peterson. According to Peterson, *Elements of Victory* was begun over dinner, brought back to the office, and then worked on further over a beer after midnight.

Bliss critiqued Peterson's work on the booklet. "Well, Art, I don't like this part and I like that and this is correct," Bliss would say. He could irritate Peterson. "I think it is too academic," said Bliss, who knew from long experience how to speak to grassroots Republicans. "So that really ticked me off, you know, because I was trying to rebuild the party up a little, but he was right, probably," said Peterson. "We've got to modify it," Bliss would tell his assistant. So they ordered another beer and figured out how to put Peterson's words into the language of the Republican operatives they were meant to influence.

The outgoing academic and the shy Bliss had their own special chemistry at these late-night encounters. "We were different.... His favorite expression was, 'Art, you are a real tonic for me.' That's what he called me, his 'tonic,'" recalled Peterson.[12]

Chapter 50

Bliss Says "No" to Nixon

As 1966 progressed, it was the Democrats' turn to face difficulties. President Lyndon Johnson's popularity was declining.[1] Ray Bliss sensed that the Republicans were making a comeback and so was former vice president Richard Nixon.

Nixon's political career seemed to be over after he lost the close 1960 presidential race and then the 1962 governor's race in California. But by 1966, Nixon was in the process of creating a "New Nixon." He cast himself as a loyal Republican soldier eager to do battle on behalf of candidates for Congress. He coyly rejected any suggestion that he was just warming up for 1968 when he would try again for the presidency. "I am a political realist. I do not expect to be a candidate again. I am motivated solely by a desire to strengthen the party so that whoever we nominate in 1968 can win," Nixon said.[2]

Representative Bill Ayres from Akron had no doubts that Nixon would run for president again, and Ayres likely shared his views with Bliss. Nixon and Ayres were longtime friends, so it was natural that Ayres called Nixon's new office in New York for a political speech in 1963. "He didn't say that [he was running for president], but of course that was on his mind," said Ayres.

Nixon and Ayres both expected Barry Goldwater to be the Republican candidate in 1964 and they also expected him to lose to Democratic incumbent John F. Kennedy. After that, the fight would open for the 1968 GOP nomination, when Nixon still would be relatively young. "He [Nixon] talked about the thing to do would be to get out and work for the Congress [Republican candidates] in 1966, which is exactly what he did," said Ayres.[3]

Bliss welcomed Nixon's help in campaigning for other Republican candidates, but the national chairman did not want to show favoritism toward any potential 1968 presidential candidates—of which there were many. It was not long, however, before Nixon's ambitions and Bliss's view of his role as national chairman collided.

Bliss later provided his side of the showdown with Nixon to Ben Maidenburg, executive editor and publisher of the *Akron Beacon Journal.*

> One day Maurice Stans [a Nixon fundraiser] came to my office [at Republican national headquarters] and asked me to authorize half the cost of a couple of airplanes to take Nixon and a bunch of newspapermen on a tour of 32 states.
>
> I said I could not spend the national committee's money for one candidate, that I had to think of the whole party, not any one candidate, and that I felt the GOP National Committee would back me to the hilt.
>
> Stans pleaded with me, but I said, 'Hell no.'
>
> A couple of days later, Nixon called me from New York and repeated the request. I told him what I had told Stans. Nixon became absolutely furious. He used language that I had never heard him use before, or since. He was really foul-mouthed.
>
> But I stuck to my guns. Finally, when I could get a word in edgewise, I told Dick that I knew of some people who wanted him to be President and who, if approached, would no doubt come up with the money. I gave Nixon the names, and Stans and Nixon and others picked up the needed money.[4]

Arthur Peterson recalled the telephone conversation between Bliss and Nixon. One day he and Bliss returned from lunch to find that an "urgent call" from Nixon had come in. "I want you to hear this," Bliss told Peterson, as Bliss turned on the speaker phone in his office and returned Nixon's call.[5]

Nixon and Bliss exchanged pleasantries, but soon the former vice president began pressing his request for the funds to rent the airplanes. Bliss thanked Nixon for what he was doing to help Republican candidates, but said the request would be impossible to fulfill. The conversation heated up. "It was obvious from the tone of his voice that Nixon was infuriated. He became more and more demanding and threatening. Ray Bliss drew heavily on his omnipresent cigarette, but remained outwardly calm. Only the increasing redness of his face revealed his furor within," Peterson remembered.

Nixon gave up, but not without a fiery and threatening good-bye: "All right, Ray, but remember this, I don't forget these things."

Bliss was not cowed by the threat. "Ray and I went over that [the conversation] several times after that and laughed about it," said Peterson.[6]

Bliss may have had a second reason for refusing Nixon's request. Josephine Good, who had worked at party headquarters with Bliss, said he wanted to make sure that the staff was taken care of financially. The party did not have a lot of extra money at the time Nixon made his request, Good recalled. "And this is one thing I always thought was so great about Mr. Bliss. He had a lot of respect for the staff. He felt responsible for the staff and he was going to be sure that he always had a payroll for them. He had the money in the bank but he wouldn't give it to Nixon because he felt he was saving that...for operation of headquarters in case there was a lag in contributions," Good reported.[7]

In his memoirs, Nixon gave a brief and sanitized version of how Bliss handled his request: "RNC Chairman Ray Bliss refused our request for committee funds to rent a plane on the ground that this would be showing favoritism for me over other potential presidential candidates. So we raised the money on our own. It was a political miracle that we were able to do it all by ourselves."[8]

A more detailed account from Nixon's perspective came in 2006 from Thomas Roeser, a former political operative. In a blog post, Roeser discussed a visit Nixon made to Chicago in 1966 to headline a fundraiser for Republican David Reed, an African American running for a US House seat.[9]

Roeser made clear that he believed Nixon's willingness to make the trip was related to his presidential ambitions: "Nixon was crossing the country helping Republican candidates for Congress in order to pick up due-bills for collection at the next presidential go-round in 1968."

Roeser said that on Reed's behalf he helped arrange "a small cocktail party with light nibbles for the guests and passed the word that Nixon would be on hand." Before Nixon arrived at the party, however, Nicholas Ruwe, Nixon's advance man, approached Roeser. "One look at his face—of abject terror—and my blood froze," wrote Roeser. Roeser asked Ruwe what had happened.

"Listen.... You and me—we got trouble. Maybe we got to cancel this thing," Ruwe said. Roeser asked why. "Nixon is up in the suite now. He just got a call from Ray Bliss," Ruwe said. "Ray Bliss just dropped a bomb on us," Ruwe continued. "He just told Nixon that Nixon has to pay all the bills from his national trips himself—that the RNC won't cover them. This despite the fact that Nixon was told earlier that the RNC would."

Ruwe told Roeser that Bliss's decision was influenced by another prominent Republican and Nixon rival for the presidential nomination.

"Nelson Rockefeller is raising hell with Bliss because Nixon is getting a free ride so Bliss pulled the plug on it. Do you realize that this means Nixon is stuck with the tab of well over $100,000—well over that!" Ruwe said. Nixon was furious, said Ruwe. "He told me to make plane arrangements to get the hell out of here tonight! He's in a terrible—dreadful—temper and I don't blame him," said Ruwe.

Roeser and Ruwe went up to Nixon's suite to see if they could persuade Nixon to attend the fundraiser. They found Nixon on the telephone with Bliss. "He ignored me, held the receiver away from his ear and said in a guttural whisper to Ruwe: 'Bliss' and pointed meaningfully to it," said Roeser.

Roeser provided what he said was the "substance" of what he heard Nixon tell Bliss: "Ray—let me say this. I was told all my trips would be paid for—was told it. Listen to me: WAS TOLD IT! I'll tell you this, Ray! Tell you this, Ray! Tell you this, Ray! I'll make good on all my bills...I'll either pay for them myself or by god I'll raise the money. But I want you to know this. You better goddamn hope..." Roeser then paraphrased Nixon: "and he [Nixon] expressed the thought that if he ever, ever got near the presidential nomination much less the presidency, Ray Bliss would be hiking his ass back to Ohio."

After the call with Bliss ended, Nixon's diatribe continued: "Slam went the receiver! Then, standing up, came a long tirade of injustices and ingratitude from all he had helped."

Ruwe exploited Nixon's hurt feelings to persuade him to attend the fundraiser. "Yes," said Ruwe, "and here you are ready to speak for another black candidate! And will the blacks on the South Side [of Chicago] vote for you again? Hell no!" Ruwe told Nixon that the "people who have always gone after you" were counting on Nixon to back out of the fundraiser.

Ruwe's psychology worked, according to Roeser: "Nixon turned suddenly calm, ashen. 'Yes,' he said.... 'I'm going to give this thing everything I got and afterward—.'"

Ruwe brought Bliss back into the conversation: "And afterward, you're going to grab Ray Bliss by the collar and give him a..."

Nixon agreed and then proceeded to the planned fundraiser and, according to Roeser, "gave a speech I will long remember" about the Republican Party's commitment to civil rights and Reed's virtues as a candidate.

Nixon biographer Stephen Ambrose sympathized with Nixon. "As Nixon was the only Republican campaigning nationally in 1966, he had good reason to resent Bliss' decision," Ambrose wrote in his Nixon biography.[10] Ambrose said that Nixon did not forget and forgive. "He [Nixon] carried a grudge. He had a long memory," Ambrose later recalled.[11]

Historian Rick Perlstein was less kind to Nixon, writing that Nixon "hit up the Republican National Committee for a free airplane because, he said, he would be working for the party's sake, not his own. Fortunately for the other 1968 contenders, RNC chair Ray Bliss, who had a keen ear for bullshit, made him rent one, out of the half million dollars raised by Stans."[12]

Nixon, as Bliss said he would, found the resources to stay on the campaign trail. He seemed to be everywhere, campaigning for every Republican candidate who wanted his help. During the last week of June, he spoke in Chicago, Detroit, Flint, and Bay City in Michigan; Roanoke, Virginia; and Washington, DC.[13]

Bliss's first national election as chairman was in 1966. He arrived at headquarters in Washington, DC, about 7:30 P.M. on election night, November 8, after flying in from Akron. Early in the evening, when television networks were projecting winners, based on voting samples, Bliss was in his cautious mode. "I'm not interested in projected winners," he told an aide. "I want to see definite winners. Don't get carried away by TV predictions."[14]

The Republicans were definite winners up and down the ticket. The GOP picked up forty-seven seats in the US House of Representatives and three in the US Senate. They added eight governorships. The GOP made large gains in state legislatures, and in every major city the Republicans cut the Democratic vote margins substantially compared to 1962.

By 1:25 A.M. on November 9, Bliss sat at his desk, eating a hot dog, sipping a beer and, in the words of one observer, "grinning like a happy cat."[15]

The results prompted Bliss to hail Thruston Morton, a US senator from Kentucky and a former national chairman, who was seated nearby.

"I'd say we're on our way, Thrus," Bliss said.

"You damn betcha we are," drawled the Kentuckian. "It's a new ball game and it's been a long time coming."

The next day Bliss told reporters: "This press conference…will be a little different from my first one, when you were asking me if the Republican Party would survive."

"It looks to me," he boasted, "as if we have a live elephant."[16]

Chapter 51

Tightrope Walking

For Ray Bliss, 1967 began on a positive note. The Capitol Hill Club, a Washington, DC, Republican organization, conducted a poll of its members on national GOP leaders. It found the shy, bespectacled Akron insurance man had become the sixth most popular Republican in the country. Bliss trailed only a handful of current or former office holders.[1]

David Broder described the only tool Bliss had available to achieve this success: "All the new chairman had was a license to walk the tightrope among conflicting rivalries while trying to build the shattered hulk of the Grand Old Party." Bliss, concluded Broder, was an "A-1 Tightrope Walker."[2]

The year also ended well for Bliss. As in 1965, the Republicans won a number of big city mayoral races, including John Ballard's reelection in Akron. The GOP candidate narrowly lost in Philadelphia, but cut the Democratic margin of victory from 65,000 four years earlier to 10,000.[3]

In between, walking the tightrope became an everyday task for Bliss when it came to managing the GOP's many constituencies.

One notable Republican success in 1966 had been the election of Edward Brooke to the US Senate from Massachusetts, the first black person to be popularly elected to Congress's upper chamber. Many black voters had backed the "party of Lincoln" and there were still a significant number of black Republicans in northern states, represented by groups such as the National Negro Republican Assembly (NNRA).[4]

In the 1930s, however, black voters began shifting toward the Democratic Party of Franklin Delano Roosevelt. An important exception was in the South, a solidly Democratic region, where the Jim Crow laws kept most blacks away from the polls. Blacks voted decisively Democratic in 1964, when Barry Goldwater opposed the Civil Rights Act. In a reversal of historic patterns, five of the six states the Republicans carried were in Dixie.

Bliss wanted Republicans to win a larger share of the black vote, an expectation consistent with his "big city" strategy. His approach to black voters was pragmatic, said John Bibby. "His experience in Ohio had indicated that you could get some votes. There was some potential," Bibby said.[5]

The downside was potentially alienating white voters, especially in the South—so Bliss was walking a racial tightrope. Soon after becoming national chairman, Bliss heard from black Republican leaders complaining that the new chairman was not doing enough. "When Bliss came in we all said we'd wait and see. We've waited and so far we've seen nothing," said George Fowler, chairman of the New York State Commission on Human Rights. "Frankly, we're angry about it."[6]

In the summer of 1965, Bliss met with the leaders of the NNRA in Washington, DC. W. O. Walker of Cleveland, director of Ohio's Department of Industrial Relations, was quoted as saying, "It was the unanimous opinion of our group that we had a constructive meeting today."[7]

Arthur Peterson helped prepare for the meeting and also attended. Bliss told Walker and the others that he would try to help them organize Republicans in black areas. Also, the chairman made an effort to include "articulate black leaders" on the national Republican Party tapes he would send to radio stations to be used as public service announcements. "Bliss was unwilling to go beyond what he could say and do," said Peterson. The chairman would not promise to do more for black Republicans than he could deliver.[8]

In 1966, Bliss appointed an advisory group of twelve black leaders, reactivated the Republican National Committee's minorities division, and hired Clarence Townes, a black insurance man from Richmond, Virginia, to direct it.[9] "He gave him [Townes] a budget and some limited staff. He [Townes] traveled and met with folks," said Bibby.[10] Townes's division eventually worked in nineteen states, including several in the South.

Early in his chairmanship, Bliss also heard from Republicans about the danger of wooing black voters. "Let me say that you people are still following the Democrats' advisors and instead of gaining the Negro vote, which is impossible, you are alienating a sizeable White vote. In my opinion the White vote that you are going to lose is no longer confined to the South," wrote G. W. Gulmon of Natchez, Mississippi.[11]

Bliss approached the task of seeking white votes in the South with the same caution he used in seeking black votes. Bliss was leery of "fishing expeditions" into southern elections.[12] Although the region had been shifting slowly toward the Republicans, there were still many places where the "party of Lincoln" was viewed with great suspicion. Besides, Bliss did not want the GOP too closely associated with some prominent southern Republicans, such as Senator Strom Thurmond of South Carolina, the presidential nominee of the segregationist Dixiecrat Party in 1948, who had switched from Democrat to Republican in 1964.

"Ray's problem was with some of the southern state chairmen and national committee people who had been supporters of Goldwater in 1964," Bibby said. "Ray placed great importance on personal loyalty and he did not consider either to be among his loyal supporters. A southern operation was a bit difficult for him therefore because he also believed strongly in working through regular channels—i.e., the state chairmen and national committee members." Despite these problems, "Bliss was supportive of expanding the party in the South and he provided financial and staff support to I. Lee Potter of Virginia, who ran the southern operation while Ray was chairman," Bibby said.[13] A 1967 success was the election of Republican Louie Nunn in Kentucky, the first Republican governor in twenty years.

Haley Barbour, who served as chairman of the Republican National Committee from 1993 to 1997 and later as governor of Mississippi, said Bliss's greatest continuing legacy in the South was the training programs he set up for state and local parties. Barbour benefited from them personally in 1968 when he dropped out of college to work on Richard Nixon's presidential campaign.

"He [Bliss] emphasized the building up of the party at the grassroots and at the state level by having trained people on the ground," Barbour said. "And so training was a huge element in what we saw of what the RNC was doing. And candidly, for years thereafter in Mississippi, we had, I mean, dozens of party leaders at the county level who had all gotten active when Bliss was chairman and had been trained as grassroots, local party, nuts and bolts leaders.... So, to me, Ray Bliss's great legacy to the party was the training." The training schools Barbour attended did not feature high-blown theories. They focused on "essentially nuts and bolts organizational training—find 'em [voters], vote 'em, count 'em," said Barbour.[14]

Another tightrope Bliss walked was with the Young Republicans (YRs). The leadership of this group of Republicans younger than forty was dominated by Goldwater supporters. Indeed, the draft Goldwater movement had been based on YR machinery. In 1966, a group of New Jersey YRs known as the "Rat Finks" embarrassed the GOP by writing—and singing—racist, anti-Semitic, and anti-Catholic songs. Initially, the YR leadership refused to sanction the offenders. In June 1966, Bliss stepped in with a strongly worded resolution from the Republican National Committee condemning the Rat Finks' extremism.[15]

These divisions were evident in Ohio as the 1967 YR convention approached in June. On one side was Donald "Buz" Lukens, later a member of the US House of Representatives from Ohio, then part of the conservative leadership. On the other side, Roger W. Tracy Jr., later Ohio tax commissioner, was head of the Ohio YRs and a Bliss ally.

A convention preview news story predicted a rough time for Bliss. "Every time Akron's Ray Bliss thinks of the next few days, his head hurts," said the story in the *Akron Beacon Journal*. "It's because the National Young Republican Federation meets in Omaha…to elect officers and politick as only the Young Republicans can politick.…One of its favorite pastimes is rattling the nuts and bolts that hold the GOP together."[16]

Tracy wanted to soothe Bliss's headache. He was the campaign manager for Ohioan Jim Betts of suburban Cleveland, who was running for chairman of the national Young Republicans as the "unity" candidate. The Ohioan was the decided underdog to Jack McDonald of Tennessee, the candidate of the conservative faction known as the "syndicate."

While the YRs behaved as if they were an independent entity, the Republican National Committee controlled their budget, which amounted to $150,000 in presidential election years. Bliss hinted that he might cut the money off if the group did not get in line, or maybe even recommend withdrawing recognition of the group as an official arm of the Republican Party.[17] The "syndicate" put up a defiant front. "We'd just become an independent organization," an unnamed representative of the group said. "We'd set up our own fund-raising system. That would give Bliss a bigger headache than he's got now."[18]

Unofficially, Ohio GOP chairman John Andrews had been working for weeks to line up support for Betts from outside Ohio, but the gambit failed. "We got routed," Tracy said of Betts's candidacy for chairman. "We put up a valiant fight. The criticism of us is that we were liberal."[19]

Besides electing McDonald as chairman, the "syndicate" also succeeded in defeating amendments to the group's constitution that would have given Bliss and the Republican National Committee more control over the group.[20]

Bliss did not want to alienate YRs, nor did he want the organization to become a tool for one of the candidates seeking the 1968 presidential nomination—as it had been in 1964. That was clearly on the verge of happening.

"All week the colored gas filled balloons have soared high over the convention floor where the Republicans are meeting, dangling a huge 'Reagan in '68' sign," reported Robert Feldkamp of the *Akron Beacon Journal.* "The sign is symbolic of a new love affair that has hit this city between the YRs and California Governor Ronald Reagan."[21]

Bliss's initial reaction was to ignore what amounted to a repudiation of his effort to gain more control over the YR group for the national committee. "If they don't want to join the team, that's OK with me," Bliss said. "I'm concerned with the electorate which is a lot bigger than this outfit."[22]

Despite his public statements, Bliss kept negotiating. His control of the national party's spending gave him a bargaining chip. By September, a truce between the McDonald-led YRs and the Republican National Committee was announced. Bliss seemed to have won most of the assurances he had sought in Omaha. The YRs agreed not to use any funds directly or indirectly "to promote any candidate for public office prior to the 1968 Republican convention or prior to a primary election."[23]

Not all young conservatives were unhappy with Bliss. Howard Phillips, who would serve in the Nixon administration and was a three-time presidential nominee of the Constitution Party, joined the national committee staff in 1965. He ran Opportunities Unlimited, a group Bliss founded to help attract college students to the GOP. "Ray Bliss was a great man, one of the finest men I've ever met," Phillips later said. "Extraordinary devotion to his task; extraordinary integrity. I loved working for him. I was proud to be associated with him."[24]

At the founding meeting of Opportunities Unlimited at the University of Wisconsin, Bliss said to young voters: "We do not demand that you submit to policies already established by leaders of the preceding generation. Because the Republican Party is the minority, it has fewer people seeking to advance to positions of leadership. Hence your chances of rising rapidly to a leadership role are not only excellent but certain."[25]

Bliss later remembered: "When I was scheduled to appear at the University of Wisconsin, I recall my staff saying we had better cancel that meeting because I would be picketed. When I arrived, there were 20–30 students picketing against the Vietnam war. I stopped to chat and told the students, 'I will make you a proposition. I'll pay for your lunch if you come in and listen to what I have to say. You don't have to agree with me, just listen.' So in they came.... When I was finished the students that were picketing led a standing ovation."[26]

In his personal life, however, Bliss was not an exemplar of racial, religious, or ethnic reconciliation. Peterson said that he and Bliss would argue about race and religion: "Ray had some compartmentalization in his mind with Jewish voters and black voters." Bliss considered Peterson a liberal and would try to needle him by making objectionable remarks. "There are really good black friends of mine and then there are niggers," Bliss opined. "There are really good Jewish friends of mine and then there are kikes." Bliss used racial and religious slurs to manifest "real concern" about what he considered "overly aggressive behavior" by Jews and the "underachieving" of blacks, said Peterson. "He was so put off by those two characteristics [overly aggressive behavior and underachieving], that these words [nigger and kike] expressed a kind of disgust," said Peterson. "Then he had to attach those to people. He found it helpful to personalize it." Peterson concluded that Bliss's "spirit was right but he was reflecting his culture in many ways," he said. "I don't think he felt it was wrong."[27]

On the subjects of race and religion, Bliss was a man of his time—including his upbringing in Akron in the early twentieth century. The Rubber City was a cultural melting pot, with racial, religious, and ethnic prejudice as the downside of such diversity. One aspect of this environment—anti-Catholic sentiment—had a major impact on Bliss's life.

At the same time, Bliss was not insensitive to the country's racial and religious problems. Bliss admired his political mentor in Akron, James Corey, for standing up to the Ku Klux Klan in the 1920s. Bliss wanted blacks to have the right to vote, which they had not had in the South. Meanwhile, his lifelong partners in the insurance agency were Jews. He was deeply suspicious of contemporary extremists, such as the John Birch Society, who assigned Jews a central place in their conspiracy theories.

Bliss found himself walking another tightrope in an area of his strength: the National Federation of Republican Women (NFRW). Phyllis Schlafly of Alton, Illinois, was running for president of the NFRW against Gladys O'Donnell of Long Beach, California. Schlafly had gained national attention by writing a book, *A Choice Not an Echo*, in support of Goldwater's 1964 presidential campaign and later became a leading antifeminist. O'Donnell was a pioneer among female aircraft pilots and later served in the Nixon administration.[28]

Officially, Bliss remained silent on the race to lead the half-million-member federation. But he and John Andrews feared that a victory by Schlafly would reopen the wounds of 1964.[29] It could not have pleased Bliss that the Ohio Federation of Republican Women favored Schlafly. Katherine Kennedy Brown, Ohio's national committeewoman, nominated Schlafly from the floor of the NFRW national convention in Washington, DC.

With Bliss's and Andrews's help behind the scenes, moderate Republican women, such as Elly Peterson of Michigan, defeated Schlafly. O'Donnell prevailed, with 1,910 votes to Schlafly's 1,494.[30]

The NFRW convention was raucous. "It was marked by days and nights of credentials challenges and charges and counter-charges over everything from voting fraud to the creation of phantom federation clubs to the busing in of delegates."[31]

Schlafly's husband sat in the gallery with other nondelegates and led the shouting when the convention took voice votes. The noise from the gallery became deafening on a crucial, final voice vote—on whether to refer to the executive board a motion challenging the election results. Dorothy Elston, then the federation president, ordered everyone but the delegates to clear the convention hall; the results were later upheld by the NFRW's board of directors.

The Schlafly forces were not good losers and demanded that Bliss intervene, but Bliss would not be drawn into the disagreement: "The women's federation, like the Young Republicans, is an autonomous organization, with its own constitution, its own bylaws and its own rules."[32]

Schlafly wrote a bitter letter of complaint to Bliss on June 6, 1967. "Your spokesmen have repeatedly proclaimed your neutrality in the matter of the NFRW contest. Lest Republicans be tempted to agree with the Bard's famous words that you 'doth protest too much'... it is time to produce some hard evidence of your neutrality," she wrote. It was not the first time that staffers at the Republican National Committee had done her wrong, Schlafly complained.[33]

She demanded an accounting of how the national committee staffers who worked against her were paid by the national committee. She also complained about being denied the second-best suite in the convention hotel, to which she should have been entitled as first vice president of the women's group. There had been earlier evidence that Bliss was working against her and for O'Connell, she continued.

Schlafly then tried hoisting Bliss with his own twin petards of avowed neutrality and pursuit of Republican unity: "There is nothing personal about this; it is just a matter of principle. If we are to have Republican victories in 1968, conservatives must be assured by you that their money will not again be spent to attack other Republicans."

Bliss's tightrope walking had just one goal—winning elections. He was pleased enough at his efforts to poke fun at himself and the Republicans' political situation at a fundraiser in Cleveland. "Two years ago...I felt like a man being fed to the lions," Bliss said. "We had the worst split in the party since Bull Moose days, and every time I went to a Republican meeting, a minister prayed for divine guidance for the national chairman."

"Believe me, he needed it!"[34]

Chapter 52

A Medium and a Message

A major challenge for Ray Bliss was planning the 1968 Republican National Convention. He wanted the convention to showcase a united party and to launch a successful general election campaign—unlike the 1964 convention, which had failed on both counts.

The first priority was picking the host city. Josephine Good, as part of her work at the national committee, prepared charts that showed how each of six competing cities measured up on criteria ranging from the quality of hotels to the political makeup of the region's officeholders.[1]

On September 8, 1967, the Republican National Committee voted to hold the convention in Miami Beach, Florida, accepting the recommendation of the site selection committee headed by Bliss.[2]

Republicans had not held a convention in a southern city since 1864, and that was Baltimore in Maryland, a border state. One benefit of Miami Beach was its potential appeal to southern voters. Governor Claude Kirk Jr., elected in 1966, was Florida's first Republican governor since Reconstruction. At the same time, Miami Beach's reputation for charm, glamour, and celebrities dimmed its association with southern conservatism.[3]

The Republican National Committee required the host city to contribute $650,000 to help pay for the convention. Miami Beach offered $800,000—$650,000 in cash and $150,000 in goods and services.[4] "The money was terribly important," said Good, but facilities mattered as well.[5] "Even if a city offered $1 million or $2 million in cash but didn't have the facilities or the rooms available, I wouldn't select it," Bliss said early in the process. "On the other hand, a city with an ideal hall and ideal rooms but not enough money would have to be considered very highly."[6]

First, there had to be a convention hall with seating for 14,000, including 1,200 box seats. The hall had to be air conditioned. There had to be at least three rooms near the convention floor to accommodate 50 to 100 people for caucuses. There had to be accommodations for television and radio coverage. Two or three interview rooms were needed near the convention floor. Parking for 1,000 cars was required.[7]

As party chairman, Bliss could not control political conditions, but he could make sure the site had everything needed to make the event run efficiently, while meeting the demands of television and keeping the delegates comfortable. He could focus relentlessly on the details, just as he had done for thirty years.

Representatives from all the cities had to answer a battery of questions:

Describe seating in convention hall—permanently fixed or portable, color, padded or otherwise, width between rows, level, etc. Are box seats different? How many seats in each box?
What are the restroom facilities? Will portable equipment be necessary?
What arrangements are made for cleaning the hall?
Describe public address system and acoustics in convention hall.
Number of public telephones.
Will special cables for television be necessary?
Is there a permanent or portable stage or platform? Describe in detail.

Those questions were just for the convention hall. There was a separate list of requirements for hotels, including the following:

10,000 first class rooms near convention hall, or within reach of fast transportation to convention hall.
    Each state must have at least one suite available for state headquarters. Size of suite will vary according to size of state delegation.
    Each candidate for the office of President or Vice President establishes campaign headquarters at one of the central hotels. It is impossible to determine in advance these requirements, but space should be available for at least four to six candidates.

Bliss and his site committee also wanted to know how delegates would get around in the convention city. The committee requested detailed information on transportation:

Description of all types of transportation available, including fares.
Distance to be traveled from hotel center to convention hall.
What special arrangements would be made to handle convention traffic.
Location of airport and distance from airport to hotel center.
Location of railroad stations and distance to hotel center.
Number of airlines operating in city.

Bliss personally inspected hotel rooms—no trivial matter to Bliss. He wanted party leaders to be well taken care of in the premier hotels but he also wanted delegates to be in a good mood once the convention started.[8] "People sometimes got irritated because he was so fussy about the hotels," said Good, "but he said if people come to any kind of meeting, be it the convention or a national committee meeting, and they have trouble with their reservation or any trouble with the hotel they start out unhappy. They stay unhappy. They grump about everything. They're difficult to get along with."[9]

No detail escaped Bliss's attention. He asked Arthur Peterson to come with him to Miami Beach in early 1968 to look over the convention hall and surrounding facilities.[10]

"I think it has great possibilities," Peterson said.

Bliss, however, was not satisfied. "It needs about 30 more urinals," he told Peterson. "These architects don't know anything about gout."

The convention managers heard from Bliss and responded. "They put 'em [the urinals] in," said Peterson. The extra urinals were portables. Bliss worried about how they would look. The convention director had begun to understand Bliss and had a sense of humor, said Good.

"Mr. Bliss, they'll be beautiful," he said.[11]

Bliss arrived in Florida on July 29 before the convention started to make sure the stage was properly set. He got his first official look at the nearly completed Republican convention facilities. Bliss was generally pleased, but the wooden folding chairs in the spectator areas bothered him. They didn't have cushions.

"This is awful late to get cushions, isn't it?" he asked the convention hall manager.

"Well, maybe the governor can use his influence in getting them for us."

Governor Claude Kirk said that he might solve the problem by getting some cushions from a beer company that supplied them at athletic events.[12]

The flamboyant Florida governor and the understated national chairman made an odd couple. During a preconvention ceremony, Kirk wore a "flaming red coat and striped white pants," according to one newspaper account.[13] Bliss didn't have anything "flaming red" in his gray wardrobe.

Kirk at one point spotted a purple flower on a table, grabbed it, and tried to stick it in a buttonhole in Bliss's lapel. When he couldn't locate a buttonhole, Kirk found a paper clip and attached it to Bliss's suit.

"How does that look?" asked Kirk.

A bystander said it made the conservative Bliss look like one of the "flower people."

"Well," sighed Bliss, "flower people vote and I hope they vote Republican."[14]

One thing about Kirk probably gave Bliss pause. Kirk smoked a pipe. Bliss generally did not like or trust pipe smokers, said Peterson. It was one of Bliss's idiosyncrasies. "They're pontificators," Bliss would say of pipe smokers. Bliss's own choice of tobacco products—cigarettes—was all right by his standards, anyway. "Cigarette smokers are doers," said Bliss.[15]

Voters could be persuaded through the medium of a well-executed convention, but the party's message mattered too. Here Bliss was more interested in doing than pontificating: he wanted a party platform that showcased Republican unity and attracted voters.

When Bliss asked Peterson to be the chief of staff for the platform-writing committee, he told him that "the platform is going to be the Republican Coordinating Committee Report," with its consensus positions developed by a cross-section of GOP leaders. Achieving this result required clever politics.

As national chairman, Bliss made temporary platform committee assignments that the convention would be expected to ratify. But there was soon bickering over the platform among elected Republicans.[16] Governor John Chafee of Rhode Island, head of the Republican Governors Association, wanted to "modernize" the Goldwater platform from the 1964 convention, while Representative Melvin Laird of Wisconsin, who had chaired the 1964 platform committee, did not.[17]

This was just the kind of intraparty sniping that Bliss wanted to avoid. To accomplish unity, the chairman pulled off a "sneaky," according to Peterson. "He [Bliss] always was leery of the congressional people," said Peterson. "Strategically, he understood that you had to work with them and he understood also that you had to let them be the spokespersons.... They [the governors] didn't think the [Capitol] Hill people appreciated all the difficulties the states were going through. They [governors] had some of their own agenda items," said Peterson.[18]

Bliss appointed Senator Everett Dirksen of Illinois, the Senate minority leader, as chairman of the committee—and made Governor Chafee the vice chairman. The panel's public face was the congressional leadership, but the governors had a critical role.[19]

When Dirksen and his aides wanted to take over the staffing of the committee, said Peterson, Bliss called Dirksen at home to discuss the problem. "He [Bliss] did that, I guess, because of my pleading. I mean I was almost in tears. I was frustrated," said Peterson. The next morning, Dirksen told the platform committee how things were going to be done: "I just wanted to say that all the stuff that Art has been doing and the committee has been doing, we are going to go along with that...I think some of you had some different ideas, but we will not do that."[20]

Deft staff work by Peterson put many of the Republican Coordinating Committee's positions into the draft document. "It would be difficult indeed," Peterson wrote later, "for any platform committee to completely cast aside the position papers prepared by such an impressive and representative group as the Coordinating Committee, particularly since these positions appeared to serve candidates so well in the highly successful Republican campaign of 1966."[21]

As the convention approached, public bickering among platform committee members had disappeared. The committee convened in Miami Beach on August 6 and adopted the draft document. Calling for a "Republican Resurgence," the platform highlighted the challenges facing the nation and identified broad approaches to addressing the nation's major problems.[22]

Its something-for-everybody approach drew sarcasm from journalist Arthur Krock, writing in the *New York Times:* "Laboring in the perfumed sweat of Miami Beach, the Republicans have constructed a platform on which their Presidential nominee can run in all directions and probably will." Krock, however, offered some faint praise: "In sum, the platform was adequate but not notable as a standard political treadmill on which the representatives of nearly every party faction can run without falling off."[23]

Bliss no doubt agreed.

Chapter 53

The Politics of Turmoil

Ray Bliss's plan to use the 1968 Republican convention to showcase party unity was complicated by an ugly mood in the country. Americans were sharply divided on both foreign and domestic issues. Historian James Patterson labeled 1968 "the most turbulent year."[1]

A major controversy was the Vietnam War. Already unpopular, the conflict took a dramatic turn for the worse on January 30 when the Communist forces launched the "Tet Offensive" (named after the beginning of the lunar year) against American and South Vietnamese troops and installations, including the US Embassy. Although the allies eventually gained the upper hand, the "victory" brought more questions than answers. Over the next several months, antiwar protests escalated across the county, especially on college campuses. Both the war and the protests divided Americans.

The increasingly tense situation on civil rights exploded on April 4, when the Reverend Martin Luther King Jr. was assassinated in Memphis, Tennessee. The tragic killing of the nation's most prominent civil rights leader and an advocate of nonviolent protest unleashed several days of riots in major American cities, including Washington, DC. This civil unrest followed major race riots in 1967 in Detroit and Newark, New Jersey. It also encouraged black militancy, including a shootout between the Black Panther Party and the police in Oakland, California, on April 6. White backlash to the civil rights movement escalated.

Another source of unrest was the rise of a "counterculture" among young people who rejected traditional values. From long hair and unkempt clothing to drug use and sexual liberation, the counterculture angered conservatives in both political parties, reinforcing a perception of permissiveness. The women's movement was challenging gender roles. Increasing crime rates in major cities added to the sense of disorder.

As was his custom, Bliss said little publicly about the growing unrest. He was sensitive, however, to the feelings of black employees at the Republican National Committee when King was assassinated, said Josephine Good. "The next day [after King's assassination] all the black people at the committee were very upset," said Good. "They all had come to work. They had pictures of Martin Luther King. Mr. Bliss told everybody to go home."[2]

Arthur Peterson said that he personally supported American involvement in Vietnam, but that Bliss "really didn't know what to think about that. He was in one sense against the war.... He was concerned about the waste of funds and material and so forth. He just felt it was a waste. You couldn't have guns and butter," said Peterson.[3]

Bliss was not very sympathetic to the people rioting in the big cities, although he didn't dwell on the subject, said Peterson. "He would say, 'What are these people doing? What are they doing to themselves?'" Peterson recalled.

There was a practical reason for Bliss to avoid taking public positions on these issues. "He felt there were Republicans on both sides of both issues," said Peterson. As national chairman, his job was to provide neutral turf for all Republicans. He wanted to unite, not divide the party.

The Republican Party had been fractured in 1964, and now it was the Democrats who seemed to be coming apart. Rivals to President Lyndon Johnson rose from several quarters.[4]

First, Senator Eugene McCarthy of Minnesota announced his candidacy for president on November 30, 1967, based on opposition to the Vietnam War and with backing from college students. Then on February 8, 1968, former Alabama governor George Wallace declared his independent candidacy for the White House, hoping to tap the resentments of southern and working-class whites.

The March 12 primary in New Hampshire was a big surprise: President Johnson only narrowly defeated Senator McCarthy. Then on March 16, Senator Robert Kennedy of New York, the brother of the late president John F. Kennedy, entered the race, banking on his appeal to liberals and minority voters. On March 31, President Johnson said he would not seek reelection. With Johnson out, Vice President Hubert Humphrey stepped forward on April 27, strongly backed by big city party leaders and labor unions.

Six weeks later, tragedy struck again. Senator Kennedy was shot while celebrating his victory in the California presidential primary and died soon afterward. On August 10, Senator George McGovern of South Dakota entered the campaign to rally Kennedy's supporters.

Meanwhile, Bliss kept careful tabs on the GOP candidates and the nomination process. "He wanted a fair playing field for everyone," said Peterson. Bliss got upset with him when Peterson voiced an opinion about who would make the best candidate.[5]

An early favorite for the GOP nomination was former vice president Richard Nixon, but he soon had competition from both wings of the party.[6] His initial rival was Michigan governor George Romney from the liberal wing, but Romney's campaign began to fade in the fall of 1967, when he tried to explain his opposition to the Vietnam War, claiming he had been "brainwashed" by American officials. His campaign was not pretty, as Ohio governor James Rhodes noted: "Watching George Romney run for the Presidency was like watching a duck try to make love to a football."[7]

Romney ended his campaign on February 28, 1968, two weeks before the March 12 primary in New Hampshire. Nixon formally announced his candidacy on February 1, and with Romney's exit, won New Hampshire decisively. He campaigned without formal opposition for most of the spring. Another rival, New York governor Nelson Rockefeller, felt pressure to enter the race. On March 21, Rockefeller declared that he would not campaign for the nomination—only to reverse himself on April 30. Rockefeller narrowly defeated Nixon in the Massachusetts primary, but otherwise fared poorly in the remaining contests.

Another possible rival was Governor Ronald Reagan of California, a favorite of conservatives. Although Reagan also performed poorly in most primaries, he was the "favorite son" candidate of his home state and its numerous delegates. Reagan did not formally enter the race until the GOP convention opened on August 5. An unofficial joint effort by liberal Rockefeller and conservative Reagan to stop Nixon had little effect.[8]

As in 1964, the Ohio Republicans adopted a "favorite son" strategy, with Governor James Rhodes as the candidate. Rhodes calculated that the nomination would take more than one ballot—which would have made Ohio's 58 delegates crucial and allowed Rhodes to be a kingmaker.[9]

At a press conference on the eve of the Republican convention in Miami Beach, reporters peppered Bliss with questions.[10]

"You talked about unity a moment ago," one reporter said. "The Republican Party has had problems with unity. Now in the upcoming convention do you think you'll have that problem again?"

"We have no problems next to what the Democrats have, in my judgment," Bliss responded.

Bliss said the outcome of the convention was uncertain. "Well, with all the favorite sons we have, assuming they have their names put into nomination, or consent to their name being placed in nomination, it would appear that we at this point have an open convention and that anything could happen," he said.

As usual, Bliss declined to go anywhere near endorsing a candidate or even assessing the strengths and weaknesses of the contenders. "I've made no attempt to assess the strength of the candidates state by state for the reasons I outlined to you earlier that I'm impartial in this contest.... As National Chairman I must refrain from becoming involved," he explained.

In a trademark statement, Bliss said: "I can't forecast at this point whether it will go past the first ballot or won't."

Chapter 54

Ray Bliss's Convention

It was "Ray Bliss's convention."

That's how William Brock later described the gathering August 5–8 in Miami Beach. At that time, Brock was a congressman from Tennessee and backing former vice president Richard Nixon for the presidential nomination.[1] He went on to serve as Republican national chairman from 1977 to 1980.

On August 5, 1968, Chairman Bliss gaveled the Republican National Convention to order. "If it accomplishes nothing more, the 1968 Republican convention will go down in history for one achievement," Ben Maidenburg reported. "Chairman Ray Bliss banged the gavel opening the hooraw at precisely 10 a.m. And the oldest of the old-timers said it was the first convention in memory to start on time."[2]

Bliss wanted the programs to proceed at a brisk pace, said Arthur Peterson. The clergymen who gave the daily invocations drew Bliss's wrath. Each was supposed to spend just two or three minutes invoking the blessing of a higher being. The Catholic priest who gave the invocation the first night, however, went on for five or six minutes, said Peterson. "Bliss was steaming that night," Peterson said. A Jewish rabbi and a Protestant layman also exceeded their time limits. Finally, an Episcopal priest kept his opening prayer within the allotted time. "I told you the only people you can trust are Episcopalians," snorted Bliss, saluting his adulthood faith.[3]

Bliss's speech on the convention's opening night highlighted the GOP's progress under his chairmanship. It was out of character for Bliss to speak, but it was important to describe the dramatic changes that had taken place since 1965.[4] "At that time there were those who said that come 1968 the Republicans would have to hire someone to accept its Presidential nomination. At least three distinguished gentlemen with us in this city tonight present living proof of the fallacy of that contention.... And those who, three years ago, placed such confidence and such faith in the other party now are crying out almost desperately for new leadership and new programs which will face up squarely to the problems so rapidly eroding our nation."

Bliss described the progress as not just good for Republicans, but vital to the health of the two-party system that he valued so highly. "Since the founding of the Republic our two-party system has furnished the flesh and blood for the skeleton of our Constitutional system. If this system fails, our Governmental system fails with it." GOP no longer meant just Grand Old Party, according to Bliss: "It is the G-O-P which is the Government of the People."

Bliss then summarized successes the party had enjoyed at the ballot box, noting that for the first time, the party had made gains in three straight elections. "Now some individuals say that politics is a matter of luck as far as wins and losses are concerned, but I learned many years ago that the harder you work in politics the luckier you get," Bliss told the convention.

The delegates came from the party's grass roots, and Bliss wanted them to know that those roots were the party's strength. "And not for one minute throughout my career have I doubted that in politics, as in business firms and labor organizations, you must build from the bottom up, not from the top down," Bliss said. "From purely a practical-politics point of view, then our job as Republicans from now until November 5 must be from the precinct, through the ward, through the city, through the county and state. If we win enough offices at the bottom, the very impact of these victories makes it possible to win at the top."

Bliss praised the work of the platform committee, but reminded the delegates: "The individuals who are chosen to be our presidential and vice presidential nominees must be given the complete, unswerving and vigorous support of all Republicans. Whatever may be a personal disappointment of the moment must be burned and forgotten."

"We can provide the means to achieve for the United States stability, fidelity, honor, dignity, tolerance and opportunity. I believe with all my heart that it is the Republican Party and the Republican Party alone at this moment which can make the Impossible Dream possible," he said.

Bliss's speech set the stage, but he did not rely on words alone to convey to the convention audience and millions of Americans watching the proceedings on television that the Republican Party now represented diverse points of view. The lineup of first-day speakers made the point. It included conservative Barry Goldwater, the party's 1964 presidential nominee, and liberal Thomas Dewey, the party's unsuccessful nominee in 1944 and 1948. Former president Eisenhower was critically ill, but made a brief speech remotely from his hospital room.

New York City mayor John Lindsay introduced the keynote speaker, Washington governor Daniel J. Evans. The program also featured Senator Edward W. Brooke of Massachusetts and Gladys O'Donnell, president of the National Federation of Republican Women.

Convention participants from Ohio got special attention. Charles Kurfess, the Republican speaker of the Ohio House of Representatives, led the Pledge of Allegiance to the Flag on the convention's opening day. "Ray took care of Ohio," Kurfess remembered years later. Kurfess savored the experience: "What the hell?" he said. "Have you ever been on national television?"[5]

As national chairman, Bliss had the authority to appoint extra pages at the convention, and he included Thaddeus Garrett Jr., a black high school student from Akron. "I was like a kid in a candy store," Garrett recalled. Pages were supposed to be as invisible as possible at the convention, leaving the spotlight to the party luminaries whom Bliss wanted the public to get to know. Because of his race, Garrett stuck out in the sea of predominantly white faces. Garrett, however, compounded the problem. He couldn't resist seeking autographs from the senators. His supervisor called Garrett aside and said: "I just got a call from the chairman [Bliss] on the platform and he told me to tell you that he sees you on television too much.'"

"That was all that needed to be said to me," said Garrett. "I was back in the shadows for the rest of the convention."[6]

As much as Bliss focused the convention on uniting the party, he could not insulate it from the turbulence in the nation. The Reverend Ralph Abernathy, who had taken over as president of the Southern Christian Leadership Conference after the assassination of Dr. Martin Luther King Jr. earlier that year, led a protest of about sixty-five poor persons, mostly blacks, outside the convention headquarters at the Fontainebleau Hotel on August 6, the second day of the convention. Abernathy said the protestors came from the "51st State of Poverty."

Abernathy, at a press conference, made a pitch for the nomination of New York governor Nelson Rockefeller for president, although he did not formally endorse him and did not expect the Republicans to choose him.[7] Bliss did his best to placate Abernathy and his followers. A Bliss emissary handed Abernathy forty-three tickets to the convention.

"Good news, Hosea," Abernathy shouted to Hosea Williams, an aide. "Forty-three tickets for the poor people." At about 10 P.M. on the day of the protest, Abernathy led the ticketed demonstrators inside the convention hall where they sat for a while in four sections of the spectator area, without causing a stir.[8]

Josephine Good said that Bliss figured out how to get the protesters inside the hall. "I don't know how he [Bliss] did it because every seat was taken. He made arrangements for Abernathy and his party to come in and sit down at the convention. That was a smart thing to do, you know. He personally maneuvered some people, was able to get them to move out of their seats and gave them [Abernathy and the others] good seats....It cooled things down more than created a problem," said Good.[9]

Abernathy associates arrived just in time to hear Senator Everett Dirksen of Illinois ask for the ratification of the 1968 GOP party platform. "Republicans roared approval" when asked to approve the platform Bliss had worked so hard to build.[10]

While Bliss successfully avoided disruption inside the convention hall, riots broke out in Miami Beach and nearby Miami.[11] On the final day of the convention, August 8, racial violence erupted in which three blacks were killed and eighteen persons were injured. The disorder in Miami spread to within a mile of the convention hall. The National Guard was called to quell looting and arson that broke out downtown.

It was a sign of the troubling and confusing time in the nation's history that as the bloody disturbances raged outside, Republican delegates inside the convention hall turned to selecting their presidential ticket.

When the delegates voted, Nixon prevailed on the first ballot, with more delegates than Rockefeller and Reagan combined. In a show of party unity, delegates were allowed to switch their votes to back the winner. Rockefeller and Reagan both endorsed Nixon.

The Ohio delegation, it turned out, missed the boat, voting for favorite son Governor Rhodes on the first ballot. For the second straight convention, Rhodes's behavior had produced controversy. When the convention ended, the Ohio delegates went home to "promote a national ticket they neither asked for nor helped assemble."[12]

However, Nixon's next decision—his choice for a vice-presidential running mate—almost upended the campaign before it started. He chose Maryland governor Spiro T. Agnew. The initial reaction from many of the delegates was "Spiro Who?"

Bliss tried to keep his feelings in check. "He just didn't know much about him [Agnew]," said Peterson. "He just shook his head and didn't comment." According to Peterson, he and Bliss later ran into a top Nixon aide and asked how Agnew had been chosen. The aide told Bliss that Nixon believed that "Reagan was coming on strong." To head off Reagan's charge, Nixon "made a deal" with some of Reagan's potential supporters, including southerners. Bliss, upon hearing the explanation, "just closed his eyes, shook his head and said 'OK,'" Peterson said.[13]

In his acceptance speech, Nixon sought to lift party spirits and to send the faithful back to their communities filled with enthusiasm.

"We're going to win," he said to pandemonium. "And I say let's win one for Ike."[14] On this sentiment, Bliss and Nixon agreed.

Chapter 55

Ray Bliss Keeps His Job

Right after the national convention ended—on August 9, 1968—Ray Bliss was reelected as chairman of the Republican National Committee. Because of Bliss's high party standing, the decision attracted little attention. But this expression of party unity masked tensions between Bliss and Nixon.

Bliss told his version of these events to Ben Maidenburg of the *Akron Beacon Journal.* "About a year before the 1968 Republican convention," Maidenburg wrote, "Bliss started hearing rumblings that he would be replaced before the convention." Members of the Republican National Committee also heard these rumblings and came to Bliss's defense. Governor Henry Bellmon of Oklahoma was upset enough to arrange a meeting in New York with him, Bliss, and Nixon "a couple of months or so" before the convention. The meeting was scheduled for half an hour but went on for an hour and a half instead, Bliss told Maidenburg.

Bellmon asked Nixon: "Do you intend to replace Bliss before the convention?"

"Absolutely not," Nixon replied, according to Maidenburg. "Bliss has done this and that, and accomplished this and that for the party, and I wouldn't dream of replacing him now, or at any time."[1]

A November 1968 news story in the *Akron Beacon Journal* reported a meeting between Nixon and Bliss, this one in July before the convention.[2] The source of the story was Bliss's friends.

"Bliss is keeping his own counsel as to why he was ready to chuck his job nearly five months ago. But conversations with the Akronite's friends make it possible to piece the story together," the story reported. It cast Bliss as the catalyst for his possible departure as national chairman. It said that Bliss had sought the meeting with Nixon after first telling a few associates that he was making arrangements to quit as national chairman and move back to Akron right after the convention.

"He was tired and discouraged," said the story. "Some of what is happening inside the Nixon machine in New York is said to have upset Bliss. Precisely what isn't clear, but Republican fund-raising is believed to be a factor."

Robert Feldkamp had already reported that by July 4, 1968, Bliss had been "angry enough" to make plans to quit. "Bliss associates prevailed, however, and urged him to stay on at least until the inauguration—if the eventual nominee wanted him." Instead of quitting, Bliss met with Nixon and "later told friends there was no question in his mind that Nixon wanted him to stay as chairman, at least for the rest of the year."[3]

Bliss and Nixon agreed that Nixon's personal campaign for president would be run out of New York but that what Bliss called the "broad aspects" of the campaign would be run from national headquarters in Washington, DC.

Presidential candidates, however, do not want and will not permit an independent-minded national party chairman to tell them how to do things, Bliss said in 1974. "I don't agree with the philosophy, but the practical aspects are that in both parties at the national level the candidate picks somebody that will completely be subservient to his interest." This was particularly true with Nixon, Bliss recounted: "I knew Nixon like a book. I'd known him since '48. I knew all his weaknesses, his assets and everything about him. I knew he wouldn't be happy or wouldn't want anybody not totally under his command running his campaign. You've got to recognize the facts of life."

Bliss's role in the Nixon campaign began taking shape. John Mitchell, a top Nixon aide and law partner, soon met Bliss in Washington, DC. "What's your view as to how we should set up the campaign?" Mitchell asked. "Should we move the offices to Washington, keep them in New York or what?"

Bliss saw no benefit in suggesting that the campaign headquarters be moved to Washington, DC. "Well, they had a whole staff of New Yorkers and they were high priced and lived high. Well, I could see all the campaign money going down the drain feeding them if they brought them into Washington. It's simpler to leave 'em in New York," Bliss recalled.

Bliss said he reached an agreement with the Nixon campaign on what his role would be. "I had a minimum of conflict with them because I well knew how he operated, so I took on the areas which they would feel they didn't want to fool with like getting out the votes and running down to St. Louis and meeting with the ward leaders…that type of thing. And getting some money and trying to help out our general array of candidates," Bliss said.[4]

Rumors about Bliss's departure persisted as the convention approached. Sometime after the New York meeting, according to Maidenburg, Mitchell called on Bliss and asked: "Do you plan to quit before the convention?" This angered Bliss. "I'll be goddamned if I'll quit before the convention. I've brought the party this far and I'm going to see it through," the chairman told Mitchell.

The tensions increased at the convention itself. Nixon was unhappy about the behavior of the Ohio delegation. Because he couldn't get first ballot support from the Ohio delegation, Nixon had to "deal" with the southerners more than he wanted to, Bliss told Maidenburg. Otherwise, Nixon feared that California governor Ronald Reagan might gain enough support to deny Nixon the nomination.[5]

Arthur Peterson recalled that toward the end of the convention Nixon supporters "took a sort of straw vote" among national committee members and the support for Bliss was "obvious." The effort to remove Bliss was a "trial balloon," said Peterson. "It fell quickly."[6]

While Bliss was understandably upset by the persistent pressure to resign, it had been common for the party's presidential nominee to name his own national chairman after the convention.[7]

The same day that Bliss was reelected national chairman, he chaired a joint meeting of the Republican National Committee and Republican National Finance Committee on how the party committees, the Nixon presidential campaign, and the national committee would work together during the general election campaign. Nixon and Agnew were in attendance along with key campaign officials John Mitchell, Maurice Stans, and Richard Kleindienst. A press conference followed.[8]

A division of labor had been arranged between the organizations. Nixon's committee would handle scheduling, for example. "They can do it easier than we can do it," said Bliss. "My men wouldn't know whether Nixon wants a breakfast meeting or a dinner meeting. They [Nixon's committee] know all that. They'll handle the agency program on TV and his personal advertising. They'll handle as I see it the public relations that relates directly to the presidency."

Bliss said he "would do what [he had] been doing, the broad aspects of it like building the Party base." Bliss continued: "The arrangements have been discussed but we have to work out the fine details and eliminate duplication between the two committees; that's when arguments start."

Bliss was asked whether he thought "the meshing of these two organizations will go without any hitches."

His answer reflected Bliss's professional approach to politics. "Of course it's like business," he responded, "...you have misunderstandings and problems as you move along and it's all the same in politics; we have to work them out. I've had some experience dealing with parallel organizations in the past and sure you have something develop now and then and have some misunderstandings, but you sit down and say all right this is your area and this is my area. I don't see anything insurmountable about it."

A reporter also asked Bliss if Nixon would have someone specifically assigned to work with the national committee.

"Yes, he's planning to ask Mr. Kleindienst," said Bliss, referring to Richard Kleindienst of Arizona. "He [Kleindienst] was the former state chairman, seven or eight years, of Arizona. He's had the experience on the practical side and in the last two campaigns he's been involved in the delegate side of the campaign. So he will have some understanding of the thinking of party members, which is important."

Bliss also announced that Maurice Stans, who had been Nixon's campaign committee finance chairman, was taking over as chairman of the national Republican Party's Finance Committee, replacing Lucius Clay, who had held the post since 1965.

Nixon and Bliss were prepared as a tough general election campaign began.

Chapter 56

Nixon Wins a Squeaker

The Republicans left Miami Beach unified and organized. In contrast, the divided Democrats experienced further disarray at their national convention in Chicago, August 26–29, 1968. Inside the convention hall, the Democrats nominated Vice President Hubert Humphrey, even though he had not competed in a single primary. He chose Senator Edward Muskie of Maine as his running mate. Outside the hall, protesters and police clashed, generating disturbing images broadcast on television. The 1968 Chicago convention was as much a public relations disaster for the Democrats as the 1964 San Francisco convention had been for the GOP.[1]

A wild card was the American Independent Party and its presidential ticket of former Alabama governor George C. Wallace and retired air force general Curtis LeMay. After the 1964 election, some conservatives had advocated for a separate conservative party instead of sticking with the Republicans. Now they had another choice. It was unclear whether the new party hurt Democrats or Republicans more.[2]

Nixon enjoyed a big lead in the public opinion polls over Humphrey as the fall campaign began, with Wallace a distant third.[3]

Nixon campaigned on behalf of the "silent majority" and the grievances of Americans troubled by racial, cultural, and economic change and the resulting unrest. He argued for "law and order," criticized "Great Society" social programs, and claimed he had a "secret plan" to end the Vietnam War. Nixon's vice-presidential running mate,

Spiro Agnew, soon became controversial. Agnew used ethnic slurs and made disparaging comments about big cities—"If you've seen one slum, you've seen them all." Agnew attacked the news media, calling reporters "nattering nabobs of negativism."

After Labor Day, George Wallace began to gather steam, showing appeal not only in the South but also among working-class whites in the North. Wallace claimed there wasn't "a dime's worth of difference" between the major political parties. He demanded an end to racial desegregation, attacked the counterculture, and espoused aggressive military action to win the Vietnam War. Wallace's running mate, General Curtis LeMay, provoked controversy by advocating the use of tactical nuclear weapons in Vietnam. But Wallace also defended New Deal social programs, such as Social Security.

Hubert Humphrey had been seeking the presidency for as long as Nixon and was a seasoned campaigner. The Democrat rallied the party in defense of civil rights, the Great Society, and the New Deal. Humphrey staked out his own positions on the Vietnam War, and tried to separate himself from President Johnson. He declared his willingness to end the bombing of North Vietnam as part of peace negotiations to end the war.

Then on October 31, President Johnson announced that the United States would stop bombing North Vietnam. This "October surprise"—less than a week before election day—angered Nixon, who accused the administration of playing politics with the war. Soon afterward, Senator Eugene McCarthy, a leader of the antiwar Democrats, endorsed Humphrey.

As suspense built, Bliss kept busy doing all he could to keep Nixon and the Republicans ahead. Nixon was aware of what Bliss was doing and appreciated the national chairman's skills, said Herbert G. Klein, who was a senior member of Nixon's 1968 campaign team. "He always regarded Ray Bliss as the ultimate of a professional workman in the political field. He was the blue collar mechanic who could put any kind of organization together," said Klein.[4]

Klein recalled that after Nixon won the nomination, Bliss came to New York for Saturday morning campaign meetings and also met with the leaders of a Nixon-Agnew citizens' group set up to appeal to dissident Democrats and independents. Bliss advised Nixon to continue his heavy use of television right up to election eve and joined those who counseled Nixon to stay away from televised debates with Humphrey.[5]

At Nixon's request, Bliss personally visited several large cities to supervise final get-out-the-vote drives, including Cleveland, Philadelphia, Chicago, St. Louis, Los Angeles, Boston, and Detroit. He had not forgotten the lesson he had tried to teach the Republican Party with his Big City report. "In 1960 we lost some of the large electoral-vote states by very narrow margins because we lost the big cities there by big margins," Bliss told reporters. "The job is to lift our strength in Republican areas and reduce our loss ratio, as I call it, in the big cities," he explained during an interview in mid-October.[6]

There was another reason besides getting out the vote for visiting big cities, Bliss told a separate news conference in Cleveland. He wanted to make sure that Republicans didn't become the victim of ballot fraud. There had been reports in 1960 in Chicago, for example, that voting totals had been manipulated to favor Democrat John F. Kennedy. There had been "allegations," Bliss said, that not all the votes for Nixon had been "properly counted."[7]

The key to preventing fraud was manning every precinct with observers, Bliss said. "In 1960, we had thousands of precincts unmanned across the nation." He declined to single out Chicago for special attention at the news conference, not wanting to alienate any Democrats who might be considering a vote for Nixon.[8]

Bliss made sure that Ohio, always a battleground in presidential elections, got special attention. A 247-mile Nixon train caravan through the state in late October was said to be Bliss's idea. Nixon was believed to be ahead in Ohio before the train expedition, but Bliss said it would help his image by putting him "closer to the people" as the campaign came to a close.[9]

For his work, Bliss had a permanent staff of 145 and about 50 part-time employees. His budget was a little less than $3 million, but Bliss said he would end up spending less than that. The national committee also made $1 million available to the Nixon campaign after the Republican convention in August.[10]

On election night, Bliss, known for his caution, turned into an optimist. "I'm confident Richard Nixon is going to be elected," Bliss said from party headquarters in Washington, DC, shortly after midnight. Two hours later, after several rounds of telephone calls, he made the same call, but added: "But boy it's a squeaker."[11]

Years later Bliss recalled his election night projections.[12] By 4:30 A.M. on Wednesday, November 6, the television stations still were saying the outcome of the election was in doubt. A newscaster from ABC, an old friend, called Bliss and asked, "Ray, would you give us a projection on the outcome?"

"Certainly," answered Bliss, who predicted a Nixon win. He went down some of the states where the results still were in doubt for the newscaster—Illinois, Missouri, and California. Bliss had been receiving his own reports from these and other states. In Illinois, for example, he knew that the downstate vote for Nixon had been heavy, offsetting the Democratic advantage in Chicago.

Bliss contrasted his accurate projections with John Mitchell's inability to call the outcome. "Meanwhile, Mitchell was fiddling around," Bliss said in 1974. "Poor

John Mitchell, he didn't even know what a precinct committeeman was. That was his problem. He was fiddling around with palatial New York headquarters stuff…ducking all over the lot about the big outcome issues."

Nixon won on November 5, 1968, but the margin was very close.[13] He received 43.4 percent of the popular vote, while Humphrey got 42.7 percent and Wallace 13.5 percent. Although Nixon received a lower percentage of the popular vote than when he lost to John F. Kennedy in 1960, his vote margin was about five times greater than Kennedy's was in 1960—some 500,000 ballots in 1968 versus about 100,000 eight years before.

However, Nixon won the Electoral College with 301 votes, about the same number as Kennedy received in 1960. Humphrey received 191 votes, while Wallace got 46 from the southern states of Alabama, Arkansas, Georgia, Louisiana, and Mississippi—the same number (but not from all the same places) that Goldwater won in 1964. On balance, the Wallace vote hurt Humphrey more than Nixon, helping Nixon carry all the other southern states except Texas, the home state of President Johnson. But had Humphrey and Wallace won states with 32 more electoral votes between them, they would have denied Nixon the 270 he needed to win. That would have thrown the election into the Democrat-controlled House of Representatives.

Analyst Victor Riesel traced the origins of Nixon's win in 1968 back to the Big City report. "The plan called for slicing into Democratic control of the nation's 10 biggest megalopolises.…Nixon and Bliss believed they needed only to take anywhere from 5 to 10 percent more big-city votes than they did in 1960," wrote Riesel. In big city after big city, Nixon vastly increased the Republican presidential vote over what Barry Goldwater had received in 1964. "Bliss is especially proud of his siege of Richard Daley's bailiwick," wrote Riesel.[14] Goldwater had lost Chicago by 674,000 votes; Nixon narrowed that to 390,000. Nixon carried Illinois, among the 44 states Goldwater had lost in 1964.

Much to Bliss's disappointment, the GOP gained just five seats in the US House of Representatives.[15] Votes for Nixon or Wallace did not translate into votes for Republican congressional candidates in many districts, especially in the South. In some states, such as Ohio, court-ordered redistricting ended up helping the Democrats.

The Republicans did pick up five seats in the US Senate. Bliss must have been pleased by the departure of Democrat Frank Lausche from the Senate. Lausche, the incumbent, lost the primary to challenger John Gilligan of Cincinnati. Then Bliss's old friend Republican Bill Saxbe defeated Gilligan in the general election.

Bliss was satisfied with the overall outcome. "When I became chairman in 1965, I was asked if we could survive as a force in the nation," Bliss recalled in a postelection interview. "In my fondest dreams I didn't visualize that we would be knocking on the door of the White House in 1968. Now we have elected a president. It's phenomenal."[16]

Bliss talked about how rebuilding the party had helped win the election. The issues had benefited Nixon, Bliss conceded, but he ticked off party activities that made a difference too: registering voters and getting them to the polls; ballot security; seminars for campaign managers, research, and public relations workers; data processing and information retrieval machines; use of "truth squads" to check on what opponents were saying and to provide the Republican view; programs to attract youth and ethnic voters to the Republican side; and providing tapes and slides of Republicans and Republican messages to two thousand radio and TV stations. A radio or TV reporter could dial a national committee number and have a recording fed to him or her that was ready for use in a newscast.

"The coordination was better than in any other campaign in my memory.... Nixon did his share. We did our share. The people in the precincts did their share.... That produces victory," the national chairman said.

Despite his positive public comments, Bliss privately harbored concern about helping Nixon win. Returning home after election night, Bliss told his wife: "I don't know whether I did the country a service or a disservice."[17]

Ray Bliss (left) and Barry Goldwater (second from right), 1965. Bliss became national chairman with the backing of defeated GOP presidential candidate Barry Goldwater, his vice-presidential running mate William Miller (second from left), and his national chairman, Dean Burch (right). (Courtesy of the *Akron Beacon Journal*)

National Chairman Ray Bliss, 1965. The moment Bliss (left) was elected chairman of the Republican National Committee, along with his wife, Ellen Bliss (center). (From the Ray C. Bliss Papers. Courtesy of Archival Services, University Libraries, The University of Akron)

Ray Bliss (left) and John Andrews (right), 1965. After working with Bliss for many years, Andrews succeeded Bliss as Ohio GOP chairman. (From the Ray C. Bliss Papers. Courtesy of Archival Services, University Libraries, The University of Akron)

Dark days for the GOP, 1965. Ray Bliss's (center) first news conference after becoming national chairman, where he outlined his plans to rebuild the GOP. (Courtesy of the Ohio History Connection [P391])

Ray (top) and Ellen (bottom) Bliss, 1965. Candid snapshots of the Blisses shortly after Ray became Republican National Chairman. (From the Ray C. Bliss Papers. Courtesy of Archival Services, University Libraries, The University of Akron)

Salute to Ray Bliss, 1965. A poster advertising simultaneous fundraising held in Ohio cities to raise funds for the Republican National Committee shortly after Bliss became national chairman. (From the Ray C. Bliss Papers. Courtesy of Archival Services, University Libraries, The University of Akron)

Ray Bliss (left) and Arthur Peterson (right), 1966. Political scientist Peterson worked for Bliss in Ohio and at the Republican National Committee in Washington, DC. (From the Ray C. Bliss Papers. Courtesy of Archival Services, University Libraries, The University of Akron)

Ray Bliss (front center) and the GOP congressional leadership, 1966. Following a pattern set in Akron and Columbus, Ohio, Bliss meet regularly with the congressional leadership as national chairman. (From the Ray C. Bliss Papers. Courtesy of Archival Services, University Libraries, The University of Akron)

Democrat Hubert H. Humphrey, 1968. Vice President Humphrey visits with children in Elizabeth Park while campaigning in Akron. (Photo by Opie Evans. From the Opie Evans Papers. Courtesy of Archival Services, University Libraries, The University of Akron)

Ray Bliss and Richard Nixon, 1968. Bliss worked hard to elect Republican Nixon to the White House in 1968. But soon after the election, Nixon sought to remove Bliss as national chairman. (AP Photo/Charles Tasnadi)

Chapter 57

Rumors Spread: "Bliss Is Out!"

On Sunday, November 17, 1968, an *Associated Press* news story reported "President-elect Richard Nixon is considering replacing National Chairman Ray Bliss in an overhaul of the Republican party organization." Written by Jack Bell, a political journalist on friendly terms with Bliss, the story cited "associates of Nixon."[1]

Ray Bliss later told Ben Maidenburg his version of the story: "About the third Sunday after the election, Bliss was in his office in Washington, and with him several staff people, and they brought in a copy of the Washington paper, on the front page of which was an article by Jack Bell....It said Bliss was to be fired." Later that same day, Nixon aide Herbert Klein, appearing on *Meet the Press*, predicted that Nixon would clean out the "old hands," reinforcing the Bell story.[2]

Bliss was troubled by these reports, but perhaps not surprised.[3] William Vance of the *Akron Beacon Journal* later reported: "The vision that danced before Ray's thick-lensed glasses was one of John Bailey, the 'paper' chairman of the Democratic Party during the Kennedy-Johnson years."[4]

As national chairman, Bailey took his orders from the White House. Bliss and his wife once saw Bailey and his wife at a Washington, DC, cocktail party. "Ray, you are getting along wonderful," Bliss recalled Bailey telling him. "You're winning. My advice to you is never have a president."[5]

Years later Bliss discussed the difference between being the local and state GOP chairman and being national chairman. As Summit County GOP chairman, "the [Akron] mayor was the man I selected and everybody knew it....I applied the same theory at a state level."[6] The system worked because Bliss for the most part controlled the playing field: candidates for local and state offices had separate campaign committees that were subordinate to the party committees—headed by Bliss.

Conditions were different for a president and a national chairman. The president had to run a national campaign with his own committee, political advisers, and financial backers. Such an organization rivaled the influence of the party committee. Once in office, a president made political decisions and appointments important to Republicans in all fifty states. Members of the national committee deferred to the White House, not the national chairman, because they "might want a federal job or they might want to get their nephew a job," Bliss said.

Such deference limited the national chairman's authority. "The national chairman was just a figurehead that the president picked and he sat over there and was handling, you know, shining shoes for people and so on. Those were the facts of life," said Bliss. "He's an errand boy for the president of the United States."

Although it had been difficult, Bliss had found a way to work with Richard Nixon during the campaign, but now he faced a stiffer challenge. The president-elect wanted a new national chairman. Just two days after the 1968 election, Nixon told his aides that Bliss was one of the Republican leaders who would "have to go."[7] Herbert Klein recalled that the actual decision to replace Bliss had been made during the fall campaign.[8]

But according to John Sears, a Nixon campaign aide, Bliss's fate had been sealed two years earlier. "Nixon wanted him replaced ever since 1966 because he [Bliss] had refused to give Nixon a plane as he campaigned for congressional candidates. That was the genesis of it. You know everybody understood that if Nixon won he was going to get replaced." Nixon was sensitive to such slights. "Nixon was quick to think that everybody was against him," said Sears. "Certainly Bliss qualified by what happened in '66."[9]

According to Sears, Nixon and his advisers also wanted a different kind of chairman: "I think there was a feeling that now that we had the presidency we should get someone who could be more of a public relations, out-front kind of person." In Bliss's terms, Nixon wanted a "speaking chairman," not an "office chairman."

Democrats still controlled both houses of Congress, and Republicans needed someone outside the White House to make the president's case, said Sears. "He [Nixon] wanted to stand above the battle and so you think you need somebody in a place like the national chairmanship who can speak in a more political vein," Sears added.

After the election, the Nixon camp quickly settled on a "two-chairman" plan for the Republican National Committee, with a "name chairman" as a spokesman for the White House and the party, and a second "purely political mechanic" to run day-to-day operations.[10]

The person to fill the "mechanic" spot was quickly identified as Murray Chotiner, a longtime Nixon campaign adviser. There was more debate on the "spokesman" position. The initial choice was Bud Wilkinson, a former University of Oklahoma football coach and sportscaster.[11]

Another issue was how to deal with Bliss. Nixon asked his aides to "find out what Bliss wants" in terms of a patronage job so Bliss could be moved elsewhere. No one knew what post might satisfy Bliss.[12] Despite having no strategy, the Nixon team began a campaign to pressure Bliss into resigning.

On November 18, John Mitchell, Nixon's campaign manager, was directed to talk with Bliss immediately "in view of the Bell story," published the day before.[13] Mitchell contacted Bliss, Maidenburg reported, in person and by telephone: "By now, Bliss was really wrought up. He told Mitchell: 'You tell Dick that I'll resign when I choose. If he tries to force me out, then I'll take it to the national committee.'"[14]

Based on his experience with Nixon, Bliss decided he would "just sit tight" and see what happened next.

Much of the discussion in the Nixon camp was summarized in a memo by Sears, dated November 22, 1968. Addressed to Nixon, the memo called for a sweeping presidential takeover of the Republican National Committee as well as the Republican US House and Senate campaign committees and the Republican Governors Association. "The power and authority of the Presidency must be brought to bear on the National Committee to completely remodel it, both in terms of personnel and function," wrote Sears. Sears agreed with the two-chairman plan, but foresaw political resistance: "It must be expected that this will generate a certain amount of internal dissension in the party itself."[15]

Like a number of Nixon's aides, Sears displayed little respect for Bliss's political skills—many Nixon operatives referred to Bliss as "old nuts and bolts."[16] But Sears acknowledged support for Bliss among party loyalists. "Ray Bliss, while he certainly can't win any confrontations with RN [Nixon], has a few cards to play. Quite wrongly, most of the state chairmen believe that he has done a good job and see no reason to replace him. He has cultivated their loyalty assiduously against the time when someone might try to replace him." But Sears was uncertain about how to remove Bliss. "Were he a different kind of fellow, we could kick him upstairs somewhere, but I can't think of any place where he could do a decent job."[17]

Richard Kleindienst, the Nixon campaign's liaison with the Republican National Committee in 1968, wrote a related memo on how to replace Bliss.[18] The best solution, wrote Kleindienst, would be a "voluntary resignation" after "a meeting with an emissary from the President-elect." If that didn't happen, the next step would be a resolution from a member of the Republican National Committee declaring the chairmanship vacant, with a follow-up motion deferring to Nixon:

"I move that the senior member of the Committee in years of age appoint a committee of five persons to wait upon the President-Elect for the purpose of determining his wishes as to the designation of a suitable person to be elected as Chairman of the RNC."

Kleindienst also detailed what the new chairman should be like—and the description did not fit Bliss: "I believe that the new Chairman, in addition to being loyal and compatible with the President, should project youthfulness and dynamic-articulated vigor. Within the next four years, young people are going to be more and more politically significant and the persons of the 'old politics' (such as myself) are going to be less and less significant."

The best time for changing leaders, Kleindienst argued, would be about the same time Nixon was inaugurated on January 20. "First, it would coincide with the new administration. Second, if removal became controversial, it would be submerged in the other events and festivities of the Inauguration." The next best time would be six months later—in June—at the end of the "so-called 'honeymoon period' of the new administration." Bliss, Kleindienst wrote, did not want to resign by January 20 "for reasons solely of personal image and pride."

Kleindienst did not anticipate a fight with Bliss, but was uncertain. "He would be foolish not to do so [resign] upon request. Whether he would openly resist is a matter of conjecture." Kleindienst urged immediate action, arguing that Bliss would not engage in an "open contest" with Nixon, but instead would pursue "a contest of confusion and indecision."

The word of Bliss's likely ouster set the national rumor mill spinning. A number of stories followed, based on information from "unnamed sources," but clearly close to the president-elect.

One account appeared on November 18 in the *New York Daily News*, headlined with the kind of play on words that made the tabloid popular in the nation's largest city: "Nixon May Kiss Off Bliss for a More-Blistery Boss."[19] The story left Bliss dangling at Nixon's mercy.

"The question of whether to replace Bliss, a nuts and bolts pro, and bring in a more commanding figure who could generate greater interest has not yet been resolved, sources here indicated." The anonymous sources allowed Nixon to distance himself from the report of Bliss's possible demise. The story said, "A Nixon spokesman said that the report of the possible departure of Bliss is a speculative one and that there would be no comment on it."

Although Bliss was said to be "upset and mystified" by the rumors, he avoided public comment. The spokesman at Republican headquarters, Fred Morrison, had little to say about Bliss's future other than "I don't know." Nixon's team did nothing to quell the rumors. Ronald Ziegler, a Nixon press aide, said, instead, that "nothing would be served" by discussing Bliss's future.[20]

Bliss had public defenders, including Jim Fain, editor of the *Dayton Daily News*. Although the newspaper tended to endorse Democratic candidates, Fain and Bliss respected each other. Fain may have presented some of Bliss's views.

On November 19, right after the rumors started, Fain wrote: "The reason Nixon may want Bliss out is simple: Nixon likes to run his own political machinery and Bliss is nobody's stooge. This motive had nothing to do with effectiveness; it has to do merely with who is in charge." Dismissing the idea that Nixon wanted a more effective national committee, Fain wrote, "Bliss is the super-technician of politics. He is the most effective nuts-and-bolts man in the politics business. Nixon, a connoisseur of such things, knows that." If Nixon wanted Bliss out, Bliss would go willingly. "He has run the course pretty well in politics and would not mind a quieter life," Fain wrote.[21]

But instead of asking Bliss for his resignation, the Nixon team continued the soap opera. At a November 20 meeting, they discussed seeking to "build up some counter-heat to Bliss" and the need to "move on Bliss." But a week later, they were still debating what kind of job could be offered to Bliss.[22]

As Sears's and Kleindienst's memos had anticipated, the rumors of Bliss's ouster generated a strongly negative reaction. After Jack Bell's November 17 article, according to Maidenburg: "Bliss started getting phone calls from all over the country. He was urged to stick it out and that if Nixon tried to fire him, the committee would back Bliss to the hilt."[23]

On December 6, columnists Rowland Evans and Robert Novak described a broad "backlash" against Nixon. "The backlash has encompassed pro-Bliss state chairmen, national committeemen, governors, members of Congress, and other Republican notables," said the column. "Telegrams of protest from party leaders such as these are cascading into Nixon's Pierre Hotel headquarters on Fifth Avenue."[24]

Evans and Novak told of a Republican state chairman who had slipped into Washington, DC, to meet with Bliss. The chairman told Bliss that he and others would stand by him and urged him not to buckle under to Nixon. "Bliss replied that he had no intention of resigning—even though, he [Bliss] added, that was precisely what the Nixon-inspired leaks were trying to accomplish."

The columnists also reported that an unnamed Republican governor asked if Bliss would mind "if a quiet campaign to retain him were started?" In response, "Bliss hemmed and hawed a bit, sucking on a chain-smoked cigarette, then said that, although he himself naturally couldn't take part in such a campaign, he would have no objections."

Other GOP leaders were more vocal. Wisconsin Chairman Ody Fish, head of the GOP state chairmen's organization, was described as "almost beside himself with anger." Don Ross, the Nebraska national committeeman who had helped engineer Bliss's election as national chairman in 1965, said simply that Nixon "can't be serious."[25]

Bliss got strong backing from Ohio. "The general reaction is that it is unfair to treat Bliss in this manner after a period of years in which he brought the party to the point where a candidate like Nixon could step in and win," said Summit County GOP chairman D. E. "Gene" Waddell. Ohio Republican chairman John Andrews said he "surely would hope Ray will be kept" as national chairman. Ohio governor James Rhodes—who did not always see eye to eye with Bliss—said that the national chairman had "done an outstanding job." Ohio secretary of state Ted W. Brown said, "Any Republican candidate who has gone through a general election with Bliss as the leader—statewide or nationally—could not help but realize his abilities and qualifications as a producer." Brown added, "The party owes him a debt of gratitude."[26]

Ohio millionaire developer and sportsman John Galbreath—one of the Ohio Republicans whom Bliss had dressed down after they backed the ill-fated right-to-work initiative in 1958—was said to be angry with Nixon, as was Cleveland restaurateur Vernon Stouffer. Both were major contributors to Nixon's campaign.[27]

Evans and Novak concluded that backlash from Republicans revealed "shocking hostility for their own brand-new president." Even Nixon's advisers admitted (privately) that they had blundered: "While these Nixon men agree with his [Nixon's] plan to find a more articulate, telegenic national chairman than old-pro technician Bliss could ever be, they admit Nixon blundered in leaking his intentions." The Nixon camp was still searching for a way to remove Bliss.[28]

In the midst of this controversy, Bliss maintained a public silence, even when he came back to Akron in early December to oversee election recounts as a member of the Summit County Board of Elections.

"I'm just not discussing it," Bliss said of his future as chairman. "I'm not saying I won't discuss it eventually, but at this point I'm just not saying anything about it." Bliss stuck to this position as he headed out to the Republican Governors Association conference in Palm Springs, California. "Yes," Bliss said softly. "I'm just not discussing it."[29]

In another memo to Nixon, Sears anticipated trouble from Bliss at the Republican governors' meeting: "Ray Bliss will speak to the governors on Saturday (December 7) for about 45 minutes. No one seems to know exactly what he expects to say to them. There is speculation that he will try to get a resolution passed, but the governors are requesting that he be kept on as National Chairman of the Republican Party. If this appears to be the case by tomorrow, we shall get a couple of our friends to submarine the resolution on the grounds that the National Chairmanship is a matter that is entirely up to the President."[30]

Some governors backed Bliss. Governor Tom McCall of Oregon said that he did not understand "how a man who has been successful in electing a president should be thrown out on his ear." But California governor Ronald Reagan had a different view. While Bliss had done a "wonderful job," Reagan made it clear that "if Nixon wants a replacement, he will get no real argument out of the governors."[31]

Just as Sears had proposed, a resolution supporting Bliss was set aside. One report noted: "The ostensible reason is that this might seem an improper interference with the prerogative of President-elect Richard M. Nixon to name a national chairman on his own.... In the background, however, is the fact that Bliss had not been supportive enough of the effort by Republican governors to influence the 1968 party platform."[32]

The same story reported that Bliss had "quietly put into motion a campaign" to keep his job. Without consulting Nixon, he rescheduled a February meeting of the Republican National Committee to January 17, 1969, in Washington, DC—just three days before the presidential inauguration on January 20.[33]

At the time, Bliss maintained it would just be a "regular" meeting to discuss the election results. But he later told Maidenburg that he scheduled the meeting of the national committee "on purpose," just to show the Nixon camp that he wasn't going to be "tossed out."[34]

The public sparring continued after the Republican governors' meeting. Akron congressman Bill Ayres predicted that Bliss would stay as chairman "as long as he wants the job." Ayres had been talking to Nixon aides in New York.[35] Ayres said he told them that a "nuts and bolts" chairman like Bliss would be more helpful in the long run to members of Congress and other Republican office seekers than would the younger, public relations type of chairman Nixon was said to be seeking as Bliss's replacement.

On December 9, Nixon aide Herbert Klein appeared again on *Meet the Press* and, when asked about Bliss's status, said Bliss "has not had a discussion with the President-elect and therefore there has been no decision on whether he will be kept or not. A lot will depend on how the national committee will be restructured. A decision will have to be reached either way in January."[36]

The struggle continued in the New Year. In yet another memo to Nixon, dated January 2, Sears reported that "friends of Bliss" had been asked to approach the chairman about leaving, including Congressman Ayres. The memo said the message to Bliss was clear: "It would be a mistake to fight [Nixon] over the Chairmanship and that all such a fight would produce is disunity in the Party with little real hope that Ray would be kept on as National Chairman." Furthermore, the memo said, Bliss "should stop directing press attention to the situation and stop encouraging members of the National Committee and those holding public office to call and write the Nixon people, urging them to retain him."[37]

Not all Bliss's friends urged an early exit. According to Alex Arshinkoff, Everett Dirksen of Illinois, the Republican leader in the US Senate, told Bliss, "If you can hold on until June, you'll be fine."[38]

On January 3, Robert Feldkamp of the *Akron Beacon Journal* reported that Bliss was digging in his heels. "Among his friends," wrote Feldkamp, "Bliss' stubborn streak is well-known." Nixon's silence had strengthened Bliss's resolve to keep his job instead of resigning as a matter of course after the inauguration. "And while he could still find himself out of a job next month," reported Feldkamp, "Bliss won't go quietly."[39]

As Kleindienst's memo had warned, the soap opera had reached a state of "confusion and indecision."[40] Only Nixon himself could resolve it.

Chapter 58

A Meeting at the Pierre Hotel

As the backlash over ousting Ray Bliss intensified, Bryce Harlow offered to help. Nicknamed "Mr. Integrity," Harlow had served in the Eisenhower White House and now was on Nixon's staff. Harlow and Bliss were good friends, having worked together in Ohio politics when Harlow was the lobbyist for Cincinnati-based Procter & Gamble.[1]

Harlow conferred with John Sears, the Nixon campaign aide, and presented a new approach for removing Bliss in a memo to Nixon dated December 2, 1968. It began by agreeing with the president-elect's goal: "The National chairman must be one with whom you can work satisfactorily and will perform the 'spokesman' role you desire; obviously, therefore, Ray Bliss must be replaced."[2]

However, the timing of the move would be "critically important," Harlow wrote. "If this is done before the Inauguration (Jan. 20)...the resentments that you kindle will be, we believe, severe and very harmful to you. We strongly urge that this matter be so handled as not to injure you."

Forcing the two-chairman team of Bud Wilkinson (as public spokesman) and Murray Chotiner (as inside mechanic) on the Republican National Committee immediately "will blow the lid off," Harlow warned. "I am gravely concerned over the likely adverse reactions."

To reduce negative fallout, Harlow recommended that Nixon and Bliss have a face-to-face meeting. Nixon could then explain to Bliss "the circumstances that have arisen, assure him of your determination that his replacement will be done in a way that will protect him from personal embarrassment, and that he should then meet with the press and lay to rest the stories that he is being forced out." Harlow offered to "lay the groundwork" for such a meeting by talking with Bliss. He thought Bliss might exit by February 1969 or shortly thereafter.

Given Nixon's sensitivity to slights, Harlow went out of his way to establish his good intentions: "I regret the feeling of compulsion that prompts me to send this memorandum when I feel sure you will not be pleased by what it says. I do feel, however, that I owe it to you to report frankly when I am convinced that an action that is about to be taken can be very harmful to you. This is such an instance."

By mid-December, Nixon had accepted Harlow's suggestion, with specific "guidelines." One was finding an appropriate patronage job for Bliss, such as an ambassadorship. Another guideline was for Harlow to tell Bliss he had to go.[3]

"During the first Nixon term," reported Lamar Alexander, then an aide to Harlow and later a US senator from Tennessee, "when it was time to fire Ray Bliss…they sent Bryce to do it." Harlow became the "emissary of the president-elect" that Richard Kleindienst had recommended in his November 1968 memo.[4]

Harlow and Bliss had dinner in Washington, DC, on December 16. In a December 19, 1968, memo to H. R. "Bob" Haldeman, Nixon's top aide, Harlow outlined Bliss's conditions for leaving the job.

Bliss believed that he was entitled to stay as chairman through the January 20 presidential inauguration and be "accorded the consideration traditionally accorded to the Party Chairman." If those conditions weren't met, trouble awaited. "If it is desired to remove him before Inauguration, he will fight it—'win, lose, or draw.' His belief is that such an issue should not be joined; he cannot see why anyone would wish to." After the inauguration, "he seeks only to find a graceful exit," Harlow explained. "He repeated a number of times that all he wants is not to go out of office with 'his tail between his legs.'"

"My opinion is that at the earliest practical date [Nixon] should request Bliss to come in for a meeting," wrote Harlow. "I recommend an absolutely candid discussion, kept as friendly as possible, then set in motion graceful procedures by which Bliss can depart in reasonable time without a confrontation."

Harlow also reported that Bliss showed "little interest" in an ambassadorship.[5]

According to Maidenburg, Bliss's own version of the December meeting matched Harlow's memo.[6]

Bliss told Harlow what he had said to John Mitchell earlier—that he would resign when he chose, and if Nixon pushed things, he would make a fight out of it before the national committee.

Harlow later described his role in the effort to force Bliss out. "I was very close to Bliss. That is why they picked me to plunge in the sword. The news almost broke his heart. I suffered with him. I virtually forced the President to see him. I had Ray come to New York to the President's office."[7]

It took a few weeks to set up the New York meeting. For one thing, Nixon was not quite ready. "I talked to Bryce," Nixon told his aides in a December 31 meeting. "Our ducks are not in a row yet, so will talk to Bliss later." Haldeman's notes from a New Year's Day meeting read, "Don't meet with Bliss until the deal is ready."[8] But Nixon was soon ready to get Bliss out of the job, as he indicated in a January 7 memo to Haldeman: "It is imperative that we move on the Bliss matter this week. If we let it drag until the Inauguration [January 20] he will just stay on because we do not have an alternative."[9]

On January 2, Sears wrote to Nixon, stressing Bliss's pride: "Bliss is mainly concerned with saving face and will not fight over the chairmanship if a way can be found for him to make his exit which will not be embarrassing to him." Bliss wanted to leave the job on his own terms. Sears noted: "Bliss wants very much to be given great credit for the success of the party over the last four years and, if he is to retire from office, to have it done in such a way that it appears to be his decision rather than ours."[10]

The rest of Sears's January 2 memo offered detailed recommendations on how a Nixon-Bliss meeting should proceed.

In "Phase I" of the conversation, Nixon was to compliment Bliss on the recovery of the party during the last four years. He should discuss the Republican Coordinating Committee, which would "make Bliss happy because he views the Republican Coordinating Committee as his invention and the instrument through which unity was obtained." He should also solicit Bliss's advice on national committee operations.

The compliments were to be just a warm-up. "All of this shouldn't be more than 15 minutes and is geared to soften him [Bliss] up for Phase II."

In "Phase II," Nixon was to politely tell Bliss that a new type of national chairman was needed. Sears provided Nixon with a detailed script for breaking the news: "Ray, this National Committee situation has been a hard thing for me to think through. If we had gained control of the Congress, there would have been no problem since the Administration would have the necessary spokesmen to sell itself and the

Party to the people.... Therefore I have no alternative but to use the National Chairmanship as a means of supplying this partisan aspect."

Then Nixon should raise the possibility of a new job for Bliss. "Of course, I would very much like to have you join the Administration and be available on an informal basis to advise me on the affairs of the party."

Nixon was to pause and wait for Bliss to respond.

Sears assumed that Bliss would agree to leave because "this is as close as he wishes to come to being fired," and that he would ask about what jobs were available.

The memo also discussed how to handle Bliss's departure publicly.

"RN [Nixon] should make it clear at the outset that he would not wish the public or anyone else to think that Bliss was being asked to resign and that in any event, it would be only right for everyone to understand that Ray's staying or leaving was a matter of his [Bliss's] decision."

Sears suggested that Bliss and Nixon issue separate statements after the meeting. Neither would say that Bliss was leaving the job.

Bliss's statement would say that he had met with Nixon for "about an hour" and discussed the Republican Party and its future. Nixon was very appreciative of Bliss's "service to date," Bliss would say, and offered him the option of staying as chairman or taking a job in the administration. Bliss would also say he wanted to consider a third alternative, returning to his insurance business in Ohio.

Bliss would conclude by saying he wanted to make this decision "in private" during his "first vacation in four years" after the inauguration. He would then report his choice to the president and the public.

In his statement, Nixon would make parallel points, praising Bliss's service and record, and noting that Bliss would soon report his choice among the three options. Nixon would end by saying: "I know it will be a difficult one for him to make, I shall only be unhappy that he cannot do all three."

Like Harlow, Sears foresaw a positive ending. "In late February, Bliss can return from sabbatical, make his decision to join the Administration (or hopefully retire) public, endorse his successor, and fly away." As a possible sweetener, Sears suggested that Nixon participate in a dinner honoring Bliss's service to the party. "It is odd, but these things mean a great deal to Bliss and they don't really cost us anything."

Sears urged "utmost secrecy" about the plan: "If none of us violate this, he [Bliss] should cooperate since I am sure that he will not wish to embarrass himself by owning up to the fact he's being dumped."

The Nixon camp may not have accepted all of Sears's recommendations, but subsequent events seemed to follow the script fairly closely. The point about Bliss's pride was widely recognized. H. R. Haldeman, Nixon's top aide, noted this point in a January 8 memo to John Ehrlichman, another Nixon aide: "One of the hang ups of Ray Bliss is that he is most anxious to be accorded the customary courtesies of the National Chairman at the inaugural. He says that these include sitting in the Presidential box at the parade, and going with the President to all of the Inaugural balls, and being presented there.... In view of our efforts to work out the other problems, it probably would be wise to accord him these courtesies, if at all possible."[11]

Nixon and Bliss finally met on January 10 at the Pierre Hotel, Nixon's temporary headquarters in New York City. Harlow and press aide Ron Ziegler were in attendance. There is no transcript of the hotel meeting, but some of what happened can be pieced together from later reports.

The meeting wasn't announced until a few minutes before Bliss arrived and was billed as a discussion of inaugural plans and "general party matters." Evans and Novak later wrote that Nixon, Bliss, and Harlow talked politics for two hours—a longer meeting than Sears had anticipated.[12]

In an interview years later, Harlow described the meeting, and it appears that Nixon used at least part of Sears's script. "Ray, it is not because of you, you know that," Nixon said. "We have spent our lives together in politics." Nixon went on: "It is because we've got to get someone now who is a hard hitting partisan speaker...and it is going to have to be the chairman of the National Committee."[13]

"You are not that kind of a chairman," added Nixon, "you do nuts and bolts, put it together and make it work. You've been great at that, but now we have to get someone who can drive home the issues, attack the Democrats, fight the problems, and that is not how you do business."

Maidenburg's account from Bliss also reveals part of Sears's script: Bliss said that Nixon thanked him for his hard work, and said, "I think you deserve the best and I'm ready to offer you anything you like."[14]

"Like what?" Bliss asked—much as Sears's script had anticipated. Nixon offered Bliss the chairmanship of any regulatory commission or an ambassadorship "to most any country in the world," Bliss said. Harlow confirmed the offer of an ambassadorship—despite Bliss's previous lack of interest in such a post.[15]

According to Maidenburg, Bliss told Nixon that he wouldn't take a commission job because he had a "very healthy insurance agency" back in Akron, and if anyone with business before the commission bought an insurance policy from his agency "there would be hell to pay."[16]

Regarding an ambassadorship, Bliss said he would talk with Mrs. Bliss and let Nixon know.

According to Alex Arshinkoff, Bliss told Nixon he was not wealthy enough to pay the costs of being an ambassador.[17] Maidenburg reported that Nixon brought up the ambassadorship to Denmark. This embassy had a private endowment, so "an envoy could easily live on his income."[18] As Nixon talked about Denmark, with its royalty, pomp, and circumstance, his eyes just "glowed and glowed," Bliss later recalled.[19]

Bliss also told Nixon, according to Maidenburg, that his insurance income was sufficient "and anyway, one day he wanted to retire from Washington and go home and have some peaceful existence."[20] Nixon warned Bliss that he would miss being in the nation's capital.

So the second and third options for a Bliss exit outlined by Sears—a job in the administration and returning to his Akron insurance business—came up in the conversation. Apparently, the first option—Bliss staying on as national chairman—came up near the end of the meeting. Perhaps Nixon waited in vain for Bliss to take the hint and offer his resignation.[21]

Maidenburg recounted what Bliss told Nixon about the chairmanship: "I was polite, but I let Dick know that I felt I had done a good job for the committee, and that I was not going to be forced out. I told him I would retire one day, but I would pick the day and he needn't worry—it wouldn't be far off—either April or June—maybe not till September…I wanted to get the (1970) congressional campaigns put together."[22]

Bliss said that Nixon was "most affable in his offers and tried hard to sell me."[23] And Harlow also reported that Nixon was as "considerate as he could be."[24]

Nixon may have been too considerate: he did not seal the deal for Bliss's departure. Evans and Novak concluded that Nixon "buttered up Bliss with so much praise (calling his organizational work 'superb') that the chairman thought the President-elect was letting him write his own departure ticket—later, when things had calmed down, perhaps June or July or some other time."[25]

Harlow later wondered: "I wasted the President's personal time being nice to Bliss. Or did I?"[26]

According to Sears, Nixon never explicitly told Bliss that he had to leave as national chairman. "Nixon couldn't fire anybody," said Sears. Nixon would demand that someone be fired but then "he couldn't do it himself."[27]

John Ehrlichman, a top Nixon aide, confirmed this tendency: "The president was very inept at firing people, notoriously inept. And I've always thought of it as someone killing a chicken with a spoon. Just really stretched it out and made it twice as painful as it ordinarily would be."[28]

A good example, Ehrlichman recalled, was Nixon's treatment of Senator Robert Dole of Kansas, one of Bliss's successors as Republican national chairman. In 1972, Nixon was running for reelection and wanted to replace Dole as chairman with George H. W. Bush of Texas. When summoned to see Nixon, Dole announced that he wouldn't leave because being "dumped" by the president would hurt him back in Kansas.

"Typically the President stopped talking and said, 'Well, work it out with Haldeman,'" Ehrlichman said.

This all resulted in an elaborate "Kabuki performance," with Dole being persuaded to resign as chairman after Nixon did some fundraisers for him for his Senate reelection campaign. Dole's departure and replacement by Bush was delayed until after Nixon's second inauguration in 1973.

At an impromptu press conference right after the 1968 Pierre Hotel meeting with Nixon, Bliss did not behave like a man who had been fired. He emerged with a smile and broke his public silence on the chairmanship. With Harlow and Ziegler present, he discussed only the first option described in Sears's memo—staying on as chairman.

"The President-Elect expressed complete satisfaction with the job being done by me as Republican National Chairman, complimented me on the job I've done and the National Committee has done in the past four years in uniting our Party and helping to achieve the recent victory and he expressed the desire that I continue on as Republican National Chairman," Bliss said, according to a transcript of the press conference.[29]

"Do you plan to do so?" one reporter asked.

"Yes, sir," Bliss responded.

Bliss dodged, however, when reporters attempted to determine how long he planned to stay on as national chairman.

"So do you expect to have an active role in the 1970 election?" a reporter asked.

"Who knows what the future holds?" responded Bliss. "I'm not pinning down any dates as to how long I'm going to serve."

Bliss did his best to change the subject: "I'm not going to discuss the Chairmanship any further," said Bliss. "I stated what he [Nixon] said. He asked me to remain on as Chairman, expressed satisfaction with the job I was doing, complimented me on it and I will continue as Chairman of the Republican National Committee."

The reporters probed for any Bliss-Nixon friction. "Haven't you been perhaps a little bit disappointed that the President-Elect hasn't attempted to knock down these rumors that you're going to be replaced?" one asked—a reasonable question given the rumors that Bliss was out as chairman.

"Well of course they were speculative stories and it's my understanding that he [Nixon] has refused to respond to speculative stories," Bliss responded cautiously. "There has never been any direct statement from [the] President-elect on it."

The reporters probed more: "Wouldn't it have been helpful to you if he had knocked down these reports?" But Bliss still wouldn't take the bait, saying, "Well I'm not going to discuss what might or might not have been. I'm here to discuss the meeting of today and tell you the facts relating to it."

The press conference also touched on the upcoming inauguration, and Bliss's comments indicated that the Nixon advisers had been correct in believing that Bliss wanted to attend as chairman.

"What will your role now be, in the inauguration?" a reporter asked.

"Well, it's the normal role of a National Chairman where you participate in certain events, attend certain events, etc.," said Bliss. "It will be the role that the Chairman has enjoyed in the past. The same prerogatives."

The reporters asked Bliss about the need for someone at the national committee who could be a spokesman for the president, the concept that Nixon and his aides had been promoting privately.

Bliss's answer did not sound as if he were on the same page as the Nixon team. "Well when you boil it down you have many people in our Party competent to speak on the issues," said Bliss.

Before the press conference ended, a reporter again pressed Bliss to be specific about his future at the national committee: "Would it be fair to say that after your meeting with Mr. Nixon you think all these rumors are utterly talk? What is the impression you have after the meeting with the President-elect?"

Bliss had the last word: "Well, all I can tell you is what he [Nixon] said to me. I said that."

Nixon did not speak to reporters, but his spokesman, Ron Ziegler, backed up Bliss's account of the meeting. Ziegler said: "I don't know how long continue means, but continue is an ongoing word."[30]

The press conference was widely seen as resolving the public standoff between Bliss and Nixon—to Bliss's advantage. "Nixon's vote of confidence in the canny political pro," wrote Feldkamp of the *Akron Beacon Journal*, "ended six weeks of intense speculation that the President-elect was going to fire Bliss and put in a younger, more attractive spokesman for the party."[31]

Many journalists saw it as a long-term solution. "Bliss Agrees to Stay as Chairman" was the headline in the *Washington Post.* It reported that Bliss had agreed to "continue indefinitely." The *New York Daily News* went farther, quoting Bliss as saying "I am going to stay on indefinitely." Neither of these statements appeared in the news conference transcript.[32]

Republican leaders in Congress and around the country welcomed the news that Bliss would stay on. Congressman Bill Ayres said: "I don't like to say 'I told you so,' but I told you so."[33]

Feldkamp of the *Akron Beacon Journal* was a longtime Bliss watcher, however, and he picked up on Bliss's refusal to pin down how long he would stay as chairman. He also noted that Nixon "seemed to maintain a slight coolness toward the chairman." The president-elect, for example, allowed no pictures to be taken of him and Bliss and did not join the chairman after the meeting when Bliss talked to reporters.[34]

"Still, unclear, however," wrote Feldkamp, "is just how long the Bliss-full mood will last."

"Sheer disaster" is how columnists Evans and Novak later described the press conference from the point of view of the President-elect.[35] Even before Bliss's news conference at the Pierre Hotel, unnamed Nixon sources said that Bliss's authority as party chairman "had been weakened by the public controversy" and hoped Bliss would resign gracefully.[36]

Evans and Novak concluded: "Things were back where they had been right after the election. When the Nixon team moved from the Pierre to the White House, the matter remained unresolved with yet greater difficulties ahead."[37]

The presidential inauguration provided a brief break for all concerned.

Chapter 59

Chairman for an Inaugural

The January 20, 1969, inauguration of President Richard Nixon marked a stunning turnaround for the Republican Party, nearly written off as irrelevant just four years before. Nixon and Bliss set aside their conflict over the national chairmanship to celebrate the pinnacle of each man's professional career.

A prelude to the inauguration was a meeting of the Republican National Committee in Washington, DC, on January 17, 1969. It was the committee's first meeting since the 1968 general election. Bliss had rescheduled it as part of his struggle with Nixon over his future as national chairman. But the issue seemed to have been settled at the Pierre Hotel meeting, so Republicans turned to celebration with gusto.

In a moment of personal triumph, Bliss brought the meeting to order almost twenty years to the day after his election as Ohio chairman in 1949 and twenty-six years after he became Summit County chairman in 1942.[1]

Bliss was proud of the successes of the national committee, but also humble: "We have come a long way, simply because all of you have been cooperative, tolerant, and helpful, understanding of a chairman in a difficult role....I am so grateful to you and thank you from the bottom of my heart."[2]

Committee members gave their chairman a standing ovation.

Nixon sent a telegram extolling Bliss's virtues. "I know that each member of the national committee shares my appreciation and esteem for our chairman, Ray

Bliss.... His skill in rebuilding our party from its low fortunes four years ago to its present strength has been unmatched in the history of Republican leadership."

Nixon then issued his first public statement on Bliss's future. "As you are aware, on my request he [Bliss] has agreed to remain in his post to help maintain our forward momentum so that we can build a nationwide majority party with the strength and dedication to meet the many challenges confronting our nation."[3]

Bliss also praised Nixon at the meeting. "Let's set one thing straight once and for all. As Chairman of your Committee, I have great confidence that Dick Nixon with his background and experience in domestic and international affairs is the best trained man ever elected to the White House and is going to be one of our great presidents."[4]

Bliss also offered a warning. "In my judgment—and remember this. Now we've got a changed role in the National Committee. We have the presidency now. And certainly there are some things going to happen that you may not like, but let's play on his team together.... We must keep this party united, and the way to do it—Nixon is the spokesman, the administrator, the President, and we've got to back him up with everything we've got to preserve that job in '72. And I'm sure that the job he will do will help make it easier for us to win in the coming elections."[5]

Nixon's and Bliss's statements appeared to confirm the Pierre Hotel meeting. But both were also consistent with the recommendations from Nixon aides on a graceful exit for Bliss. When reporters asked, Bliss said his job was no different than that of a member of the cabinet, who serves at the pleasure of the president.[6]

In the "Chairman's Report" to the national committee, Bliss began by listing the accomplishments and activities of the party under his watch. Using maps of the United States, he pinpointed Republican victories at the state and local levels. Then Bliss showed the locales of the numerous conferences, workshops, and seminars held for party leaders. These included meetings focused on research, electronic data processing, public relations, big city and county officials, and campaign management. He also detailed efforts to reach out to young people, college professors, senior citizens, women, black, and ethnic voters. Bliss highlighted the "Votewagon" tour for voter registration, special efforts to woo white-collar voters and encourage absentee ballots for Americans living or serving abroad, and ballot security programs.[7]

Bliss's fascination with the nuts and bolts of politics was on display when he described "new techniques we can use to modernize our operation."[8] One example was a new "retrieval machine," an electronic device that quickly sorted and collated news sources on a particular topic. In 1968, it covered some 25,000 items and could produce up-to-date information for campaigns in just a few hours—instead of the eighteen days taken to perform the same task previously.

Bliss also showed off new "deluxe" printing and collating machines to process mail. GOP headquarters received thousands of letters a month that required a response, and the party sent out millions of pieces of direct mail. The new equipment allowed hundreds of personalized letters a day to be printed and mailed. It also allowed for the managing of addresses, printing materials, and assembling of political mailings—seventy-five pieces a minute.[9]

In conclusion, Bliss was cautiously optimistic about the 1970 congressional elections: "I think we can gain ground. I am honest about it: if we are willing to put forth the effort. But it is going to take all of us doing just what we have done over the past. There will be many things—now remember, we're in. But there will be many things you can find fault with. Now let's not be faultfinders.... We won; now let's not throw it away by creating divisions in our ranks."[10]

The national committee put an exclamation point on the event by reaffirming Bliss as chairman and raising his salary from $32,000 to $40,000 a year.

At the inauguration, Bliss was shown great respect, as befitting one of the architects of the Republican victory. He and Ellen were seated on the inaugural platform, on the right side of Row E, the furthest of five rows from the podium. Bliss and his wife were in seats 6 and 8. Next to them were Mr. and Mrs. J. Willard Marriott, the hotel magnate and inaugural chairman and his wife. Several members of Nixon's new cabinet, including Attorney General John Mitchell, were on the left side of the aisle.[11]

Nixon took the oath of office from fellow Californian Chief Justice of the Supreme Court Earl Warren. The two Democrats who had just relinquished power—Lyndon Johnson as president and Hubert Humphrey as vice president—and newly inaugurated vice president Spiro Agnew—looked on as Nixon began his seventeen-minute speech.[12]

After the close 1968 election it was a time for the new president to bring the country together. "We have endured a long night of the American spirit," Nixon said. "But as our eyes catch the dimness of the first ray of dawn, let us not curse the remaining dark. Let us gather the light."[13]

Evidence of the unrest that was tearing the nation apart was nearby. Demonstrators opposed to the Vietnam War "hurled sticks, stones, bottles, cans, obscenities and a ball of tin foil" at the president and others in his new administration during the parade from the Capitol to the White House. There were even smoke bombs. By the end of the day, eighty-one protesters were arrested for disorderly conduct.[14]

Nixon's conciliatory tone was reminiscent of Bliss's work to unify the Republican Party, while the turbulent backdrop revealed the difficulty of the task.

To visitors from Akron, Bliss was a conquering hero. The *Akron Beacon Journal* sent Betty Jaycox, longtime women's editor, to provide a personal account of the celebration.[15] Jaycox was the unofficial chronicler of Akron's high society, a fact that Bliss certainly was aware of.

At an inaugural concert at Constitution Hall in Washington, DC, Jaycox sat with Ray and Ellen Bliss, just two boxes away from the presidential box. The Bliss box was full of family and Akron friends. The group, besides Jaycox, included Summit County Republican chairman D. E. "Gene" Waddell and his wife, Barbara; and Ellen Bliss's sisters: Jean Wade and her two daughters, Kate and Julie; and Louise Earley and her husband, Lawrence.

"President-elect Nixon beamed Ray's way several times," Jaycox reported.

She noticed that those who greeted Bliss used a single name—"chairman."

Jaycox interviewed Mrs. Bliss on the chairman situation. "Didn't you worry when Ray was going through the uncertainty of Nixon perhaps appointing another chairman?" asked Jaycox.

"Of course I did," said Mrs. Bliss. "It wasn't easy."

"Did you pretend you weren't a bit worried to bolster his morale?" Jaycox followed up.

"Well," said Ellen, "I didn't pretend not to worry, but I am a very quiet worrier, so it didn't bother Ray a bit."

Jaycox was convinced that Bliss's future as national chairman no longer was in doubt. "Nobody need worry about Ray Bliss anymore," Jaycox reported. "The National Chairman of the Republican Party is now on the sunny side of the Republican street."

Chapter 60

Bliss "Retires" as National Chairman

Glowing tributes at the Republican National Committee and smiles at the presidential inauguration provided only temporary calm for Ray Bliss. Nixon's aides, now in the White House, had not given up on ousting him.

Initially, Nixon felt the matter was settled at the Pierre Hotel, pending Bliss's choice of a patronage appointment. H. R. Haldeman, now White House chief of staff, disagreed. On January 24, just four days after the inaugural, he described Bliss as an "urgent problem," and his handwritten notes from a White House meeting said "need some devious way to solve the problem."[1]

A week later, on January 30, there was still no word from Bliss. Bryce Harlow, now congressional liaison, told a White House meeting that "Bliss has to go now—can't be left to drift." The discussion turned once again to what kind of patronage post Bliss might accept.[2]

Nixon had to be convinced of the need for prompt action. On January 31, Haldeman wrote in his diary: "P [Nixon] refusing to recognize that he did not set Bliss's departure as a firm thing" at the Pierre Hotel. Haldeman then reported a decision: "Finally settled on a procedure, either Ambassador now, or out in June, with Murray Chotiner coming in now as number two man."[3]

Nixon soon became frustrated with Bliss. On February 4, Haldeman's diary said: "Back to the Bliss matter at staff meeting, P [Nixon] mad at his attitude, decided only way to deal with him is to set deadline about Ambassadorship for this week, and if he refuses it, and to leave, force Chotiner on him, and deal with Rogers Morton on all politics." Haldeman's meeting notes were even more explicit: "ignore Bliss."[4]

The White House had found its "devious way" to deal with Bliss, and the tool, Murray Chotiner, was already on hand. As part of the inauguration planning, Chotiner was given an office at Republican national headquarters. His job was "doling out inauguration tickets to deserving politicians." The Nixon team told national committee staffers that Chotiner would be gone on January 21, the day after the inaugural. But Chotiner had no intention of leaving.[5]

Murray Chotiner was a key operative in Nixon's political career. He managed Nixon's first campaign for the US House of Representatives in 1946 and his 1950 US Senate campaign, and was active in the 1952 presidential campaign when Nixon was the vice-presidential candidate. Sidelined by an investigation of government contracts involving him, Chotiner was absent from Nixon's campaigns in 1956 and 1960, but he returned as part of Nixon's unsuccessful 1962 campaign for California governor and then participated in the 1968 presidential campaign.[6]

Evans and Novak described Chotiner as "the most interesting personality in Nixon's political camp: aggressive, egocentric, a professional among amateurs, brilliant, overbearing, ruthless, engaging, habitually guilty of overkill, constantly enlarging his area of operation. Painted in sinister colors by the press, he was both a public relations problem for Nixon and an invaluable campaign strategist."[7]

Chotiner's loyalty was to Nixon personally, not to the Republican Party. He had a reputation as an effective campaigner but also as a "hatchet man."[8] He was also one of the first paid campaign consultants and contributed the chapter "Managing the Campaign" in *Politics U.S.A.*, where Bliss had written on the role of a state party chairman.

Chotiner wrote that a winning candidate needed to be "clean" (free of scandal), "clear" (on the issues), "constructive" (committed to results), and "courageous" (willing to be aggressive). His example of courage was Richard Nixon and his statements in the 1950 US Senate campaign. "I have been advised not to talk about communism," Nixon said. "But I am going to tell the people of California the truth and this is one thing we cannot stop talking about as long as the menace of international communism faces us here in the United States."

Chotiner went on to describe the difference between "truth and a smear" and "how to attack" in campaigns. Attacks should be based on the facts of an opponent's record and should be directed at an opponent's weaknesses. Once underway, the campaign should "just keep hammering and hammering on those weak points until your opponent can no longer exist in the election drive." Nixon used this approach and the issue of communism to defeat Democrat Helen Gallagher Douglas in 1950.[9]

The day after the 1968 election, according to Evans and Novak, Nixon asked Chotiner what he wanted to do: "Chotiner, hardly one to downgrade himself, replied he would like to replace Bliss as Republican National Chairman. Taken aback, Nixon said that, of course, was impossible, and the matter was dropped."[10]

Nixon's top aides did not want Chotiner in the White House, where he would be a political liability as well as a rival for power. Many were also keenly aware of Chotiner's limitations. Aides recommended a "strong man over Chotiner" because there could be "no nonsense" and "no hacks" at the Republican National Committee.[11] Among the most vocal critics was Bryce Harlow, who wrote in his December 2 memo to Nixon: "Without in any way derogating Murray Chotiner (whom I barely know), it does seem to me that his appointment to the Committee under existing circumstances would be a serious reverse for you personally. I have a strong suspicion that it would revive a lot of old canards that you have most successfully laid to rest, particularly this year."[12]

Chotiner's arrival at GOP party headquarters before the presidential inauguration did not please Bliss. For one thing, Chotiner was not the sort of character Bliss wanted anywhere near the national committee. Also, Bliss disliked being watched by the Nixon camp as had happened during the 1968 campaign.

Ben Maidenburg reported Bliss's account of what happened next. "In early December, Bliss was in his office and Murray Chotiner stalked in." "Stalked in" were Bliss's exact words, wrote Maidenburg.[13] Chotiner said to Bliss: "They want you to appoint me either assistant GOP national chairman or associate national chairman. Of course, you will make the public decisions and statements, but not until you have gotten my approval of them. In other words, you'll be the front man and I'll run the show."

According to Maidenburg, "Bliss was so surprised he nearly fell off his chair." But Bliss was not too surprised to respond to Chotiner.

"I'm not going to do it, and, anyway, the [national] committee wouldn't accept you in a thousand years," said Bliss.

Chotiner then tried to be diplomatic. "Look, I'm going to go back to California to close up my office, and I've been promised this job and I'd just like to reach an understanding with you."

"I told him to get out," Bliss told Maidenburg.

Bliss now knew first-hand about one part of the two-chairman plan. It was then, Maidenburg wrote, that Bliss decided to reschedule the Republican National Committee meetings to January 17, right before the presidential inauguration.

Meanwhile, the Nixon camp had settled on a person for the top spot in the two-chairman plan to replace Bliss: Maryland US Congressman Rogers C. B. Morton. From Nixon's point of view, Morton was a good choice as a "speaking" chairman. Telegenic and articulate, he also wanted to continue his congressional career while serving as national chairman. In addition, his brother was Thruston Morton, who had served as a congressman and US senator from Kentucky as well as Republican national chairman. The Morton brothers and Bliss were good friends.[14]

Morton's name first surfaced publicly as a possible successor to Bliss on January 10, 1969—the very day that Nixon and Bliss were meeting at the Pierre Hotel. Unnamed sources told columnists Evans and Novak that Bliss would likely stay until after the presidential inauguration, but they insisted that Bliss would be leaving soon and Morton was the likely successor.[15]

Rogers Morton came to see Bliss soon after the December Bliss-Chotiner confrontation, according to Maidenburg.[16]

"Ray, are you going to resign?" Morton asked.

"I'm going to but it won't be till April—maybe June or later," said Bliss. "The national committee wants me to hang on, but I'm getting tired of all this and if Nixon will just lay off, I'll satisfy him pretty soon."

"In that case, let me tell you what has happened," Morton said. He told Bliss that Nixon had wanted to nominate Morton as secretary of interior and floated the idea at the Republican Governors Association conference on December 6 (where the Nixon and Bliss forces were sniping at each other). However, the western governors strongly objected to an easterner for the job, so Nixon abandoned Morton in favor of Alaska governor Walter Hickel. Nixon then asked Morton to serve as Republican national chairman. Morton was terribly embarrassed by the whole thing, wrote Maidenburg.

Now Bliss knew first-hand about the other part of the two-chairman plan.

According to Maidenburg, Bliss saw Morton as a good successor as national chairman, and this fact influenced Bliss's subsequent decisions.[17]

After the inauguration, Chotiner had not been idle. He stayed in his office at Republican headquarters and began doing postelection political chores. "When the White House called," reported William Vance of the *Akron Beacon Journal*, "it was Chotiner, not Bliss, who was answering the phone."[18]

One incident particularly embarrassed Bliss, Vance reported. Akron school superintendent Martin Essex had been invited to Washington to discuss becoming US commissioner of education. It would have pleased Bliss if a candidate from his hometown had been appointed. Bliss, however, was out of the loop, a bad place to be in Washington, particularly if a president of your own party is in the White House. It turned out that the job had already been offered to someone else—while Essex was still discussing the post with officials.

Even so, Chotiner's position at national headquarters was becoming "untenable," according to Evans and Novak: he lacked a permanent job at the national committee and Bliss could be a formidable opponent. So Chotiner must have welcomed Nixon's decision to "force Chotiner on Bliss."[19]

Late one afternoon in early February, Chotiner walked down to Bliss's office at Republican national headquarters, according to Evans and Novak. "Blunt as always, Chotiner propositioned Bliss in words to this effect: Ray, I've been promised by the White House that I will run the National Committee as No. 2 man here, and I have got to get going. I've promised jobs to people, and they're pressing me. Now, Ray, you can stay on as National Chairman if you want, but I can't wait a minute to take over the machinery."

Evans and Novak wrote that Bliss was "deeply shaken" by this second confrontation with Chotiner, who later took credit for forcing Bliss out.[20]

Bliss called Haldeman to arrange a meeting at the White House, Evans and Novak reported. When Bliss learned that Nixon wanted Chotiner put on the national committee payroll, he said he would resign.[21]

A February 9 memo from Haldeman to Nixon basically confirms these accounts, although it differs in some details. Haldeman reported that Bliss called him from Ohio on the evening of February 8. Bliss "said he wanted to make this whole situation as pleasant as possible and that, of course, he did not have any intention of staying on as National Chairman in any event." Bliss was concerned, however, about "sudden pressure" being put on him to make a decision because he wanted to talk with his wife before taking any action. "Bliss also said he was not interested in being ambassador to Denmark but would rest and return to his insurance business in Akron," wrote Haldeman.

Bliss wanted to meet Nixon and report his decision personally, and then make a public announcement that he was leaving the chairmanship in mid-April. He would also appoint Murray Chotiner as "associate chairman." But Bliss was uneasy with Chotiner, Haldeman wrote.

"Bliss gives his word that he will do whatever is asked of him and that he will carry out instructions from us, but he is very concerned that until he actually leaves he continue to be National Chairman. He was somewhat disturbed by Chotiner's approach in informing him that when Chotiner came in it would be clearly understood that he [Chotiner] would take over totally."

According to Haldeman, Bliss would accept Chotiner's control in fact, but not in appearance. "He assures us that he will make whatever moves Chotiner asks him to make, but wants them to be Bliss' moves rather than Chotiner's during this interim period."

Bliss still preferred a June—rather than April—departure, but was willing to leave in April. Haldeman concluded that an April departure "certainly is safer."[22]

Haldeman's February 9 memo to Nixon may have contained some wishful thinking on his part. A week later, the situation was still unresolved, so he wrote to Ehrlichman: "On the Ray Bliss matter, I will try to reach him Monday and report to you on the results of the call. If I fail, however, it should be followed up and quickly and firmly by you."[23]

During the week between Haldeman's first and second memos, Bliss was in frequent communication with the White House. There are also credible reports that Bliss and Nixon met as Bliss requested. However, there is no official record of such a meeting and it was not mentioned in Bliss's account to Maidenburg.

It could be that an informal meeting took place. The president's busy schedule had many opportunities for a brief discussion with Bliss. But Bliss may have come to the White House and been met by a top aide instead of the president. This pattern fits with Nixon's hands-off approach to firing people.[24]

In any event, the White House's hopes were fulfilled at the end of the week. "I talked with Chairman Bliss last night on the phone and it is my understanding that he is prepared to go ahead with the exchange of letters [with Nixon]," wrote Haldeman in a second memo to Erhlichman.[25]

Chotiner was still a sticking point. "Ray is ready and willing to appoint Chotiner Deputy Chairman, but wants it clearly understood that he, Bliss, retains the full authority of the Chairmanship until he actually leaves office. It may be a little hard for Chotiner to accept this and it is imperative that we make sure he does so that the thing does not blow up during this next six-week period," wrote Haldeman.

However, Chotiner had to realize the situation was "delicate" and make some concessions to Bliss. "I do think there may be some problems as far as personnel is concerned, and it is probably better to let Ray keep on the people he wants to keep, or give them notice now so that they can plan to leave at the time Ray does rather than trying to get them out before Ray goes," Haldeman added.

Without Chotiner in the picture, Bliss "might have been able to ride out the storm and delay his retirement for a decent interval," reported Vance of the *Akron Beacon Journal*. But a deeper problem was Nixon's repeated lack of communication with Bliss. "Raymond Charles Bliss, a proud but pragmatic man," concluded Vance, "knew it was a situation that neither he nor his beloved party could long endure."[26]

On February 17, Bliss wrote to Nixon announcing his "retirement"—as opposed to "resignation"—as national chairman. The effective date was April 15, making Bliss's term as national chairman almost exactly four years. Nixon wrote back accepting.[27]

Such letters in high-profile controversies usually mask the truth, and these were no different. They read like correspondence between best friends. Bliss even made it sound like he was leaving despite Nixon's desire that he remain on the job.

"While I appreciated very much your suggestion at our Jan. 10 meeting at the Pierre Hotel in New York that I continue as Chairman of the Republican National Committee, I have given it much thought and have concluded that I will retire as Chairman in April and return to my private business."

Bliss wrote that the timing would give the new chairman time to get ready for the elections in 1969 and 1970. Without naming Chotiner, he wrote that "you may find it desirable to appoint a representative of your administration to work closely with me until the new Chairman is elected."

Bliss said that he was "looking forward" to meeting with Nixon when the president returned from a trip to Europe. The next paragraph seemed to sum up Bliss's true feelings about the job he had spent a lifetime preparing for: "The last four years have been the most important and satisfying of my life since they provided me an opportunity to rebuild the Republican Party and help elect you President of the United States."

Bliss made sure that Nixon knew he would not air their disagreements: "You may be assured of my continued support and dedication to the principles of the Republican Party which you so ably espouse."

Then he ended it: "With warm regards and high esteem, I am sincerely yours, Ray."

If anything, Nixon outdid Bliss with accolades of praise. There was no hint of the president's months-long effort to force Bliss out or of Bliss's resistance. Nixon wrote that "I have read with great personal regret your February 17 letter advising me of your decision to leave the National Chairmanship in mid-April."

Nixon did all he could to avoid the impression that Bliss had been fired: "In our Party's six score years we have never had a Chairman more dedicated than you have been, more professionally competent, or with a record of greater achievement than yours. It is also true that no Chairman has won more respect throughout our Party's ranks than you have won since you took up the reins of leadership in 1965. You have, therefore, every reason for full satisfaction as you leave this high post. I join our entire Party membership in saluting you for a job extraordinarily well done."

Nixon wrote that he did not want Bliss to just fade away: "In accepting your decision I must request that you remain available as our counselor despite your retirement, because you offer our Party far too much professional skill to remove yourself entirely from our common cause."

The president promised to "designate a representative" to work with Bliss at the national committee and said that they would meet after his European trip "to discuss the Committee's requirements for the future."

Nixon personalized the exchange by bringing their spouses into the conversation: "Pat (Mrs. Nixon) joins me in warmest greetings to Ellen (Mrs. Bliss) and in congratulations to both of you for having so ably served our Party and our country for so many years."

He signed it, "Sincerely, Dick Nixon."

Bliss kept his hometown newspaper, the *Akron Beacon Journal*, informed of his plans. It splashed the breaking news on the front page the next day with a five-column headline, "Ray Bliss Will Resign as GOP Chief April 15." A box with the story identified it as a "Beacon Journal Exclusive" and bragged that "the exchange of letters was confirmed by the White House more than an hour after the *Akron Beacon Journal* broke the story in its early editions."[28]

Bliss's decision caught Ohio allies by surprise. D. E. "Gene" Waddell, the Summit County Republican chairman, told Vance he didn't hear from Bliss directly until a day after Bliss sent his letter to Nixon. "There's a right way and a wrong way and Bliss usually does it the right way," said Waddell. "That's why he didn't let this leak out before getting a reply from Nixon."[29]

Evans and Novak wrote that the exchange of letters came "when most Republican politicians thought the Bliss problem had been safely resolved for at least several months."[30] National political reporters were stunned by the announcement. The news stories that followed were filled with speculation on its causes and consequences. The White House's two-chairman plan with Morton and Chotiner was soon common knowledge.

The most revealing story was by David Broder on February 19: "Chotiner says that whoever becomes Chairman will concentrate on speechmaking and 'meeting the public' while he (Chotiner) runs the headquarters as 'deputy chairman or associate chairman or executive director or whatever they choose to call it.'"[31]

Rogers Morton did not like this approach. He told the White House that he would become chairman "on the condition that President Nixon abandon plans to name Murray Chotiner the number two man."[32]

"They got the cart before the horse. There is a need for competent professional people on the staff, but I feel strongly...that whoever is chairman ought to select his own staff. There has to be a single line of authority," Morton told a reporter.[33]

Instead of running the Republican National Committee, Chotiner ended up in an "obscure post in the bureaucracy" as general counsel in the Office of Special Trade Representative.[34]

According to Maidenburg, Bliss "brought Morton in, privately, and briefed him thoroughly before he took office."[35]

It was time for Bliss to say good-bye to Washington, DC.

Chapter 61

Farewell to Washington

Republicans from all over the country let Ray Bliss know that he would be missed as national chairman. Nixon's one-time rival for the Republican presidential nomination, New York governor Nelson Rockefeller, sent Bliss a glowing tribute.

"You brought to the chairmanship a high order of professional competence, untiring, around-the-clock diligence and a single-minded devotion to its welfare above and beyond any special interest, faction or consideration," Rockefeller wrote. "But by all odds the greatest contribution that you made—and it was indispensable to the great victory we enjoyed last year—was the unity which you brought to the party through the confidence you inspired and held on the part of all its elements."[1]

No doubt Bliss appreciated such compliments, but he drew his strength from the grass roots of the GOP. Members of the Republican National Committee praised the chairman who looked out for their interests, coached them, and led the party to victory.

"One of the highlights of a successful election year during our 1966 campaign was your visit to Casper where you imparted a tremendous degree of enthusiasm to our party workers," wrote Robert F. Gosman, national committeeman from Wyoming. Nelda Brown, the national committeewomen from Kentucky, wrote, "Thanks from all Kentucky Republicans for the many long hours spent rebuilding our party." McDill "Huck" Boyd, who represented Kansas on the national committee, said he wrote to Bliss with "tears in my heart." Florence Cauble, a national committeewoman from Georgia, sent a tribute that must have especially pleased Bliss because of his almost religious devotion to the virtues of the two-party system: "Not only Republicans—but all Americans owe you a deep debt of gratitude for the years of your life devoted to rebuilding the 2-party system."[2]

This sentiment was bipartisan in nature. David Broder recalled a social event in early 1969 while Bliss was "awaiting the formalities of the purge" as national chairman. There probably were more Democrats than Republicans at the event, but that didn't matter. "The Democrats he had just helped turn out of power surrounded him and praised his craftsmanship, while marveling that Nixon would so cavalierly discard such an asset," Broder wrote. Bliss "was a hero that night, even to the Democrats, because he was much more than a partisan. He was a pro."[3]

President Nixon honored Bliss in a way that only a president can: with a reception and black-tie dinner at the White House. Held on April 13, 1969, it also served to welcome Rogers Morton, soon to become the new national chairman.

A *New York Times* account of the two-hour gala included a picture of four smiling couples: President Nixon and First Lady Pat; Vice President Spiro Agnew and his wife, Judy; Ray and Ellen Bliss; and Morton and his wife, Anne. After the picture was taken, the four couples greeted the guests before dinner, with the Nixons in the Blue Room; the Agnews in the Red Room; and the Blisses and Mortons in the Green Room. A buffet dinner was then held in the State Dining Room.[4]

Among three hundred guests were four cabinet secretaries, four former GOP national committee chairmen, and key Bliss allies Ody Fish, Don Ross, Fred Scribner, and J. Willard Marriott. White House staffers Bryce Harlow and John Sears—who had played a major role in Bliss's exit—were also present, as was Bliss's colleague Arthur Peterson. Governor James Rhodes, GOP chairman John Andrews, and national committeewoman Martha Moore represented the state of Ohio. Ellen Bliss's sisters, Louise Earley and Jean Wade, and her brothers, Francis and Bill Palmer, were among the guests, along with other Akron friends, including Ben Maidenburg of the *Akron Beacon Journal.*

The event provided a picture of unity and a seamless transition in leadership that suited Nixon's purpose as much as Bliss's.

Akron congressman Bill Ayres was there as well. "Well, it was run just like a regular state dinner and Ray and Ellen were the guests of honor," said Ayres. It had all the regal trappings that appealed to Nixon. "They had strolling violins and the whole shooting match," said Ayres. It was not out of character for Nixon to honor someone with whom he disagreed. "Nixon would do nice things for people he didn't necessarily like," said Ayres. "It was sort of like a farewell. 'I'm through with this one now, that's it.' It was sort of like a guest who had overstayed his welcome," Ayres added.⁵ In this vein, President Nixon rejected the first draft of a perfunctory White House note thanking Bliss for his service to the Republican Party. "Too short," Nixon wrote on the draft. "Warm it up. Refer to Ohio in 1960."⁶

Bliss appreciated the honor, despite initial skepticism. He later told Maidenburg it was the first time a person other than a high foreign dignitary had ever been "wined and dined" in the State Dining room. Maidenburg asked Bliss: "But how could you accept this after the way he treated you? It's like giving some bum a six-inch steak just before they hang him." According to Maidenburg, Ray and Ellen discussed the dinner at length, "both feeling it was a sham and shame." But in the end, they decided to attend.

Bliss admitted he was initially upset by Nixon's plans to make it a "full-dress" dinner. Bliss told him, "I don't have too many friends in Akron and Ohio that can come up with more than a black tie." An unhappy Nixon agreed to the less formal black-tie dinner.⁷

Bliss was more comfortable a day later when he gave his final speech as national chairman to the annual meeting of the National Federation of Republican Women. It was the same group to which he had given his first speech as chairman in April 1965. From his early days as a local Republican leader in Akron, Bliss had placed a high value on the work, much of it volunteer, done by women campaign workers.

The NFRW appreciated him in return. The meeting had an "unprecedented registration of nearly 5,000 women," the *Chicago Tribune* reported. Bliss reminded his audience "that every pundit in the country said that we couldn't win in 1968, but we did." He emphasized what he considered the key to political success. "These are changing times and a changing world, but one rule that doesn't change is that work wins elections."

Bliss briefly slipped out of his cautious mode to take a mild poke at the president and the presidential aides who wanted a smooth-talking, "speaking" chairman: "I may not have the voice of an Enrico Caruso or the charisma of a Clark Gable but we won a couple just the same."⁸

A few days earlier, Bliss had held a good-bye reception for the press. William Vance of the *Akron Beacon Journal* reported that about a hundred reporters enjoyed cocktails and a buffet table twenty yards long, loaded with food and a melting ice elephant. "The ruddy-faced, chain-smoking chairman said a fond farewell Tuesday night to the Washington press corps he once feared would tear him to shreds within six months after assuming command of the shattered GOP," Vance wrote.

Jovial and relaxed, Bliss told his guests their coverage had been fair. "And," he added with a huge grin, "I never gave you a headline you had to retract."

A reporter asked Bliss, "Any regrets, Ray?"

"None," Bliss replied.

Asked how involved he would be in politics back home in Akron, "It depends," Bliss replied, with a hint of mystery, "how I feel when I get there."[9]

At the April 15 meeting of the Republican National Committee, Rogers Morton was elected as chairman to succeed Bliss. Bliss then departed for an all-paid ocean cruise. It gave Bliss a well-deserved vacation from national politics.

When Bliss returned to Akron, he found a friendly sign on the door to his insurance company, Tower Agencies, Inc. "Welcome Home! 20 years of absenteeism is ENUF!!" A small red carpet was stuck to the floor with masking tape to make Bliss's re-entrance a regal one.

"Good morning," Bliss said with a smile as he walked inside to his private office, sniffed the roses that Madge Doerler had ordered, and dropped into his leather chair. Having worked with Bliss in politics and business, she shared his obsession with details, fretting that the roses wouldn't arrive on time. They did and she was pleased.

Charlie Sacks, a partner in Bliss's insurance agency, fretted too. "I figured Ray liked strudel, so guess what?" asked Sacks. "They don't send us very much strudel for the luncheon." If Bliss complained about a strudel shortage, it went unrecorded. He felt at home in Akron.

"He can be counted a real patriot," exclaimed Doerler. "I know I get kind of maudlin about it. But his political work was an effort of love—a love for his country. And now he's earned a vacation."

"I was looking forward to coming home," said Bliss.[10]

A little more than a month after his return to Akron, Bliss put himself on display for a testimonial dinner "honoring" him. At $125 a ticket, the dinner attracted 700 guests, then a record attendance for a Republican fund-raising event in Summit County. The proceeds totaled more than $80,000, half going to the county party and the other half divided between the state and national committees.

The speaker for the evening was Senator Hugh Scott of Pennsylvania, the number two Republican leader in the Senate. He had also served as Republican national chairman in 1948 and 1949, about the time Bliss had become Ohio state chairman.

While the testimonial nature of the dinner masked its real purpose—raising money—at least one of the guests had come purely out of respect for Bliss: the Summit County Democratic chairman Robert Blakemore. Blakemore, who served with Bliss on the county board of elections, joked that he was on "an intelligence mission" to find out who the major Republican contributors were.

A picture from the dinner appearing in the *Akron Beacon Journal* showed a smiling Bliss, his left arm draped around Representative Bill Ayres from Akron and his right arm around Senator Scott. He was in an upbeat, almost lighthearted mood."

"I hope Bill Ayres will remember me because if I don't survive in my insurance business I may need his clearance for a postal job," Bliss cracked.

Chapter 62

Setting the Record Straight

Ray Bliss was back in Akron, but he was hardly out of GOP politics. He had left one political job, Republican national chairman, but he still held other positions—Ohio's national committeeman, a member of the Ohio Republican Executive and Central Committee and the Summit County Republican Central Committee, and a seat on the Summit County Board of Elections.

Bliss's return home and his plans for the future were big news in Akron. Abe Zaidan, a reporter for the *Akron Beacon Journal,* had shown up at Bliss's insurance office, uninvited, to get an update for the paper's readers. "We don't think Mr. Bliss is going to want to give any interviews this morning," one of Bliss's assistants cautioned Zaidan. Zaidan hung around, however. He and Bliss began to talk about ordinary things—how Bliss was feeling, was he ready to get back to selling insurance?

"He was very circumspect at the beginning," said Zaidan, "sort of toyed with a pencil on his desk." As they talked, however, Bliss loosened up. According to Zaidan, the exit from Washington, DC, had been humiliating and their talk gave Bliss a chance to tell his version and discuss his future.

The newspaper treated the ninety-minute interview as a major news event. The front-page headline must have pleased Bliss: "Ray Bliss: The 'Retired' Mr. GOP Will Still Keep a Hand in Politics." Zaidan nicely summed up the essence of the community's returning hero in the first paragraphs of his story:

In the staged and starry world of national politics, where men are events and events often seem bigger than life, let alone men, Raymond Charles Bliss was easily mistaken for a misfit.

Uncommonly shy, and self-conscious about an image that added up to little more than a pudgy, round-faced man with a fleshy nose and slicked-back hair, Bliss had to be content to make political history off-stage while the headliners took the bows.

That was all right with him. And after a generation of quietly stage-managing winners—the last four years as Republican National Chairman—Bliss just as quietly slipped out of the theater and came home to Akron, satisfied that he had done his best, earned his pay and, most of all, helped restore the two-party system after the GOP had been crushed in 1964.

In Bliss's telling, the decision to come back to Akron had been his, not Nixon's. Bliss was not in a brooding mood, reported Zaidan. He said, "I chose my own time and place to resign."

> "I had intended leaving after the [Republican] convention," Bliss said. "I never went to Washington with any ambition of staying there permanently. I know everybody wants to know why I picked April to resign. Well, it rounded out a four-year term. If I had stayed on longer, there would have been the 1970 elections and then we would have 1972 coming up. So I said I couldn't stay. It was a simple choice of getting out now or staying through 1972—and I just didn't want to do that."

There was no mention of whether Nixon would have resisted a Bliss attempt to stay on. Also left unsaid was how he felt about Nixon's tactics to force him out. But Bliss did explain why an ambassadorship or other jobs Nixon had offered him held little interest. He had grown tired of public life. "If I had accepted the European ambassadorship," he said, "it would have meant my leaving the country and running around some more. I'd be right back where I started. No, I couldn't see that for me."

The larger political world already had started buzzing about the different approach that Bliss's successor as national chairman, Representative Rogers Morton of Maryland, was taking. Morton, as Nixon had desired, became the chief political spokesman for the president's programs. Bliss wouldn't say much to Zaidan about Morton's approach. "I won't speak for Morton," said Bliss. "He's a new chairman and he'll have problems just as I did. I'm not going to put a stone in his path."

Bliss did talk about the way he had done things as chairman. He made the case for the type of national chairman that President Nixon did not want, a nuts-and-bolts "office chairman" who put campaigns together, while letting the candidates and officeholders do the talking.

Bliss was proud of the Republican record while he was chairman.

"If you believe as I do that our government must be built from the bottom up, then that is what has been done in the past four years.

"Since 1964, the Republicans have gone from 17 to 31 governors—the highest since 1920...; we have gone from 32 to 43 Senate seats and from 140 to 192 House seats, in each case the highest since 1956; we gained control of both houses in 20 state legislatures, the highest since 1954. In 1964, the Republicans controlled seven. We also gained 648 state legislators, 1,400 county offices and nearly 100 mayors since 1964," said Bliss.

Control of the state legislatures mattered, Bliss reminded Zaidan. "The state legislature is very important because it controls redistricting and affects congressional seats. And now we hold the most congressional seats since 1956."

Nixon's election as president, interestingly, did not rate top billing in Bliss's list of successes. He mentioned it nearly as an afterthought. "And we also elected a president," said Bliss.

By the time of the interview, newspaper columnists and other analysts had had five months to digest the November 1968 election results. In analyzing why Nixon won, some put more emphasis on Americans dissatisfaction with former President Lyndon Johnson and the Democrats than on the revamped Republican Party Bliss had engineered.

Bliss's thirty years as a successful party leader made him a credible voice in this debate. "The record of the opposition party is bound to have an impact," Bliss said. "You always pick up a certain amount of anti-votes. But I've never seen an election analysis in which the majority of the votes cast for the winner were anti-votes. The better the organization, the more you will be able to exploit the opportunity handed you by the opposition. And where this really counts is in close elections."

This success hadn't been a one-person job, Bliss emphasized. "I don't want to leave the impression that I rebuilt this Party myself. It took a lot of hard work by a lot of people. It took good candidates. And it took financial responsibility in running the party."

Bliss took pride in the $1.5 million the national committee had in the bank when he left—compared to the $341,000 he found in the treasury when he came to Washington. "If we had 50 programs on the drawing boards," he noted, "but couldn't afford all of them, we assigned priorities. If we were going to preach financial responsibility as a Party, we had to practice it. And, remember that we set out to raise money at a time when people were reading in the newspapers that the party was dead."[1]

Chairman Morton, Bliss's immediate successor, later spoke highly of Bliss's work, even though his approach differed: "I couldn't possibly have accomplished what I've done if I hadn't inherited a fine organization from Ray Bliss. I've succeeded him but I can't replace him."[2]

Bliss told Zaidan that his emphasis on nuts and bolts didn't mean that he didn't care about issues. "I'm deeply interested in issues," said Bliss. "But as a party, we're out to win—not to fight with each other over ideologies. Once a chairman starts sounding off on issues people begin to feel that you are using your position unfairly for personal issues."[3] A good example was Bliss's Republican Coordinating Committee, which gave the fractured Republicans a common voice on issues.

"Ray really liked to win," concluded Madge Doerler, "that is why we won so often." But he did not want to win just to win. "He was an old fashioned values guy; he wanted to do something for his community and his country," Doerler added. Winning elections was just the first step in good government. "In this way, Ray felt he had achieved a measure of success at every level of politics," she said.[4]

The national chairman's job had required Bliss's attention, 24 hours a day, seven days a week. He was looking forward to shifting to a lower gear. "I've been up to my ears in politics for years," Bliss told Zaidan. "You do not control your own time under those circumstances. Events cause you to constantly move from one thing to another. You're not able to plan on anything. I don't know how many times I had planned on taking a vacation or a trip during a theoretically lull period. But something always caused me not to make the arrangements. From now on, I'll be on my own time and will pick and choose what I want to do."

What Bliss also wouldn't do was peddle his political skills and connections to high places for a profit. For him, there had been one reason to get involved—to protect the GOP and the two-party system. Bliss had turned down an offer to write a political column for a national publication and indicated that he would be satisfied with earning a good living from his insurance agency. "I've been living out of a suitcase for 20 years and I just want to settle down and start living like a human being," said Bliss.[5]

Many of Bliss's friends agreed that he had chosen the right time to return to Akron. D. E. "Gene" Waddell, chairman of the Summit County Republican Party, said that Bliss intended to return to Akron after Nixon's election. But Bliss wanted to decide on his own when to leave.[6]

Bliss "stayed on against his will" after the election, said Doerler. He was "not really happy in Washington" and didn't like the "cocktail parties" and "phonies." The latter apparently included Nixon himself: Bliss later said that Nixon "attached great importance to what I call the phony things in life."[7]

David Broder quoted "Bliss friends" to the effect that Bliss would have quit at the presidential inaugural if Nixon had not pressured him publicly. One said, "It's not the kind of job you stay in if you are not wanted."[8] These perspectives are consistent with Bliss's statement upon becoming national chairman that he didn't plan on making it a career.

But other friends had a different view. Arthur Peterson said, "I think he [Bliss] would have liked to stay. That's my gut feeling."[9] Fellow political scientist and former Bliss aide Robert Huckshorn agreed: "He was unhappy that he was leaving. He did not think the job was done."[10]

John Sears said that Bliss didn't want to leave. "He was trying to keep his job. He was quite happy as national chairman. It was a job that seemed to fit him at the time. He had done a good job, I think, of keeping the party sort of together after the '64 election and I think he felt it was a good position for him."[11]

William Vance wrote that Bliss "wanted very much to stay." There was a condition, however: Bliss wanted the job "as long as he was going to be his own guy."[12]

Bliss seemed to endorse this view in an interview after he retired with Ben Maidenburg, saying he had wanted to stay and organize the upcoming congressional campaign.[13] Winning control of Congress was a goal that had eluded Bliss as national chairman.

Clyde Mann said that Bliss had hoped for a longer tenure as national chairman. After all, his success in Ohio and in Akron was in part a product of his longevity as party leader, a pattern that built on the work of his predecessors, Ed Schorr and Jim Corey. But Mann concluded, "Bliss would not be regimented. He could not be controlled. He could not be bought. He demanded complete control of party operations."[14]

In 1965, Evans and Novak reported: "After six months on the job, Ray Bliss' honorable dream of becoming permanent national chairman, as he was permanent state chairman in Ohio, seems farther than ever from realization." But they concluded: "As long as Bliss can endure the ordeal, he can remain as national chairman."[15]

By February 1969, Bliss had decided it wasn't worth enduring any longer and began a new chapter in his life.

Chapter 63

Politics as an Avocation

Ray Bliss never had much time for hobbies. He had played bridge in college and a little golf in the 1930s, but gave up the games as his political involvement increased. He later tried growing roses but said that ended "because the beetles beat me to them."[1] Dining out with friends was as close to a pastime as Bliss had for most of his career.

Without the title "chairman" for the first time in almost thirty years, Bliss decided he would treat politics as "an avocation and not a vocation."[2] He would work in politics out of personal interest rather than as a professional obligation.

One challenge was near and dear to Bliss's heart: reversing the decay of the Ohio Republican Party. Bliss had spent sixteen years as state chairman building a modern party organization, but while he served as national chairman, Governor James Rhodes had taken control of the party and made it a tool of his office. It had lost most of the independence Bliss had insisted on maintaining even while Republicans served in the governor's office. It no longer recruited and nurtured new candidates or raised money to help Republicans up and down the ticket.

Bliss described this state of affairs at a private luncheon in 1979:

> "We [Republicans] won [in the 1950s and 1960s] because we built up a stable of candidates and put on aggressive campaigns. But nobody's willing to do that anymore. There's been no leadership in Ohio to get a stable of candidates or to find people to finance campaigns.

"To have a strong party organization, you have to have a strong chairman. He can't be the lackey of the governor. John Andrews and Earl Barnes [two Republican state chairmen who followed Bliss] had different ideas than I did. They thought the party ought to work closely with the governor. But Jim Rhodes never did anything unless it was to support Jim Rhodes."[3]

In 1969, President Nixon had wanted to do a similar thing, making the Republican National Committee a tool of the White House.

Another challenge was division among Ohio Republican candidates, something Bliss had struggled against his entire career. Governor Rhodes was finishing up his second four-year term in 1970 and was term-limited. This led to two contested primary races.

One was for the seat of retiring Senator Stephen Young, a Democrat. Young had been elected to the Senate as a result of the 1958 Right-to-Work disaster, defeating Bliss ally and Republican incumbent John Bricker. In 1970, Governor Rhodes sought the GOP Senate nomination against Representative Robert Taft Jr., the son of the legendary Senator Robert A. Taft. Bliss had a tense relationship with Rhodes, but was close to the Tafts.

The other primary contest was for the Republican candidate for governor. The top contenders were state auditor Roger Cloud and US Representative Donald "Buz" Lukens. Bliss was familiar with Cloud, who had served as the Speaker of the Ohio House of Representatives. Lukens was a strident Goldwater conservative who had tangled with Bliss when he was national chairman.

On primary day, Taft edged out Rhodes, winning just over half the vote to capture the GOP nomination for the US Senate seat. Cloud also got half the vote to win the GOP gubernatorial primary over Lukens and another candidate.[4]

Yet another challenge was from strong Democratic candidates in 1970. For the Senate, Cleveland businessman Howard Metzenbaum won the nomination, beating former astronaut John Glenn, who Bliss had tried to recruit for the GOP. For governor, Representative John Gilligan of Cincinnati won easily. Two years earlier, Gilligan had upset the legendary Frank Lausche, a Bliss nemesis, in the Democratic Senate primary, but had lost the general election.[5]

But the Republicans had an even bigger challenge than weak organization, divisive primaries, or strong Democratic opponents: a scandal in state government.

In what was known as the "statehouse loan scandal" or the "Crofters scandal," a Columbus loan-arranging company had persuaded Republican state officials to make millions of dollars in questionable loans to two private companies. In return for arranging the loans, the insiders received "finders'" fees. Auditor Cloud and other statewide officials were implicated.[6]

By June 1970, there were reports that Bliss had been approached about returning as state chairman in light of the dire Republican prospects for the fall election. Bliss put a stop to such talk: "Some people have told me 'We'd like to have you as chairman again' but I wouldn't consider any of the talks serious," said Bliss, adding, "I made it clear when I came back here [Akron] that I wasn't interested in any more full-time political jobs."[7]

But Bliss agreed to help the Republicans by touring the state to raise money and to try to unify the party. At one meeting in Toledo, the party received a pledge of $50,000 after a Bliss visit. At events in Canton and Cleveland, persons who previously had refused to contribute gave after hearing from Bliss. In a meeting of party leaders from northeastern Ohio, Bliss admonished the downcast Republicans to pick themselves up, quit squabbling, and go after the Democrats.[8]

"We have to start a forward movement to win the election in November. We are all aware of the problems we have in the state. We've had times of adversity. We've overcome it in the past and we can do it again," Bliss said to a standing ovation. He praised Cloud and Taft as two men who can "run on their records."[9]

None of it made much difference. Gilligan easily defeated Cloud for governor, getting 54 percent of the vote. The Democrats also won the offices of attorney general, treasurer, and auditor. These victories gave the party control of the Ohio Apportionment Board, the body charged with drawing state legislative districts after each ten-year federal census.[10] The Democrats were poised to improve upon their 1970 state legislative gains in the future.

Nationally, the Democrats picked up twelve seats in the US House of Representatives. One Republican loss hit home for Bliss: Bill Ayres, whom Bliss had recruited back in 1950 to represent the Akron area, lost to Democrat John F. Seiberling, the grandson of F. A. Seiberling, cofounder of the Goodyear Tire & Rubber Company.[11]

The Vietnam War was a major issue in the campaign. Ayres backed American involvement, while Seiberling marched with antiwar protesters. The nation was bitterly divided on the issue, especially in the Akron area because of what had happened on May 4 at Kent State University, just twelve miles away. Four students were killed by Ohio National Guardsmen who were sent to the campus by Governor James Rhodes to restore order in the wake of antiwar protests.

Ayres's campaign used a photo of Seiberling taken soon after the shootings to suggest that the Democratic challenger was allied with campus upheavals. In the photo Seiberling was flanked by two long-haired students. The strategy backfired. Seiberling handily defeated Ayres, getting more than 56 percent of the vote.[12]

There was one bright spot for Bliss on election night. Robert Taft Jr. won a very close race for the US Senate against Democrat Metzenbaum, 49.7 to 47.4 percent. The victory allowed the GOP to pick up a net of one Senate seat nationally.

Bliss's new hobby was off to a rocky start.

In 1971, Bliss became interested in the Akron mayoral campaign. He had begun his political career in the 1931 mayor's race and made his reputation in the 1937 campaign. Mayor John Ballard, whom Bliss had helped recruit for the job in 1965, had been reelected to a four-year term in 1967, due to a 1966 city charter change. But winning another four-year term was not a sure thing. Akron still was a Democratic town, and labor unions were a major force. Then there was Ballard himself, who was judged competent but uncharismatic.

"John was about as dull as dishwater," recalled Daly "Tim" Smith, who covered the 1971 mayoral race for the *Akron Beacon Journal*. The Democratic challenger was thirty-three-year old Dennis Shaul. In contrast to Ballard, Shaul "was good looking, younger. He had everything going for him. He was a rising star," said Smith.[13]

Like Bliss and Ballard, Shaul had Akron roots. He had been an altar boy at St. Vincent Catholic Church near downtown Akron, the same church where Ray and Ellen Bliss were married. A Rhodes Scholar, he had chosen to come home after graduating from Notre Dame University and Harvard Law School. He was on city council but had higher aspirations.[14]

Summit County Republicans knew they were in for a tough race and sent out a political SOS to Bliss. He responded.

Alex Arshinkoff said Bliss helped design a newspaper ad that showed Ballard's accomplishments as mayor. "I mean there was a great ad that they ran that was double page on which he [Bliss] had the entire map of Akron...[and] came up with the idea to show all of the improvements that Ballard had made—this bridge, that bridge, this fire station," said Arshinkoff.[15]

There was another key, however: the editorial endorsement from the *Beacon Journal*. Because television in Akron was dominated by stations in nearby Cleveland, the city's only newspaper played a big role in determining election outcomes. "Bliss was very involved in that election," said Ballard. "In fact, I was amazed. He was as tenacious as a bulldog with Ben Maidenburg [executive editor and publisher of the newspaper]."[16]

Still, Chairman Waddell was very worried about the endorsement. "I knew we were in deep trouble with this Dennis Shaul," recalled Waddell. "And I went to Bliss and I said, 'If we don't get that endorsement, we are going to lose this. This is going to be close enough as it is. We will lose by 5,000 votes.'"[17]

The key was John S. Knight, editor of the *Beacon Journal*. The circumstances in 1971 called for Bliss to personally tug on his long friendship with Knight. A meeting was arranged near the end of the general election campaign. Among other things, Bliss vigorously promoted the merits of the two-party system. "He really talked about the fact, you know, that this is a heavy, heavy Democrat area here. We have a Republican mayor and it gives the party a chance to survive and get other candidates to keep the two-party system alive. He pointed to his general two-party points, his two-party type speech," Waddell remembered. "And I think Jack Knight believed in that. I don't think Knight ever wanted to see a one-party circumstance."[18]

The *Beacon Journal* endorsement came on October 25, with just a week to go before the election. It was for Ballard. Smith said he had no doubt that it was Knight who made the call. The newspaper's editorial board was not a democracy, and Knight's vote was the one that counted.[19]

The headline on the endorsement editorial was both even-handed and definite: "Two Good Candidates—But Ballard Is Our Choice." The editorial did not mention the meeting between Bliss and Knight. It was clear, however, that Waddell and other Ballard supporters were right to be concerned. "The mayoral race between incumbent John Ballard and challenger Dennis Shaul has given the *Beacon Journal* pause for reflection," the lead paragraph said. Both men were "able, honest and conscientious" and "devoted to what they perceive to be the best interests of Akron and its future." The editorial added that both candidates had "substantial, though different, qualities of leadership," but that the election should turn on whether Shaul, with just two years of experience on city council, had made the case that Ballard should be replaced. Ballard's pluses, however, outweighed the minuses, even against "so attractive a candidate as his opponent," the editorial said.

The editorial finished up with a final plug for Ballard: "We admire Dennis Shaul and, should he be defeated, hope he will continue his interest in public affairs and public office. But we will vote for John Ballard in the belief that he is the better man for this office at this time."[20]

Ballard won the election by a very narrow margin—some 4,000 votes.[21] Ballard and Waddell agreed the newspaper endorsement was crucial to Ballard's 1971 victory and that Bliss's help had been crucial to getting the endorsement. "I used to make the statement that no Republican can get elected to the mayor's office without the *Beacon Journal* endorsement," Waddell remembered. "Because of Ray Bliss, Republicans didn't have to try in 1971."[22]

Bliss's new hobby was becoming more fun.

Chapter 64

Bliss, Nixon, and Watergate

Ray Bliss's new hobby included consulting with the Nixon White House. In 1970, Bliss told Ben Maidenburg that he had been summoned to the White House by "one of Dick's aides."

"What for?" asked Maidenburg.

"They want my help," said Bliss.

"Doing what?" probed Maidenburg.

"In the upcoming election campaign," Bliss replied.

"Are you going to do it?" Maidenburg wanted to know.

Bliss said he had not made up his mind, but he would probably help in some ways, "and, if so he would likely receive some kind of title."

"How the hell could you go to work for him [Nixon]," Maidenburg asked, "after the way he treated you?"

"Well, I'm still a Republican," Bliss said. "I want to see the party progress and I can't let bygones be future guidelines."[1]

As a member of the Republican National Committee from Ohio, Bliss was frequently in Washington, DC, and paid official and private visits to the White House. Bliss told the *Akron Beacon Journal* that he had several meetings and telephone conversations with Nixon's aides, including Murray Chotiner—who had pressured Bliss to exit as national chairman. Chotiner said, "Ray is very knowledgeable on the situations throughout the entire country." And he implied that Bliss was under consideration for some type of a part-time job, but "not of a political nature."[2]

Given Republican troubles in the 1970 elections, the White House had good reasons to want Bliss's help. It looked like Nixon could face a tough reelection campaign in 1972. In the spring of 1971, other White House aides who had helped oust Bliss were now trying to get him involved in the campaign.

"In order to bring Ray Bliss more strongly into camp, he should be given a part-time commission post of some kind that will give him some prestige," H. R. Haldeman, White House chief of staff, wrote to campaign aide Gordon Strachan. "This came up before, but apparently nothing has been done on it. Please follow-up and let me know on this."[3]

In December 1971, President Nixon sent a congratulatory telegram to a surprise birthday party for the sixty-four-year old Bliss, held at the Portage Country Club in Akron. After praising the former national chairman's ability and success, the telegram concluded: "I look forward to working together with you in the challenging months ahead, and I continue to rely on the qualities that have earned you this testimonial."[4]

This wooing apparently had some effect: Bliss eventually agreed to chair the Nixon campaign in Ohio. Evans and Novak reported on the courtship of Bliss in March 1972: "Ray C. Bliss, hounded out as Republican national chairman on President Nixon's personal orders three years ago, is now being wooed by campaign manager John Mitchell to serve as his liaison with state party organizations in the President's campaign." According to the column, John Mitchell, who also had managed Nixon's 1968 campaign, and Bliss had held "several confidential talks." Bliss, although "embittered by his sacking in the spring of 1969," had made clear that he was willing to get involved. Mitchell needed Bliss's help because of "increasing friction between the President's campaign apparatus and regular state party organizations."[5]

Mitchell talked with Nixon about Bliss at the White House on April 4, 1972. He explained that Bliss was needed in Ohio to "keep the Taft forces and the Rhodes forces and the rest of them." He went on to say to Nixon, "Well, Bliss is going to come back to work for me, you see, he wants the recognition.... He's not going to be the guy to come and do the nuts and bolts, but he wants the identification with you."[6] Mitchell recommended a personal meeting with Bliss.

The meeting eventually took place on May 16, 1972, in the Oval Office. A transcript reveals a cordial event, beginning with photographs of Nixon, Bliss, and Mitchell, and ending with gifts from President Nixon to Bliss, his wife, and friends back in Akron.

Bliss told the president that his insurance business had doubled since he returned home in 1969 and he couldn't do full-time political work.

"That's fine, but could you get a break?" Nixon asked.

"Well, I am trying to give a reasonable amount of time to help," said Bliss.

Nixon tried to sell Bliss on joining the campaign, first with flattery. "I understand that this is a lot, that you are such a good guy you gave much of your life to the party that you served," said Nixon.

Next Nixon tried the prospect of future business opportunities. Nixon mentioned that some of his friends might be interested in doing business with Bliss's insurance agency.

Then Nixon offered Bliss a government job. Nixon and Bliss discussed agencies, commissions, ambassadorships, or serving as the president's special envoy abroad. Nixon reminded Bliss that former national chairman Leonard Hall had been an envoy for President Eisenhower.

Bliss was polite but noncommittal. The meeting concluded with Nixon asking Bliss to work with Mitchell, make statements to the press, and help with the national convention.[7]

"The president asked me to assist in his campaign," Bliss told reporters two days later, "and I agreed to do so as a part-time consultant."[8] He elaborated to the *Akron Beacon Journal*: "I will not accept any more full-time political appointments and have repeatedly said that.... That position still stands."[9]

President Nixon was renominated at the Republican National Convention in Miami Beach—the same place as the 1968 convention. Bliss helped organize the convention, not as national chairman who ran the show, but as an adviser to the Arrangements Committee. "I'm getting more sleep now and I'm able to have dinner with my wife occasionally," Bliss said to a reporter, drinking coffee and puffing on a cigarette.[10]

The big surprise came in the Democratic Party, which also held its national convention in Miami Beach. In part because of changes in party rules on how delegates were selected, Senator George McGovern of South Dakota won the Democratic presidential nomination over better-known candidates. McGovern was perceived as too liberal for most voters in 1972, much as Goldwater had been perceived as too conservative in 1964. Like Goldwater, McGovern suffered from numerous missteps during the campaign.[11]

Nixon easily won reelection without Bliss's full-time help in 1972. The Nixon-Agnew ticket got 61 percent of the popular vote, and Nixon carried every state except Massachusetts and the District of Columbia. For the third time in a presidential election, Nixon won Ohio, but this time it was a landslide.

During the campaign, however, a scandal was brewing. It began with the June 17, 1972, break-in at the Democratic National Committee headquarters at the Watergate building in Washington. The break-in had been arranged by Nixon's Committee to Re-elect the President (CREEP). Watergate, as the scandal became known, would not go away after the election.[12]

The scandal broke wide open after the trial of the accused Watergate burglars in the spring of 1973. In short order, Nixon's top aides were forced to resign; a special prosecutor was appointed to investigate; a select committee of the US Senate conducted its own inquiry; secret tapes of conversations in the White House were discovered; and legal action was started to obtain the tapes.

In the summer of 1973, Bliss called a special meeting of midwestern Republican leaders in Washington, DC. Bliss had called a similar meeting of the group in 1965 after the Goldwater debacle. No one from the White House was invited to attend. When asked if he intended to bring up the Watergate scandal, Bliss said, "I'm not going to even bring up Watergate.... I'm going to discuss something constructive for the party."[13]

But privately Bliss was very critical of Nixon's handling of Watergate. According to Clyde Mann, Bliss was troubled by the Nixon campaign's illegal fund-raising as well as by the president's defiance of subpoenas for the White House tapes.[14] Bliss believed that Nixon had not recruited "independent-minded" professionals to staff the White House. Back in 1970, Bliss had told Ben Maidenburg: "Nixon's making a horrible mistake about one thing. He has surrounded himself with a group of 'yes men' and he never gets an argument. He hears just what they think he wants to hear."[15]

The Watergate scandal continued to expand. In the fall of 1973, evidence surfaced that the Nixon White House had engaged in illegal campaign contributions, unauthorized wire taps, and attempts to use federal agencies to punish those on a White House "enemies list." Even worse, Vice President Spiro Agnew resigned on October 10, 1973, in response to bribery and tax evasion charges from when he was Maryland governor. Nixon then nominated Gerald Ford, the Republican leader of the House of Representatives, as vice president. Ford was sworn in on December 6, 1973. In the spring of 1974, the House of Representatives began considering articles of impeachment against President Nixon, and then a federal grand jury indicted a number of White House aides. The grand jury also named Nixon as an "unindicted co-conspirator."

With these troubles mounting, Nixon pleaded for Bliss's help, according to Alex Arshinkoff. Bliss was in Washington, DC, on April 25, 1974, for a meeting of the Republican National Committee. After a White House session, Nixon asked Bliss to step into the Oval Office.

"I'm in real trouble and I think my base is evaporating," Nixon said. "I may be able to hold on if you vouch for me, Ray. People respect you."

"Well, Mr. President, I guess it gets down to a simple question," replied Bliss. "Are you guilty? Are you involved in any of this?"

Nixon said, "Ray, I'm pure in this. I'm pure as the driven snow. I had nothing to do with this. This is a Democrat plot. I am clean."

"Are you telling me that this is all hyped up?" asked Bliss.

"I had nothing to do with it....I wouldn't be around that two-bit burglary. I didn't know anything about it," claimed Nixon.

"Well, let me see what I can do," Bliss told Nixon.

Bliss went to the Capitol Hill Club, a social club for Republicans, where he ran into his friend Bryce Harlow, a White House aide who had helped negotiate Bliss's exit as national chairman in 1969. Arshinkoff related the conversation Bliss said he had with Harlow.

"Ray, you look troubled. What's the story?" asked Harlow.

"Well, I was just with Nixon and he says that they are setting him up," Bliss said. "This is all a bunch of bullshit and that he's clean and that he doesn't deserve this. And we ought to do something. This is bad for the republic. This is terrible. We'll be throwing presidents out one after another because we disagree with policy."

Harlow had bad news for Bliss, according to Arshinkoff. "Ray, he is guilty as sin. I've listened to the tapes. That son-of-a-bitch is trying to set you up one more time," said Harlow.

"To the day I die, I'll never forget what you just did here," Bliss said to Harlow. "And he [Bliss] went out to his car, packed his bags and went back to Akron," reported Arshinkoff, "and never talked to Dick Nixon again as long as he lived."[16]

By then support for President Nixon among Republican leaders was crumbling. Bliss finally broke his public silence on Nixon and Watergate: "I don't think our fortunes should be built on any one man. I don't care who he is."[17]

After an adverse ruling by the US Supreme Court on the secret tapes and formal submission of articles of impeachment to the House of Representatives, Nixon resigned the presidency on August 8, 1974.

Even if Bliss had heeded Nixon's last plea for help, it probably would not have done Nixon much good. However, many of Bliss's friends believed that Watergate never would have occurred if Bliss had stayed on as national chairman in 1969. One of the most adamant was former congressman Ralph Regula, the Republican from Stark County, Ohio, just south of Bliss's home base in Summit County. "If Richard

Nixon had kept Ray Bliss, there never would have been a Watergate," said Regula. "He would have blown the whistle the first day."[18]

US Appeals Court judge Paul C. Weick, an Akron friend and attorney for Bliss, had a similar view: "If Bliss had remained as National Chairman, in my opinion, there would not have been any burglary of the Democratic headquarters and no Watergate, as Bliss was absolutely honest and he never would have permitted it."[19]

Herbert Klein, a longtime Nixon aide who was untouched by the Watergate scandal, disagreed with Regula and Weick. Klein said it's doubtful that Bliss could have done much to stop the scandal if he had been national chairman. The Watergate break-in had been engineered by CREEP, Nixon's reelection campaign committee, not the Republican National Committee. "Ray Bliss would never have known about something like that happening. I'm convinced Nixon did not either," said Klein.[20]

John Sears, another Nixon aide, agreed with Klein. "I don't think he [Bliss] ever would have known it was going on," said Sears. "I mean, most people didn't."[21]

Bliss himself had acknowledged that the national committee had limited control over the political activities of a sitting president. But it is possible to speculate what might have happened if Nixon and Bliss had been able to forge a more cooperative relationship. As national chairman, Bliss might have found out about the proposed break-in and other "dirty tricks" before they happened. He could have threatened to resign and publicly disclose the plans if they were not called off.

This is all conjecture. It is not conjecture, however, that the Watergate scandal led to further public disillusionment with politics, and that bothered Bliss. During his tenure as national chairman, polls had shown a gradual revival of interest in the two-party system, Bliss said in a 1981 interview. "Then came Watergate and the bottom fell out. He [Nixon] nearly destroyed the two-party system in this country."[22]

Chapter 65

Ray C. Bliss and Gerald R. Ford

Vice President Gerald Ford became president on August 9, 1974, following President Nixon's resignation. Ray Bliss was pleased for both the country and the Republican Party. "It's a whole new ballgame," Bliss told Abe Zaidan of the *Akron Beacon Journal*. "I believe the party will unite behind Jerry Ford. He's a team player who will keep his lines of communication open."[1]

The respect was mutual. Ford knew first-hand what Bliss had done for the party after he became national chairman. "He was literally drafted to pull a demoralized and discouraged Republican Party together," Ford later wrote. "Ray was a quiet, hardworking, knowledgeable person who generated great confidence as to his fairness. He could be tough when the circumstances demanded such action, but it was never done by a bombastic display." Ford added, "Ray and I had a very special relationship. We were elected to our respective jobs in 1965, when the Republicans were at a very low ebb, so we seemed drawn together. This wonderful friendship is one that I will always cherish."[2]

The new president was soon engulfed in controversies of his own making. On August 20, 1974, Ford nominated former New York governor Nelson Rockefeller for vice president. Rockefeller was known as a liberal Republican and this decision angered conservatives. Then on September 8, 1974, Ford issued a blanket pardon to former president Richard Nixon. Many Americans were outraged that Nixon would not stand trial for his misdeeds.[3]

The change in the White House also meant a change at the Republican National Committee. There had been three national chairmen since Bliss left in 1969, prompting one journalist to note that the party had a "revolving-door policy" for the chairman's office.[4]

Ford tapped Mary Louise Smith, a national committeewoman from Iowa, for the top job. Smith was the first woman to head the Republican National Committee. Considered part of the party's moderate wing, she had come up from the grass roots, like Bliss, focusing on nuts and bolts and coalition building.[5]

Bliss was on the committee that formally nominated Smith for the post at a September 1974 White House meeting. Later that day, Bliss sat at the head table with Ford, Smith, and other dignitaries at a reception at the Mayflower Hotel in Washington. Mrs. Smith later remarked, "I didn't mind being called 'chairman'—that was the job title, not a description of the person who held the job. Chairman Bliss was my role model."[6]

With Ford in the White House and Smith at the national committee, Bliss was interested in helping Republicans rebound in the 1974 elections that were less than two months away. A year earlier, Bliss had offered a prescription for the ailing Republicans in 1974: "First, we've got to overcome the demoralization of Watergate…then we have got to step up our efforts to recruit clean, aggressive candidates who'll be willing to campaign hard and familiarize themselves thoroughly with the issues."[7]

Back in Ohio, the Republicans had found such a candidate: former governor James Rhodes. The Ohio Constitution limited governors to two terms, but Rhodes asked the Ohio Supreme Court to rule that this limitation meant two *consecutive* terms. The court agreed with Rhodes, and he was off and running for a third, nonconsecutive term.[8]

Bliss and Rhodes had not always gotten along, but they joined forces to help the beleaguered Republicans. Usually a behind-the-scenes operator, Bliss turned into a cheerleader for the party.

"The Ohio Republican Party, facing either the nadir of its existence or a surprising upset of Democrats on November 5, must get its loyalists to the polls with the same vigor that brought Richard Nixon victory over John F. Kennedy here [Ohio] in 1960," reported the *Akron Beacon Journal* on October 18. "That's the message Akron's Ray C. Bliss, former Republican National Chairman, brought to nearly 2,000 faithful at the Ohio Republican Convention here Thursday," the story continued. The low-key Bliss had fired up the crowd: "As the band played the Ohio State fight song, Rhodes attempted to gavel down the enthusiastic crowd. Unable to gain quiet, he finally called all members of the state ticket to the front of the stage with him for bows."[9]

Republicans fared poorly in the 1974 elections. Nationally, Democrats gained four governorships, three US Senate seats, and forty-nine seats in the US House of Representatives.[10]

The Democrats also had the upper hand in Ohio, electing a lieutenant governor, attorney general, auditor, and treasurer. They retained control of the Ohio House and took control of the state senate from Republicans.

The big exception was big: Rhodes took back the governorship for the Republicans. He defeated incumbent Democrat John Gilligan by 48.6 to 48.3 percent of the vote—a margin of some 11,000 ballots out of more than 3 million cast. Rhodes actually conceded defeat at a post-midnight press conference only to wake up in the morning as governor-elect.[11]

Meanwhile, Bliss's friendship with Ford came in handy in 1974 when state leaders sought to create a national park in the Cuyahoga River valley between Akron and Cleveland.[12] A key player in the effort to establish the park was Representative John Seiberling, an Akron Democrat. Bliss and Seiberling had little in common politically, but they shared something that transcended their political differences—a love for their hometown. In 1971, Seiberling had introduced legislation to create the park. He was then a freshman congressman and the bill went nowhere. Two years later Seiberling tried again with more success.[13]

Party lines disappeared as Ohio politicians united behind the park proposal. Seiberling's key Republican ally was Representative Ralph Regula of Stark County, south of Akron.[14] This bipartisan effort helped win approval for the park in Congress, but that was not enough. There was a well-founded fear that President Ford would veto the legislation, following the recommendation of both the US Department of the Interior and the Office of Management and Budget.

Democratic and Republican advocates for the park mounted a furious lobbying effort to win Ford's approval, including Bliss, who contacted Ford directly. Bliss warned President Ford that by vetoing the bill he would lose Ohio in the 1976 presidential election. Ford signed the bill creating the park on December 27, 1974, while on a holiday ski vacation in Vail, Colorado. Later Ford said he did not specifically remember the request from Bliss, but added: "If he [Bliss] did [send a message], I certainly considered Ray's views in deciding whether to veto or not."[15]

Seiberling acknowledged Bliss's role in helping create the park. Regula said Bliss's plea was critical: "Without Ray Bliss, there never would have been a Cuyahoga Valley national park."[16] For Bliss, creation of the park was a different way that the two-party system could work for the good of all.

After the Watergate scandal, Bliss participated in Republican debates about improving the two-party system, including campaign finance reform and changes in the selection of national convention delegates.[17] Bliss recommended that these debates be conducted behind closed doors. "I want people there to speak their mind and not be inhibited by the press," Bliss told reporters in 1973. "If they have something sensitive to say, they ought to say it."[18]

Bliss's advice was largely ignored, and the reform controversies came to a head at a meeting of the Republican National Committee in March 1975.[19] The national committee compromised on public financing for the national conventions, part of a post-Watergate law enacted by Congress. Conservatives, opposed to any federal government involvement, wanted to reject the federal money. Their motion failed, however, 90–62. Instead, the committee agreed to support a lawsuit seeking to block federal financing, but to accept the $2 million if legal action failed or the courts did not act on the lawsuit.

No compromise could be reached, however, on delegate selection. The debate focused on a "positive action" plan to encourage greater participation of women and minorities in party affairs. State parties were encouraged to conduct "outreach workshops, open hearings, and wide publicity about party affairs." Although strictly voluntary, such encouragement was too much for conservatives.

Despite his commitment to party unity, Bliss entered the fray, giving an "emotional speech," telling the committee that the national party could not afford to look "weak-kneed" on the issue of participation and inclusion. Edward Mahe Jr., the national party's executive director, tried to put a positive spin on the intraparty battling: "Put it in the paper—Republicans are fun."[20]

A divided party, however, was no fun for an appointed president seeking election to his own term. President Ford declared his candidacy for the White House on July 8, 1975—more than a year before the 1976 election.[21] The campaign finance laws, including the need to qualify for the new public financing system, were one reason for the early start. Another reason was to get ahead of any opponents for the Republican nomination.

Ford's fledgling campaign needed both a campaign chairman and a manager. Bliss's name was repeatedly mentioned for both roles.[22] Bliss said he wasn't sure what he would do for the Ford campaign, but emphasized that he would "not be getting into any full-time role." But he added, "I still have some continuing interest in politics."[23]

Bliss was listed as a member of an initial advisory group the Ford campaign announced in July. He helped organize a "Republican National Committee Task-force" in August. Its mission was to "look at the RNC staff organization to determine its productivity, its effectiveness, its imagination, and its professionalism" and report to Ford by November 1975.[24]

A strong challenger to President Ford soon emerged. In July 1975, "Citizens for Reagan" announced backing for former California governor Ronald Reagan. A key campaign operative was John Sears, the former Nixon aide who had helped oust Bliss as national chairman in 1969. By the fall of 1975, Reagan was officially in the race.

The Ford campaign was surprised by the Reagan candidacy. The president enjoyed the support of most of the Republican establishment in Washington, DC, Ohio, and across the country. Reagan had strongly backed Barry Goldwater's disastrous campaign in 1964 and lost the GOP nomination to Nixon in 1968. However, Reagan had some advantages. A former actor, he was a made-for-television candidate with an aw-shucks smiling appeal. He was a conservative with a golden tongue, appealing to a wide range of voters.

After narrowly winning the New Hampshire primary on January 27, it looked as if Ford had a clear path to the nomination. But when Reagan won the North Carolina primary on March 23, the race quickly became a see-saw affair. As the national convention neared, neither candidate had enough delegates to win the nomination.

Bliss summed up the situation in an interview from his Akron office that appeared in the *Ohio Republican News*, the official voice of the Ohio party. "At this point, we have reached a stage where the delegates have been chosen and campaigns have been waged in practically every state in the country and the die has been cast. There are strong feelings both ways as to the candidates."

Then Bliss offered a rare, public endorsement of a candidate: "I happen to be a strong supporter of President Ford because I've known him for a good many years and I think he's qualified to be president." He also added a note of hope for the divided Republicans. "We've had divisions within our party before and come back. We had a serious fight at the 1952 convention at Chicago between General Eisenhower and Senator Taft. It was a bitterly fought convention, but we won in the fall because Republicans closed ranks. It can be done again if we have the heart and will to do it."[25]

However, Bliss had heart problems of his own that kept him on the sidelines during the primaries. On February 16, 1976, he was admitted to City Hospital in Akron with a heart attack.[26] As a consequence, Bliss sat out most of the primary campaign. However, he was well enough to attend the Republican National Convention in Kansas City. According to journalist Abe Zaidan, Bliss went to each state delegation making the case for Ford, arguing that the incumbent president deserved the party's nomination.[27]

The vice presidency was a major issue at the convention. Ford had removed the incumbent vice president, Nelson Rockefeller, from the ticket in November 1975 in an attempt to appease conservatives. Meanwhile, Reagan named Senator Richard Schweiker of Pennsylvania as his vice-presidential candidate in an attempt to attract moderates. The Reagan forces then pressured Ford to name his vice-presidential running mate before balloting for the presidential nominee began. Ford, however, won a vote on a proposed rule change that would have forced him to make the early—and politically dangerous—announcement.

Bliss was relieved. He acknowledged that he had been worried about a Reagan upset for months. "I think it's a strong setback for the Reagan forces," Bliss said. "This indicates Ford has the delegates to win. I'm not as nervous as I was a year ago about this."[28]

Ford won the nomination on the first ballot, but by a narrow 117 delegate votes. Ford picked Senator Bob Dole of Kansas as his running mate, a choice that had Reagan's approval.

The Republicans left the national convention at least superficially united, but Ford was trailing the Democratic nominee, Jimmy Carter, by thirty-four points in the polls. The former governor of Georgia, Carter had won the nomination campaigning as a "Washington outsider" and continued that theme against Ford. Senator Walter Mondale of Minnesota was the vice-presidential nominee.

Ford, however, began to close the gap, and, as usual, winning Ohio was critical to Republican hopes. But Bliss was not able to do for Ford what he had done for John Ballard in the Akron mayor's race in 1971: the *Akron Beacon Journal* endorsed Carter instead of Ford for president.

Ford's comeback fell short. Carter carried Ohio 48.9 to 48.7 percent, winning by some 11,000 votes out of 4 million cast. His popular vote margin nationally was slightly higher, 50.2 percent, and he prevailed in the Electoral College, 297 to 240.[29]

There was more bad news for Ohio Republicans. In a rematch of the 1970 US Senate race, Democrat Howard Metzenbaum defeated incumbent Republican Robert Taft Jr., 49.5 to 46.5 percent.

The election results were a disappointment for Bliss. Not only had Ford and Taft lost close races, but his mentee Mary Louise Smith soon resigned as head of the national committee.

What the GOP needed was another Ray Bliss to restore the party's fortunes. Such a person was available: William E. Brock III was elected chairman of the Republican National Committee in 1977.[30]

On the surface, Bliss and Brock were a study in contrasts. Bliss came from a modest financial background and had never held public office. Brock was a millionaire, with much of his wealth coming from a family-owned candy business in Tennessee. Before becoming national chairman, he had served three terms in the US House and one term in the US Senate.

Brock successfully rebuilt the Republican Party over the next four years, paving the way for the Republican victories in 1980, including the White House and control of the US Senate. He was a worthy successor to the organizational man from Akron.[31]

Chapter 66

Citizen Bliss

After the 1976 election, Ray Bliss began phasing out of involvement in politics because of poor health. In the spring of 1978, he did not seek reelection to the Summit County Republican Central Committee. He had been an elected precinct committeeman continuously since 1932.[1] Then in November 1978, Bliss announced his resignation from the Summit County Board of Elections. "For many years, either the party's central committee or executive committee chairman has been a member of the board," said Bliss.[2]

Alex Arshinkoff called Bliss's resignation "bittersweet." "I have more respect for him [Bliss] than for anyone else in politics," said Arshinkoff. "He was the very best in his job, always insisting that we have fair and honest elections. It will be a loss to the community."[3]

Bliss may have had bittersweet feelings as well. He had joined the elections board in 1935 and served continuously for forty-two years. It was his first paying job in politics. Even when he was state and national chairman, Bliss made it a point to be at the board offices on election nights to help supervise the ballot counting.

In 1980, Bliss cut his last formal ties to the Republican Party when he announced he would not seek reelection as Republican national committeeman from Ohio, serve as a national convention delegate, or endorse any presidential candidate in 1980.[4] Bliss had been on the national committee continuously since 1952, serving twelve years as the Ohio state chairman and then sixteen years as national committeeman from Ohio, in addition to serving as national chairman from 1965 to 1969.

Brian Usher, the political writer for the *Akron Beacon Journal,* dubbed him "Citizen Bliss." Bliss seemed to like the new title. "I reserve the right to support anybody I please," he said. "I may not do anything. I don't know."[5]

As the news of his retirement spread, Bliss received numerous personal letters of praise from his peers in Republican politics.

Ody Fish, the national committeeman from Wisconsin who had helped engineer Bliss's election as national chairman in 1965, noted Bliss's achievements and added: "Aside from all that I genuinely treasured our friendship. You were motivated by the best of reasons, a desire for a better and stronger country."[6]

Arthur Peterson spoke for many: "It is difficult for me to comprehend the American political scene without you. . . . I realize that you have given everything of yourself for over half a century and it is time now that some new, younger people step into the harness to help pull the load. Nevertheless, it will not be the same."[7]

Bryce Harlow wrote about Bliss's success and humility: "Very few people I have come across over the years could have the satisfaction you are entitled to have from your contributions to our party and our country. You can't openly admit that, I suppose; yet you know it's true just as I do. Just what you did as National Chairman (and I know a heckuva lot about that!) earned you political immortality; and then, when you factor in what you did for the party in Ohio over all those years—well, like I say, you're entitled to settle back with a big grin, rub your tummy, and say, 'Well folks, I did my best and you'll have to admit it's pretty good.'"[8]

At the 1980 Republican National Convention in Detroit, Bliss received public recognition for his fifty years of service to the Republican Party. Senator Bob Dole of Kansas—one of Bliss's successors as national chairman—made the presentation.

"The individual we honor tonight has been called with admiration, but rather unfairly, a nuts and bolts man. That is too simplistic. What he really is, is a master builder, an architect of the possible. Each of us in this arena owes him a great debt, for truly we have built on his foundation," said Dole. "Thus, I am honored to present this solid gold medal to a great Republican and a great American, Chairman Ray Bliss."[9]

Even as he was honored, Bliss still focused on winning elections. After thanking the convention, he added: "And all I ask of you and those on the air tonight who believe as I do that we need a new President is redouble your efforts as you did while I was chairman, and I am sure we will have a tremendous victory in November."

Bliss's request was in part a plea for unity. In 1980, the Republicans faced the familiar divisions between conservatives and moderates.[10] Former California governor Ronald Reagan was a favorite of the conservatives, and having won most of the 1980 primaries, was about to receive the presidential nomination. But moderate Republicans feared that Reagan would lose the election to President Jimmy Carter. In fact, one moderate, Representative John Anderson of Illinois, was preparing to run as an independent in the general election, potentially hurting the GOP.

Reagan briefly considered offering the vice-presidential nomination to former President Gerald Ford, a move viewed as a "dream team" by some party leaders—but not by others, including Bliss. Instead, Reagan chose another moderate for the second spot on the ticket, primary rival George H. W. Bush. Bush was also a successor to Bliss as national chairman.

Brian Usher of the *Akron Beacon Journal* reported, "Bliss could read the political cards stacking up against Democrat Jimmy Carter better than most, but he would tolerate no overconfidence among his legions. He wanted no letting down and no wild shift to the right among the very conservative delegates who had been elected in the primaries."[11]

Bliss explained to Usher: "I can smell complacency in politics. This is my last turn at the wheel, so I wanted to go on the record so nobody will come back later and say, 'Ray, if you saw something wrong, why didn't you say so?'"[12]

Bliss's concern was warranted. The presidential race quickly tightened after the national conventions. In his first speech in retirement, Bliss addressed the Ohio Republican Convention in Columbus. The convention was upbeat, but Bliss delivered a note of realism. He reminded the delegates of Tom Dewey's close defeat in 1948 and Gerald Ford's narrow loss in 1976. "When we have won in Ohio, we have generally won it the hard way...with better candidates and hard work," Bliss said.[13]

Republicans buckled down and Reagan won the election. Nationally and in Ohio, Reagan narrowly took the popular vote, but got a landslide in the Electoral College, 489 electoral votes to just 49 for Carter. The GOP also took control of the US Senate and gained 34 seats in the US House of Representatives.[14]

After the election, Bliss was asked to serve as the honorary chairman for the governors' reception at Reagan's presidential inauguration, the same post he held at Nixon's inaugural in 1968. Bliss sounded almost grumpy about attending the festivities. "I don't really care to go," Bliss said. "I'm going because my wife and her sisters want to go. If you've been to one of them, you've been to all of them. It's just a madhouse."[15]

It would be the fifth presidential inauguration for Bliss. After Reagan's swearing in as the nation's fortieth president, Ray and Ellen Bliss attended a candlelight dinner and inaugural ball at the Kennedy Center. Although Reagan was the center of attention at the ball, he shared the spotlight with the organizational man from Akron.

Representative Ralph Regula and his wife, Mary, from Stark County south of Akron, were among the guests in the Blisses' box. Instead of dancing, the Regulas watched as senators, members of Congress, and party leaders—past and present and from all parts of the country—filed past to pay tribute to "Mr. Chairman."

"It was like holding court," Regula said later. "Ray just stayed in the box. He knew them all."[16]

Chapter 67

University Trustee

As Ray Bliss slowly moved out of Republican Party politics, he became increasingly active in the affairs of his alma mater, the University of Akron. Bliss and his wife had been active alumni since the 1930s.

In December 1970, Republican Governor James Rhodes appointed Bliss to the university's board of trustees. The appointment was to complete the term of retiring former Goodyear chairman E. J. Thomas, ending in 1974.[1]

Akron's municipal university had become a state university in 1967. Bliss helped guide the school though the aftermath of this transition. According to University of Akron official W. Richard Wright, "Ray Bliss found a new purpose and dedicated himself to the university."[2]

Bliss applied his passion for detail to his board work, recalled Madge Doerler: "We went over and over every board document before each meeting."[3]

Bliss gave the university top priority—as President Richard Nixon and Attorney General John Mitchell soon found out. When Mitchell was preparing to head up Nixon's reelection campaign in 1972, he tried to set up a Monday meeting at the White House with Nixon. Bliss, however, had scheduled a meeting of the board of trustees' development committee for that Monday, "so the President and Mitchell had to wait until Tuesday," reported Helen Carringer in the *Akron Beacon Journal* in June 1974.

Carringer had become a fan of Bliss's service to the university and made the case for Bliss's reappointment to the board of trustees when his term expired in 1974. "In the Finance Committee," wrote Carringer in the same article, "Bliss has been insistent that the university consult experts in the community for broader decision-making background and in matters of insurance he has been a watchdog but never a participant because of his own business interests." She also quoted an editorial in the *Buchtelite*, the university's student newspaper: "If any trustee ever merited reappointment to the Akron University Board of Trustees, it's Ray Bliss."

Carringer's column was directed at Governor John Gilligan, a Democrat. Historically, Democratic governors had appointed Democrats to university boards of trustees, while Republican governors had appointed Republicans—just as Rhodes did with Bliss in 1970. "While he is a 'big' man in Republican politics," Carringer wrote about Bliss, "there is nothing too little for him and his wife, Ellen, to do for their alma mater."[4]

Despite this plea, Gilligan followed precedent and appointed a Democrat. But Bliss was not off the board of trustees for long. Rhodes defeated Gilligan in the 1974 governor's race and, in June 1975, the Republican governor appointed Bliss to a full nine-year term.[5]

The board of trustees represented a cross-section of the community's political, business, and civic leadership. This diversity was reminiscent of the campus a young Bliss had encountered as a student in the late 1920s. Bliss served with fellow Republicans, such as Charles J. Pilliod, chairman of the Goodyear Tire & Rubber Co., but also with Democrats, including Robert Kidney, chairman of the Akron Labor Council, and attorney Bernard Rosen, a prominent Democrat who was a partner in a law firm with Robert Blakemore, the chairman of the Summit County Democratic Party.

However, political differences took a backseat to serving the university, which the trustees regarded as a civic duty. "There was a common bond...a common commitment to make Akron a better community. The means of doing that was through the growth of the university," said Rosen's son, attorney Gary Rosen.[6]

Like Bliss, the elder Rosen held an undergraduate degree from the University of Akron and was also fiercely proud of his alma mater. Bliss would ask younger relatives why they would want to leave Akron to attend college when they had an outstanding university in their hometown.[7] Gary Rosen said his father asked him the same question when he left Akron to seek an undergraduate degree at Tufts University in Massachusetts, adding, "My father was a tad frustrated with me."[8]

Wright recalled how Bliss worked to insulate the university from partisan politics, including patronage appointments. In one of Bliss's initial meetings as a board member, trustees were presented with the annual budget and a list of employees for their approval. Bliss held up the employee list and said, "We don't need to see this list. We hire the president and he hires everyone else—if there is a problem, we take it up with the president."[9]

Bliss's and Rosen's political connections benefited university students. In 1972, Dan Moldea, president of the student body, appeared before the board of trustees to single out the two members for their help with the student government's nonpartisan voter registration proposal. He specifically thanked Bliss, "senior member of the Summit County Board of Elections, for his guidance and understanding throughout the process."[10]

Bliss looked out for the interests of the students. At a 1978 meeting, Bliss "expressed his strong belief that holding tuition down was very important." Wright recalled what Bliss said to fellow trustees when increasing tuition was discussed. "I can remember when many of you were in school. You could barely pay your bills, worked two jobs, and had patches on your clothes. Today's students need the same opportunity," Bliss said.[11]

Bliss was also critical of a formula that the Ohio Board of Regents used to distribute money to state-supported universities. It penalized low-tuition schools such as the University of Akron.

The board meeting minutes show that Bliss took a keen interest in fund-raising and the efficient operation of the university. Bliss and his wife became donors to the university in 1972, when they established the Ray C. and Ellen P. Bliss Political Science Scholarship Fund. The couple eventually provided more than $52,000 to the fund.[12]

The scholarships were for full-time undergraduate students majoring in political science. Initially, preference was given to students from Summit County, but eventually eligibility was expanded to include students from neighboring Stark County as well as members of Bliss's fraternity. Financial need and academic achievement were not the only criteria for the scholarship. Another top priority was "participation in party organization activities." Awards were made on a bipartisan basis, and active Democratic and Republican students were encouraged to apply.

"Bliss wanted college graduates to volunteer in party politics after they graduated," recalled Wright, "like they might volunteer for Little League or the United Way."[13]

Bliss took a hands-on approach to administering the scholarship. He served on the selection committee along with a faculty member from the Political Science Department and two others from outside the university. His involvement is evident in a 1979 letter to Representative Ralph Regula from Stark County about two Republican students from Regula's area who had been awarded scholarships. "I write to let you know about the scholarship awards because I thought you might like to congratulate them as recipients," wrote Bliss, "and, last but not least, I thought you might like to have your local campaign activator keep them in mind in your next campaign."[14]

Two years earlier, in 1977, a Bliss scholarship was awarded to Charles W. Walker of Akron, an African American student, who was also blind and an orphan. "It will be a great honor to receive the Ray Bliss Scholarship," Walker wrote. "Mr. Bliss has been a great public servant. Although I have been a Young Democrat, I have been a great admirer of Mr. Bliss."[15]

Ellen Bliss later recalled her husband's satisfaction with the scholarships. "Ray believed young people mattered to the two-party system," she said. "The students reminded him of when he was in college."[16]

The University of Akron grew steadily during Bliss's tenure on the board of trustees. Enrollment increased by more than 40 percent, from 18,536 to 26,680 students. By 1981, the school had more than sixteen times the number of students as when Bliss matriculated in 1925. The university also expanded physically, acquiring, constructing, or planning fifteen new facilities. In Summit County, the projects included acquiring the "Rubber Bowl" stadium from the city of Akron, constructing the state-of-the-art E. J. Thomas Performing Arts Hall, and planning the James A. Rhodes Sports Arena.

The university reached beyond Summit County as well. In 1972, the university added a branch campus in Orrville in nearby Wayne County. In 1973, a cooperative effort of the University of Akron, Kent State University, and Youngstown State University established the Northeastern Ohio Universities College of Medicine in Rootstown, in Portage County (renamed Northeast Ohio Medical University in 2011).[17]

Bliss's service on the board of trustees was not without its own peculiar politics. There was friction between Bliss and President Dominic Guzzetta, who held the top university job from 1971 to 1984.

"Guzzetta was ambitious and insecure" said Wright. "He and Ray often locked horns behind the scenes." Wright remembered that Guzzetta was irritated at coverage in the *Akron Beacon Journal* and complained to Bliss. "Bliss told him, 'Anyone that sits in the corner office [the president's office suite] has to get along with the local newspaper…that's your job.'"

Guzzetta was not satisfied with his salary or social status. He regularly asked Bliss to help him obtain seats on corporate boards. "Ray, you know lots of CEOs, you could help me if you wanted to," Wright recalled. Bliss deflected the requests until one day he said, "Ok, Dom. I can recommend you for corporate boards, but on one condition—that you give me your letter of resignation as president of the University of Akron."[18]

While on the board of trustees, Bliss served as a member of the finance committee, chairman of the development committee, a member of the university foundation, and vice chairman when Democrat Rosen and labor leader Kidney were chairmen of the board.

On June 25, 1981, Bliss was elected chairman of the board. After the vote, Bliss read a board resolution commending the retiring chairman, labor leader Kidney, for his "wise counsel and conscientious service."

"Bob," quipped the chairman-elect, "I never thought I'd see the day when Ray Bliss would be sorry to see a Democrat leave any office."[19]

Becoming board chairman put the finishing touch to Bliss's rehabilitation at the University of Akron. Fifty years earlier, in 1931, Bliss had been expelled, charged with stuffing the ballot box in the campus May Queen election. Now he was one of the university's top leaders.

If Bliss thought about all these matters on his first day as chairman, July 22, the meeting minutes do not reflect it. Instead, the record shows the understated, pragmatic attitude that was Bliss's trademark: "Mr. Bliss thanked the Board for their expression of confidence in electing him chairman. He pledged to be tolerant of the differing views and convictions of others.... Mr. Bliss stated that he recognizes that his success as Chairman depends upon the support of his fellow Board members."[20]

The late 1970s and early 1980s had not been kind to Akron or other cities in the "Rust Belt." Bliss worried that the coming generations would not have the same opportunities he had enjoyed. Paul Poorman, then editor of the *Akron Beacon Journal*, described Bliss as a man "preoccupied with the future."

"Bliss wanted to reverse the negative momentum," Poorman wrote, "and he had a vision for how the institutions he loved could help move things ahead." He wanted the University of Akron to play a bigger role in redeveloping the economy of the city of Akron and the surrounding area. But he did not want his alma mater to turn its back on its primary role "as a school for everybody."

Bliss also wanted a re-energized two-party system that would produce leaders who would "get Ohio moving again." He hoped the Republican Party would develop new candidates with new ideas—and he wished the same for the Democrats. "Today and tomorrow are what matter, not yesterday," Bliss told Poorman.

"And bluntly," Poorman concluded, "that aspect of his thinking set him apart from some in our community. To me that will be Ray Bliss' legacy."[21]

Chapter 68

Mentor and Teacher

As Ray Bliss moved into retirement, he expanded his roles as mentor and teacher. His pupils were part of his legacy.

In 1977, the Ohio Republican Party was at a low ebb. The Democrats controlled the state legislature and most statewide offices. James Rhodes was still governor but, from Bliss's point of view, Rhodes was part of the problem. The party had lost its independence and become subordinate to the governor.

Two GOP leaders in the state senate decided to do something about the situation: James Tilling, director of research and communications for the Republican senate caucus, and Tom Van Meter of Ashland, Ohio, state senator and the assistant minority leader. "We need to go up and talk to Ray Bliss because he was the most successful nuts-and-bolts guy both in Ohio and nationally," Van Meter said to Tilling. A former political science professor at Ohio University, Tilling had heard about Bliss in the late 1950s and the 1960s when he was growing up in a 'political family' in upstate New York. "People talked about what an effective job he had done with the Ohio Republican Party," Tilling said.

Tilling and Van Meter met with Bliss at his Akron insurance office and then went to lunch at the City Club. It was the first of several meetings leading up to the 1978 election. "He was very relaxed," Tilling recalled. "He obviously was dressed formally. He always had on his coat and tie, but he was very friendly. I think he was interested in the fact that we were interested in him and what he could do to help us. He was very energetic. I don't mean necessarily jumping up and down, but intellectually, very energetic. And he had a lot of great ideas and stories and was very eager to share them."

Van Meter led off the initial conversation. He asked Bliss to describe how he had run the state party, what kinds of services the party provided to candidates, and what the senate Republican caucus could do to help itself. The senate leaders had decided that they could not expect any help from the Ohio Republican Party because it had few resources and was under Rhodes's control.

"I knew that it really distressed Ray. Because he said you'd call up down there [at state headquarters] and the phone would ring and ring and nobody would answer. They wouldn't work after 5 o'clock. To him, it was just a symptom of lack of interest. No enthusiasm. No organization. No leadership," said Tilling.

Bliss pinned some of the blame on former president Richard Nixon. "Obviously, he did not have a very high regard for Richard Nixon. He said probably nobody did more to destroy the party than Nixon. What he meant by that was not that Nixon did it on purpose. But the effect of his policies and actions...they were a death blow to the party," said Tilling.

Bliss and his visitors then came up with a strategy for the Republican Senate caucus to engineer a comeback on its own. "Basically what became clear early on in the conversation was that you didn't really have a functioning Republican Party at the state level to provide the resources that any campaign or candidate needs," said Tilling. "Somehow we would have to recreate the party model inside the Republican [Senate] caucus."

Bliss told them how to do it. First, they had to learn how to find the right candidate for each Senate district. "He was a very strong believer in the candidate, recruiting the right candidate. That candidate had to be tailored to the district. You had to find out what the voters in the district were thinking. What kind of candidate could you recruit that would reflect their views and their values," Tilling said.

Van Meter, an army veteran of the Vietnam War and a combative conservative, got the message. Using Bliss's advice, he helped recruit moderate Republicans to run in districts where successful candidates had to appeal to Democrats and independents as well as Republicans to win. In conservative districts, Van Meter recruited conservatives.

"The next thing he [Bliss] talked about was the importance of fund-raising and how it would be helpful to have a centralized fund-raising mechanism," said Tilling. "That led to the development of the Republican Senate Campaign Finance Committee and the emphasis being placed on having caucus fund-raisers instead of having each individual candidate around the state raise their own money." There had been a separate Republican Senate Campaign Finance Committee, but it had become just a shell, said Tilling.

In future state senate campaigns, Republican candidates were encouraged to raise some money on their own. The campaign finance committee, however, would raise the bulk of the money and, more importantly, put the money into the races where it was needed and where it could make a difference. This was a change.

"I remember Tom [Van Meter] told me in 1976 their policy was every candidate, regardless of whether they needed it or not, got a fixed amount out of the campaign committee, a thousand bucks, $5,000 bucks, whatever it was. We stopped that after talking to Ray, realizing we were just throwing away scarce resources and giving it to people who didn't need it," Tilling recalled.

Bliss did more than tell them how to raise the money and how to spend it. He helped them find it. The business leaders who formed the financial backbone of the party had become discouraged about giving. "They'd sort of cut back on what they were doing," said Tilling.

Senate minority leader Paul Gillmor of Port Clinton—who became involved in the sessions with Bliss—and Van Meter had been having trouble finding generous contributors. Bliss, whom the business leaders remembered from the party's better days, began making calls for the Republican senators.

"When Tom and Paul went to 'em [business leaders] and showed 'em our plan and how we thought we could make it, I know the first time around in the 1978 election there was a fair amount of skepticism....I know Tom in many instances made mention of Ray...that he had met with Ray. That was something that got their attention," said Tilling. "They understood it was the same combination of strategies that Ray had used. That helped them to understand we might have a chance," said Tilling.

The Republicans picked up three Ohio Senate seats in 1978, cutting the Democratic advantage to 18–15. In 1980, they picked up three more seats and won back the majority.

Bliss was pleased, said Tilling. "I think he was excited by the fact that he played a key role and he was helpful in us winning the Senate."

The Republicans lost control of the Ohio Senate to the Democrats in 1982 during a national recession, but regained control in 1984. The Republican majority in the state senate became the foundation for the slow rebuilding of the Ohio Republican Party in the 1980s and beyond.

While Bliss had a behind-the-scenes role in starting the revival, he wouldn't have bragged about it. "I think the thing that impressed me the most about him was that despite the fact that he was proud of his accomplishments, he still reminded me of a very modest guy," said Tilling.[1]

The late 1970s were also a challenging time for Republicans in Akron, but this was nothing new. Bliss had learned his craft by winning local elections in a strongly Democratic area. Although Bliss had resigned as GOP chairman in Summit County when he became national chairman in 1965, he had remained active in the local party and was always on the lookout for new talent. Alex Arshinkoff came to Bliss's attention.

Arshinkoff seemed an unlikely Republican. The youngest of four sons from a family of Macedonian ancestry, he was a dark-haired, swarthy ethnic in a party that often seemed to be dominated by Anglo-Saxon Protestants.[2]

Like Bliss, Arshinkoff got hooked early on politics. He followed events at City Hall, Columbus, and Washington, DC, the way other northeastern Ohio boys devoted themselves to the Cleveland Indians' baseball team. Arshinkoff was just fifteen years old and volunteering on Robert Taft Jr.'s successful 1970 US Senate campaign when he first shook hands with Bliss.

Arshinkoff grew up in Akron but graduated from Jackson High School in neighboring Stark County, where he was student council president. Upon graduation in 1973, Arshinkoff entered the University of Akron, where he pledged Phi Kappa Tau, the same fraternity to which Bliss and D. E. "Gene" Waddell, the Summit County Republican chairman, belonged.

Arshinkoff's political involvement increased quickly. In 1973, he ran for the Akron City Council as a kind of Republican sacrificial lamb in a heavily Democratic inner-city ward. He lost and then lost another bid for the same seat in 1975. Both times, however, he won the endorsement of the *Akron Beacon Journal*.

Still a college freshman, Arshinkoff was elected president of the College Republicans in 1974. In the same year, he ran for Republican precinct committeeman and won a seat on the county party's central committee. It was a good time for an ambitious, hard-working, young man to advance in the party: older Republicans were discouraged by the Watergate scandal, and recruiting newcomers was difficult.

The aspiring politician caught the eye of Summit County chairman Waddell, who sponsored Arshinkoff for a seat on the party's smaller but more influential executive committee. At that committee's first meeting, the new member was elected a party vice chairman.

Arshinkoff remembered what happened next: "Stick around, we're going to go up and have a drink with Ray Bliss," Waddell told him. For Arshinkoff, this was like having an audience with the Pope. The executive committee had met in the basement of an Akron-area restaurant, and Bliss was waiting for them upstairs.

Bliss gave Arshinkoff advice on how to run the College Republicans. Give the group a social dimension, Bliss said, just as he had done with the Young Republicans back in the 1930s. Arshinkoff took the advice and rented the local American Legion hall for a bash, complete with ten kegs of beer and a band that played 1950s hits. "When I think back on that meeting, many of the people in the [Summit County Republican] party today attended that night," Arshinkoff noted later.

He got further proof of the value of such events from his own family. Arshinkoff's father and uncles used to attend the social events Bliss put on for Summit County's Young Republicans in the 1930s. His uncle kept a memento. "He took his wallet out and took out a card, a Young Republican card from 1936," said Arshinkoff.[3]

Arshinkoff was off and organizing. Bliss became his mentor, just as Jim Corey had been for Bliss in the 1930s.

In the fall of 1974, Arshinkoff ran Republican Don Stephens's unsuccessful campaign for county auditor during the post-Watergate election. Two years later, he directed Stephens's successful campaign for reelection as a county commissioner—the only Republican countywide to win while Democrat Jimmy Carter captured the White House.[4]

Waddell found that more and more of his time was taken up with his law practice. Arshinkoff, with Bliss's support, assumed more day-to-day duties of running the local party. By 1978, Waddell decided to step down as county chairman, with the idea of turning the reins over to Arshinkoff.

A furor erupted at the party meeting when Waddell proposed Arshinkoff as his successor. Older Republicans considered him too inexperienced. But Arshinkoff had an important ally in Bliss. Bliss knew that his young protégé had, in effect, been running the party and was confident he could do the job on a full-time basis. He also fit Bliss's vision of a party open to like-minded people of all backgrounds.

Akron mayor John Ballard was among those who opposed Arshinkoff. Ballard's candidate for party chairman was former county commissioner Richard Slusser (the son of the Akron mayor Bliss helped elect in the 1940s and 1950s). Ballard helped organize two meetings of Republicans looking for an alternative to Arshinkoff.

In the heat of the battle, Ballard and Slusser charged that they hadn't received much financial help from the local party in past elections. That blast brought an unusual retort from Bliss, who seldom criticized fellow Republicans. "One present officeholder and one former officeholder have said the party organization provided them with no money," said Bliss. "They got thousands of dollars. These careless statements make it difficult to build a party."[5]

By the time the party executive committee met in June to choose a new chairman, Slusser was no longer a candidate. Turnout for the meeting—106 of 124 executive committee members—was the biggest in the party's history. Arshinkoff defeated his only opponent, restaurant owner Mark Figetakis, 90–12, with four abstentions.

Arshinkoff was pleased. "We've turned the corner," he told the executive committee. "I know it. I can feel it." At twenty-three, he became the youngest urban county Republican chairman in Ohio and possibly the nation. "I would not have been chairman if it had not been for Bliss," said Arshinkoff.[6]

After being elected chairman, Arshinkoff dropped out of college to become chairman full time. He would continue taking classes from Bliss, not from the university. "It was like the chance to study art with Michelangelo or Leonardo da Vinci," Arshinkoff said in 1987. "Most artists would quit art school in a minute for a chance like that."[7]

The mentor told his willing student what he expected, said Arshinkoff: "When I became county chairman, Bliss told me he expected two things: no surprises on the executive committee and he wanted to approve all appointments to the university's board of trustees." [8]

Arshinkoff did not achieve instant success. In 1978, the Republicans won only three of twenty-three local races. "For a week, I never went back to headquarters," said Arshinkoff. He was at home when the phone rang. "Where the hell are you?" asked Bliss. "Get your ass down here."

Arshinkoff did as he was told. Bliss gave him a constructive tongue-lashing. "In politics you're going to have big ups and big downs," Bliss told him. "You just get out there and start filling that ticket."[9]

Arshinkoff took the advice. In 1979, there were 145 races on the county ballot and the Republicans had candidates in 102 of them. The Republicans won 49, including an Akron municipal judgeship and the Akron mayor's race.

Arshinkoff continued to consult with Bliss frequently on party operations and campaigns. He was a regular visitor to Bliss's insurance office, located in the same building as party headquarters. Bliss was always teaching. "He was willing to help us daily, that was the key. I went to Bliss four or five times a day, sometimes for five or six hours," Arshinkoff said. "I'd go to him and ask advice and he would give it." In return, Bliss wanted to be kept informed. "If you want me to be there on the crash landings," Bliss said, "let me be there on the takeoffs."[10]

Those who observed Arshinkoff and Bliss close up say it was a clear case of hero worship. "He just sat at Mr. Bliss's feet like a king," said Frances Rex. "That kid ran

Main Street for us, from one end to the other. He did anything we wanted him to do. He earned the respect of a lot of people," said Rex. "Bliss had an eye for knowing people who were up and coming. He could pick out people better than anybody I know."[11]

"Alex simply adored Ray," said Madge Doerler.[12]

Bliss was demanding, she recalled. "G_dam it! Don't do that," Bliss would tell Arshinkoff in anger. But Bliss also admired Arshinkoff, both Rex and Doerler agreed.

Arshinkoff continued as county chairman into the twenty-first century and became one of the most influential Republican county chairmen in Ohio.

Bliss's mentoring extended beyond politics to an institution he loved as much as his hometown—the University of Akron. While serving a second term on the university's board of trustees, Bliss took a newly appointed member, Janet Purnell, under his wing. It had a lasting and significant effect on her life.

Purnell, a public school principal, and her husband, Norman, a lawyer, stuck out in Summit County Republican politics because they were African Americans in a party that was largely white. For the Purnells, the "party of Lincoln" was preferable to the Democrats, especially the Democrats' segregationist wing in the South. Purnell had been active in the Summit County Republican Party, and had run a solid, if losing, campaign for a seat on Akron City Council. In 1978, Governor James Rhodes appointed her to the University of Akron Board of Trustees.

Like Bliss, Purnell was a graduate of the University of Akron. She had met Bliss before her appointment, but they did not have a close relationship. That changed. "He would call me up from his insurance office," Purnell later recalled. "We'd be talking about board-related issues. That's the way he approached me to mentor me. He said that I had a lot of potential. He would offer me counsel if I was willing to accept it. He was sincere."[13]

Purnell had anticipated that she would serve on a board committee that developed educational policy. No, said Bliss. She had too much ability to select what Bliss considered the "light committees." He saw her as a future chairman of the board. The path to the chairmanship led through service on the Finance and the Building and Grounds committees.

Other board members included Akron industrial leaders, prominent attorneys, and civic leaders. Bliss told Purnell that she was too modest about her abilities. "He began giving me specific examples of his having observed me," she said. She took his advice and made her way up the ladder on the board of trustees. "I hadn't remotely envisioned me leading [the board]," she said. "I didn't in truth consider myself a peer [with other board members]."[14]

In August 1986, Purnell became the first woman to chair the board of trustees. "My election as the first female chairman of the board of trustees of the University of Akron speaks well for the professionalism and commitment of my fellow trustees," she said at the time. "I am delighted that the trustees have extended me the opportunity to pursue a higher dimension of excellence in service to my alma mater."[15]

Bliss, Purnell said, helped her get there. "The real-life experiences and interactions he manifested, those were constructive," said Purnell. "Those were unconditional, regardless of my race and gender."[16]

Chapter 69

A Pathfinder Reaches the End of the Trail

Ellen Bliss recalled having mixed emotions on New Year's Day 1981.

"I congratulated Ray and told him I was looking forward to the excitement of the new year," she said. The Republicans were returning to the White House and the Blisses would be attending Ronald Reagan's presidential inauguration. "But also I told him I was apprehensive—it was five years since his heart attack."

In 1976, his doctor had told Bliss that unless he changed his habits—including overworking—he could expect another heart attack within half a decade. "But he wouldn't have been happy if he had stopped working," Mrs. Bliss said.[1]

Bliss was trying to change lifelong habits that contributed to his heart trouble, said Madge Doerler. He had given up cigarettes and switched from beer and mixed drinks to coffee and water. Bliss's pace had slowed, but not too much. He still often worked sixteen-hour days. "He was very much doing things that had to be done. He was really keyed up about Akron U," Doerler said.[2]

Even in retirement, Bliss was constantly asked for advice by a new generation of aspiring Republican candidates. State Senator Charles R. Saxbe, the son of former US senator and US attorney general Bill Saxbe, sought Bliss's help for the 1982 Ohio attorney general's race. Representative John Ashbrook, a staunch conservative who often disagreed with Bliss, wanted his advice for the 1982 US Senate campaign.[3]

It was the passing of an old friend that really began to slow Bliss down. According to Arshinkoff, Bliss was stunned by the death of *Akron Beacon Journal* editor John

S. Knight on June 16 at the age of eighty-six. Knight and Bliss had known each other for fifty years. Knight had built a nationwide newspaper empire starting with the *Akron Beacon Journal*, while Bliss had reached similar heights leading the Republican Party at the local, state, and national levels. Despite their lofty achievements, Knight and Bliss remained at heart Akron boys.

The day after Knight died, Arshinkoff went to see Bliss in his insurance office. No matter when Arshinkoff had showed up in the past, Bliss had always seemed to be busy. This time he was sitting in his chair, reading a newspaper. Arshinkoff sensed that something was wrong. "You could feel the wind knocked out of his sail," Arshinkoff recalled. Bliss asked Arshinkoff if he knew that Knight had died. "What a tragedy," said Bliss. Then Bliss told Arshinkoff that he would be pulling back from his role as political adviser, helping Arshinkoff run the local GOP. "Look, you're pretty much on your own," said Bliss. "Every letter you need to run the party is in your file. I've written every meeting call, every financial meeting call. We've laid out your program.... You can handle it. I'm stepping away."

Arshinkoff, just twenty-six at the time, went home that night and told his parents what had happened and what he had concluded. "I told my parents that Mr. Bliss is going to die.... You could just feel it," he said.[4]

Journalist Abe Zaidan had a similar experience in early August when he and Bliss lunched at Akron's Portage Country Club. The lunch began with pleasantries, including talk of Bliss's plans to vacation in Germany and Austria. But the conversation soon took a serious turn. Bliss discussed the closing chapter of his political career. Then he began to ramble and the conversation wandered.

"Bliss had a few things he wanted to get off his chest," said Zaidan. Bliss talked about the people who had hurt him.

One was Richard Nixon. Nixon had wanted to control Bliss, and years later, Bliss still felt humiliated. Nixon's misdeeds had offended Bliss, but he felt some responsibility for having helped Nixon win the election. "He was an aberrant thinker," said Bliss, "but he was our man."

Zaidan recalled that Bliss went on at length about slights he had received over his career. James Rhodes was a source of painful memories. Rhodes would say one thing to Bliss and then get the *Columbus Dispatch* to write "nasty things" about him.

Bliss complained about associates who used local party positions for personal gain. He had concluded that lawyers should not serve as party chairmen because they couldn't resist the temptation.

"I can tell you, sir," Bliss told Zaidan, "I never did that. I never sought publicity. I never promoted myself in any way."

Bliss was especially ashamed by self-interested behavior among University of Akron officials who wanted to "make deals" for their personal advancement. A proud, honorable, and private man, Bliss was deeply disappointed by those who had put petty politics above the public, the party, or the university.

"Bliss seemed to sense his passing," Zaidan concluded. A sense of foreboding hung over the conversation.[5]

Sadly, these premonitions soon turned out to be accurate.

On August 5, Bliss attended a morning meeting of the University of Akron Board of Trustees, of which he was now chairman. Bliss reminded Madge Doerler that he hated morning meetings: "You may like morning meetings, but I don't like them. And I'm not going to have any more of them."[6]

That evening Bliss called John LaGuardia, a University of Akron official. Bliss wanted to talk about his plans for the university. Bliss told LaGuardia that removing President Guzzetta was a top priority and the effort would begin the very next day.[7]

Bliss arrived at work at 8:10 A.M. on Thursday, August 6, unexpectedly early. Shortly after 8:30, he left his office and collapsed in the corridor outside. Assistant building manager Hugh Hill found Bliss and called paramedics, who took him to Akron City Hospital. He was dead on arrival at 9:37 A.M.[8]

Dr. Arthur Dobkin, Bliss's doctor, said that he had suffered from angina pectoris (recurrent pain in the chest caused by a sudden loss of blood to the heart muscle) and a shortness of breath since a 1976 heart attack. Dr. Dobkin said he "had anticipated [this] could happen any time."

Arshinkoff was shaken by Bliss's death, despite his premonition that it was imminent. When he heard the news, Arshinkoff slumped on a couch in his office and held his head in his hands. "It was like losing my father or mother. He was my friend and mentor," Arshinkoff said. Arshinkoff turned down three television interview requests on the subject of Bliss's death. "I'm afraid I'd break down in front of 2.5 million viewers. I couldn't handle that."[9]

Tributes to Bliss quickly came in from around the country.

President Ronald Reagan, whose inauguration Bliss had attended just months before, issued a statement: "Ray Bliss understood that the strength of our democracy and the responsiveness of our government were dependent upon the vitality of the party system. He respected his party and those in his party respected him. Nancy and I convey our deepest sympathy to his family."[10]

Ohio Governor James Rhodes, never one for understatement, called Bliss "the greatest Republican leader Ohio has ever had....He was a tremendous organizer," the governor said, "and he had an enthusiasm for life and politics that was unmatched by any other person I've known."[11]

Former congressman Bill Ayres said Bliss brought dignity to politics. "He felt hard work and a thorough discussion of the issues would have people come down on the GOP's side. He never had any harsh things to say about Democrats. He just didn't agree with them."

Democratic Representative John Seiberling of Akron said: "Ray Bliss was a true professional and he was a person who always conducted his affairs honorably. I've never known him to advocate or support sleazy politics."

Al Teodosio, the Summit County Democratic chairman who had worked with Bliss on the board of elections, summed up the accolades succinctly: Ray Bliss was a "political giant."

An obituary in the *New York Times* said that Bliss "brought to the national chairmanship qualities that had succeeded in Ohio: acceptance of such new techniques as confidential polling, 15-hour workdays, tough-mindedness, discretion and the keeping of promises, a consuming desire to win elections and an eye for detail."[12]

On Monday, August 10, 1981, at St. Vincent Catholic Church in Akron, five hundred family members, friends, and admirers gathered from all over the state and nation for Bliss's funeral.[13] It was the church where Bliss and his wife Ellen had been married on Thanksgiving Day in 1959.

There were forty honorary pallbearers, representing the breadth of Bliss's career, from national, state, and local Republican officials to business and labor leaders, University of Akron officials, and lifelong friends. The six actual pallbearers came from the family.

The Reverend Thomas Corrigan, with whom Bliss had developed a friendship, conducted the twenty-five-minute memorial service. Bliss was not Catholic, so Corrigan did not conduct a formal mass. He sprinkled Holy water on the casket as he delivered a eulogy that captured Bliss's years of service to both the Republican Party and his hometown.

"For those of you who knew Ray Bliss well, no eulogy is necessary," said Father Corrigan. "For those of you who didn't, no adequate eulogy is possible.... He walked with the kings of this land and he never lost the common touch. In the field of politics, he walked where there was no path and left a trail," said Corrigan. He emphasized the high value that Bliss had placed on loyalty: "He spent himself like a candle burning out. Loyalty was not a word to be bantered about. It was a commitment. In the art of compromise, he made room for God's work."

Bliss had spent his life promoting and celebrating a political system that he believed had built a great and prosperous nation. Appropriately, clergy and mourners joined in singing "America the Beautiful" as Bliss's casket was slowly wheeled out of the downtown church. The funeral procession moved just a few blocks west to Mount Peace cemetery. Corrigan presided at the graveside services where Ray Bliss was laid to rest in the soil of the only city he ever called home.

Ray Bliss (left) and Republican Rogers C. B. Morton (right), 1969. After a brief struggle with the White House, Bliss "retired" as national chairman after four years in office. He was succeeded by Morton. (AP Photo/Charles Gorry)

Coming full circle, 1969. US Senator Hugh Scott (left), Ray Bliss (center), and Congressman Bill Ayres (right) at an Akron fundraiser. Scott was Republican national chairman when Bliss was Ohio Republican state chairman in 1950, the same year Bliss recruited Ayres to run for Congress. (Courtesy of the *Akron Beacon Journal*)

Homecoming, 1969. Ray Bliss (left) returns to Akron and his insurance business. Madge Doerler (right), a long-time political and business associate, was pleased with his return. (Courtesy of the *Akron Beacon Journal*)

Ellen Bliss (left), Ray Bliss (center), and President Gerald Ford (right). Long political allies, Bliss worked to elect Ford to the White House in 1976, but to no avail. (From the Ray C. Bliss Papers. Courtesy of Archival Services, University Libraries, The University of Akron)

Summit County Republican women. Ray Bliss believed that Republican women were a crucial strength of the party. (Courtesy of the Summit County Republican Party)

Bliss associates and Ronald Reagan. Bliss's Republican Summit county allies (from left) Roy Browne, Gene Waddell, Frances Rex, Ronald Reagan, and Alex Arshinkoff. (Photo by Herb Hott. Courtesy of the Summit County Republican Party)

Ray Bliss (left) and Republican George H. W. Bush (second from right). Bush campaigned in Akron during 1980 with the help of Ray Bliss. (Courtesy of the *Akron Beacon Journal*)

The end of the trail. Ray Bliss was honored at the 1980 Republican National Convention for his fifty years of service to the GOP. (AP Photo)

University of Akron Board of Trustees, 1981. Ray Bliss (first row, second from left) was elected chairman of the University of Akron Board of Trustees in 1981. Also pictured are Republican Janet Purnell (first row, far right) and Democrat Bob Kidney (first row, center). (From the University of Akron Photographs Collection. Courtesy of Archival Services, University Libraries, The University of Akron)

Chapter 70

Ray C. Bliss Institute of Applied Politics

A week before his death, Ray Bliss told Brian Usher, political writer for the *Akron Beacon Journal*, about his plans for an "institute of applied politics" at the University of Akron. The bipartisan institute would educate students in practical politics. "Nuts and bolts instruction would dominate the curriculum and train students to make a profession out of politics," Bliss told Usher.[1]

Bliss modeled his plans on the Institute for Practical Politics at Ohio Wesleyan University. Founded by political scientist Benjamin Arneson in 1947, its motto was "better minds for better politics." The Institute began sponsoring "Democratic Day" and "Republican Day" in 1949. Speakers for the first Republican Day included the new Ohio Republican chairman, Ray Bliss. Bliss continued participating in the program long after Arneson's death in 1953. Thanks in part to Bliss's help, political scientist Arthur Peterson became institute director in 1961.[2]

In 1980 and 1981, Peterson and Bliss exchanged letters about a practical politics institute at Bliss's alma mater.[3] Bliss also consulted Vernon Cook, a University of Akron political scientist who had previously taught with Peterson at Ohio Wesleyan. Like Arneson and Peterson, Cook was actively engaged in politics. A Democrat, Cook was elected to the Ohio House of Representatives, serving from 1972 to 1987. Bliss wanted Cook to be the new institute's first director, to instill bipartisanship.[4]

After Bliss's death, Ellen Bliss became an untiring champion for her husband's plans. The idea got off to a good start. The university board of trustees asked Cook to prepare a proposal for the "Ray C. Bliss Institute of Applied Politics." But the plan was delayed by University president Dominic Guzzetta, who balked at Bliss's request that the new institute should have a bipartisan board of advisers.[5]

In 1984, a new president of the University of Akron, William Muse, revived the plan. A resolution calling for the establishment of the institute was passed by the board of trustees in 1985.[6] Cook was slated to be the first director, with a formal launch featuring former president Gerald Ford.[7] Behind the scenes, however, trouble was brewing. University trustee George Wilson was unhappy with the choice of Cook as the first director. Fellow Republicans, Bliss and Wilson had been friends since the latter served as University of Akron student body president in 1949.[8] The controversy led President Muse to put the plans on hold.[9]

Muse then appointed a blue-ribbon advisory task force to "resolve the issues of the institute in a completely bipartisan manner." The first and only meeting of the task force occurred in November 1985. "The consensus from the group was [the institute] is a good idea," Muse reported, "and the focus should be on the nuts and bolts of practical politics—how to use the political system—and not on political philosophy."[10] The task force also recommended Cook as the first director and creation of a bipartisan advisory board.

In the fall of 1986 the institute finally started operating.[11] But Cook's tenure as director was short: he died from pancreatic cancer November 23, 1987, at sixty. The bipartisan advisory board was never appointed.

University officials did not find another director like Cook, who combined teaching with a political career. Instead, they chose political scientist John C. Green, whom Cook had hired for the institute a few months earlier. Initially, Green wanted to remain a teacher and a scholar. Mrs. Bliss finally persuaded him to take the job in 1988. "Ray was a teacher and a scholar, too," she told Green. "He would be proud to have you direct the institute."[12]

Green was still serving as director in 2017. By then, the Bliss Institute had grown to include five staff members and about half a dozen faculty, including a number of political practitioners. It was supported by an endowment of $6.2 million, drawn from the Bliss estate and other sources. Its programs included a Certificate in Applied Politics program, a Master of Applied Politics degree, an extensive internship program, and the Ray C. and Ellen P. Bliss Scholarships.[13] It also sponsored speakers, seminars, and conferences. The best known of these events were the quadrennial "State of the Parties" conferences that started in 1993.[14]

At the heart of the program are the students who carried into the future the knowledge of practical politics that Bliss mastered over his fifty-year career. These "Bliss scholars" are living examples of Bliss's continuing impact on practical politics.

Cyndra Cole's life changed during her senior year in high school in Green, an Akron suburb, when she took an advanced placement class in government. "Before that I wanted to be a biomedical engineer," said Cole. "But I took government and I loved it." In 2001, she enrolled at the University of Akron, received a Bliss scholarship, and interned for the Republican candidate for municipal clerk of court in 2003. "[I] worked my butt off in that race and we lost," said Cole.[15]

The next year, Cole managed the reelection campaign of a local Republican state representative, Mary Taylor. Taylor was heavily favored, but that did not affect the campaign. "Run like you're five points down" was Taylor's approach, said Cole— vintage Ray Bliss advice.

In 2006, Cole, a campaign veteran at twenty-two, became the political director for Taylor's campaign for state auditor. Taylor was the only Republican to win a statewide executive office, squeaking past her Democratic opponent with about 51 percent of the vote. Cole remembered watching the results that showed all other statewide candidates losing: "We were just kind of sitting there ... we are the only ones who don't have to bury our heads in the sand."

After earning a Master in Applied Politics degree in 2006, Cole joined Taylor in the auditor's office. In 2008, Cole left her government job to work for Taylor's reelection. But instead, Taylor ran for lieutenant governor on the winning ticket with gubernatorial candidate John Kasich. In 2017, Cole was teaching courses for the Bliss Institute and raising a family of three children with her husband, Randy Cole, another Bliss Institute alumnus. She did not rule out a return to politics: "I guess the idealism in me still feels like that's where I can make a difference."

Kellie Copeland's interest in politics began earlier than Cyndra Cole's, when Copeland was growing up in the Akron suburb of Tallmadge. "The trouble started when I got my first Bible," she recalled, explaining that "so much of the teachings of Jesus were about the Good Samaritan and how we are our brother's keeper."[16] These lessons led Copeland toward the Democrats.

Copeland was not a traditional student when she entered the University of Akron in 1988. She lived at home, worked full-time, and went to night school. She also found time to participate in local campaigns—which Ray Bliss would have appreciated. She received a Bliss scholarship and interned with Democratic national chairman David Wilhelm in 1994.

After receiving her bachelor's degree in political science in 1995, Copeland went to work as a field organizer for President Bill Clinton's reelection campaign. After Clinton was reelected, she took a job at the US Department of Education, before returning to Ohio to work for Vice President Al Gore's 2000 presidential campaign, the American Heart Association, and the Ohio AFL-CIO. In 2002, Copeland became executive director of NARAL Pro-Choice Ohio, a job that tested her political skills in an era when pro-life Republicans often controlled state government. In 2017, Copeland was still with NARAL.

Robert Paduchik, like Kellie Copeland, grew up in Tallmadge, but with different political beliefs. Paduchik's family background on both his mother's and father's sides traced to parts of the old Soviet Union—Ukraine and Belarus. That background made the family staunch anti-Communists with a philosophy of self-reliance—"they didn't expect anything from government, they didn't want anything from government"—that tilted them toward Republicans.[17]

Paduchik entered the University of Akron in 1984, intending to major in accounting. "I hated accounting. I got a 'C' in it. I gravitated toward political science," he recalled. In 1986, Paduchik campaigned for Lynn Slaby, the Republican candidate for the Akron-area US House seat. "I loved it…probably like a heroin addict's first high," Paduchik said.

After Slaby lost, Paduchik got involved in campus politics through his fraternity—as Ray Bliss had more than fifty years earlier. He won election as student government vice president by seven votes. He received a Bliss scholarship, volunteered for Vice President George H. W. Bush's 1988 presidential campaign, and earned a bachelor's degree in political science in 1989.

In 2000, Paduchik began to make his mark nationally by managing Texas governor George W. Bush's Ohio presidential campaign. His opposite in Vice President Gore's Ohio campaign was fellow Bliss Institute alumnus Derrick Clay. In 2001, the Bliss Institute honored both Paduchik and Clay with Honorary Certificates in Applied Politics.

A test of Paduchik's skills came four years later when he managed President Bush's 2004 reelection campaign in Ohio. Bush accentuated Ohio's importance by visiting his campaign's Columbus headquarters on election day.

"Paduchik, what's going to happen?" the president asked.

"We're going to win Ohio," Paduchik declared.

The early returns made Paduchik's guarantee look false. Democrat John Kerry was running up big victory margins in Ohio's six biggest cities—120,000 more votes than Gore's margin four years earlier. But thanks to a huge turnout in suburban and rural areas, Bush prevailed with just over 50 percent of the vote. In 2016, Paduchik agreed to manage Republican Donald Trump's successful Ohio presidential campaign, and as a consequence, was chosen as cochair of the Republican National Committee in 2017.[18]

Morris Reid, like Bob Paduchik, made his mark in presidential politics, but on the Democratic side. "My grandmother is a Democrat," Reid said.[19] Although Bliss was white and Reid was African American, their backgrounds were similar. Like Bliss, Reid was very close to his mother, who raised him and his brother as a single parent. Bliss and Reid both grew up in Akron and graduated from a city high school—Bliss from South and Reid from Central-Hower.

Reid got into politics in high school, putting up yard signs for Democrat Tom Sawyer, who was elected to the US House in 1986. Reid entered the University of Akron in 1988. He received a Bliss scholarship and in 1989 interned with Harry Meshel of Youngstown, the Democratic minority leader of the Ohio Senate. "It was my first real taste of larger politics—polling, focus groups. It was the best thing that ever happened to me. I was nineteen and twenty when I got down there," said Reid.

In 1992, Reid worked for Democrat Bill Clinton's successful presidential campaign. He followed Clinton to Washington and joined the staff of Ron Brown, the new secretary of commerce. By 1996, Reid was Brown's confidential assistant.

Then tragedy struck. On April 3, 1996, Brown's plane crashed on a trip to Croatia. Reid was asked to identify the secretary's body. "It was like the earth had opened up and was crying," Reid said.

Although Reid worked on President Clinton's reelection in 1996, Brown's death cooled Reid's interest in campaigning. Instead he worked for Mercury, a public relations and lobbying firm, rising to managing director, a post he held in 2017.

Chapter 71

Political Legacy

Ray Bliss had a wry, understated sense of humor, so it's easy to imagine his reaction to the debate that broke out among political scientists assessing his career. "There they go again," Bliss would have said, with a slight smile creasing his face, dismissing high-blown academic chatter about practical politics. Indeed, when he was inducted into Phi Sigma Alpha, a political science honorary society, in 1981, Bliss remarked that the group "would never be the same."[1]

It was Bliss's success that prompted the debate. Even before his death, Bliss had become a yardstick against which other party leaders were measured. A study published in 1976, five years after Bliss left as national chairman and five years before he retired from politics, concluded: "Ray Bliss commanded such widespread respect that he added prestige to the [national] committee by just being there." Bliss was the only chairman to receive this accolade from the Democratic and Republican leaders interviewed. The study included this detailed description:

> Bliss is a quiet, almost shy, man who does not enjoy public speaking or the spotlight of publicity. He is an intense perfectionist, capable of extended periods of concentration and attention to detail. His standards and expectations for himself and his staff are high, and he insists that the programs initiated by his office be fully and carefully executed. His consuming interest is politics. He is totally immersed in political life, and this has left him little time for outside interests or hobbies. Bliss places a high priority on personal integrity and honesty in politics. He considers himself a straight

shooter who levels with political associates and does not promise things he cannot deliver. As a political professional and an expert in organization, he attaches great importance to party loyalty. He also exercises great care to protect the organization of which he is part from real or potential opponents—without or within the party. He knows that miscalculation or mistakes on the part of a major party leader can have reverberations throughout the party structure. Consequently, he exercises great care in making decisions.[2]

Larry J. Sabato, director of the Center for Politics at the University of Virginia, succinctly summed up this view of Bliss's legacy: "When you think of 'political party leader' in American history, Ray Bliss is one of the first names that comes to mind. On the GOP side, he is considered the prototype of the ideal chairman. He had superb organizational skills, was acceptable to all factions, and was relatively ego-free, keeping himself out of the limelight."[3]

It was the length of this yardstick that was debated at a 1991 conference on Bliss held at the University of Akron.[4]

Bliss had no greater admirer than Arthur Peterson, who worked so closely with him. In Peterson's view, Bliss was an innovative party leader with unparalleled political instincts, a leader rather than just a manager. "He was indeed a master of the 'nuts and bolts' of party politics," Peterson argued, "but he was also a conceptualist, a big-picture man, a people person and even a speaker of distinction when the situation required."[5]

Bliss's strengths as a manager—attention to detail, relentless follow-through efforts, and long hours on the job—obscured the leadership he provided to the nation, according to Peterson. "His ultimate motivation was strengthening the two-party system in America. But to Bliss, parties were not an end in themselves. They were rather essential instruments toward the larger goal of efficient, effective government about which he cared passionately."[6]

Peterson rebuffed critics who suggested that Bliss was not knowledgeable or interested enough about policy issues to be a "speaking chairman" at the national committee. "That was not true!" wrote Peterson. "He could defend an issue position with the best of the party leaders in Washington.... He chose not to do so publicly because he felt that was the province of elected officeholders."[7]

Two other political scientists who worked with Bliss at the Republican National Committee shared Peterson's perspective, although not his zeal.

"For Ray Bliss," John Bibby noted, "the most effective way to achieve vigorous inter-party competition on a continuing basis was to have party organizations that could provide the infrastructure needed to win elections and to keep the party going in difficult times."[8] A key part of Bliss's legacy was a "permanent, professional and service-oriented national committee."[9] But this achievement did not come smoothly. Just as Bliss built on the work of previous Republican leaders—and his own practical experience as a county and state chairman—his successors built on his work.

"In 1965," Robert Huckshorn wrote, "the RNC had never seen anything quite like Ray Bliss."[10] Bliss's party-building efforts began to reverse the relationship between the Republican National Committee and the state committees. This process continued and was expanded by Chairman William Brock between 1977 and 1981, and largely maintained by subsequent chairmen. The national committees became an indispensable service provider to state and local parties and candidates. In the 1980s, the Democratic National Committee adopted a very similar approach.

Huckshorn maintained that this service party model was likely to continue: "The parties will be with us for some time to come and it can be anticipated that they will continue to emphasize their role as service providers for the state and local party organizations, a role pioneered by Ray Bliss."[11]

Not all political scientists had such a high view of Bliss, especially in comparison to Bliss's successor William Brock.

Tim Hames offered a biblical metaphor for the relationship between Bliss and Brock: Bliss was "John the Baptist," paving the way for the larger changes instituted by Brock about a decade later.[12] Increased fund-raising made it possible for Brock to expand services to Republicans, according to Hames. Brock used these resources to influence state and local committees, and he was willing to take sides in Republican primaries. Bliss believed the national committee should support Republican organizations and candidates, not lead them.

Paul S. Herrnson put Bliss's activities in the context of party change in response to electoral misfortune. According to Herrnson, Bliss's successful party building was an example of "reinforcement," improving the operations of the national committee within the existing structure of the party. In contrast, Brock's successful party building was an example of "renewal," redefining the national committee's role and changing the party structure. What Bliss and Brock had in common was a focus on organization rather than ideology in an era of deep party divisions. Brock's "renewal" lasted longer than Bliss's "reinforcement." President Nixon dismantled much of Bliss's program after firing him in 1969, whereas President Reagan maintained most of Brock's program after he appointed him US trade representative in 1981.[13]

In contrast to Peterson, Philip Klinkner thought Bliss was more a manager than a leader. "As RNC chairman, Ray Bliss was either unable or unwilling to challenge the traditional constraints on his office in order to alter the balance of power within the Republican Party," Klinkner concluded. "Bill Brock, on the other hand, successfully took advantage of the opportunities presented to an out-party chairman." In Klinkner's view, Brock was more aggressive from the start. Bliss was reluctant to publicly show his interest in the national chairman's job, but Brock mounted a full-scale campaign and was even willing to criticize his opponents to promote his candidacy.

Once elected, Brock rebuilt the party's grassroots organization to reach out to new groups of voters, including southerners and women, while Bliss insisted on implementing the recommendations from the Committee on Big City Politics (which Bliss chaired in 1961 and 1962). Klinkner also concluded that Brock was a more effective fundraiser, expanding a direct-mail program of small contributions and relying less on large contributors.

Most importantly, Brock did more to improve the party's image by developing and promoting Republican positions on issues. Klinkner minimized Bliss's use of the Republican Coordinating Committee to come up with Republican alternatives to President Lyndon Johnson's "Great Society" programs. Brock, meanwhile, began publication of *Commonsense*, a journal that helped Republicans use themes of family, neighborhood, community, and voluntary associations to counter "New Deal–Great Society liberalism." Brock was more willing to speak out on issues as national chairman.[14]

Among Republican chairman who came after Bliss, however, few appreciated Bliss's pioneering efforts more than Brock did.[15] After the 1980 Republican victories, Brock said of Bliss, "Our present success is due in large measure to his devotion and…leadership."[16]

Brock acknowledged that he consciously tried to carry out many of the same party-building programs that had worked for Bliss. "Obviously you watch people as good as Ray Bliss to try to learn from them," he said.[17]

Brock first had a chance to talk with Bliss at the 1968 Republican National Convention, when Brock helped coordinate the southern states for Nixon. "What you knew about Ray Bliss was that he was the master of the practical," said Brock.

Brock applauded Bliss's efforts to expand the Republicans' appeal. "He [Bliss] was the kind of person that understood you had to carry something more than suburbs and farms, that you had to work the cities, that you had to have a broadly based party. That party loyalty was of almost paramount importance. He really believed that. At least the essence of what I got from him was that loyalty was almost the sine qua non." The party could not win if voters perceived it as some kind of exclusive political club, said Brock. "He [Bliss] was one of those who said the word

Republican was good enough. Therefore, you could have Nelson Rockefeller and Richard Nixon and Barry Goldwater all in the same party."

Brock dismissed critics of Bliss's efforts to appeal to voters in big cities. Brock made a similar appeal in the 1980 campaign even though the cities were more Democratic by then. "They said the same thing about me when I had a program for blue collars, ethnics, and blacks. They said, Why go hunting? There aren't any ducks there," said Brock. Brock, like Bliss before him, proved the critics wrong in 1980. "The fact is we elected Ronald Reagan and a Republican Senate with those people who weren't supposed to be voting Republican."

Brock never lost sight of the groundwork Bliss had helped lay for him. "People have such myopic views of politics," said Brock. "He [Bliss] did not. He had a perspective that was extraordinarily wide. He really did have a sense that if we were willing to talk about the cities, if we were willing to talk about the South, about areas that were not traditionally Republican, that we could compete, even if we didn't have the resources to follow up entirely.... It gave heart to those of us in those areas and engendered a real degree of enthusiasm and support that wouldn't have come otherwise."

Bliss had admirers among Democratic operatives as well as Republicans.

James Ruvolo of Toledo served as Ohio Democratic chairman from 1983 through 1991. "He [Bliss] was the kind of political leader that all of us aspire to be," said Ruvolo. "He was pragmatic. He wasn't driven by ideology or any of the things that can sidetrack you." Bliss worked within what Ruvolo called the "moderate ideology" of the Republican Party. "In other words, he didn't resort to tricks of fanning a single issue here or there. He did it with organization, resources, with good candidate recruitment," said Ruvolo. There was a caveat to Ruvolo's praise. Bliss succeeded because "he kept the party at the center of the process." With the ascendance of candidate-centered politics and well-funded special interest groups, that would be hard to do today, Ruvolo added.[18]

Academic analysts of Bliss's legacy are also concerned with candidate-centered politics. When considering the tendency of candidates to run independently of their party, political scientist Tim Hames wrote, "One wonders what Ray Bliss would think of this situation."[19] On this point, fellow scholar John Bibby had an answer: "Candidate-centered politics, [Bliss] believed, would yield only temporary successes and fragment the political system."[20]

Gerald Austin, campaign manager for Democrat Richard Celeste's two successful campaigns for Ohio governor, said one of Bliss's greatest achievements was turning the business of raising money, recruiting candidates, developing issues, and winning elections into a profession. Before Bliss, "there was not a profession in politics," said Austin, also manager of Jesse Jackson's 1988 presidential campaign. "He turned it into a profession where people became involved in politics as a way to make a living. It wasn't just a volunteer operation."[21] Bliss admired professionalism and held himself to high standards of conduct. He would have appreciated the compliment, even from a Democrat.

The development of political professionals was not, however, universally admired. The candidate-centered politics that plagued Bliss's career may have been aided by the very professionalism Bliss championed.[22]

In 1968, journalist James M. Perry attacked "technocrats" who used polling, television, and computers to help candidates win elections. "The technocrats really don't care," wrote Perry. "Ideology, issues, human emotions—these are not their concern. Ray Bliss, chairman of the Republican National Committee, is almost a caricature of today's technocrat. 'Don't ask me about issues,' he tells reporters, and then they all repeat together 'I'm a nuts-and-bolts technician.'"[23]

This critique was not personal: "It would be unkind not to differentiate between the technocrat and his work," Perry added in a footnote. "Ray Bliss, late of an evening, highball in hand, is an interesting and even stimulating companion."

The increasing independence of candidates from party organizations continued after Bliss left politics. A good example is the independent campaigns of Ross Perot in 1992 and 1996. And another example is Donald Trump's Republican presidential nomination in 2016. Both these candidates challenged the two-party system—one from without and the other from within.

It is fitting to give Ray Bliss the last word on these matters.

In a 1976 interview, Bliss was asked about his unofficial title of "Mr. Nuts and Bolts."[24] "That came about," said Bliss, "because of my emphasis on precision in the development of political practices within the framework of party organization." Bliss went on to summarize his approach to political organizing: "I just believe in thoroughness. If you are going to take on a task, you do it well or you don't do it."

Bliss noted that many party leaders were interested in speaking out on issues and not on organization. "My primary interest was strengthening the party organization, the recruitment of strong candidates for office, the building of adequate funds to finance them, and so on."

"I'm proud of the fact that I was a nuts and bolts chairman," Bliss concluded. "I think the results in Ohio and in the nation showed that it paid off."

"Now, no chairman succeeds because of what he did alone," he added, "but because hundreds of thousands of people get in and pitch. But he has to provide the leadership and the stimulus and the vigor to the effort."

Bliss wanted to clear up one thing: "There's a mistaken notion that developed over the years that I had no interest in issues. I considered candidates' stands on issues or the party's stands on issues a very vital part of any campaign. But I felt that the chairman shouldn't unilaterally determine that position."

While he was Ohio chairman, Bliss recounted, he worked with Republican legislative leaders and gubernatorial nominees to craft an effective party platform. As national chairman, he presided over the Republican Coordinating Committee, where current and former officeholders laid the foundation for the 1968 party platform. Bliss always hoped that leaders would resist putting a "corsage" in the platform—a promise they weren't going to pursue if elected.

"You've got to have some interest in the issues," Bliss acknowledged, "and it's desirable to say, here's where we stand—here's our general position. But it has to be done in step with the candidates, because, after all, they have to make good on these commitments."

Concern with issues did not mean excluding people. "It seems to me that a party, to be an effective party, has to maintain a position of welcoming the participation of people whose views may differ from the others within the party.... I've always argued that it's the responsibility of party leaders to respect the deeply held convictions of others and I still feel that way."

The greatest legacy of the organizational man from Akron was his deep commitment to democracy and the American two-party system. The vagaries of elections aside, it is the professional practice of politics that brings these institutions to life in every generation.

Notes

Prologue

1. David Broder, "Uphill with Dodd," *Washington Post*, January 18, 1995.
2. W. Richard Wright, interview by William Hershey, May 7, 1995.
3. Ray C. Bliss, "The Role of the State Chairman," in *Politics U.S.A.*, ed. James M. Cannon (Garden City, NY: Doubleday, 1960), 160.
4. William Hershey, "The Party's Not Over," *Akron Beacon Journal, Beacon Magazine*, June 7, 1981.
5. This quotation was supplied by a former Bliss associate who carried it in his wallet.
6. Hershey, "The Party's Not Over."

Chapter 1: Akron, Ohio

1. Hershey, "The Party's Not Over."
2. Madge Doerler, interview by William Hershey, May 7, 1995.
3. George W. Knepper, *Akron, City at the Summit* (Tulsa, OK: Continental Heritage Press, 1981), 77–81.
4. Kenneth Nichols, *Yesterday's Akron: The First 150 Years* (Miami: E. A. Seemann Publishing, 1976), 12–14.
5. Knepper, *Akron*, 19–24.
6. Transcript of Ray C. Bliss at a Taft Seminar, Ohio Wesleyan University, Delaware, Ohio. June 26, 1974. Hereafter cited as Taft Seminar, 1974.
7. Nichols, *Yesterday's Akron*, 39–42.
8. Alfred D. Chandler Jr., *The Visible Hand: The Managerial Revolution in American Business* (Cambridge, MA: Belknap Press, 1993).
9. George W. Knepper, interview by William Hershey, April 25, 1995.
10. Nichols, *Yesterday's Akron*, 40.
11. Knepper, *Akron*, 94–95.
12. "Immigration & Migration in the Industrial Age, 1870–1930," *Black, White, and Beyond*, http://learn.uakron.edu/beyond/industrialage.htm.
13. Karl H. Grismer, *Akron and Summit County* (Akron, OH: Summit County Historical Society, 1952; repr., Salem, MA: Higginson Book Co., 1994), 298–99.

Chapter 2: Family Matters

1. Mary-Ann Blasio, "Ray C. Bliss: The Formative Years 1907–1937," unpublished paper, University of Akron, 1990.
2. Norma Rios, personal communication on Bliss family history, December 17, 2004.
3. Ibid.

4. Ibid.

5. Ibid. One of Ray's paternal uncles became an architect who designed some of Akron's most beautiful private homes. Another uncle became a barber and opened his own shop in 1901, a fixture downtown for the next forty years. A third uncle became an automobile mechanic and owned a garage in California. Ray Bliss's paternal aunts married businessmen.

6. Dennis E. Wieland, "The Lives and Times of the Wielands," unpublished family history, 198. Ray's maternal uncles were in the grocery business, eventually operating two stores, and his maternal aunts married small business owners.

7. Rios, personal communication.

8. Doerler interview, 1995.

9. Arthur Peterson, interview by William Hershey, April 23, 1996.

10. Rose Carlson, interview by William Hershey, June 2, 1995.

11. Carlson and Doerler interviews, 1995.

12. Madge Doerler, interview by John C. Green, September 15, 1996.

13. Carlson interview, 1995.

14. Doerler interview, 1995.

15. Keyes Beech, "Biography in Brief," *Akron Beacon Journal*, May 19, 1940; Doerler interview, 1995.

16. Carlson interview, 1995.

17. "Sabotage Seen in Office Blast," *Ohio State Journal*, April 15, 1932; Doerler, interview, 1995.

18. Carlson interview, 1995.

19. Carlson and Doerler interviews, 1995.

20. "Mother of Ray Bliss, Ill 3 Years, Dies," *Akron Beacon Journal*, January 9, 1956.

21. Hershey, "The Party's Not Over."

22. Carlson interview, 1995.

Chapter 3: The University of Akron

1. Ray Bliss to Norman Auburn, November 21, 1968. Series B (1968/69): Box 11, Folder 39. James Baker Papers, University of Akron Archives (UAA).

2. The Universalists merged with the Unitarians to form the Unitarian Universalist Association in 1961.

3. George W. Knepper, *Summit's Glory: Sketches of Buchtel College and The University of Akron* (Akron, OH: University of Akron Press, 1990), 10.

4. Ibid., 1–8; on Greeley, see http://www.britannica.com/biography/Horace-Greeley.

5. Knepper, *Summit's Glory*, 31–32.

6. Grismer, *Akron and Summit County*, 364–65.

7. Knepper, *Summit's Glory*, 89–92.

8. Knepper interview, 1995.

9. University of Akron student transcript of Ray C. Bliss provided by UA general counsel Ted Mallo, December 7, 2004.

10. "Twenty Minutes with Chairman Bliss," *The Laurel of Phi Kappa Tau*, September 1978, 4.

11. Ibid., 5.

12. Ibid., 9.

13. Ibid., 5.

14. Hershey, "The Party's Not Over."

15. Blasio, "Bliss: The Formative Years."

16. Ibid.

17. Louise Palmer Earley, interview by William Hershey, October 21, 1995.

Chapter 4: The May Queen Fiasco

1. Beech, "Biography in Brief."
2. Alexander Arshinkoff, interview by William Hershey, April 28, 1996.
3. *"Twenty Minutes,"* 5.
4. Ibid.
5. Ellen Bliss, interview by John C. Green, December 6, 1990.
6. "Twenty Minutes," 5.
7. "Akron U Sorority 'Lifts' the Pins in May Queen Rumpus," *Akron Beacon Journal*, May 12, 1931.
8. Knepper interview, 1995.
9. "Students to Vote Today in Title Race," *Buchtelite*, May 8, 1931.
10. "Ellen Palmer Disqualified by Council," *Buchtelite*, May 12, 1931.
11. Ibid.
12. "Akron U Sorority."
13. "Bliss Is Suspended; Eight-Hour Penalty Given to Two Girls," *Buchtelite*, May 15, 1931.
14. "Akron U Sorority."
15. "Ask Compromise in Bliss Fight against Ouster," *Akron Beacon Journal*, May 18, 1931.
16. Gene Jordan, "GOP's Ray Bliss Easing Out of Politics," *Columbus Dispatch Magazine*, July 6, 1980; Hershey, "The Party's Not Over."
17. Arshinkoff interview, 1996.
18. Doerler interview, 1996.
19. "Akron U Sorority."
20. See for example, "Obituaries: Bliss Rebuilt Republicans with Nixon," *United Press International*, August 7, 1981.
21. Beech, "Biography in Brief."
22. Clyde Mann, interview by John C. Green, May 1, 1990.
23. A former Bliss associate asked to remain anonymous.
24. Knepper interview, 1995.
25. Arshinkoff interview, 1996.
26. "Palmer Disqualified."
27. Robert Feldkamp, "Bliss, Man of Deliberation, Had Fastest GOP Rise," *Akron Beacon Journal*, January 13, 1965.

Chapter 5: Ray C. Bliss Meets James A. Corey

1. H. H. Harriman, "Death Ends Career of Jim Corey," *Akron Beacon Journal*, December 15, 1941.
2. Hershey, "The Party's Not Over."
3. Beech, "Biography in Brief."
4. Doerler interview, 1996.
5. Doerler interview, 1995; Robert Feldkamp, "Bliss, Man of Deliberation."
6. Hershey, "The Party's Not Over."
7. Alan L. Otten and Charles B. Seid, "The Minor Masterpiece of Ray C. Bliss," *Reporter*, February 10, 1965; David Broder, "Bliss Rides the Elephant," *New York Times Magazine*, March 21, 1965.
8. This conclusion is based on the dozens of interviews of former Bliss associates conducted by the authors; Alex Arshinkoff, interview by John C. Green, May 1, 1990.
9. Harriman, "Death Ends Career."
10. Daniel J. Coffey, John C. Green, David B. Cohen, and Stephen C. Brooks, *Buckeye Battleground: Ohio, Campaigns, and Elections in the Twenty-First Century* (Akron, OH: University of Akron Press, 2011), 5–8.

11. R. Hal Williams, *Realigning America: McKinley, Bryan, and the Remarkable Election of 1896* (Lawrence: University Press of Kansas, 2010).

12. Grismer, *Akron and Summit County,* 288.

13. Ralph M. Goldman, *The National Party Chairmen and Committees: Factionalism at the Top* (Armonk, NY: M. E. Sharpe, 1990), 194.

14. Mary Loretta Petit, "Charles Dick of Akron, Politician" (Master's thesis, Catholic University of America, 1948).

15. Grismer, *Akron and Summit County,* 680–81.

16. On the 1912 election, see http://www.britannica.com/event/United-States-presidential-election -of-1912/images-videos/Results-of-the-American-presidential-election-1912-Presidential-Candidate -Political/67679.

17. Harriman, "Death Ends Career."

18. Ibid.

19. On the 1920 election, see http://www.britannica.com/event/United-States-presidential-election -of-1920.

20. Charles Whited, *Knight: A Publisher in the Tumultuous Century* (New York: Dutton, 1988), 19.

21. Knepper interview, 1995.

22. Alexander Arshinkoff, interview by William Hershey, May 6, 1995.

23. Mark J. Price, "Local History: The Great Temple," *Akron Beacon Journal,* August 27, 2007.

24. Arshinkoff interview, 1995.

25. On the 1928 election, see http://www.britannica.com/event/United-States-presidential-election -of-1928.

Chapter 6: First Campaign Lessons

1. Ray Dorsey, "Anatomy of a Politician," *Cleveland Plain Dealer,* May 7, 1961.

2. "The Mayoralty Election," *Akron Beacon Journal,* October 31, 1931.

3. Feldkamp, "Bliss, Man of Deliberation."

4. H. Earl Wilson, "Cox, Making Third Fight for Mayor's Chair, Believes Long War against Bosses Will Yield Him Coveted Prize," *Akron Beacon Journal,* October 18, 1931.

5. "Sparks Is Elected Mayor with a Plurality of 3,835," *Akron Beacon Journal,* November 3, 1931.

6. Ray C. Sutliff, "Myers Challenges Old Adage: 'They Never Come Back,'" *Akron Beacon Journal,* October 17, 1933.

7. Ray C. Sutliff, "I. S. Myers Defeats Earl Cox for Mayor," *Akron Beacon Journal,* November 7, 1933; "Ray Bliss Named to Zoning Board," *Akron Beacon Journal,* January 9, 1934.

8. On the 1932 election, see http://www.britannica.com/event/United-States-presidential-election -of-1932.

9. Whited, *Knight,* 37.

10. Ibid., 65.

11. Arshinkoff interview, 1995.

12. Ibid.

13. George Wilson to Ray Bliss, January 14, 1965, Box 37: Item 5, Ray and Ellen Bliss Papers, UAA.

Chapter 7: Climbing the Political Ladder

1. Beech, "Biography in Brief."

2. Dorsey, "Anatomy of a Politician."

3. "Sport Program, Baby-Test Mark Summit Outing," *Akron Beacon Journal,* August 23, 1933.

4. Grismer, *Akron and Summit County*, 490; Elisabeth Hurley, interview by John C. Green, June 1, 1999.
5. "Who Was 'In' Who Wasn't on That Bliss Appointment Stirs Debate," *Akron Beacon Journal*, September 15, 1934.
6. Doerler interview, 1995.
7. Ibid.
8. Arshinkoff interview, 1995.
9. Beech, "Biography in Brief."
10. "Three Announce Political Hopes," *Akron Beacon Journal*, May 1, 1935.
11. Jean M. Converse, *Survey Research in the United States: Roots and Emergence, 1890–1960* (Berkeley: University of California Press, 1987); Becky Wilson Hawbaker, "Taking 'the Pulse of Democracy': George Gallup, Iowa, and the Origin of the Gallup Poll," *Palimpsest*, 74 (1993): 98–118.
12. Dorsey, "Anatomy of a Politician."
13. Ibid.
14. "Schroy Defeats Witwer, GOP Takes City Council," *Akron Beacon Journal*, November 11, 1935.
15. "Fraternity Alumni Group Names Bliss," *Akron Beacon Journal*, September 9, 1934.
16. Arshinkoff interview, 1995.
17. Beech, "Biography in Brief."
18. On the 1936 election, see http://www.britannica.com/event/United-States-presidential-election -of-1936.
19. Doerler interview, 1995.

Chapter 8: The Test Tube City

1. Robert Morehead, "The Test Tube City," *Nation's Business*, February 1938.
2. Daniel Nelson, "The CIO at Bay: Labor Militancy and Politics in Akron, 1936–1938," *Journal of American History* 31 (December 1984): 567–68.
3. Nelson, "CIO at Bay," 566.
4. J. Curtis Brown Sr., ed., *A Mighty Fine Union: A URW Golden Anniversary History*. Washington, DC: United Rubber, Cork, Linoleum & Plastic Workers of America, AFL-CIO. September 12, 1985, 3–4.
5. Brown, *Mighty Fine Union*, 13–14.
6. Ibid.
7. Whited, *Knight*, 40.
8. Daniel Nelson, "The Great Goodyear Strike of 1936," *Ohio History* 92 (1983): 6–36.
9. Knepper, *Akron*, 134–35.
10. Thomas T. Spencer, "Auxiliary and Non-Party Politics: The 1936 Democratic Presidential Campaign in Ohio," *Ohio History Journal*, http://resources.ohiohistory.org/ohj/browse/displaypages.php?display []=0090&display[]=114&display[]=128.
11. Morehead, "Test Tube City."
12. Alfred W. Jones, *Life, Liberty, and Property: A Story of Conflict and a Measurement of Conflicting Rights* (Akron, OH: University of Akron Press, 1999), 32.
13. Nelson, "CIO at Bay," 573.
14. Ibid., 575.
15. Jones, *Life, Liberty, and Property*, 108–9.
16. Arshinkoff interview, 1996.

Chapter 9: The 1937 Akron Mayoral Campaign

1. Nelson, "CIO at Bay," 576.

2. Nelson Lichtenstein, *Walter Reuther: The Most Dangerous Man in Detroit* (New York: Basic Books, 1997), 54–55.

3. Arshinkoff interview, 1995.

4. "Browder Backs F.D.R. Policies," *Akron Beacon Journal*, September 24, 1937.

5. "Words Fly in Ballot War," *Akron Beacon Journal*, September 25, 1937.

6. Nelson, "The CIO at Bay," 576.

7. Arshinkoff interview, 1996.

8. James S. Jackson, "URW Bitterly Assail Davey," *Akron Beacon Journal*, September 13, 1937.

9. Arshinkoff interview, 1996.

10. H. H. Harriman, "Says Davey Liquor Agents Are Aiding Schroy's Drive," *Akron Beacon Journal*, October 20, 1937; Patrick McMahon, "Charge State Aids Schroy; New Deal Club Hits Judge," *Akron Beacon Journal*, October 14, 1937.

11. H. H. Harriman, "Elect Schroy, Urges Bixler," *Akron Beacon Journal*, September 13, 1937.

12. Patrick McMahon, "Patterson Hits at 'Hobgoblins,'" *Akron Beacon Journal*, October 12, 1937.

13. "Schroy or Patterson," *Akron Beacon Journal*, October 27, 1937.

14. Arshinkoff interview, 1996.

15. H. H. Harriman, "Patterson Gets 36,095 votes; Labor Candidates Take 4 Seats on Council," *Akron Beacon Journal*, November 3, 1937.

16. Harriman, "Patterson Gets 36,095 votes."

17. Nelson, "CIO at Bay," 577–85.

18. Arshinkoff interview, 1995.

Chapter 10: A Quest for Party Unity

1. On the 1938 elections, see http://www.encyclopedia.com/doc/1G2-3468301186.html.

2. Carlson interview, 1995.

3. Beech, "Biography in Brief."

4. Doerler interview, 1996.

5. Ibid.

6. Stephen Hess and David Broder, *The Republican Establishment* (New York: Harper and Row, 1967), 43.

7. "DeWoody, Bliss Confer on Jobs," *Akron Beacon Journal*, January 24, 1939.

8. Arshinkoff interview, 1995.

9. H. H. Harriman, "Schroy Elected," *Akron Beacon Journal*, November 8, 1939.

10. H. H. Harriman, "GOP Is Split by Party Feud," *Akron Beacon Journal*, September 9, 1940.

11. "DeWoody, Bliss Greet Bricker; Peace Hinted," *Akron Beacon Journal*, September 24, 1940.

12. William S. White, *The Taft Story* (New York: Harper and Row, 1954), 115.

13. On Wendell Willkie, see http://www.britannica.com/biography/Wendell-Lewis-Willkie.

14. On the 1940 election, see http://www.britannica.com/event/United-States-presidential-election-of-1940.

15. H. H. Harriman, "Harter Defeats Schroy by Over 5,000," *Akron Beacon Journal*, November 5, 1941.

16. Doerler interview, 1996.

Chapter 11: Ray Bliss Becomes County Chairman

1. H. H. Harriman, "Young GOP Crowd Annihilates Rivals," *Akron Beacon Journal*, December 21, 1941.

2. H. H. Harriman, "Ballot Board Picks Officers," *Akron Beacon Journal*, December 21, 1941.

3. H. H. Harriman, "Bliss Elected to Head GOP," *Akron Beacon Journal*, August 20, 1942.

4. H. H. Harriman, "Bliss Answers DeWoody Charges," *Akron Beacon Journal*, August 26, 1942.

5. Harriman, "Young GOP Crowd."

6. On the 1942 election, see http://journals.cambridge.org/action/displayAbstract?fromPage=online& aid=8730159&fileId=S0003055400043264.

7. H. H. Harriman, "Slusser Wins by 9,812 Votes," *Akron Beacon Journal*, November 3, 1943.

8. Jordan, "GOP's Ray Bliss."

9. Arshinkoff interview, 1995.

10. Minutes, Summit County Republican Executive and Central Committees, June 15, 1944, and December 6, 1946. Made available by Chairman Alexander Arshinkoff, 2004.

Chapter 12: Strengthening the Local Party

1. "Twenty Minutes," 9.

2. Doerler interview, 1995.

3. Ibid.

4. Hershey, "The Party's Not Over."

5. Frances Rex, interview by William Hershey, July 19, 1995.

6. Ibid.

7. Jordan, "GOP's Ray Bliss."

8. Doerler interview, 1995.

9. Arshinkoff interview, 1995.

10. Ray C. Bliss, "Election Aftermath: How Republicans See the Future," *U.S. News and World Report*, November 15, 1965.

11. Doerler interview, 1995.

12. Arshinkoff interview, 1996.

13. Doerler interview, 1996.

14. Clyde Mann, "Ray Bliss: He Believes in Peace," *Akron Beacon Journal*, February 17, 1957.

15. Doerler interview, 1995; Lee Leonard, "Old Pro Retires from Panel," *Sarasota Herald-Tribune*, July 19, 1980.

16. "Sieber Assails Bliss Leadership," *Akron Beacon Journal*, August 13, 1942.

17. "Photo Finish," *Akron Beacon Journal*, November 8, 1945.

18. Taft Seminar, 1974.

19. Doerler interview, 1995.

20. Arthur Peterson, interview by William Hershey, December 79, 2004.

21. Arshinkoff interview, 1995.

22. Doerler interview, 1996.

23. Minutes, Summit County GOP, May 23, 1944.

24. Doerler interview, 1996.

25. Minutes, Summit County GOP, April 6, 1945.

26. Doerler interview, 1996.

27. Minutes, Summit County GOP, January 3, 1944, and August 1, 1944.

28. Doerler interview, 1996.

29. "1949 Campaign [Summit County]." Series I: Box 5, Folder 30. Ray C. Bliss Papers. MSS768. Ohio History Connection (OHC), Columbus, Ohio.

Chapter 13: Growing Recognition

1. H. H. Harriman, "Akronite's Choice Held Significant," *Akron Beacon Journal*, August 6, 1944.

2. "Planks in Party Invited by Bliss," *Akron Beacon Journal*, August 13, 1944.

3. Doerler interview, 1995.

4. H. H. Harriman, "He's Ready: Youth, Training Give Bliss Background for GOP Spot," *Akron Beacon Journal*, October 21, 1945.

5. Peterson interview, 1996.

6. Hess and Broder, *Republican Establishment*, 50.

7. Jordan, "GOP's Ray Bliss."

8. Doerler, 1996; Broder, "Bliss Rides the Elephant."

9. Minutes, Summit County GOP, June 15, 1944, and August 1, 1994.

10. Minutes, Summit County GOP, December 16, 1943.

11. On the 1944 election, see http://www.britannica.com/event/United-States-presidential-election -of-1944.

12. "Appoint Bliss to Committee," *Akron Beacon Journal*, January 21, 1945; "GOP Group Visits Akron," *Akron Beacon Journal*, May 14, 1945.

13. Harriman, "He's Ready."

14. H. H. Harriman, "Ray Bliss Declines to Run," *Akron Beacon Journal*, November 9, 1945.

15. Doerler interview, 1996.

16. Mann interview, 1990.

17. Arshinkoff interview, 1996.

18. Harriman, "He's Ready."

Chapter 14: Ray Bliss Gets a Day Job

1. Doerler interview, 1996.

2. Articles of Incorporation, Tower Agencies, Inc., October 21, 1947. Ohio Secretary of State (#204608).

3. "'Hy' Harris, Legal Aid's First Head," *Akron Beacon Journal*, March 3, 1969.

4. "Charles Sacks, Lawyer, Civic Leader," *Akron Beacon Journal*, December 25, 1972.

5. "Death Takes 'Hy' Subrin, Akron Attorney, Teacher," *Akron Beacon Journal*, August 16, 1974.

6. Articles of Incorporation, 1947.

7. Doerler interview, 1995.

8. Doerler interview, 1996.

9. "Madge Emily (Heacock) Doerler," *Akron Beacon Journal*, February 23, 2011.

10. Wright interview, 1995.

11. Doerler interview, 1995. Analysis of Bliss's personal financial records found in the Ray and Ellen Bliss papers at UAA and the Ray Bliss papers at OHC support this conclusion.

Chapter 15: The Great Defeat of '48

1. On the 1946 election, see http://ashbrook.org/publications/oped-busch-06-1946.

2. H. H. Harriman, "Slusser Wins Second Term," *Akron Beacon Journal*, November 7, 1945.

3. "Labor Scores," *Akron Beacon Journal*, November 5, 1947.

4. Richard Norton Smith, *Thomas E. Dewey and His Times* (New York: Simon & Schuster, 1984), 494.

5. Will Muller, "Ohio's Republican Chairman Converts Gimmicks into Votes," *Detroit News*, May 28, 1957.

6. William Hershey, "For Truman the Luck Started Here?," *Akron Beacon Journal*, September 24, 1992.

7. Bernard Rosen, interview by William Hershey, April 15, 1995.

8. "When All the Experts Got It Wrong: Harry Truman's Upset Presidential Victory, 1948," http:// www.austincc.edu/lpatrick/his1302/WhenAllTheExperts1.html.

Chapter 16: Ray Bliss Becomes State Chairman

1. "Bliss Named in GOP Leader Fight," *Akron Beacon Journal*, November 18, 1948.
2. H. H. Harriman, "Bliss Set to Head Ohio GOP," *Akron Beacon Journal*, January 28, 1949.
3. Doerler interview, 1996.
4. Harold A. Stacy, "Bliss Pledges New GOP Formula as He Takes Over Party Reins," *Columbus Dispatch*, February 10, 1949.
5. "Minutes of Meeting of the Republican State Executive and Central Committee" and "Mr. Ray Bliss, Chairman: Following is a rough draft of the notes taken by me at the meeting of the committee," February 9, 1949. Series I: Box 18, Folder 2. Bliss papers, OHC. The second document is unlikely to have been written by Bliss because his remarks are reported in detail.
6. Taft Seminar, 1974.
7. Stacy, "Bliss Pledges."
8. Clyde Mann, "Bliss and Hanhart Again Party Chiefs," *Akron Beacon Journal*, May 18, 1954.
9. "GOP Chairman Bliss," *Akron Beacon Journal*, February 10, 1949.

Chapter 17: Strengthening the State Party

1. Frank Avren, interview by William Hershey, May 2, 1996.
2. H. H. Harriman, "Bliss Set for GOP Shakeup," *Akron Beacon Journal*, March 28, 1949.
3. Ray Mitten, "Bliss Seeks Large Vote," *Akron Beacon Journal*, June 19, 1949.
4. John H. Kessel, "Ray Bliss and the Development of the Ohio Republican Party," in *Politics, Professionalism, and Power: Modern Party Organization and the Legacy of Ray C. Bliss*, edited by John C. Green (Lanham, MD: University Press of America, 1994), 49.
5. Muller, "Ohio's Republican Chairman."
6. Mann interview, 1990.
7. Muller, "Ohio's Republican Chairman."
8. Ray C. Bliss, Statement before the United States Senate, Committee on Rules and Administration, Sub-committee on Privileges and Elections, January 7, 1952.
9. Harriman, "Bliss Set for GOP Shakeup."
10. Kessel, "Ray Bliss," 50.
11. "Bliss Calls Session on GOP Policy," *Akron Beacon Journal*, April 27, 1949.
12. Broder, "Bliss Rides the Elephant."
13. Avren interview, 1996.
14. Frederick M. Wirt, "The Organization Man in Politics: Ray Bliss and the 1960 Election," in *Politics, Professionalism, and Power: Modern Party Organization and the Legacy of Ray C. Bliss*, edited by John C. Green (Lanham, MD: University Press of America, 1994), 65.
15. Kessel, "Ray Bliss," 54.
16. Ibid., 51.
17. John Kessel, "Road to the Mansion: A Study of the 1956 Gubernatorial Campaign in Ohio" (PhD diss., Ohio State University, 1958), 311.
18. "Bliss Road to State Chairmanship Opened by Slusser Decision," *Akron Beacon Journal*, February 13, 1949.
19. H. H. Harriman, "Slusser Has Habit of Winning by 10,000 in Mayoral Elections," *Akron Beacon Journal*, November 6, 1949.
20. "Top Party Men Back Bliss' Plans," *Akron Beacon Journal*, June 16, 1949.

Chapter 18: Taft and TV

1. James T. Patterson, *Mr. Republican: A Biography of Robert A. Taft* (Boston: Houghton Mifflin, 1972), 461.
2. Taft Seminar, 1974.
3. Hershey, "The Party's Not Over."
4. Muller, "Ohio's Republican Chairman."
5. Hershey, "The Party's Not Over."
6. Muller, "Ohio's Republican Chairman."
7. George W. Knepper, *Ohio and Its People* (Kent, OH: Kent State University Press, 1989), 382.
8. Avren interview, 1996.
9. Hershey, "The Party's Not Over."
10. Muller, "Ohio's Republican Chairman."
11. Kessel, "Ray Bliss," 52–54.
12. Bliss, "Role of a State Chairman," 159.
13. Kessel, "Ray Bliss," 51.
14. Muller, "Ohio's Republican Chairman."
15. William Ayres, interview by William Hershey, April 22, 1995.
16. Avren interview, 1996.
17. Ayres interview, 1995.
18. H. H. Harriman, "Bliss Cites Dem Edge in Jobs," *Akron Beacon Journal*, February 13, 1950.
19. Bliss, Statement to US Senate, 1952.
20. On the 1950 election, see https://en.wikipedia.org/wiki/United_States_Senate_elections,_1950 and https://en.wikipedia.org/wiki/United_States_House_of_Representatives_elections,_1950.

Chapter 19: Mr. Republican Loses White House Bid

1. "Bliss Star Rises with Taft Victory," *Akron Beacon Journal*, November 9, 1950; "Bliss' Finesse," *Akron Beacon Journal*, November 9, 1950.
2. Wright interview, 1996.
3. Ayres interview, 1995.
4. "Bliss to Give Tops to Top GOP Brass," *Akron Beacon Journal*, September 20, 1951.
5. H. H. Harriman, "Last 2-Booth Count Decides Mayors' Race," *Akron Beacon Journal*, November 7, 1951.
6. Bliss, Statement to US Senate, 1952.
7. Ibid.
8. H. H. Harriman, "See Bliss Being Groomed for Spot in Taft Plans," *Akron Beacon Journal*, February 12, 1951.
9. Clyde Mann, "Bliss Ignored in Strategy," *Akron Beacon Journal*, July 15, 1952.
10. David Halberstam, *The Fifties* (New York: Villard Books, 1993), 211.
11. Mann, "See Bliss Being Groomed"; White, *Taft*, 174–79.
12. White, *Taft*, 180–81.
13. On Adlai Stevenson, see http://www.britannica.com/biography/Adlai-E-Stevenson.

Chapter 20: Ohio Likes Ike

1. H. H. Harriman, "Election Victories Rewarded," *Akron Beacon Journal*, July 11, 1952.
2. Ray C. Bliss to Arthur Summerfield, July 12, 1952. Series I: Box 10, Folder 42. Bliss Papers, OHC.
3. Clyde Mann, "Name Bliss One of GOP Strategists," *Akron Beacon Journal*, September 7, 1952.
4. "Twenty Minutes," 6.

5. Alvin Silverman, "2 Whistle Stops Put Back for Ike," *Cleveland Plain Dealer*, September 23, 1952.

6. Ray C. Bliss to Eisenhower Campaign, September 20, 1952. Series I: Box 11, Folder 3. Bliss Papers, OHC.

7. Ray C. Bliss to Martin Coyle, September 26, 1952. Series I: Box 11, Folder 3. Bliss Papers, OHC.

8. Daniel M. Ogden Jr. and Arthur L. Peterson, *Electing the President*, rev. ed. (San Francisco: Chandler, 1968), 253–58.

9. On 1952 election, see http://www.britannica.com/event/United-States-presidential-election-of-1952.

Chapter 21: The Organizational Man in Action

1. Ray C. Bliss to Florence Morris, January 15, 1953. Series I: Box 11, Folder 6. Bliss papers, OHC.

2. Doerler interview, 1996.

3. Don Strouse, "I Like to Do Things People Say Can't Be Done," *Akron Beacon Journal*, January 31, 1953.

4. "Midwest GOP Names Bliss," *Akron Beacon Journal*, January 20, 1953.

5. Robert J. Huckshorn, *Party Leadership in the States* (Amherst: University of Massachusetts Press, 1976), 171–79.

6. Paul R. Leach, "Bliss Considered by GOP for National Chairman," *Akron Beacon Journal*, March 29, 1953.

7. Clyde Mann, "GOP Party Job Not for Me—Bliss," *Akron Beacon Journal*, April 1, 1953.

8. "Bliss vs. Schorr," *Akron Beacon Journal*, June 23, 1952; Richard L. Maher, "Schorr's Wings Clipped by Ohio GOP," *Cincinnati Enquirer*, December 9, 1952.

9. "Lausche Strengthened by Assembly Actions," *Akron Beacon Journal*, June 21, 1951.

10. William B. Saxbe, *I've Seen the Elephant* (Kent, OH: Kent State University Press, 2000), 43.

11. William Saxbe, interview by William Hershey, September 20, 1995.

12. Hal Conefry, "Saxbe Named Speaker of Ohio House," *Columbus Citizen*, December 9, 1952.

13. Saxbe interview, 1995.

14. Mann interview, 1990.

15. Kessel, "Ray Bliss," 56.

16. Mann interview, 1990.

17. Clyde Mann, "10-Year Republican Rule Broken as 81,433 Ballot," *Akron Beacon Journal*, November 4, 1953.

18. White, *Taft*, 269–70.

19. Taft Seminar, 1974.

Chapter 22: George Bender and a Judas Goat

1. Clyde Mann, "Bliss 'Farm System' Gives GOP Surplus of Able Candidates," *Akron Beacon Journal*, January 23, 1955.

2. Doerler interview, 1995.

3. Clyde Mann, "Ray Bliss in Middle of Battle over GOP Senate Nomination," *Akron Beacon Journal*, January 3, 1954; Clyde Mann, "Bender Endorsement Seen Causing Rift in Ohio GOP Party," *Akron Beacon Journal*, January 8, 1954.

4. Ray C. Bliss to Andrew Hale, October 26, 1954. Series I: Box 16, Folder 24. Bliss papers, OHC.

5. Bliss to Hale, 1954.

6. Hal Conefry, "Both Bliss and Bender Deny Rift," *Akron Beacon Journal*, April 1, 1954.

7. "Bender Outburst Adds Coals to Bliss Feud," *Akron Beacon Journal*, September 9, 1952.

8. Bliss to Hale, 1954.

9. Saxbe, *I've Seen the Elephant*, 53–54.

10. John Andrews, interview by William Hershey, May 22, 1995.

11. Saxbe interview, 1995.

12. Clyde Mann, "Saxbe to Run against Bender," *Akron Beacon Journal*, January 13, 1954.

13. Clyde Mann, "Saxbe Jolts Ohio Peace Hope," *Akron Beacon Journal*, January, 14, 1954.

14. Clyde Mann, "Saxbe Claims Bliss Goes Out If Bender Wins Nomination," *Akron Beacon Journal*, March 13, 1954.

15. Conefry, "Both Bliss and Bender."

16. Milt Freudenheim, "Saxbe Rips Bliss as GOP 'Killer,'" *Akron Beacon Journal*, April 15, 1954.

17. Andrews interview, 1995.

18. Saxbe, *I've Seen the Elephant*, 57–58.

19. Reed Smith, "GOP Gives Clevelander 58,000 Lead," *Akron Beacon Journal*, May 5, 1954.

20. Arshinkoff interview, 1995.

Chapter 23: Success and Sorrow

1. Clyde Mann, "Bliss Hailed as GOP's Top Leader," *Akron Beacon Journal*, November 6, 1954.

2. Ibid.

3. Ibid.

4. Clyde Mann, "Compensation Bills Deadlock Broken by Bliss' Efforts," *Akron Beacon Journal*, July 3, 1955.

5. On O'Neill, see http://www.ohiohistorycentral.org/w/C._W._O'Neill.

6. Kessel, "Ray Bliss," 49–50.

7. Jordan, "GOP's Ray Bliss."

8. Clyde Mann, "O'Neill's Campaign Damaged by Rumors He Would Oust Bliss," *Akron Beacon Journal*, January 29, 1956.

9. Arshinkoff interview, 1995.

10. Jordan, "GOP's Ray Bliss."

11. "Mother of Ray Bliss."

12. Doerler interview, 1995.

13. Ibid.

Chapter 24: A Republican Governor—At Last

1. Michael R. Beschloss and Vincent Virga, *Eisenhower: A Centennial Life* (New York: HarperCollins, 1990), 134–35.

2. "Can Win without Ike—Bliss," *Akron Beacon Journal*, November 14, 1955.

3. Tom Wicker, *One of Us: Richard Nixon and the American Dream* (New York: Random House, 1991), 193.

4. Ibid, 199.

5. Clyde Mann, "Bliss Rips Lausche as 'Straddler,'" *Akron Beacon Journal*, June 26, 1956.

6. W. H. Lawrence, "Eisenhower and Nixon Are Renominated," *New York Times*, August 22, 1956.

7. Michael Curtin, "The O'Neill-DiSalle Years, 1957–1963," in *Ohio Politics*, edited by Alexander P. Lamis (Kent, OH: Kent State University Press, 1994), 43.

8. "Bliss Heads Ohio GOP Fourth Time," *Akron Beacon Journal*, May 22, 1956.

9. Kessel, "Ray Bliss," 57.

10. Ibid., 423.

11. Ibid., 346–53.

12. Ibid., 325–29.

13. On the 1956 election, see http://www.britannica.com/event/United-States-presidential-election -of-1956.

14. "Bliss Back in Running to Succeed Hall," *Akron Beacon Journal*, January 12, 1957.

15. "Bliss Takes Self out of Chairman Contest," *Akron Beacon Journal*, January 16, 1957.

Chapter 25: A Rocky Start and a Showdown

1. Michael Pavick, interview by William Hershey, May 1, 14, 17, 1996.

2. Clyde Mann, "O'Neill Pay Raise Switch 'Shocks' Leaders of GOP," *Akron Beacon Journal*, April 7, 1957.

3. Ibid.

4. Ibid.

5. Keith McNamara, interview by William Hershey, May 5, 1996.

6. Clyde Mann, "Mild Rebellion within Ohio GOP Soon Quelled," *Akron Beacon Journal*, July 26, 1956.

7. Clyde Mann, "Krenzler Pushing to Fill Ray Bliss' Shoes—Sometime," *Akron Beacon Journal*, February 17, 1957.

8. Arshinkoff interview, 1995.

9. Saxbe interview, 1995.

10. Mann, "Krenzler Pushing."

11. Ibid.

12. Ibid.

13. Arshinkoff interview, 1995.

14. "Bliss: Ability Comes First in Patronage," *Akron Beacon Journal*, January 22, 1953.

15. Doerler interview, 1995.

16. Arshinkoff interview, 1995.

17. Ibid.

18. Jordan, "GOP's Ray Bliss."

19. Arshinkoff interview, 1995.

20. Jordan, "GOP's Ray Bliss."

Chapter 26: Business Defies Bliss

1. "GOP Committee Election Information: When Republicans Talk to Laboring Groups, We Should Say...," August 1, 1960. Box 40, Folder 1. Ray and Ellen Bliss papers, UAA.

2. Curtin, "O'Neill-DiSalle Years," 48.

3. Lichtenstein, *Walter Reuther*, 295.

4. Michael B. Hissam, "C. William O'Neill and the 1958 Right-to-Work Amendment" (senior honors thesis, Ohio State University, June 2005), 51.

5. Hissam, "William O'Neill," 59–60.

6. "Nation Has Eyes on Ohio Right to Work Campaign—Verity," *News Bulletin* of Ohio Chamber of Commerce, Columbus, Ohio, 12, no. 7 (June 1958).

7. Arshinkoff interview, 1995.

8. John Mahaney, interview by William Hershey, May 13, 1996.

9. "Presentation of the 1958 Campaign in Ohio Voter Attitudes on Issues and Candidates," March 20, 1958. Series I: Box 7. Bliss paper, OHC. The poll was based on approximately 10,000 questionnaires sent to more than 150 communities across Ohio.

10. Pavick interview, 1996; the following details of Pavick's career and relationship with Bliss are from the interview.

11. Hissam, "William O'Neill," 73.

12. Ibid., 44–45.

13. Richard O. Davies, *Defender of the Old Guard John Bricker and American Politics* (Columbus: Ohio State University Press, 1993), 196.

14. Davies, *Defender of the Old*, 196.

15. Charles Kurfess, interview by William Hershey, July 16, 1995.

16. Joseph Alsop, "Ideological Gymnasts in Cincinnati and the Election," *Cincinnati Enquirer*, November 10, 1958.

Chapter 27: The Right-to-Work Disaster

1. Hissam, "William O'Neill," 76.

2. J. C. Marion to C. William O'Neil, October 29, 1958. Box 43. C. William O'Neill Papers. MSS 342. Ohio History Connection, Columbus, Ohio.

3. Davies, *Defender of the Old*, 200.

4. Mann interview, 1990; Davies, *Defender of the Old*, 199.

5. Hissam, "William O'Neill," 64.

6. Ibid., 75–76.

7. Michael Curtin, *Ohio Politics Almanac* (Kent, OH: Kent State University Press, 1996), 89.

8. Davis, *Defender of the Old*, 199.

9. Howard Metzenbaum, interview by William Hershey, September 11, 1995.

10. Hissam, "William O'Neill," 64.

11. David Eugene Waddell, interview by William Hershey, May 6, 1995.

12. Hissam, "William O'Neill," 83.

13. John H. Fenton, "The Right-To-Work Vote in Ohio," *Midwest Journal of Political Science* 3 (August 1959): 243.

14. Fenton, "Right-to-Work," 253.

Chapter 28: Ray Bliss Rebuilds—Again

1. Clyde Mann, "Bliss Blames RTW for GOP Debacle," *Akron Beacon Journal*, November 5, 1958.

2. "Bliss Preens GOP for '60 Election," *Akron Beacon Journal*, January 11, 1959.

3. William Hershey, "Down on the Farm with John Galbreath," *Akron Beacon Journal Beacon Magazine*, January 24, 1982.

4. Ibid.

5. Andrews interview, 1995.

6. Arshinkoff interview, 1995.

7. Andrews interview, 1995.

8. Clyde Mann, "Bliss to Have 'Experts' Aid GOP County Chiefs," *Akron Beacon Journal*, January 28, 1959.

9. Andrews interview, 1995.

10. Wirt, "Organization Man," 70.

11. Ibid., 71.

12. Ray C. Sutliff, "Vital Decisions on City Election Near for GOP Leaders," *Akron Beacon Journal*, May 17, 1959.

13. Waddell interview, 1995.

14. Bliss, "Role of the State Chairman," 169–70.

15. Waddell interview, 1995.

16. Hershey, "The Party's Not Over."
17. Ibid.

Chapter 29: Wedding Bells

1. Arshinkoff interview, 1995.
2. Earley interview, 1995.
3. Clyde Mann, interview by William Hershey, May 13, 1995.
4. Earley interview, 1995.
5. Blasio, "Ray Bliss."
6. Ayres interview, 1995.
7. Della Mann, interview by William Hershey, May 13, 1995.
8. "RCB House Construction, 1955–1957." Series I: Box 16, Folder 6. Bliss papers, OHC.
9. Earley interview, 1995.
10. Della Mann interview, 1995.
11. Mann interviews, 1995, 1990.
12. Della Mann interview, 1995.
13. "Ray Bliss to Wed Ellen Palmer Today," *Akron Beacon Journal,* November 26, 1959.
14. Della Mann interview, 1995.
15. Earley interview, 1995.
16. Marion Geyer, "Felicitations Pour in for Blisses," *Akron Beacon Journal,* November 27, 1959.
17. Mann interview, 1995.

Chapter 30: Politics Writer

1. James M. Cannon to Ray C. Bliss, January 26, 1959. Series I: Box 19, Folder 5. Bliss papers, OHC.
2. James M. Cannon, ed., *Politics U.S.A.* (Garden City, NY: Doubleday, 1960), vii–xi.
3. Bliss, "The Role of the State Chairman," 160. All quotations in this chapter come from this source.

Chapter 31: Presidential Politicking

1. Broder, "Bliss Rides the Elephant." According to Ellen Bliss, an excellent description of the Ohio Republican Party under Bliss is found in Michael Barone, Grant Ujifusa, and Douglas Matthews, *The Almanac of American Politics 1972* (Washington, DC: Gambit Press, 1972), 610–11. On Bliss's role in modernizing the Ohio Republican Party, see Brian M. Conley, "States and the Making of the 'Service' Party: The Case of the Postwar Ohio Republican Party," *Journal of American Studies* 45 (2011): 519–37.
2. "Alcorn Quits, Bliss May Get Top GOP Post," *Akron Beacon Journal,* April 1, 1959.
3. Clyde Mann, "Bliss Takes Self out of Top GOP Picture," *Akron Beacon Journal,* April 2, 1959.
4. "GOP Picks Chicago, Morton," *Akron Beacon Journal,* April 11, 1959.
5. Clyde Mann, "Bliss Says Nixon Holds His Fire," *Akron Beacon Journal,* May 17, 1960.
6. Robert E. Hoyt, "Rocky over Nixon? Unlikely, Says Bliss," *Akron Beacon Journal,* June 9, 1960.
7. "Vote Nixon, Shun Bender, Bliss Urges," *Akron Beacon Journal,* April 15, 1960.
8. "Bender Defeat Hailed by Bliss," *Akron Beacon Journal,* May 4, 1960.
9. Theodore White, *The Making of the President 1960* (New York: Atheneum, 1962), 197–98.
10. Ogden and Peterson, *Electing the President,* 78–79.
11. White, *Making of the President 1960,* 206.
12. Clyde Mann, "Ohioans Still Grumbling," *Akron Beacon Journal,* July 29, 1960.

13. "Hit Bliss Actions at Convention," *Akron Beacon Journal*, July 31, 1960.

14. Clyde Mann, "'Demotion' Irritates C. J. Brown," *Akron Beacon Journal*, August 7, 1960.

Chapter 32: Ray Bliss's Masterpiece

1. White, *Making of the President 1960*, 52.

2. Wirt, "Organization Man," 76.

3. Broder, "Bliss Rides the Elephant."

4. Ray C. Bliss to Staff, September 6, 1960. Series I: Box 11, Folder 30. Bliss papers, OHC.

5. Eugene P. O'Grady, interview with William Hershey, May 6, 1996.

6. Wirt, "Organization Man," 65.

7. Ibid., 66.

8. Ibid., 68.

9. Ibid., 67.

10. Ibid., 65.

11. Broder, "Bliss Rides the Elephant."

12. "Field Men and Reports," October 6, 1960. Series I: Box 2, Folder 20. Bliss papers, OHC.

13. Taft Seminar, 1974.

14. Ibid.; "Bliss Credits Polls for Ohio Victory," *Akron Beacon Journal*, January 19, 1961.

15. Taft Seminar, 1974.

16. Ibid.

17. Wicker, *One of Us*, 254.

18. Taft Seminar, 1974.

19. Robert Kotzbauer, "Bliss Wants to Change the Subject," *Akron Beacon Journal*, January 29, 1961.

20. Taft Seminar, 1974.

21. On the 1960 election, see http://www.britannica.com/event/United-States-presidential-election -of-1960.

22. "Bliss Organization Won Ohio for GOP," *Akron Beacon Journal*, January 3, 1961.

23. White, *Making of the President 1960*, 333.

24. Ibid., 21.

25. Richard M. Nixon to Ray C. Bliss, December 14, 1960. Series I: Box 11, Folder 18. Bliss papers, OHC.

Chapter 33: A Big City Assignment

1. Robert E. Hoyt, "Bliss Shy As GOP Raves," *Akron Beacon Journal*, January 7, 1961.

2. Ibid.

3. Ibid.

4. Broder, "Bliss Rides the Elephant."

5. Ray C. Sutcliff, "Bliss Would Be GOP Chief, If—," *Akron Beacon Journal*, January 8, 1961.

6. Cabell Phillips, "GOP Loss Is Laid to the Big Cities," *New York Times*, February 26, 1961.

7. Thomas Flinn, "How Mr. Nixon Took Ohio: A Short Reply to Senator Kennedy's Question," *Western Political Quarterly* 15 (June 1962): 274–79.

8. Ray C. Bliss, "Report of the Committee on Big City Politics," January 12, 1962. Republican National Committee. In *Papers of the Republican Party*, edited by Paul L. Kesaris (Frederick, MD: University Publications of America, 1987).

9. Bliss, "Big City Politics," Preface, 1–2.

10. Bliss, "Big City Politics," Subcommittee on Party Organization and Candidate Recruitment, 4–47.

11. Bliss, "Big City Politics," Subcommittee on Labor, Business, Professional and Independent Groups, 1–12.

12. Bliss, "Big City Politics," Subcommittee on Ethnic and Minority Voters, 1–6.

13. Bliss, "Big City Politics," Subcommittee on Public Relations, Surveys and Educational Methods, 1–29.

14. Robert Kotzbauer, "Bliss Chooses 6 to Help Recruit Workers for GOP," *Akron Beacon Journal*, July 25, 1962.

15. "Anticipating Bliss's Report," *Akron Beacon Journal*, October 19, 1961; "GOP Unit Rejects Goldwater Plan," *Akron Beacon Journal*, May 18, 1961. On the conservative perspective, see M. V. Hood III, Quentin Kidd, and Irwin L. Morris, "The Republican Party in the South: From Radical Fringe to Conservative Mainstream," *The Oxford Handbook of Southern Politics* (Oxford: Oxford University Press, 2012), 336.

Chapter 34: Ray C. Bliss and James A. Rhodes

1. Flinn, "How Mr. Nixon," 274.

2. Brian Usher and Michael Cull, "A Man Named Rhodes," *Akron Beacon Journal*, March 5, 1978.

3. Ibid.

4. Tom Diemer, Lee Leonard, and Richard G. Zimmerman, *James A. Rhodes: Ohio Colossus* (Kent, OH: Kent State University Press, 2014), 31.

5. Richard G. Zimmerman, "Rhodes's First Eight Years, 1963–1971," in *Ohio Politics*, edited by Alexander P. Lamis (Kent, OH: Kent State University Press, 1994), 59.

6. Usher and Cull, "A Man Named Rhodes."

7. Arshinkoff interview, 1995.

8. James A. Rhodes, interview by William Hershey, October 13, 1995. Robert Kotzbauer, "All's Not Peaceful in the GOP Camp," *Akron Beacon Journal*, April 8, 1961.

9. Arshinkoff interview, 1995.

10. Rhodes interview, 1995.

11. Arshinkoff interview, 1995.

12. Rhodes interview, 1995.

13. "Bliss Sees Stiff Ohio Fight for GOP," *Akron Beacon Journal*, May 11, 1962.

14. Zimmerman, "Rhodes's First Eight Years," 61.

15. See O. F. Knippenburg, "Bliss Booklet Shows GOP Strategy," *Columbus Citizen Journal*, May 31, 1966; Arshinkoff interview, 1995.

16. Curtin, "O'Neill-DiSalle Years," 53–54.

17. Zimmerman, "Rhodes's First Eight Years," 67; Usher and Cull, "A Man Named Rhodes."

18. Arshinkoff interview, 1995.

19. Rhodes interview, 1995.

20. Curtin, "O'Neill-DiSalle Years," 57.

21. Zimmerman, "Rhodes's First Eight Years," 68.

22. Kurfess interview, 1995.

23. "Ignorance Isn't Bliss—Just Ask Ohio Dems," *Akron Beacon Journal*, November 22, 1962.

24. On the 1962 election, see Andrew Busch, *Horses in Midstream: U.S. Midterm Elections and Their Conse-quences, 1894–1998* (Pittsburgh: University of Pittsburgh Press, 1999), 145–48.

25. Arshinkoff interview, 1995.

Chapter 35: Recruitment Matters

1. On Glenn, see Frank Van Riper, *Glenn: The Astronaut Who Would Be President* (New York: Empire Books, 1983).

2. Ray C. Bliss to J. Willard Marriott, October 25, 1963. Series I: Box 16, Folder 30. Bliss papers, OHC.
3. Arshinkoff interview, 1995.
4. Robert Feldkamp, "Glenn Race May Start in Akron," *Akron Beacon Journal*, February 9, 1964.
5. Ibid.
6. John Glenn, interview by William Hershey, August 15, 1996.
7. Ray C. Bliss to Joe Bartlett, January 15, 1964. Series I: Box 16, Folder 31. Bliss papers, OHC.
8. Arshinkoff interview, 1995.
9. "Professors to Help Draft GOP Policy," *Akron Beacon Journal*, June 3, 1962.
10. Peterson interview, 1995.
11. Ellen Bliss interview, 1990.
12. George Hinman to Nelson Rockefeller, December 14, 1962. Nelson A. Rockefeller personal papers, Politics—George L. Hinman. 04/J.2.1—005 #0025: Bliss, Ray C. Rockefeller Archive Center (RAC). http://dimes.rockarch.org/FA346/collection.
13. Abe Zaidan, interview by John Green, May 9, 2012.
14. Hinman, December 14, 1962.
15. Arshinkoff interview, 1995.
16. "Man behind the Desk," *Time*, November 23, 1962.

Chapter 36: Trouble in San Francisco

1. For details of this effort see F. Clifton White, *Suite 3505: The Story of the Draft Goldwater Movement* (New Rochelle, NY: Arlington House, 1967),
2. Robert Feldkamp, "Bliss IS NOT Hostile to Goldwater Candidacy," *Akron Beacon Journal*, September 19, 1963.
3. Robert Kotzbauer, "Bliss Acclaimed as Goldwater Derides 'Frontier,'" *Akron Beacon Journal*, February 2, 1962.
4. Arshinkoff interview, 1995.
5. Kotzbauer, "Bliss Acclaimed."
6. "President Kennedy's assassination—Ray Bliss statement. Nov. 22, 1963." Series I, Box 18, File 51. Bliss Papers. OHC.
7. On the 1964 primaries, see https://presidentialcampaignselectionsreference.wordpress.com /overviews/20th-century/1964-overview/.
8. Waddell interview, 1995.
9. "Bliss Wins over Rowe by 4–1 Vote," *Akron Beacon Journal*, May 6, 1964; Robert Feldkamp, interview by William Hershey, January 6, 1997.
10. "Ray C. Bliss to All Males," March 5, 1964. Series I: Box 3, Folder 19. Bliss Papers, OHC.
11. Theodore White, *The Making of the President 1964* (New York: Harper Collins, 1965), 157–60.
12. Robert Feldkamp, "Glenn Rumor Pot Is Boiling," *Akron Beacon Journal*, May 31, 1964.
13. W. Richard Wright, interview by John C. Green, April 1, 1990.
14. Robert Feldkamp, "How Rhodes Pulled Rug from under Bliss," *Akron Beacon Journal*, July 12, 1964.
15. John McMullan, "Ohio Delegation's Release Kills Last Scranton Bid?," *Akron Beacon Journal*, July 10, 1964.
16. Arshinkoff interview, 1995.
17. Feldkamp, "How Rhodes Pulled."
18. Ibid.
19. John S. Knight, "Goldwater as Nominee Gives GOP New Vigor," *Akron Beacon Journal*, July 19, 1965.

20. "Rhodes-Bliss Buddies," *Akron Beacon Journal*, July 16, 1964.

21. Robert Feldkamp, "Was Caucus Slap at Bliss?," *Akron Beacon Journal*, July 14, 1964.

22. On Goldwater's acceptance speech, see http://www.speeches-usa.com/Transcripts/barry_goldwater -1964rnc.html.

23. Robert Kotzbauer, "Bliss Removes Personal Roadblock for Taking National GOP Helm," *Akron Beacon Journal*, June 23, 1964; "Bliss' Chances for National Chairman now are 50–50," *Akron Beacon Journal*, July 13, 1964.

24. Stephen Shadegg, *What Happened to Goldwater?* (New York: Holt, Rinehart, and Winston, 1965), 172–73.

25. Robert Feldkamp, "Bliss Still Boils over Barry Camp Pressure," *Akron Beacon Journal*, July 16, 1964.

26. Kotzbauer, "Bliss Removes Personal."

27. Ayres interview, 1995.

28. Kotzbauer, "Bliss Removes Personal."

29. Ray C. Bliss to Rose Kincaid, June 25, 1964. Series I: Box 16, Folder 32. Bliss Papers, OHC; Robert Feldkamp, "Ray Wants to Call All the Shots," *Akron Beacon Journal*, June 26, 1964.

Chapter 37: The Goldwater Debacle

1. Wright interview, 1995.

2. Robert Taft Jr. to Ray C. Bliss, July 20, 1964. Series I: Box 16, Folder 32. Bliss papers, OHC.

3. Mrs. Roy C. Ahern to Ray C. Bliss, July 23, 1964. Series I: Box 16, Folder 32. Bliss papers, OHC.

4. Clyde Mann to Ray C. Bliss, July 20, 1964. Series I: Box 16, Folder 32. Bliss papers, OHC.

5. "Bliss Will Keep State GOP Post," *Akron Beacon Journal*, July 21, 1961.

6. Richard M. Nixon to Ray C. Bliss, August 24, 1964. Series I: Box 16, Folder 33. Bliss papers, OHC.

7. Robert H. Feldkamp, "Will Barry's Boys Team with Ohio GOP?" *Akron Beacon Journal*, July 17, 1964.

8. Ibid.

9. "Bliss Gets Key Post in Campaign," *Akron Beacon Journal*, July 29, 1964.

10. "See Bliss Choice as 'Practical,'" *Akron Beacon Journal*, July 30, 1964.

11. White, *Making of the President 1964*, 335.

12. Lee Edwards, *Goldwater: The Man Who Made a Revolution* (Washington, DC: Regnery, 1995), 329.

13. White, *Making of the President 1964*, 337.

14. Ayres interview, 1995.

15. James T. Patterson, *Grand Expectations: The United States, 1945–1974* (Oxford: Oxford University Press, 1996), 558.

16. White, *Making of the President 1964*, 351.

17. On the 1964 election, see http://www.britannica.com/event/United-States-presidential-election -of-1964.

18. The following comments are recorded in Edwards, *Goldwater*, 344.

Chapter 38: Plotting for Bliss

1. William McGaffin and James McCartney, "How Goldwater Was Forced to Accept Bliss for Burch," *Akron Beacon Journal*, January 13, 1965.

2. McGaffin and McCartney, "How Goldwater."

3. Hess and Broder, *Republican Establishment*, 41.

4. Peterson interview, 1996.

5. McGaffin and McCartney, "How Goldwater."

6. Ibid.

7. Ibid.

8. Barry M. Goldwater with Jack Casserly, *Goldwater* (New York: Doubleday, 1988), 166.

9. Mary C. Brenna, *Turning Right in the Sixties* (Chapel Hill: University of North Carolina Press, 1995).

10. Barry Goldwater to Members of the Republican National Committee, December 26, 1964. Series I: Box 16, Folder 33. Bliss papers, OHC.

11. McGaffin and McCartney, "How Goldwater."

12. Ibid.

13. Hess and Broder, *Republican Establishment*, 42.

14. McGaffin and McCartney, "How Goldwater."

15. Ibid.

16. Ibid.

17. Walter R. Mears, "'Bliss-For-Chairman' Move Is Rolling," *Akron Beacon Journal*, January 8, 1965; Earl Mazo, "Eisenhower Proposes a Revamped National Organization to Lead Republican Party," *New York Times*, January 6, 1965.

18. McGaffin and McCartney, "How Goldwater."

19. Edwards, *Goldwater*, 368.

20. Earley interview, 1995.

21. Personal communication from Mary Burtzloff, archivist, Eisenhower Presidential Library and Museum. Meeting is recorded in the Appointment Books series of Eisenhower's Post-Presidential Papers.

22. "Twenty Minutes," 9.

23. "Tuesday Morning Release," January 12, 1965. Series I, Box 19, Folder 2. Bliss papers, OHC.

24. "Says Bliss Will Replace Burch after a Short Wait," *Akron Beacon Journal*, January 12, 1965.

25. "Statements made in Phoenix, AZ," January 12, 1965. Series I, Box 19, Folder 1. Bliss papers, OHC.

26. Ibid.

27. Ibid.

28. Ibid.

29. Ibid.

30. "Ray C. Bliss statement," January 12, 1965. Box 19, Folder 2. Bliss papers, OHC.

31. Nick Thimmesch, *The Condition of Republicanism* (New York: W. W. Norton, 1968), 55; "GOP's Burch Yields, Bliss to Take Helm," *Cleveland Plain Dealer*, January 13, 1965.

32. Robert H. Feldkamp, "Bliss Has Last Laugh," *Akron Beacon Journal*, January 17, 1965.

Chapter 39: Ray Bliss Becomes National Chairman

1. Earl Mazo, "Goldwater Asks for Unity in GOP," *New York Times*, January 22, 1965.

2. Robert H. Feldkamp, "It's Official Now: Bliss Named GOP Chairman," *Akron Beacon Journal*, January 22, 1965.

3. Mazo, "Goldwater Asks for Unity."

4. "Ohio's Ray Bliss: The GOP Picks a Chairman," *Newsweek*, January 25, 1965, 25.

5. "The Ideal Choice," *Akron Beacon Journal*, January 13, 1965.

6. Tom Wicker, "Goldwater Aftermath," *New York Times*, January 16, 1965.

7. McCartney and McGaffin, "How Goldwater."

8. Earl Mazo, "Burch's Resignation Split the Goldwater Bloc," *New York Times*, January 14, 1965, 39.

9. Taft Seminar, 1974.

10. Ibid.

11. Broder, "Bliss Rides the Elephant."

12. Feldkamp, "It's Official Now."

13. Ibid.
14. Ibid.
15. "Ray C. Bliss statement before the national committee meeting, Chicago, Illinois." January 22, 1965. Series I: Box 1, Folder 13. Bliss papers, OHC.
16. Robert Feldkamp, "I'm No Miracle Man," *Akron Beacon Journal*, January 23, 1965.
17. Broder, "Bliss Rides the Elephant."
18. Paul Gapp, "Calls Bliss 'April Fool Present to GOP,'" *Akron Beacon Journal*, April 28, 1965.
19. Feldkamp, "I'm No Miracle Man."

Chapter 40: Good-Bye Columbus

1. Robert Kotzbauer, "Won't Stay as State GOP Leader, Bliss Announces," *Akron Beacon Journal*, January 21, 1965.
2. Ibid.
3. Ibid.
4. Robert Feldkamp, "Ohio GOP Power Struggle Looms," *Akron Beacon Journal*, January 14, 1965.
5. Robert Feldkamp, "Bliss Man Stays in Control of Ohio GOP Funds," *Akron Beacon Journal*, February 9, 1965.
6. "Test of Party Leadership," *Akron Beacon Journal*, March 10, 1965.
7. This and the following quotations and summaries of speeches given at the Republican legislative dinner are taken from "Transcript of remarks made at the Republican Legislative Dinner at the Fort Hayes Hotel, Ray C. Bliss presiding," March 17, 1965. Series I: Box 1, Folder 12. Bliss papers, OHC.
8. Broder, "Bliss Rides the Elephant."

Chapter 41: Mr. Bliss Goes to Washington

1. Robert Feldkamp, "Full Day for Ray," *Akron Beacon Journal*, April 2, 1965.
2. Ibid.
3. Peterson interview, 1996.
4. "The Chairman Speaks: Address by the Honorable Ray C. Bliss, Chairman, Republican National Committee Before the 13th Annual Republican Women's Conference, April 1, 1965." Republican National Committee. In *Papers of the Republican Party*, edited by Paul L. Kesaris (Frederick, MD: University Publications of America, 1987).
5. Feldkamp, "Full Day for Ray."
6. Robert H. Feldkamp, "GOP 'Really Starting to Move Now'—Bliss," *Akron Beacon Journal*, February 13, 1966.
7. Ibid.
8. Robert H. Feldkamp, "Hoopla a la Ayres Greets Area GOP Ladies in DC," *Akron Beacon Journal*, April 1, 1965.
9. Robert Feldkamp, "GOP Shows Ohio New 'All-American Face,'" *Akron Beacon Journal*, June 10, 1965.
10. Ibid.
11. Ibid.
12. Taft Seminar, 1974.
13. Bliss, "Election Aftermath."
14. Peterson interview, 1996.
15. Taft Seminar, 1974.
16. Feldkamp, "GOP Shows Ohio."

Chapter 42: Fixing the Finances

1. "GOP Broke before June?" *Akron Beacon Journal*, April 13, 1965.
2. Taft Seminar, 1974.
3. "New GOP Boss Gets Double Salary," *Delaware County, PA, Daily Times*, April 9, 1965.
4. "Allen/Scott Report," April 9, 1965. Series II: Box 25, Folder 12. Bliss papers, OHC; Robert Feldkamp, "Ray's Pay Same as Burch's," *Akron Beacon Journal*, May 2, 1965.
5. "Allen/Scott Report," May 5, 1965. Series II: Box 25, Folder 11. Bliss papers, OHC.
6. On Lucius Clay, see http://www.britannica.com/biography/Lucius-D-Clay.
7. Robert S. Boyd, "Barry's Society Harmful to GOP," *Akron Beacon Journal*, June 19, 1965.
8. David Wise, "GOP Unhappy over New Barry Club?" *Akron Beacon Journal*, June 15, 1965.
9. Boyd, "Barry's Society."
10. John Bibby, interview by William Hershey, May 8, 1997.
11. Philip E. Meyer, "GOP Gets Fund-Raising Ideas from Dollar Backers," *Akron Beacon Journal*, August 20, 1965.
12. Ibid.
13. Ibid.
14. Hess and Broder, *Republican Establishment*, 47.
15. Brian Conley, "Route to '66: Ray Bliss, the 1966 Election, and the Development of the Republican Service Party," *American Review of Politics* 31 (2010): 81.
16. "Excerpts of Remarks by Republican National Chairman Ray C. Bliss at the GOP Victory Dinner, Statler Hilton Hotel, Hartford, Connecticut, Monday, February 28, 1966." Nelson A. Rockefeller personal papers, Politics—George L. Hinman. 04/J.2.1—095 #0654: Bliss, Ray C. RAC.
17. Conley, "Route to '66," 81.

Chapter 43: Bliss Survives a Scandal

1. Arshinkoff interview, 1995.
2. Peterson interview, 1996.
3. Josephine Good, interview by William Hershey, June 27, 1995.
4. "Bliss Fires Top GOP Assistant," *Akron Beacon Journal*, June 23, 1965.
5. Peterson interview, 1996.
6. "Bliss Fires Top GOP Assistant."
7. Rowland Evans and Robert Novak, "The Ordeal of Ray Bliss," *Saturday Evening Post*, November 6, 1965.
8. "Bliss Asks Resignation of Administrative Aide," June 23, 1965. Series II, Box 100, File 11. Bliss Papers, OHC.
9. Ibid.
10. "Lyndon, Hubert Take Poke at GOP Desk Affair," *Akron Beacon Journal*, June 25, 1965.
11. Peterson interview, 1996.
12. Feldkamp, "GOP 'Really Starting.'"
13. Peterson interview, 1996.

Chapter 44: A Single Voice

1. Jack Bell, "Bliss Reveals GOP Plans to Regain Big Cities' Vote," *Akron Beacon Journal*, June 29, 1965.
2. Hess and Broder, *Republican Establishment*, 48–50.
3. Bell, "Bliss Reveals GOP Plans."
4. Ibid.

5. Hess and Broder, *Republican Establishment*, 51–53. Also see Cornelius Cotter, "The National Committees and Their Constituencies," in *Practical Politics in the United States*, edited by Cornelius Cotter (Boston: Allyn and Bacon, 1969), 17–41.

6. Bliss, "Chairman Speaks."

7. Roscoe Drummond, "See Many GOP Factions Trying to Revive Party," *Akron Beacon Journal*, April 24, 1965.

8. Evans and Novak, "Ordeal of Ray Bliss."

9. Joel Fisher, "The Role of the National Party Chairmen in American Politics" (PhD diss., Claremont Graduate School and University Center, June 1, 1968), 154.

10. Taft Seminar, 1974.

11. Ibid.

12. Ogden and Peterson, *Electing the President*, 135.

13. The discussion of Eisenhower's role as a Bliss supporter is from Taft Seminar, 1974.

14. Arshinkoff interview, 1996.

15. Bibby interview, 1997.

16. Good interview, 1995.

17. Peterson interview, 1996.

18. Jack Bell, "Scranton Backs Bliss Try to Mend Splintering Party," *Akron Beacon Journal*, August 31, 1965.

19. Ibid.

20. Hess and Broder, *Republican Establishment*, 51–53.

21. John J. Pitney Jr., "Republican Alternatives to the Great Society," in *Politics, Professionalism, and Power: Modern Party Organization and the Legacy of Ray C. Bliss*, edited by John C. Green (Lanham, MD: University Press of America, 1994), 205–17.

Chapter 45: Denouncing Extremism

1. Patterson, *Great Expectations*, 408.

2. Barbara S. Stone, "The John Birch Society: A Profile," *Journal of Politics* 36, no. 1 (1974): 184–97.

3. Fisher, "Role of the National," 159.

4. Peterson interview, 1996.

5. Lawrence E. Davies, "Bliss Asks Republicans to Shun Membership in Radical Groups," *New York Times*, November 6, 1965.

6. Group Research Inc., based in Washington, DC, collected material that focused on right-wing groups and activities. Columbia University Libraries, Archival Collections, "Group Research, Inc. records, 1955–1965."

7. "Brief Position Papers and Other Documents Relating to the Republican Coordinating Committee," 1965–1966, prepared under the direction of the Republican National Committee, 5–6. In *Papers of the Republican Party*, edited by Paul L. Kesaris (Frederick, MD: University Publications of America, 1987).

8. Hess and Broder, *Republican Establishment*, 52.

9. David C. Attridge to Ray C. Bliss, December 29, 1965. Series II: Box 28, Folder 22. Bliss papers, OHC.

10. J. H. Blitzer Jr. to Ray C. Bliss, November 29, 1965. Series II: Box 28, Folder 22. Bliss papers, OHC.

11. Peterson interview, 1995.

12. "Bliss Ill, 'Probably Fatigue,'" *Akron Beacon Journal*, November 6, 1965.

Chapter 46: A Hometown Win

1. Peterson interview, 1997.

2. Robert Feldkamp, "Erickson's Regime 'Inept'—Ballard," *Akron Beacon Journal*, June 3, 1965.

3. Waddell interview, 1995.

4. "Role in Gambling Inquiry Gave Ballard His Big Break," *Akron Beacon Journal,* May 23, 1965.

5. "Briley for Senator," *Toledo Blade,* October 11, 1962.

6. John Ballard, interview by William Hershey, February 24, 1997.

7. "Poll Fails to Sway Ballard," *Akron Beacon Journal,* April 2, 1963.

8. Ballard interview, 1997.

9. Waddell interview, 1995.

10. Ballard interview, 1997.

11. Waddell interview, 1995.

12. Robert Feldkamp, "Ballard to Seek GOP Nomination for Akron Mayor," *Akron Beacon Journal,* May 23, 1965.

13. Robert Feldkamp, "Race for Mayor Narrows to Two," *Akron Beacon Journal,* May 24, 1965.

14. "Big Vote Could Have Killed Us—Sheppard Aide," *Akron Beacon Journal,* September 8, 1965.

15. Ballard interview, 1997.

16. Robert Feldkamp, "Ballard Defines Campaign Slogan: 'Citizens Come First,'" *Akron Beacon Journal,* August 26, 1965.

17. "Labor Not Cool to Me—Ballard," *Akron Beacon Journal,* October 12, 1965.

18. "They Dial for Votes," *Akron Beacon Journal,* October 14, 1965.

19. Thaddeus A. Garrett Jr., interview by William Hershey, May 2, 1995.

20. Robert Feldkamp, "Sheppard Rips Erickson—'Lost Touch with People,'" *Akron Beacon Journal,* October 13, 1995.

21. Robert Feldkamp, "Ballard Wins by 20,000 Dems Keep Council Reins," *Akron Beacon Journal,* November 3, 1965.

22. "Bliss: Ballard Victory Example for GOP," *Akron Beacon Journal,* November 3, 1965.

Chapter 47: New York, New York, A Republican Town

1. David Broder, "Bliss Helped Nudge Lindsay," *Washington Star,* May 14, 1965.

2. Richard M. Flanagan, *Robert Wagner and the Rise of New York City's Plebiscitary Mayoralty: The Tamer of the Tammany Tiger* (New York: Palgrave Macmillan, 2014).

3. On Lindsay, see http://www.britannica.com/biography/John-V-Lindsay.

4. Broder, "Bliss Helped."

5. Arshinkoff interview, 1995.

6. Broder, "Bliss Helped."

7. Thomas P. Ronan, "Lindsay Says He Will Run against Wagner to Halt 'Decline and Fall' of City," *New York Times,* May 14, 1965.

8. Thomas P. Ronan, "Bliss Pledges Aid to Lindsay's Race," *New York Times,* May 15, 1965.

9. "To Politics with Love," *New York Times,* May 15, 1965.

10. Ray Price, interviews by William Hershey, March 31 and April 2, 1997.

11. "The Bliss Technique," *Akron Beacon Journal,* May 17, 1965.

12. Peterson interview, 1997.

13. Richard L. Madden, "Lindsay Chosen by Acclamation at GOP Meeting," *New York Times,* May 28, 1965.

14. Richard Witkin, "Liberals Choose Lindsay to Lead a Fusion Ticket; Beame Joins the Contest," *New York Times,* June 29, 1965.

15. On the 1965 election, see https://en.wikipedia.org/wiki/New_York_City_mayoral_election,_1965.

16. James McCartney, "Lindsay's Victory in New York Gives GOP Shot in Arm," *Akron Beacon Journal*, November 3, 1965.
17. "Bliss: Ballard Victory Example."

Chapter 48: The Elements of Victory

1. Bliss, "Election Aftermath."
2. *Elements of Victory*, Chairman's Report to The Republican National Committee, January 31, 1966. Republican National Committee. In *Papers of the Republican Party*, edited by Paul L. Kesaris (Frederick, MD: University Publications of America, 1961). Also see Richard Dougherty, "Bliss Unfolds Big City Plan," *Akron Beacon Journal*, December 29, 1965.
3. John Bibby, interview by John C. Green, November 23, 2004.
4. *Elements of Victory*.
5. "Determined Republican: Raymond Charles Bliss," *New York Times*, January 13, 1965.
6. Fisher, "Role of the National," 175.
7. *Elements of Victory*.
8. Knippenburg, "Bliss Booklet."
9. *Elements of Victory*.
10. O. F. Knippenburg, "State Demos Swipe GOP's Prize Recipe," *Dayton Daily News*, August 20, 1967.
11. William Vance, "Ohio Dems Take Bliss Handbook as 1970 Guide," *Akron Beacon Journal*, July 30, 1967.
12. Fisher, "Role of the National," 172.

Chapter 49: A Tiger in the Tank

1. Feldkamp, "GOP 'Really Starting.'" Robert Feldkamp, "Bliss Outlines 9-Point Plan 'Basic' to GOP Comeback," *Akron Beacon Journal*, February 4, 1966.
2. "Area GOP Chiefs Plan DC Talks," *Akron Beacon Journal*, March 2, 1966.
3. Hess and Broder, *Republican Establishment*, 49.
4. "Speaking Engagement of Chairman Ray C. Bliss." Personal communication from James Baker.
5. Hess and Broder, *Republican Establishment*, 49.
6. Peterson interview, 1995.
7. Hess and Broder, *Republican Establishment*, 44.
8. Peterson interview, 1995.
9. Good interview, 1995.
10. Sara Fitzgerald, *Elly Peterson: "Mother" of the Moderates* (Ann Arbor: University of Michigan Press, 2011), 93.
11. Good interview, 1995.
12. Peterson interview, 1995.

Chapter 50: Bliss Says "No" to Nixon

1. Patterson, *Great Expectations*, 637.
2. Stephen Ambrose, *Nixon: The Triumph of a Politician, 1962–1972*, vol. 2 (New York: Simon and Schuster, 1990), 81.
3. Ayres interview, 1995.
4. Ben Maidenburg, "Why Nixon Fired Bliss as GOP Chairman," *Akron Beacon Journal*, August 7, 1981. At Bliss's request, a newspaper story based on the interview was not published until after Bliss's death on August 6, 1981.

5. Arthur L. Peterson, "Ray C. Bliss: Leader or Manager?" in *Politics, Professionalism, and Power: Modern Party Organization and the Legacy of Ray C. Bliss,* edited by John C. Green (Lanham, MD: University Press of America, 1994), 85.

6. Peterson interview, 1995.

7. Good interview, 1997.

8. Richard Nixon, *RN: The Memoirs of Richard Nixon* (New York: Simon and Schuster, 1978), 337.

9. The source of this material is http://blog.tomroeser.blogspot.com/2006/12/flashback-richard-nixon-comes-to-aid-of.html.

10. Ambrose, *Nixon,* 84.

11. Stephen Ambrose, interview by William Hershey, April 8, 1997.

12. Rick Perlstein, *Nixonland: The Rise of a President and the Fracturing of America* (New York: Scribner, 2008), 85.

13. Ambrose, *Nixon,* 85.

14. Robert S. Boyd and Robert H. Feldkamp, "What a Night for Ray Bliss!" *Akron Beacon Journal,* November 9, 1966.

15. Ibid.

16. Hess and Broder, *Republican Establishment,* 54.

Chapter 51: Tightrope Walking

1. "Bliss Sixth in GOP Popularity," *Akron Beacon Journal,* November 27, 1966.

2. David Broder, "Bliss: A-1 Tightrope Walker," *Akron Beacon Journal,* November 28, 1967.

3. "Bliss, in Akron, Hails 'Trend of Republican Resurgence,'" *Akron Beacon Journal,* November 8, 1967.

4. Leah Wright Rigueur, *The Loneliness of the Black Republican: Pragmatic Politics and the Pursuit of Power* (Princeton, NJ: Princeton University Press, 2014).

5. Bibby interview, 1997.

6. Richard Dougherty, "Negro GOP Faction Charges Snub by Bliss," *Akron Beacon Journal,* July 11, 1965.

7. "Negro GOP Group Meets with Bliss," *Akron Beacon Journal,* August 27, 1965.

8. Peterson interview, 1997.

9. On Townes, see Leah M. Wright, "Conscience of a Black Conservative: The 1964 Election and the Rise of the National Negro Republican Assembly," 2009, http://wesscholar.wesleyan.edu/div2facpubs/90.

10. Bibby interview, 1997.

11. G. W. Gulmon to Ray C. Bliss, October 4, 1965. Series II: Box 26, Folder 3. Bliss papers, OHC.

12. Kenneth Crawford, "The GOP Corner," *Newsweek,* April 1968. Also see Jack Nelson, "Bliss Ducks Questions on Racism, Birch Society," *Los Angeles Times,* September 26, 1965.

13. Bibby interview, 2004.

14. Haley Barbour, interview by William Hershey, April 19, 1995.

15. Fisher, "Role of the National," 162–68.

16. "It's Headache Time Again for Ray Bliss," *Akron Beacon Journal,* June 18, 1967.

17. Robert Feldkamp, "Young GOP, Bliss Head for Showdown," *Akron Beacon Journal,* June 21, 1967.

18. Ibid.

19. Roger Tracy, interview by William Hershey, May 1, 1995.

20. Robert H. Feldkamp, "Young Republicans Reject Bigger Controls for Bliss," *Akron Beacon Journal,* June 23, 1967.

21. Ibid.

22. Robert Feldkamp, "Let 'Em Fight, Says Bliss; Can He Win This Way?" *Akron Beacon Journal,* June 25, 1967.

23. "Bliss Wins Pledge from Young GOP," *Akron Beacon Journal*, September 10, 1967.
24. On Howard Phillips, see http://www.gwu.edu/~action/philint.html#04.
25. Fisher, "Role of the National," 176.
26. "Twenty Minutes," 8.
27. Peterson interview, 1997.
28. "Bliss Gets Votes Protest by Women," *Akron Beacon Journal*, May 8, 1967.
29. William Vance, "No Bliss on the Far Right," *Akron Beacon Journal*, July 9, 1967.
30. "Bliss Won't Intervene in Women's Election," *Washington Star*, May 9, 1967.
31. Fitzgerald, *Elly Peterson*, 113.
32. "Bliss Won't Intervene," 1967.
33. Phyllis Schlafly to Ray C. Bliss, June 6, 1967. Series II: Box 53, Folder 33. Bliss papers, OHC.
34. William Vance, "And No Hitting in Clinches," *Akron Beacon Journal*, June 18, 1967.

Chapter 52: A Medium and a Message

1. Good interview, 1997.
2. "GOP's Site Selection Panel Picks Miami Beach," *New York Times*, July 27, 1967.
3. Warren Weaver Jr., "Miami Beach Tops Nominating Sites," *New York Times*, April 4, 1967.
4. Theodore H. White, *The Making of the President 1968* (New York: Atheneum, 1969), 237.
5. Good interview, 1997.
6. "$800,000 Miami Bid for '68 Convention of GOP Is Highest," *New York Times*, February 22, 1967.
7. "Miami Beach Convention Meeting," September 22–23, 1967. Series II: Box 82, Folder 19. Bliss papers, OHC.
8. "Subcommittee on Housing," 1968. Series II: Box 83, Folder 2. Bliss papers, OHC.
9. Good interview, 1997.
10. Peterson interview, 1997.
11. Good interview, 1997.
12. Mel Ziegler, "Kirk Gets a Cushiony Job in Blissful Breeze Batting," *Miami Herald*, July 28, 1968.
13. "Rocky Rally Suffers from Feeling against Gov. Kirk," *Akron Beacon Journal*, August 4, 1968.
14. Drew Pearson and Jack Anderson, "The Claude Kirk Mystique—Or Could It Be Mistake," *Akron Beacon Journal*, August 7, 1968.
15. Peterson interview, 1997.
16. Vera Glaser, "GOP Governors are Outmaneuvered in Bid to 'Modernize' '68 Platform," *Philadelphia Evening Bulletin*, February 27, 1968.
17. Robert B. Semple Jr., "GOP Governors Will Press Convention Fight," *New York Times*, December 14, 1967.
18. Peterson interview, 1997.
19. Robert S. Boyd, "Bliss Rights GOP Platform," *Akron Beacon Journal*, May 30, 1968.
20. Peterson interview, 1995.
21. Ogden and Peterson, *Electing the President*, 83–84.
22. For the 1968 Republican platform, see http://www.presidency.ucsb.edu/ws/print.php?pid=25841.
23. Arthur Krock, "Party Platform for All: Republicans' Draft Viewed as Allowing the Candidate to Run in All Directions," *New York Times*, August 7, 1968.

Chapter 53: The Politics of Turmoil

1. See Patterson, *Great Expectations*, chapter 22.

2. Good interview, 1997.

3. Peterson interview, 1997.

4. See White, *Making of the President 1968* on the dynamics of the campaign.

5. Peterson interviews, 1997 and 2004.

6. White, *Making of the President 1968*, 59–60.

7. Ibid., 61.

8. Robert Feldkamp, "For Reagan, a Day to Say 'I Declare,'" *Akron Beacon Journal*, August 6, 1968.

9. William Vance, "Ohioans Going Away Mad?" *Akron Beacon Journal*, August 9, 1968.

10. "Transcript of Press Conference," August 4, 1968. Series II: Box 81, Folder 5, Bliss papers, OHC.

Chapter 54: Ray Bliss's Convention

1. William Brock, interview by William Hershey, October 3, 1995.

2. Ben Maidenburg, "... But at Least It Started on Time," *Akron Beacon Journal*, August 7, 1968.

3. Peterson interview, 1997.

4. "1968 Republican National Convention," August 1968. Series II: Box 80, Folder 28. Bliss papers, OHC.

5. Kurfess interview, 1995.

6. Garrett interview, 1995.

7. Vincent J. Burke, "Abernathy Leads '51st State' Inside," *Akron Beacon Journal*, August 7, 1968.

8. Thomas A. Johnson, "Governor Lauded by Rights Leader," *New York Times*, August 7, 1968.

9. Good interview, 1995.

10. Burke, "Abernathy Leads."

11. Martin Waldron, "Curfew Ordered in Most of Miami," *New York Times*, August 10, 1968.

12. William Vance, "Here's the Story behind the Story of Ray Bliss," *Akron Beacon Journal*, February 23, 1969.

13. Peterson interview, 1997. This explanation is consistent with the account Nixon provided in his memoirs. Nixon, *RN*, 386.

14. Ambrose, *Nixon*, 175.

Chapter 55: Ray Bliss Keeps His Job

1. Maidenburg, "Why Nixon Fired Bliss."

2. "Bliss Was Ready to Quit GOP Post Last Summer," *Akron Beacon Journal*, November 24, 1968.

3. Robert Feldkamp, "Bliss 'Upset, Mystified' By Ouster Reports," *Akron Beacon Journal*, November 19, 1968.

4. Taft Seminar, 1974.

5. Maidenburg, "Why Nixon Fired Bliss."

6. Peterson interview, 1997.

7. Feldkamp, "Bliss 'Upset, Mystified.'"

8. See "Executive Session, Joint Meeting of the Republican National Committee and the Republican National Finance Committee," Eden Roc Hotel, Miami, FL., August 9, 1968, In *Papers of the Republican Party*, edited by Paul L. Kesaris (Frederick, MD: University Publications of America, 1987), 75; and "Transcript of the Press Conferences, Eden Roc Hotel, Miami, FL.," August 9, 1968. Series 2: Box: 148, Folder: 3. Ray Bliss Papers, OHC.

Chapter 56: Nixon Wins a Squeaker

1. Patterson, *Great Expectations*, 694–97.

2. Ibid., 698–99.

3. See White, *Making of the President 1968* on the dynamics of the 1968 campaign.

4. Herbert G. Klein, interview by William Hershey, May 5, 1997.

5. Robert J. Havel, "Bliss Acclaims Nixon's Victory as Phenomenal," *Cleveland Plain Dealer*, November 10, 1968.

6. David Hess, "Could That Frown Be Real, Mr. Bliss?" *Akron Beacon Journal*, October 11, 1968.

7. "Bliss Goal: 'Ballot Security,'" *Akron Beacon Journal*, October 12, 1968.

8. James N. Naughton, "Ballot Security Is Goal of Bliss," *Cleveland Plain Dealer*, October 12, 1968.

9. Robert H. Feldkamp, "Behind GOP's Easy Purr, a Master Mechanic," *Akron Beacon Journal*, October 31, 1968.

10. Havel, "Bliss Acclaims Nixon's Victory."

11. Robert H. Feldkamp, "Confident Bliss Is Like Broken Record," *Akron Beacon Journal*, November 6, 1968.

12. Taft Seminar, 1974.

13. On the 1968 election, see http://www.britannica.com/event/United-States-presidential-election-of-1968.

14. Victor Riesel, "Bliss-Krieg of Cities Won Race for Nixon," *Tampa Tribune*, November 23, 1968; Robert Boyd, "GOP Scraps Barry's Plan, Seeks Urban Votes," *Akron Beacon Journal*, February 29, 1968.

15. "Bliss Predicts GOP Will Gain House Control," *Akron Beacon Journal*, January, 21, 1966.

16. Havel, "Bliss Acclaims."

17. Hershey, "The Party's Not Over."

Chapter 57: Rumors Spread: "Bliss Is Out!"

1. Jack Bell, "Nixon Considers Bliss Replacement," Associated Press, November 17, 1968.

2. Maidenburg, "Why Nixon Fired Bliss."

3. Feldkamp, "Bliss 'Upset, Mystified.'"

4. William Vance, "Bliss in Akron—Mum on Ouster Report," *Akron Beacon Journal*, December 3, 1968.

5. Taft Seminar, 1974.

6. Ibid.

7. H. R. Haldeman Handwritten Meeting Notes, November 7, 1968. White House Special Files (WHSF), Box 41, Folder 10. Richard Nixon Presidential Library (NPL). https://www.nixonlibrary.gov/forresearchers/index.php. In addition to Bliss, fundraiser J. Clifford Folger and Congressman Bob Wilson, chairman of the Republican congressional campaign committee, were also to be replaced.

8. Klein interview, 1997.

9. John Sears, interview by William Hershey, May 7, 2013. Also see Rowland Evans and Robert Novak, "Why Bliss Will Be Replaced," *Akron Beacon Journal*, November 27, 1968, and Bruce Boissat, "Nixon to Make Over the GOP," *Akron Beacon Journal*, December 2, 1968.

10. H. R. Haldeman Handwritten Meeting Notes, November 8–10, 1968. WHSF, Box 41, Folder 9, NPL.

11. Ibid.

12. H. R. Haldeman Handwritten Meeting Notes, November 11, 1968. WHSF, Box 41, Folder 10. NPL.

13. H. R. Haldeman Handwritten Meeting Notes, November 11, 1968. WHSF, Box 41, Folder 9. NPL.

14. Maidenburg, "Why Nixon Fired Bliss."

15. John Sears to RN, November 22, 1968. WHSF, Box 20, Folder 6. NPL.

16. See Patrick J. Buchanan, *The Greatest Comeback: How Richard Nixon Rose from Defeat to Create the New Majority* (New York: Penguin Random House, 2014), 56–57. For the complaints Nixon staffers had about Bliss, see Rowland Evans and Robert Novak, *Nixon in the White House: The Frustration of Power* (New York: Random House, 1971), 31.

17. John Sears to RN, November 22, 1968.

18. R. G. Kleindienst to RN, undated (found following Sears 11/22/1968 memo). WHSF, Box 20, Folder 6. NPL. Kleindienst opposed Bliss, according to Maidenburg, "Why Nixon Fired Bliss." During the 1968 campaign, Kleindienst served as liaison to the Republican National Committee and was tasked in part with keeping an eye on Bliss.

19. Charles Rabb, "Nixon May Kiss Off Bliss for a More-Blistery Boss," *New York Daily News*, November 18, 1968.

20. Feldkamp, "Bliss 'Upset, Mystified.'"

21. Jim Fain, "Bliss Will Go Willingly If Given Nixon Heave Ho," *Dayton Daily News*, November 19, 1968.

22. H. R. Haldeman Handwritten Meeting Notes, November 20 and November 27, 1968. WHSF, Box 41, Folder 10 and Folder 8. NPL.

23. Maidenburg, "Why Nixon Fired Bliss."

24. Rowland Evans and Robert Novak, "Bliss Purge Backlash Sweeps Up Pile of Trouble for President-Elect," *Washington Post*, December 6, 1968.

25. Ibid.

26. William Vance, "Nixon Owes Bliss Explanation—Waddell," *Akron Beacon Journal*, November 20, 1969.

27. Robert H. Feldkamp, "Nixon's Silence Has Bliss Friends Steaming," *Akron Beacon Journal*, November 23, 1968.

28. Evans and Novak, "Bliss Purge Backlash."

29. Vance, "Bliss in Akron."

30. John Sears to RN, undated (1968). WHSF, Box 18, Folder 12. NPL.

31. "Keep Bliss, Three Republican Governors Urge," *Akron Beacon Journal*, December 5, 1968.

32. Warren Weaver Jr., "GOP Governors Dodge Bliss Issue," *Akron Beacon Journal*, December 7, 1968.

33. Ibid.

34. Maidenburg, "Why Nixon Fired Bliss."

35. Robert H. Feldkamp, "It's Definite: Bliss Stays, Says Ayres," *Akron Beacon Journal*, December 10, 1968.

36. R. W. Apple Jr., "Laird Reported Choice of Nixon to Head Defense," *New York Times*, December 9, 1968.

37. John Sears to RN, January 2, 1969. WHSF, Box 20, Folder 7. NPL.

38. Arshinkoff interview, 1995.

39. Robert Feldkamp, "Bliss to Run Show, Won't Be Muzzled," *Akron Beacon Journal*, January 3, 1968.

40. Kleindienst to RN, 1968.

Chapter 58: A Meeting at the Pierre Hotel

1. Bob Burke and Ralph G. Thompson, *Bryce Harlow: Mr. Integrity* (Oklahoma City: Oklahoma Heritage Association, 2000), 17.

2. Bryce Harlow to RN, December 2, 1968. WHSF, Box 7, Folder 4. NPL.

3. John Ehrlichman to John Sears, December 17, 1968. WHSF, Box 21, Folder 17. NPL.

4. Lamar Alexander, interview by Timothy Naftali, June 27, 2007, 5. https://www.nixonlibrary.gov/virtuallibrary/documents/histories/alexander-2007-06-27.pdf. Alexander may be referring to the Harlow-Bliss meeting on December 16, but he could be referring to another Harlow-Bliss meeting, perhaps in February 1969.

5. Bryce Harlow to H. R. Haldeman, December 19, 1968. White House Central Files (WHCF)-Staff Member and Office Files (SMOF): Bryce Harlow, Box 4, Folder "Transition Office: Memorandum: (12/19/1968–12/31/1968)." NPL.

6. Maidenburg, "Why Nixon Fired Bliss."

7. Kenneth W. Thompson, ed., *The Nixon Presidency*, vol. 1 (Lanham, MD: Rowman & Littlefield, 1987), 250.

8. H. R. Haldeman Handwritten Meeting Notes, December 31, 1968, and January 1, 1969. WHSF, Box 36, Folder 16. NPL.

9. Richard Nixon to H. R. Haldeman, January 7, 1969. WHSF, Box 1, Folder 36. NPL.

10. Sears, January 2, 1969.

11. John Ehrlichman to H. R. Haldeman, January 8, 1969. WHSF, Box 32, Folder 8. NPL.

12. Evans and Novak, *Nixon in the White House*, 32.

13. Thompson, *Nixon Presidency*, 250.

14. Maidenburg, "Why Nixon Fired Bliss."

15. Thompson, *Nixon Presidency*, 250.

16. Maidenburg, "Why Nixon Fired Bliss."

17. Arshinkoff interview, 1995.

18. Maidenburg, "Why Nixon Fired Bliss."

19. Hershey, "The Party's Not Over."

20. Maidenburg, "Why Nixon Fired Bliss."

21. Evans and Novak, *Nixon in the White House*, 32.

22. Maidenburg, "Why Nixon Fired Bliss."

23. Ibid.

24. Thompson, *Nixon Presidency*, 250.

25. Evans and Novak, *Nixon in the White House*, 32.

26. Thompson, *Nixon Presidency*, 250.

27. Sears interview, 2013.

28. John Ehrlichman, interview by *Frontline*, PBS, May 28, 1996. http://www.pbs.org/wgbh/pages/frontline/shows/choice/bob/erlichman.html.

29. Transcript of Ray C. Bliss Press Conference, New York City, January 10, 1969. Box 8, Folder 17. Ray and Ellen Bliss Papers, UAA. For Harlow's summary of the press conference, see Briefing Summary, January 10, 1969. WHSF, Box 20, Folder 7. NPL.

30. "Bliss Agrees to Stay as Chairman," *New York Post*, January 11, 1969.

31. Robert Feldkamp, "Nixon Calls Bliss Superb," *Akron Beacon Journal*, January 11, 1969.

32. "Bliss Agrees to Stay as Chairman," *Washington Post*, January 11, 1969; Jerry Greene, "Why Bliss Is Leaving Post," *New York Daily News*, February 21, 1969. It is possible that Bliss told reporters privately that his tenure was indefinite.

33. Feldkamp, "Nixon Calls Bliss Superb."

34. Ibid.

35. Evans and Novak, *Nixon in the White House*, 32.

36. Rowland Evans and Robert Novak, "Rep. Morton of Maryland Is Called Likely Successor to GOP's Bliss," *Washington Post*, January 10, 1969, A23. Also see Robert Boyd, "Bliss, Nixon Get Together—'On Final Inaugural Plans,'" *Akron Beacon Journal*, January 10, 1969, A19.

37. Evans and Novak, *Nixon in the White House*, 33.

Chapter 59: Chairman for an Inaugural

1. Robert Feldkamp, "Nixon: Bliss Talents Tops in GOP Annals," *Akron Beacon Journal*, January 18, 1969.

2. "Transcript of Proceedings, Luncheon, January 17, 1969. Meeting of the Republican National Committee." Republican National Committee. In *Papers of the Republican Party*, edited by Paul L. Kesaris (Frederick, MD: University Publications of America, 1987), 75.

3. E. W. Kenworthy, "Nixon Telegram Endorses Bliss," *New York Times*, January 18, 1969.

4. Transcript of Proceedings, 1969, 51.

5. Ibid., 74–75.

6. David Broder, "Bliss Foresees Congress Gain for GOP in 1970," *Washington Post*, January 18, 1969.

7. Transcript of Proceedings, 1969, 52–75.

8. Ibid., 55.

9. Ibid., 70.

10. Ibid., 75.

11. "Inauguration Seating Arrangement," *New York Times*, January 20, 1969.

12. Robert B. Semple Jr., "Nixon, Sworn, Dedicates Office to Peace; Offers a Role to Young and Disaffected and a Chance to 'Black as Well as White,'" *New York Times*, January 21, 1969.

13. Richard Milhous Nixon: First Inaugural Address. US Inaugural Address ..., http://www.bartleby.com/124/pres58.html.

14. Ben A. Franklin, "Soldiers Back Up Police; 81 Protesters Are Seized," *New York Times*, January 21, 1969.

15. Betty Jaycox, "An Evening of Pure 'Bliss,'" *Akron Beacon Journal*, January 20, 1969.

Chapter 60: Bliss "Retires" as National Chairman

1. H. R. Haldeman Handwritten Meeting Notes, January 24, 1969. WHSF-SMOF: H. R. Haldeman. Box 32, Folder H (Notes Jan–June '69, Part I [2 of 8]). NPL.

2. H. R. Haldeman Handwritten Meeting Notes, January 30, 1969. WHSF-SMOF: H. R. Haldeman. Box 32, Folder H (Notes Jan–June '69, Part I [2 of 8]). NPL.

3. Haldeman Diaries, January 31, 1969. NPL.

4. Haldeman Diaries, February 4, 1969; H. R. Haldeman Handwritten Meeting Notes, February 4, 1969. WHSF-SMOF: H. R. Haldeman. Box 32, Folder H (Notes Jan–June '69, Part I [2 of 8]). NPL.

5. Evans and Novak, *Nixon in the White House*, 71.

6. On Chotiner, see http://www.nytimes.com/1974/01/31/archives/murray-chotiner-nixon-mentor-dies-campaign-aide-since-46-and.html.

7. Evans and Novak, *Nixon in the White House*, 71.

8. Vera Glaser and Malvina Stephenson, "Revelations of Nixon's 'Hatchet Man,'" *San Francisco Chronicle*, December 28, 1970, 12.

9. Murray Chotiner, "Managing the Campaign," in *Politics U.S.A.*, edited by James M. Cannon (Garden City, NY: Doubleday, 1960), 199–229.

10. Evans and Novak, *Nixon in the White House*, 71.

11. "H. R. Haldeman Handwritten Meeting Notes," November 12 and 11, 1968. WHSF Box: 41, Folder 10. NPL.

12. Harlow to RN, 1968.

13. Maidenburg, "Why Nixon Fired Bliss."

14. On Morton, see http://bioguide.congress.gov/scripts/biodisplay.pl?index=m001021.

15. Evans and Novak, "Rep. Morton ... Likely Successor."

16. Morton's meeting with Bliss may have preceded Bliss's dinner with Harlow on December 16, 1968.

17. Maidenburg, "Why Nixon Fired Bliss."

18. Vance, "Here's the Story Behind."

19. Evans and Novak, *Nixon in the White House*, 72.

20. White House documents suggest that this confrontation between Chotiner and Bliss may have taken place on February 6. Handwritten meeting notes from February 7 say "Bliss out today" (he was in Akron, Ohio) and from February 8 say "Chot[iner] in charge of RC—right now." H. R. Haldeman Handwritten Meeting Notes, February 7 and 8, 1969. WHSF-SMOF: H. R. Haldeman. Box 32, Folder H (Notes Jan–June '69, Part I [2 of 8]). NPL.

21. Evans and Novak, *Nixon in the White House*, 72.

22. H. R. Haldeman to Richard Nixon, February 9, 1969. WHSF-SMOF: H. R. Haldeman. Box 152, Folder "Memoranda for the President's File Jan. 69." NPL.

23. H. R. Haldeman to John Ehrlichman, February 17, 1969. WHSF-SMOF: H. R. Haldeman, Box 46, Folder "Memos/John Ehrlichman (Feb. 1969)." NPL. This memo may be misdated—Bliss's letter of resignation is also dated February 17.

24. If Bliss had a White House meeting, it may have been with H. R. Haldeman or Bryce Harlow rather than with Nixon. In any event, one of Bliss's aides recounted Bliss's reaction to the encounter but asked not to be identified.

> Bliss told us he was being called to the White House and he knew he was going to be fired ... and he came back and he called us into his office and he closed the door and he was pacing up and down behind the desk, chain smoking.
> We finally said, "Ray, what happened?"
> "The SOB. He told me I'd done a great job but it was time to move on and he wanted me to be ambassador to Denmark. I told him to stick Denmark up his ass and walked out."

Although Nixon is the implied source of Bliss's dismissal, it is unclear who actually delivered the message to him.

25. H. R. Haldeman memo to John Ehrlichman, February 17, 1969. WHSF-SMOF: H. R. Haldeman, Box 46, Folder "Memos/John Ehrlichman (Feb. 1969)." NPL. This memo may be misdated—Bliss's letter of resignation is also dated February 17.

26. Vance, "Here's the Story Behind."

27. Ray Bliss, "Letter of Resignation as Chairman of the Republican National Committee," February 17, 1969, *The American Presidency Project*, http://www.presidency.ucsb.edu/ws/?pid=2395. Richard Nixon, "Letter Accepting Resignation of Ray C. Bliss as Chairman of the Republican National Committee," February 17, 1969, *The American Presidency Project*, http://www.presidency.ucsb.edu/ws/?pid=2395.

28. William Vance, "Ray Bliss Will Resign as GOP Chief April 15," *Akron Beacon Journal*, February 18, 1969.

29. William Vance, "Bliss' Political Chums in Dark on Resignation," *Akron Beacon Journal*, February 19, 1969.

30. Evans and Novak, *Nixon in the White House*, 73.

31. David Broder, "Bliss Yields to Nixon, Resigns as GOP Chief," *Washington Post*, February 19, 1969.

32. Roulhac Hamilton, "Morton to Take GOP Post If Nixon Drops Chotiner," *Columbus Dispatch*, February 26, 1969.

33. Ibid.

34. Evans and Novak, *Nixon in the White House*, 74.

35. Maidenburg, "Why Nixon Fired Bliss."

Chapter 61: Farewell to Washington

1. Nelson Rockefeller to Ray Bliss, April 14, 1969. Nelson A. Rockefeller Personal Papers, Politics: George L. Hinman. 04/J.2.1—095 #0654—Bliss, Ray C. RAC.

2. "A Tribute to Ray Bliss," April 10, 1969. Bliss Institute of Applied Politics.

3. David Broder, "Bliss Remembered," *Washington Post*, August 12, 1981.
4. "Nixons Greet Republicans by the Hundreds," *New York Times*, April 14, 1969.
5. Ayres interview, 1995.
6. Wicker, *One of Us*, 254. Another version of the letter was included in "A Tribute to Ray Bliss," 1969.
7. Maidenburg, "Why Nixon Fired Bliss."
8. Louise Hutchison, "Team Play Wins Elections, Bliss Tells Women," *Chicago Tribune*, April 16, 1969.
9. William Vance, "We Won a Couple Just the Same: Bliss," *Akron Beacon Journal*, April 9, 1969.
10. Abe Zaidan, "Roses and Strudel for Bliss," *Akron Beacon Journal*, April 18, 1969.
11. Joe Rice, "Sen. Scott Praises Bliss, Sees GOP Senate Control," *Akron Beacon Journal*, May 23, 1969.

Chapter 62: Setting the Record Straight

1. Abe Zaidan, "Ray Bliss: The 'Retired' Mr. GOP Will Still Keep a Hand in Politics," *Akron Beacon Journal*, April 20, 1969.
2. Joe Rice, "Quarterback Styles Differ—But GOP Game the Same," *Akron Beacon Journal*, June 18, 1969.
3. Zaidan, "Ray Bliss."
4. Doerler interview, 1996.
5. Zaidan, "Ray Bliss."
6. Waddell interview, 1995.
7. Doerler interview, 1996.
8. Broder, "Bliss Yields to Nixon."
9. Peterson interview, 1996.
10. Huckshorn interview, 1995.
11. Sears interview, 2013.
12. Vance, "Here's the Story Behind."
13. Maidenburg, "Why Nixon Fired Bliss."
14. Mann interview, 1990.
15. Evans and Novak, "The Ordeal of Ray Bliss."

Chapter 63: Politics as an Avocation

1. Evans and Novak, "The Ordeal of Ray Bliss"; Hershey, "The Party's Not Over."
2. Zaidan, "Ray Bliss."
3. Lee Leonard, "Ohio GOP Has Weakened," *Sandusky Register*, August 17, 1981.
4. "Bliss Is 'Neutral' in Primary," *Akron Beacon Journal*, March 20, 1970.
5. Curtin, *Ohio Politics Almanac*, 58.
6. Hugh C. McDiarmid, "The Gilligan Interlude, 1971–73," in *Ohio Politics*, edited by Alexander P. Lamis (Kent, OH: Kent State University Press, 1994), 89.
7. Lacy McCrary and Joe Rice, "Bliss Approached to 'Take Over,'" *Akron Beacon Journal*, June 14, 1970.
8. Joe Rice, "Ray Bliss to Assist State GOP Drive," *Akron Beacon Journal*, July 8, 1970; Joe Rice, "Bliss Gives Big Lift to GOP Fund Drive," *Akron Beacon Journal*, August 13, 1970.
9. Joe Rice, "Bliss Gives Ohio GOP Something to Cheer About," *Akron Beacon Journal*, July 9, 1970; Joe Rice, "Bliss to GOP Heads: 'We're Down, Not Out,'" *Akron Beacon Journal*, August 14, 1970.
10. Richard E. Lightner, "Democrats Win Reapportionment Board Control," *Akron Beacon Journal*, November 4, 1970.
11. Joe Rice, "After 20 Yrs.—Ayres Falls," *Akron Beacon Journal*, November 4, 1970.
12. Larry Fields, "Ayres 'Last Hurrah' a Bitter Growl," *Akron Beacon Journal*, November 4, 1970.
13. Daly "Tim" Smith, interview by William Hershey, June 18, 2013.

14. Daly Smith, "Dennis Shaul 'Sounds Like a Republican,'" *Akron Beacon Journal*, October 28, 1971.

15. Arshinkoff interview, 1995.

16. Ballard interview, 1997.

17. Waddell interview, 1995.

18. Ibid.

19. Smith interview, 2013.

20. "Two Good Candidates—But Ballard Is Our Choice," *Akron Beacon Journal*, October 25, 1971.

21. Daly Smith, "Shaul Defeated by 4,194 Votes," *Akron Beacon Journal*, November 3, 1971.

22. Waddell interview, 1995.

Chapter 64: Bliss, Nixon, and Watergate

1. Maidenburg, "Why Nixon Fired Bliss."

2. Joe Rice, "No Longer Boss, But Ray Bliss Still Keeps Busy," *Akron Beacon Journal*, August 20, 1972.

3. H. R. Haldeman to Gordon Strachan, April 22, 1971. WHSF: SMOF: Box 296, NPL.

4. Daly Smith, "Nixon Wire Hails Bliss on Birthday," *Akron Beacon Journal*, December 11, 1971.

5. Rowland Evans and Robert Novak, "Mitchell Woos Bliss for Campaign Role," *Akron Beacon Journal*, March 5, 1972.

6. Transcript of White House conversations between Richard Nixon and John Mitchell, April 4, 1972. Miller Center, University of Virginia. http://millercenter.org/expressionengine.php/presidential recordings/nixon/P200.

7. Transcript of White House conversation between Richard Nixon, John Mitchell, and Ray Bliss, May 16, 1972. Miller Center.

8. "Bliss to Aid Nixon's '72 Campaign," *Akron Beacon Journal*, May 18, 1972.

9. Abe Zaidan, "Bliss: No Full-Time Role in Nixon Drive," *Akron Beacon Journal*, May 17, 1972.

10. Rice, "No Longer Boss."

11. On the 1972 election, see http://www.britannica.com/event/United-States-presidential-election -of-1972.

12. Patterson, *Great Expectations*, 778–82.

13. "Ray Bliss Calls Pow Wow of Midwest GOP Chiefs," *Akron Beacon Journal*, July 28, 1973.

14. Mann interview, 1990.

15. Maidenburg, "Why Nixon Fired Bliss."

16. Arshinkoff interview, 1995. The RNC met on April 25, 1974, at the White House and Bliss was in attendance.

17. James McCartney, "Showdown at the DC Corral," *San Francisco Chronicle*, April 28, 1974.

18. Hershey, "The Party's Not Over."

19. "Memoirs of Senior Circuit Judge Paul C. Weick." Box 8, Folder 17. Ray and Ellen Bliss papers, UAA. Bliss held similar views, telling a reporter that "Watergate would not have occurred if the party had remained in the hands of political pros." Abe Zaidan, "Bliss Sees GOP's Rebirth, Calls Ford a Team Player," *Akron Beacon Journal*, August 9, 1974.

20. Klein interview, 1997.

21. Sears interview, 2013.

22. Hershey, "The Party's Not Over."

Chapter 65: Ray C. Bliss and Gerald R. Ford

1. Abe Zaidan, "Bliss Sees GOP's Rebirth."

2. Gerald Ford to William Hershey, May 5, 1981. Box 8: Folder Ray and Ellen Bliss Papers, UAA.

3. On these controversies, see http://www.britannica.com/biography/Gerald-Ford.

4. David Broder, "Short Terms of GOP Heads," *Washington Post,* January 23, 1973.

5. Suzanne O'Dea, *Madam Chairman: Mary Louise Smith and the Republican Revival after Watergate* (Columbia: University of Missouri Press, 2012).

6. Mary L. Smith, interview by John C. Green, October 20, 1989.

7. David Hess, "Bliss Closed GOP Sex-Quota Debate," *Akron Beacon Journal,* September 11, 1973.

8. Hugh C. McDiarmid, "The Gilligan Interlude, 1971–1975," in *Ohio Politics.*

9. Ronald D. Clark, "Repeat 1960 Effort, Bliss Tells GOP," *Akron Beacon Journal,* October 18, 1974.

10. On the 1974 election, see https://library.cqpress.com/cqalmanac/document.php?id=cqal74-1222893.

11. Hugh C. McDiarmid, "The Gilligan Interlude, 1971–1975," in *Ohio Politics.*

12. Ron Cockrell, *A Green Shrouded Miracle: The Administrative History of Cuyahoga Valley National Recreation Area, Ohio* (Omaha, NE: National Park Service, US Department of the Interior, Midwest Regional Office, 1992).

13. Ibid.

14. John Seiberling, interview by William Hershey, May 29, 1997.

15. Hershey, "The Party's Not Over."

16. Regula and Seiberling interviews, 1997.

17. John C. Green, "Politics, Professionalism, and Power: Introduction," in *Politics, Professionalism, and Power: Modern Party Organization and the Legacy of Ray C. Bliss,* edited by John C. Green (Lanham, MD: University Press of America, 1994), 9.

18. Hess, "Bliss Closed GOP Sex-Quota Debate."

19. R. W. Apple Jr., "GOP Panel Splits on Party Reform," *New York Times,* March 6, 1975.

20. Ibid.

21. R. W. Apple Jr., "Ford Plans Formal Entry into '76 Race This Month," *New York Times,* June 8, 1975.

23. Douglas Balz, "Bliss Will Help Steer Ford Drive," *Akron Beacon Journal,* July 11, 1975.

24. On the 1976 GOP primaries, see https://en.wikipedia.org/wiki/Republican_Party_presidential _primaries,_1976.

25. *Ohio Republican News,* "Ray C. Bliss: Ohio National Committeeman Bliss Goes on the Record," June 25, 1976.

26. "Bliss in Hospital," *Akron Beacon Journal,* February 22, 1976.

27. Zaidan interview, 2012.

28. Abe Zaidan and Ronald D. Clark, "They're Ready for a Victory Party," *Akron Beacon Journal,* August 18, 1976.

29. On the 1976 elections see, http://www.britannica.com/event/United-States-presidential-election -of-1976.

30. On Brock see http://tennesseeencyclopedia.net/entry.php?rec=137.

31. David Broder, "Bliss Rivaled Hanna as a GOP Innovator," *Columbus Dispatch,* August 12, 1981.

Chapter 66: Citizen Bliss

1. Abe Zaidan, "Rhodes' View, Voters Now 'Owe Him One,'" *Akron Beacon Journal,* March 26, 1978.

2. Abe Zaidan, "Bliss to Leave Board of Elections," *Akron Beacon Journal,* November 22, 1978.

3. Ibid.

4. "Bliss Cuts Party Ties," *Akron Beacon Journal,* February 16, 1980.

5. Hershey, "The Party's Not Over."

6. "Retirement Letters": Ody Fish to Ray C. Bliss, February 18, 1980. Box 8, Folder 20. Ray and Ellen Bliss papers, UAA.

7. "Retirement Letters": Arthur Peterson to Ray C. Bliss, February 26, 1980. Box 8, Folder 20. Ray and Ellen Bliss papers, UAA.

8. "Retirement Letters": Bryce Harlow to Ray C. Bliss, May 16, 1980. Box 8, Folder 20. Ray and Ellen Bliss papers, UAA.

9. "Republicans Honor Ray Bliss," *Akron Beacon Journal*, July 17, 1980. "Senator Bob Dole's Speech—Republican Nat'l Convention—1980." Box: 14, Folder 21. Ray and Ellen Bliss papers, UAA. In addition to serving as chairman of the Republican National Committee, Bliss also served as a member of the committee and executive committee, 1952–80; vice chairman twice, 1960–65 and 1970–80; and member of the advisory committee, 1977–80. He served on the convention arrangement committee for the national committee in one capacity or another in 1960, 1964, 1968, 1972, 1976, and 1980.

10. On the 1980 GOP convention, see https://en.wikipedia.org/wiki/1980_Republican_National_Convention.

11. Brian Usher, "GOP 'Sage' Bliss Devoted Life to Party," *Akron Beacon Journal*, August 6, 1981.

12. Brian Usher, "Bliss Warns of Dewey-Like Overconfidence," *Akron Beacon Journal*, July 15, 1980.

13. Brian Usher, "Ray Bliss' Message Finds Receptive Ears in Ohio GOP," *Akron Beacon Journal*, September 21, 1980.

14. On the 1980 election results, see http://www.britannica.com/event/United-States-presidential-election-of-1980.

15. Marilynn Marchione, "The Glitter Fades for Old Washington Hands," *Akron Beacon Journal*, January 18, 1981.

16. Hershey, "The Party's Not Over."

Chapter 67: University Trustee

1. "Bliss AU Trustee as Two Retire," *Akron Beacon Journal*, December 9, 1970.

2. Wright interview, 1995.

3. Doerler interview, 1995.

4. Helen Carringer, "AU May Soon Lose a Dedicated Trustee," *Akron Beacon Journal*, June 9, 1974.

5. "Bliss Named to AU Board," *Akron Beacon Journal*, June 9, 1975.

6. Gary Rosen, interview by William Hershey, October 3, 2013.

7. Doerler interview, 1996.

8. Rosen interview, 2013.

9. Wright interview, 1990.

10. Minutes, University of Akron Board of Trustees, September 27, 1972.

11. Wright interview, 1990.

12. "Blisses Create AU Scholarship Fund," *Akron Beacon Journal*, April 12, 1972.

13. Wright interview, 1990.

14. "Bliss Scholars": Ray C. Bliss to Ralph Regula, May 25, 1979. Box 8, Folder 2. Ray and Ellen Bliss papers, UAA.

15. "Bliss Scholars": Charles Walker to Ray C. Bliss, March 15, 1977. Box 8, Folder 2. Ray and Ellen Bliss papers, UAA.

16. Ellen Bliss interview, 1990.

17. Donn Gaynor, "Bliss Vows Drive for Med College," *Akron Beacon Journal*, December 10, 1970.

18. Wright interview, 1990.

19. "Bliss Elected President of Akron U Board," *Akron Beacon Journal*, June 25, 1981.

20. Minutes, University of Akron Board of Trustees, July 22, 1981.

21. Paul A. Poorman, "Bliss' Forte: He Looked Forward," *Akron Beacon Journal*, August 9, 1981.

Chapter 68: Mentor and Teacher

1. James Tilling, interview by William Hershey, December 11, 1995.
2. John Funk, "A Tale of Two Alexanders," *Akron Beacon Journal, Beacon Magazine,* October 25, 1987.
3. Arshinkoff interview, 1995.
4. Funk, "A Tale of Two Alexanders."
5. Abe Zaidan, "Arshinkoff Wins Election to Head GOP in Summit," *Akron Beacon Journal,* June 28, 1978.
6. Ibid.
7. Funk, "A Tale of Two Alexanders."
8. Arshinkoff interview, 1995.
9. Ibid.
10. Ibid.
11. Rex interview, 1995.
12. Doerler interview, 1995.
13. Janet Purnell, interview by William Hershey, May 7, 1997.
14. Ibid.
15. Patrick Cole, "Purnell Is First Woman to Head AU Trustees," *Akron Beacon Journal,* August 7, 1986.
16. Purnell interview, 1997.

Chapter 69: A Pathfinder Reaches the End of the Trail

1. Ellen Bliss interview, 1990.
2. Doerler interview, 1995.
3. Usher, "Sage of Akron."
4. Arshinkoff interview, 1995.
5. Zaidan interview, 2012.
6. Doerler interview, 1995.
7. John LaGuardia, interview by John C. Green, September 7, 1999.
8. Mary Grace Poidomani, "Bliss Not Accustomed to Defeat," *Akron Beacon Journal,* August 7, 1981.
9. Brian Usher, "Summit GOP Chief Lost a Mentor in Bliss," *Akron Beacon Journal,* August 9, 1981.
10. Bernard Weinraub, "Ray Bliss Dies in Ohio at 73; Rebuilt GOP After '64 Rout," *New York Times,* August 7, 1981.
11. "He Was a Rebuilder of the Grand Old Party," *Akron Beacon Journal,* August 6, 1981; "GOP Architect Ray Bliss, 73, Praised in Death," *Sandusky Register,* August 7, 1981.
12. Weinraub, "Ray Bliss Dies."
13. Brian Usher and Marilynn Marchione, "Politicians, Friends Bid Farewell to Bliss," *Akron Beacon Journal,* August 12, 1981.

Chapter 70: Ray C. Bliss Institute of Applied Politics

1. Brian Usher, "A Bliss Dream to Become an Asset for Akron," *Akron Beacon Journal,* August 9, 1981.
2. On the Arneson Institute, see http://politics.owu.edu/arnesonInstitute.html. "Wesleyan Sets 'Republican Day' in Delaware Thursday," *Mansfield News-Journal,* March 20, 1949, 16. Verne Edwards, "Ray Bliss Impressed Delawareans," *Delaware Gazette,* August 25, 1981.
3. Arthur Peterson to Ray C. Bliss, December 17, 1980; Ray C. Bliss to Arthur Peterson, January 28, 1981; Arthur Peterson to Ray C. Bliss, February 16, 1981; Arthur Peterson to Ray C. Bliss, March 8, 1981. Box 8, Folder 14. Ray and Ellen Bliss papers, UAA.
4. On Cook, see https://en.wikipedia.org/wiki/Vernon_Cook.

5. "A Proposal for the Establishment of the Ray C. Bliss Institute of Applied Politics," March 1982. Bliss Institute of Applied Politics. Lou Hirsh, "Politics Program Planned in Honor of Bliss," *The Buchtelite*, August 13, 1981.

6. Minutes, University of Akron Board of Trustees, March 27, 1985. "A Proposal for the Establishment of the Ray C. Bliss Institute of Applied Politics," March 1985. Bliss Institute of Applied Politics.

7. "Guest for Golf, Not Speech," *Akron Beacon Journal*, August 19, 1985.

8. Maureen Brown, "Rift at Akron U Delays Birth of Ray Bliss Politics Institute," *Akron Beacon Journal*, August 8, 1985; Maureen Brown, "Newsmaker/George Wilson, Controversial Akron U Board Member," *Akron Beacon Journal*, August 9, 1985.

9. "Trustee Oversteps Role in Dispute at Akron U," *Akron Beacon Journal*, August 11, 1985; "Wilson Defends Role as Trustee," *Akron Beacon Journal*, August 19, 1985.

10. Memo to Board of Trustees from William V. Muse, November 18, 1986. Bliss Institute of Applied Politics.

11. William Canterbury, "AU Plans for Bliss Institute in Fall," *Akron Beacon Journal*, February 27, 1986. "A Proposal for the Establishment of the Ray C. Bliss Institute of Applied Politics," December 1985. Bliss Institute of Applied Politics.

12. Ellen Bliss interview, 1990.

13. On the Bliss Institute, see https://uakron.edu/bliss/.

14. Daniel J. Coffey, David B. Cohen, and John C. Green, eds., *The State of the Parties: The Changing Role of Contemporary American Parties*, 7th ed. (Lanham, MD: Rowman & Littlefield, 2014). The previous six editions were also published by Rowman & Littlefield.

15. Cyndra Cole, interview by William Hershey, August 13, 2013.

16. Kellie Copeland, interview by William Hershey, August 7, 2013.

17. Robert Paduchik, interview by William Hershey, August 12, 2013.

18. William Hershey, "Trump's Nuts and Bolts Guy," *Akron Beacon Journal*, January 21, 2017.

19. Morris Reid, interviews by William Hershey, May 17, 1997; August 9 and August 22, 2013.

Chapter 71: Political Legacy

1. Ray C. Bliss to Arthur Peterson, April 8, 1981. Ray and Ellen Bliss papers, Box 8, Folder 14, UAA.

2. Huckshorn, *Party Leadership in the States*, 217–18, 285n21. An insightful description of Bliss's character and achievements was written for *Readers Digest* at about the time that Bliss resigned as national chairman and was apparently never published. A typescript is found in "RCB—Personal—Political (1969–1979)." Series III, Box 167, File 17. Bliss Papers, OHC.

3. Larry Sabato email to William Hershey, August 8, 2013.

4. David Broder, "Why Democrats Don't Know Their Own Mind," *Washington Post*, September 18, 1991; papers delivered at this conference were published in Green, *Politics, Professionalism, and Power*.

5. Peterson, "Ray C. Bliss: Leader or Manager," 83.

6. Ibid., 82.

7. Ibid., 91.

8. Bibby, "Party Leadership," 19.

9. Ibid., 32.

10. Huckshorn, "National Committee Leadership," 39.

11. Ibid., 46.

12. Tim Hames, "Strengths and Limitations: The Republican National Committee from Bliss to Brock to Barbour," *in Politics, Professionalism, and Power: Modern Party Organization and the Legacy of Ray C. Bliss*, edited

by John C. Green (Lanham, MD: University Press of America, 1994), 151. Also see Daniel J. Galvin, *Presidential Party Building: Dwight D. Eisenhower to George W. Bush* (Princeton, NJ: Princeton University Press, 2010).

13. Paul S. Herrnson, "Party Leadership and Party Organizational Change," in *Politics, Professionalism, and Power: Modern Party Organization and the Legacy of Ray C. Bliss*, edited by John C. Green (Lanham, MD: University Press of America, 1994), 196. Also see Paul S. Herrnson, *Party Campaigning in the 1980s* (Cambridge, MA: Harvard University Press, 1988).

14. Philip A. Klinkner, "A Comparison of Out-Party Leaders: Ray Bliss and Bill Brock," in *Politics, Professionalism, and Power: Modern Party Organization and the Legacy of Ray C. Bliss*, edited by John C. Green (Lanham, MD: University Press of America, 1994), 135–48. Also see Philip A. Klinkner, *The Losing Parties: Out-Party National Committees, 1956–1993* (New Haven, CT: Yale University Press, 1994).

15. On Bliss and Brock, see Brian Conley, "Party People: Bliss, Brock and the Rise of the Modern Republican Party" (PhD diss., New School University, 2008).

16. David Broder, "Bliss Remembered."

17. Brock interview, 1995. The following quotations are from this interview.

18. James Ruvolo, interview with William Hershey, August 7, 2013.

19. Hames, "Strengths and Limitations," 165.

20. Bibby, "Party Leadership," 19.

21. Gerald Austin, interview by William Hershey, August 7, 2013.

22. David Menefee-Libey, "Embracing Campaign-Centered Politics at the Democratic Headquarters," in *Politics, Professionalism, and Power: Modern Party Organization and the Legacy of Ray C. Bliss*, edited by John C. Green (Lanham, MD: University Press of America, 1994), 167–85.

23. James M. Perry, *The New Politics: The Expanding Technology of Political Manipulation* (New York: Clarkson N. Potter, 1968), 18.

24. *Ohio Republican News*, "Ray C. Bliss," 1976, 3–4.

Bibliography

A

Akron Beacon Journal. "Akron U Sorority 'Lifts' the Pins in May Queen Rumpus." May 12, 1931.
—————. "Alcorn Quits, Bliss May Get Top GOP Post." April 1, 1959.
—————. "Anticipating Bliss's Report." October 19, 1961.
—————. "Appoint Bliss to Committee." January 21, 1945.
—————. "Area GOP Chiefs Plan DC Talks." March 2, 1966.
—————. "Ask Compromise in Bliss Fight Against Ouster." May 18, 1931.
—————. "Bender Defeat Hailed by Bliss." May 4, 1960.
—————. "Bender Outburst Adds Coal to Bliss Feud." September 9, 1952.
—————. "Big Vote Could Have Killed Us—Sheppard Aide." September 8, 1965.
—————. "Bliss: Ability Comes First in Patronage." January 22, 1953.
—————. "Bliss AU Trustee as Two Retire." December 9, 1970.
—————. "Bliss Back in Running to Succeed Hall." January 12, 1957.
—————. "Bliss: Ballard Victory Example for GOP." November 3, 1965.
—————. "Bliss Calls Session on GOP Policy." April 27, 1949.
—————. "Bliss' Chances for National Chairman now are 50–50." July 13, 1964.
—————. "Bliss Credits Polls for Ohio Victory." January 19, 1961.
—————. "Bliss Cuts Party Ties." February 16, 1980.
—————. "Bliss Elected President of Akron U Board." June 25, 1981.
—————. "Bliss' Finesse." November 9, 1950.
—————. "Bliss Fires Top GOP Assistant." June 23, 1965.
—————. "Bliss Gets Key Post in Campaign." July 29, 1964.
—————. "Bliss Gets Votes Protest by Women." May 8, 1967.
—————. "Bliss Goal: 'Ballot Security.'" October 12, 1968.
—————. "Bliss Heads Ohio GOP Fourth Time." May 22, 1956.
—————. "Bliss Ill, 'Probably Fatigue.'" November 6, 1965.
—————. "Bliss, in Akron, Hails 'Trend of Republican Resurgence.'" November 8, 1967.
—————. "Bliss in Hospital." February 22, 1976.
—————. "Bliss Is 'Neutral' in Primary." March 20, 1970.
—————. "Bliss Named in GOP Leader Fight." November 18, 1948.
—————. "Bliss Named to AU Board." June 9, 1975.
—————. "Bliss Organization Won Ohio for GOP." January 3, 1961.

———. "Bliss Predicts GOP Will Gain House Control." January 21, 1966.

———. "Bliss Preens GOP for '60 Election." January 11, 1959.

———. "Bliss Road to State Chairmanship Opened by Slusser Decision." February 13, 1949.

———. "Bliss Sees Stiff Ohio Fight for GOP." May 11, 1962.

———. "Bliss Sixth in GOP Popularity." November 27, 1966.

———. "Bliss Star Rises with Taft Victory." November 9, 1950.

———. "Bliss Takes Self out of Chairman Contest." January 16, 1957.

———. "Bliss to Aid Nixon's '72 Campaign." May 18, 1972.

———. "Bliss to Give Tops to Top GOP Brass." September 20, 1951.

———. "Bliss vs. Schorr." June 23, 1952.

———. "Bliss Was Ready to Quit GOP Post Last Summer." November 24, 1968.

———. "Bliss Will Keep State GOP Post." July 21, 1961.

———. "Bliss Wins over Rowe by 4–1 Vote." May 6, 1964.

———. "Bliss Wins Pledge from Young GOP." September 10, 1967.

———. "Blisses Create AU Scholarship Fund." April 12, 1972.

———. "Browder Backs F.D.R. Policies." September 24, 1937.

———. "Can Win without Ike—Bliss." November 14, 1955.

———. "Charles Sacks, Lawyer, Civic Leader." December 25, 1972.

———. "Death Take 'Hy' Subrin, Akron Attorney, Teacher." August 16, 1974.

———. "DeWoody, Bliss Confer on Jobs." January 24, 1939.

———. "DeWoody, Bliss Greet Bricker; Peace Hinted." September 24, 1940.

———. "Fraternity Alumni Group Names Bliss." September 9, 1934.

———. "GOP Broke before June?" April 13, 1965.

———. "GOP Chairman Bliss." February 10, 1949.

———. "GOP Group Visits Akron." May 14, 1945.

———. "GOP Picks Chicago, Morton." April 11, 1959.

———. "GOP Unit Rejects Goldwater Plan." May 18, 1961.

———. "Guest for Golf, Not Speech." August 19, 1985.

———. "He Was a Rebuilder of the Grand Old Party." August 6, 1981.

———. "Hit Bliss Actions at Convention." July 31, 1960.

———. "'Hy'" Harris, Legal Aid's First Head." March 3, 1969.

———. "Ignorance Isn't Bliss—Just Ask Ohio Dems." November 22, 1962.

———. "It's Headache Time Again for Ray Bliss." June 18, 1967.

———. "Keep Bliss, Three Republican Governors Urge." December 5, 1968.

———. "Labor Not Cool to Me—Ballard." October 12, 1965.

———. "Labor Scores." November 5, 1947.

———. "Lausche Strengthened by Assembly Actions." June 21, 1951.

———. "Lyndon, Hubert Take Poke at GOP Desk Affair." June 25, 1965.

———. "Madge Emily (Heacock) Doerler." February 23, 2011.

———. "Midwest GOP Names Bliss." January 20, 1953.

———. "Mother of Ray Bliss, Ill 3 Years, Dies." January 9, 1956.

———. "Negro GOP Group Meets with Bliss." August 27, 1965.

———. "Photo Finish." November 8, 1945.

———. "Planks in Party Invited by Bliss." August 13, 1944.

———. "Poll Fails to Sway Ballard." April 2, 1963.

———. "Professors to Help Draft GOP Policy." June 3, 1962.

———. "Ray Bliss Calls Pow Wow of Midwest GOP Chiefs." July 28, 1973.

———. "Ray Bliss Named to Zoning Board." January 9, 1934.

———. "Ray Bliss to Wed Ellen Palmer Today." November 26, 1959.

———. "Republicans Honor Ray Bliss." July 17, 1980.

———. "Rhodes-Bliss Buddies." July 16, 1964.

———. "Rocky Rally Suffers from Feeling against Gov. Kirk." August 4, 1968.

———. "Role in Gambling Inquiry Gave Ballard His Big Break." May 23, 1965.

———. "Says Bliss Will Replace Burch after a Short Wait." January 12, 1965.

———. "Schroy Defeats Witwer, GOP Takes City Council." November 11, 1935.

———. "Schroy or Patterson." October 27, 1937.

———. "See Bliss Choice as 'Practical.'" July 30, 1964.

———. "Sieber Assails Bliss Leadership." August 13, 1942.

———. "Sparks Is Elected Mayor with a Plurality of 3,835." November 3, 1931.

———. "Sport Program, Baby-Test Mark Summit Outing." August 23, 1933.

———. "Test of Party Leadership." March 10, 1965.

———. "The Bliss Technique." May 17, 1965.

———. "The Ideal Choice." January 13, 1965.

———. "The Mayoralty Election." October 31, 1931.

———. "They Dial for Votes." October 14, 1965.

———. "Three Announce Political Hopes." May 1, 1935.

———. "Top Party Men Back Bliss' Plans." June 16, 1949.

———. "Trustee Oversteps Role in Dispute at Akron U." August 11, 1985.

———. "Two Good Candidates—But Ballard Is Our Choice." October 25, 1971.

———. "Vote Nixon, Shun Bender, Bliss Urges." April 15, 1960.

———. "Who Was 'In' Who Wasn't on That Bliss Appointment Stirs Debate." September 15, 1934.

———. "Wilson Defends Role as Trustee." August 19, 1985.

———. "Words Fly in Ballot War." September 25, 1937.

Alexander, Lamar. Interview by Timothy J. Naftali, June 27, 2007. https://www.nixonlibrary.gov
/virtuallibrary/documents/histories/alexander-2007-06-27.pdf.

Alsop, Joseph. "Ideological Gymnasts in Cincinnati and the Election." *Cincinnati Enquirer*, November 10, 1958.

Ambrose, Steven. *Nixon: The Triumph of a Politician, 1962–1972, vol. 2.* New York: Simon and Schuster, 1990.

Apple, R. W., Jr. "Ford Plans Formal Entry into '76 Race This Month." *New York Times*, June 8, 1975.

———. "GOP Panel Split on Party Reform." *New York Times*, March 6, 1975.

———. "Laird Reported Choice of Nixon to Head Defense." *New York Times*, December 9, 1968.

B

Balz, Douglas. "Bliss Will Help Steer Ford Drive." *Akron Beacon Journal*, July 11, 1975.

Barone, Michael, Grant Ujifusa, and Douglas Matthews. *The Almanac of American Politics 1972.* Washington, DC: Gambit Press, 1972.

Bartleby. "Richard Milhous Nixon: First Inaugural Address." Last modified January 31, 2017. http://www.bartleby.com/124/pres58.html.

Beech, Keyes. "Biography in Brief." *Akron Beacon Journal*, May 19, 1940.

Bell, Jack. "Bliss Reveals GOP Plans to Regain Big Cities' Vote." *Akron Beacon Journal*, June 29, 1965.

———. "Nixon Considers Bliss Replacement." *Associated Press*, November 17, 1968.

———. "Scranton Backs Bliss Try to Mend Splintering Party." *Akron Beacon Journal*, August 31, 1965.

Beschloss, Michael R., and Vincent Virga. *Eisenhower: A Centennial Life*. New York: HarperCollins, 1990.

Black, White, and Beyond. "Immigration & Migration in the Industrial Age, 1870–1930." Last modified May 26, 2015. https://learn.uakron.edu/beyond/industrialage.htm.

Blasio, Mary-Ann. "Ray C. Bliss: The Formative Years 1907–1937." Unpublished manuscript, last modified 1990.

Bliss Institute of Applied Politics. "Memo to Board of Trustees from William V. Muse." November 18, 1986.

———. "A Proposal for the Establishment of the Ray C. Bliss Institute of Applied Politics." December 1985.

———. "A Proposal for the Establishment of the Ray C. Bliss Institute of Applied Politics." March 1982.

———. "A Proposal for the Establishment of the Ray C. Bliss Institute of Applied Politics." March 1985.

———. "Transcript of Ray C. Bliss at a Taft Seminar, Ohio Wesleyan University." June 26, 1974.

———. "A Tribute to Ray Bliss." April 10, 1969.

Bliss, Ray C. "The Chairman Speaks: Address by the Honorable Ray C. Bliss, Chairman, Republican National Committee Before the 13th Annual Republican Women's Conference, April 1, 1965." In *Papers of the Republican Party*, edited by Paul L. Kesaris. Frederick, MD: University Publications of America, 1987.

———. "Election Aftermath: How Republicans See the Future." *U.S. News and World Report*, November 15, 1965.

———. "Elements of Victory, Chairman's Report to The Republican National Committee, January 31, 1966." In *Papers of the Republican Party*, edited by Paul L. Kesaris. Frederick, MD: University Publications of America, 1961.

———. "Letter of Resignation as Chairman of the Republican National Committee." February 17, 1969. *The American Presidency Project*. http://www.presidency.ucsb.edu/ws/?pid=2395.

———. Papers. Ohio History Connection, Columbus, OH.

———. "Report of the Committee on Big City Politics." In *Papers of the Republican Party*, edited by Paul L. Kesaris. Frederick, MD: University Publications of America, 1987.

———. "The Role of the State Chairman." In *Politics U.S.A.*, edited by James M. Cannon. Garden City, NY: Doubleday, 1960.

Bliss, Ray C., and Ellen Bliss, Papers. University of Akron Archives, Akron, OH.

Boissat, Bruce. "Nixon to Make Over the GOP." *Akron Beacon Journal*, December 2, 1968.

Boyd, Robert S. "Barry's Society Harmful to GOP." *Akron Beacon Journal*, June 19, 1965.

———. "Bliss, Nixon Get Together—'On Final Inaugural Plans.'" *Akron Beacon Journal*, January 10, 1969.

———. "Bliss Rights GOP Platform." *Akron Beacon Journal*, May 30, 1968.

———. "GOP Scraps Barry's Plan, Seeks Urban Votes." *Akron Beacon Journal*, February 29, 1968.

Boyd, Robert S., and Robert H. Feldkamp. "What a Night for Ray Bliss!" *Akron Beacon Journal*, November 9, 1966.

Brenna, Mary C. *Turning Right in the Sixties*. Chapel Hill: University of North Carolina Press, 1995.

Broder, David. "Bliss: A-1 Tightrope Walker." *Akron Beacon Journal*, November 28, 1967.
———. "Bliss Foresees Congress Gain for GOP in 1970." *Washington Post*, January 18, 1969.
———. "Bliss Helped Nudge Lindsay." *Washington Star*, May 14, 1965.
———. "Bliss Remembered." *Washington Post*, August 12, 1981.
———. "Bliss Rides the Elephant." *New York Times Magazine*, March 21, 1965.
———. "Bliss Rivaled Hanna as a GOP Innovator." *Columbus Dispatch*, August 12, 1981.
———. "Bliss Yields to Nixon, Resigns as GOP Chief." *Washington Post*, February 19, 1969.
———. "Short Terms of GOP Heads." *Washington Post*, January 23, 1973.
———. "Uphill with Dodd." *Washington Post*, January 18, 1995.
———. "Why Democrats Don't Know Their Own Mind." *Washington Post*, September 18, 1991.
Brown, Maureen. "Newsmaker/George Wilson, Controversial Akron U Board Member." *Akron Beacon Journal*, August 9, 1985.
———. "Rift at Akron U Delays Birth of Ray Bliss Politics Institute." *Akron Beacon Journal*, August 8, 1985.
Brown, Sr., J. Curtis, ed. *A Mighty Fine Union: A URW Anniversary History*. Washington, DC: United Rubber, Cork, Linoleum & Plastic Workers of America, AFL-CIO, 1985.
Buchanan, Patrick J. *The Greatest Comeback: How Richard Nixon Rose from Defeat to Create the New Majority*. New York: Penguin Random House, 2014.
Buchtelite. "Bliss Is Suspended; Eight-Hour Penalty Given to Two Girls." May 15, 1931.
———. "Ellen Palmer Disqualified by Council." May 12, 1931.
———. "Students to Vote Today in Title Race." May 8, 1931.
Burke, Bob, and Ralph G. Thompson. *Bryce Harlow: Mr. Integrity*. Oklahoma City: Oklahoma Heritage Association, 2000.
Burke, Vincent J. "Abernathy Leads '51st State' Inside." *Akron Beacon Journal*, August 7, 1968.

C
Cannon, James M ., ed. *Politics U.S.A.* Garden City, NY: Doubleday, 1960.
Canterbury, William. "AU Plans for Bliss Institute in Fall." *Akron Beacon Journal*, February 27, 1986.
Carringer, Helen. "AU May Soon Lose a Dedicated Trustee." *Akron Beacon Journal*, June 9, 1974.
Chandler, Alfred D., Jr. *The Visible Hand: The Managerial Revolution in American Business*. Cambridge, MA: Belknap Press, 1993.
Chotiner, Murray. "Managing the Campaign." In *Politics U.S.A.*, edited by James M. Cannon. Garden City, NY: Doubleday, 1960.
Clark, Ronald D. "Repeat 1960 Effort, Bliss Tells GOP." *Akron Beacon Journal*, October 18, 1974.
Cleveland Plain Dealer. "GOP's Burch Yields, Bliss to Take Helm." January 13, 1965.
Cockrell, Ron. *A Green Shrouded Miracle: The Administrative History of Cuyahoga Valley National Recreation Area, Ohio*. Omaha, NE: National Park Service, US Department of the Interior, Midwest Regional Office, 1992.
Coffey, Daniel J., John C. Green, David B. Cohen, and Stephen C. Brooks. *Buckeye Battleground: Ohio, Campaigns, and Elections in the Twenty-First Century*. Akron, OH: University of Akron Press, 2011.
Coffey, Daniel J., David B. Cohen, and John C. Green, eds. *The State of the Parties: The Changing Role of Contemporary American Parties*. 7th ed. Lanham, MD: Rowman & Littlefield, 2014.
Cole, Patrick. "Purnell Is First Woman to Head AU Trustees." *Akron Beacon Journal*, August 7, 1986.
Conefry, Hal. "Both Bliss and Bender Deny Rift." *Akron Beacon Journal*, April 1, 1954.
———. "Saxbe Named Speaker of Ohio House." *Columbus Citizen*, December 9, 1952.

Conley, Brian "Route to '66: Ray Bliss, the 1966 Election, and the Development of the Republican Service Party." *American Review of Politics* 31 (2010): 67–89.

———. "States and the Making of the 'Service' Party: The Case of the Postwar Ohio Republican Party." *Journal of American Studies* 45 (2011): 519–37.

Converse, Jean M. *Survey Research in the United States: Roots and Emergence, 1890–1960.* Berkeley: University of California Press, 1987.

Cotter, Cornelius. "The National Committees and Their Constituencies." In *Practical Politics in the United States,* edited by Cornelius Cotter, 17–41. Boston: Allyn and Bacon, 1969.

Crawford, Kenneth. "The GOP Corner." *Newsweek,* April 1968.

Curtin, Michael. *Ohio Politics Almanac.* Kent, OH: Kent State University Press, 1996.

———. "The O'Neill-DiSalle Years, 1957–1963." In *Ohio Politics,* edited by Alexander P. Lamis. Kent, OH: Kent State University Press, 1994.

D

Delaware County, PA, Daily Times. "New GOP Boss Gets Double Salary." April 9, 1965.

Davies, Lawrence E. "Bliss Asks Republicans to Shun Membership in Radical Groups." *New York Times,* November 6, 1965.

Davies, Richard O. *Defender of the Old Guard John Bricker and American Politics.* Columbus: Ohio State University Press, 1993.

Diemer, Tom, Lee Leonard, and Richard G. Zimmerman. *James A. Rhodes: Ohio Colossus.* Kent, OH: Kent State University Press, 2014.

Dorsey, Ray. "Anatomy of a Politician." *Cleveland Plain Dealer,* May 7, 1961.

Dougherty, Richard. "Bliss Unfolds Big City Plan." *Akron Beacon Journal,* December 29, 1965.

———. "Negro GOP Faction Charges Snub by Bliss." *Akron Beacon Journal,* July 11, 1965.

Drummond, Roscoe. "See Many GOP Factions Trying to Revive Party." *Akron Beacon Journal,* April 24, 1965.

E

Edwards, Lee. *Goldwater: The Man Who Made a Revolution.* Washington, DC: Regnery, 1995.

Edwards, Verne. "Ray Bliss Impressed Delawareans." *Delaware Gazette,* August 25, 1981.

Ehrlichman, John. Interview by *Frontline.* PBS, May 28, 1996. http://www.pbs.org/wgbh/pages/frontline/shows/choice/bob/erlichman.html.

———. White House Special Files: Staff Member and Office Files. Richard Nixon Presidential Library and Museum, Yorba Linda, CA.

Evans, Rowland, and Robert Novak. "Bliss Purge Backlash Sweeps Up Pile of Trouble for President-Elect." *Washington Post,* December 6, 1968.

———. "Mitchell Woos Bliss for Campaign Role." *Akron Beacon Journal,* March 5, 1972.

———. *Nixon in the White House: The Frustration of Power.* New York: Random House, 1971.

———. "The Ordeal of Ray Bliss." *Saturday Evening Post,* November 6, 1965.

———. "Rep. Morton of Maryland Is Called Likely Successor to GOP's Bliss." *Washington Post,* January 10, 1969.

———. "Why Bliss Will Be Replaced." *Akron Beacon Journal,* November 27, 1968.

F

Fain, Jim. "Bliss Will Go Willingly If Given Nixon Heave Ho." *Dayton Daily News,* November 19, 1968.

Feldkamp, Robert. "Ballard Defines Campaign Slogan: 'Citizens Come First.'" *Akron Beacon Journal*, August 26, 1965.

————. "Ballard to Seek GOP Nomination for Akron Mayor." *Akron Beacon Journal*, May 23, 1965.

————. "Ballard Wins by 20,000 Dems Keep Council Reins." *Akron Beacon Journal*, November 3, 1965.

————. "Behind GOP's Easy Purr, a Master Mechanic." *Akron Beacon Journal*, October 31, 1968.

————. "Bliss Has Last Laugh." *Akron Beacon Journal*, January 17, 1965.

————. "Bliss IS NOT Hostile to Goldwater Candidacy." *Akron Beacon Journal*, September 19, 1963.

————. "Bliss, Man of Deliberation, Had Fastest GOP Rise." *Akron Beacon Journal*, January 13, 1965.

————. "Bliss Man Stays in Control of Ohio GOP Funds." *Akron Beacon Journal*, February 9, 1965.

————. "Bliss Outlines 9-Point Plan 'Basic' to GOP Comeback." *Akron Beacon Journal*, February 4, 1966.

————. "Bliss Still Boils over Barry Camp Pressure." *Akron Beacon Journal*, July 16, 1964.

————. "Bliss to Run Show, Won't Be Muzzled." *Akron Beacon Journal*, January 3, 1968.

————. "Bliss 'Upset, Mystified' By Ouster Reports." *Akron Beacon Journal*, November 19, 1968.

————. "Confident Bliss Is Like Broken Record." *Akron Beacon Journal*, November 6, 1968.

————. "Erickson's Regime 'Inept'—Ballard." *Akron Beacon Journal*, June 3, 1965.

————. "For Reagan, a Day to Say 'I Declare.'" *Akron Beacon Journal*, August 6, 1968.

————. "Full Day for Ray." *Akron Beacon Journal*, April 2, 1965.

————. "Glenn Race May Start in Akron." *Akron Beacon Journal*, February 9, 1964.

————. "Glenn Rumor Pot Is Boiling." *Akron Beacon Journal*, May 31, 1964.

————. "GOP 'Really Starting to Move Now'—Bliss." *Akron Beacon Journal*, February 13, 1966.

————. "GOP Shows Ohio New 'All-American Face.'" *Akron Beacon Journal*, June 10, 1965.

————. "Hoopla a la Ayres Greets Area GOP Ladies in DC." *Akron Beacon Journal*, April 1, 1965.

————. "How Rhodes Pulled Rug from under Bliss." *Akron Beacon Journal*, July 12, 1964.

————. "I'm No Miracle Man." *Akron Beacon Journal*, January 23, 1965.

————. "It's Definite: Bliss Stays, Says Ayres." *Akron Beacon Journal*, December 10, 1968.

————. "It's Official Now: Bliss Named GOP Chairman." *Akron Beacon Journal*, January 22, 1965.

————. "Let 'Em Fight, Says Bliss; Can He Win This Way?" *Akron Beacon Journal*, June 25, 1967.

————. "Nixon: Bliss Talents Tops in GOP Annals." *Akron Beacon Journal*, January 18, 1969.

————. "Nixon Calls Bliss Superb." *Akron Beacon Journal*, January 11, 1969.

————. "Nixon's Silence Has Bliss Friends Steaming." *Akron Beacon Journal*, November 23, 1968.

————. "Ohio GOP Power Struggle Looms." *Akron Beacon Journal*, January 14, 1965.

————. "Race for Mayor Narrows to Two." *Akron Beacon Journal*, May 24, 1965.

————. "Ray Wants to Call All the Shots." *Akron Beacon Journal*, June 26, 1964.

————. "Ray's Pay Same as Burch's." *Akron Beacon Journal*, May 2, 1965.

————. "Sheppard Rips Erickson—'Lost Touch with People.'" *Akron Beacon Journal*, October 13, 1995.

————. "Was Caucus Slap at Bliss?" *Akron Beacon Journal*, July 14, 1964.

————. "Will Barry's Boys Team with Ohio GOP?" *Akron Beacon Journal*, July 17, 1964.

————. "Young GOP, Bliss Head for Showdown." *Akron Beacon Journal*, June 21, 1967.

————. "Young Republicans Reject Bigger Controls for Bliss." *Akron Beacon Journal*, June 23, 1967.

Fenton, John H. "The Right-To-Work Vote in Ohio." *Midwest Journal of Political Science* 3 (1959): 241–53.

Fields, Larry. "Ayres 'Last Hurrah' a Bitter Growl." *Akron Beacon Journal*, November 4, 1970.

Fisher, Joel. "The Role of the National Party Chairmen in American Politics." PhD diss., Claremont Graduate School and University Center, 1968.

Fitzgerald, Sara. *Elly Peterson: "Mother" of the Moderates*. Ann Arbor: University of Michigan Press, 2011.

Flanagan, Richard M. *Robert Wagner and the Rise of New York City's Plebiscitary Mayoralty: The Tamer of the Tammany Tiger*. New York: Palgrave Macmillan, 2014.

Flinn, Thomas. "How Mr. Nixon Took Ohio: A Short Reply to Senator Kennedy's Question." *Western Political Quarterly* 15 (1962): 274–79.

Franklin, Ben A. "Soldiers Back Up Police; 81 Protesters Are Seized." *New York Times*, January 21, 1969.

Freudenheim, Milt. "Saxbe Rips Bliss as GOP 'Killer.'" *Akron Beacon Journal*, April 15, 1954.

Funk, John. "A Tale of Two Alexanders." *Akron Beacon Journal, Beacon Magazine*, October 25, 1987.

G

Galvin, Daniel J. *Presidential Party Building: Dwight D. Eisenhower to George W. Bush*. Princeton, NJ: Princeton University Press, 2010.

Gapp, Paul. "Calls Bliss 'April Fool Present to GOP.'" *Akron Beacon Journal*, April 28, 1965.

Gaynor, Donn. "Bliss Vows Drive for Med College." *Akron Beacon Journal*, December 10, 1970.

Geyer, Marion. "Felicitations Pour in for Blisses." *Akron Beacon Journal*, November 27, 1959.

Glaser, Vera. "GOP Governors are Outmaneuvered in Bid to 'Modernize' '68 Platform." *Philadelphia Evening Bulletin*, February 27, 1968.

Glaser, Vera, and Malvina Stephenson. "Revelations of Nixon's 'Hatchet Man.'" *San Francisco Chronicle*, December 28, 1970, 12.

Goldman, Ralph M. *The National Party Chairmen and Committees: Factionalism at the Top*. Armonk, NY: M. E. Sharpe, 1990.

Goldwater, Barry M., and Jack Casserly. *Goldwater*. New York: Doubleday, 1988.

Green, John C. "Politics, Professionalism, and Power: Introduction." In *Politics, Professionalism, and Power: Modern Party Organization and the Legacy of Ray C. Bliss*, edited by John C. Green. Lanham, MD: University Press of America, 1994.

Greene, Jerry. "Why Bliss Is Leaving Post." *New York Daily News*, February 21, 1969.

Grismer, Karl H. *Akron and Summit County*. Salem, MA: Higginson Book Co., 1994. First published by Summit County Historical Society, 1952.

Group Research, Inc. records, 1955–1965. Columbia University Libraries Archival Collections, New York, NY.

H

Halberstam, David. *The Fifties*. New York: Villard Books, 1993.

Haldeman, H. R., Collection. Richard Nixon Presidential Library and Museum, Yorba Linda, CA.

———., Diaries Collection. Richard Nixon Presidential Library and Museum, Yorba Linda, CA.

———., White House Special Files: Staff Member and Office Files. Richard Nixon Presidential Library and Museum, Yorba Linda, CA.

Hames, Tim. "Strengths and Limitations: The Republican National Committee from Bliss to Brock to Barbour." In *Politics, Professionalism, and Power: Modern Party Organization and the Legacy of Ray C. Bliss*, edited by John C. Green. Lanham, MD: University Press of America, 1994.

Hamilton, Roulhac. "Morton to Take GOP Post If Nixon Drops Chotiner." *Columbus Dispatch*, February 26, 1969.

Harlow, Bryce, White House Special Files: Staff Member and Office Files. Richard Nixon Presidential Library and Museum, Yorba Linda, CA.

Harriman, H. H. "Akronite's Choice Held Significant." *Akron Beacon Journal*, August 6, 1944.

———. "Ballot Board Picks Officers." *Akron Beacon Journal*, December 21, 1941.

———. "Bliss Answers DeWoody Charges." *Akron Beacon Journal*, August 26, 1942.

———. "Bliss Cites Dem Edge in Jobs." *Akron Beacon Journal*, February 13, 1950.

———. "Bliss Elected to Head GOP." *Akron Beacon Journal*, August 20, 1942.

———. "Bliss Set for GOP Shakeup." *Akron Beacon Journal*, March 28, 1949.

———. "Bliss Set to Head Ohio GOP." *Akron Beacon Journal*, January 28, 1949.

———. "Death Ends Career of Jim Corey." *Akron Beacon Journal*, December 15, 1941.

———. "Elect Schroy, Urges Bixler." *Akron Beacon Journal*, September 13, 1937.

———. "Election Victories Rewarded." *Akron Beacon Journal*, July 11, 1952.

———. "GOP Is Split by Party Feud." *Akron Beacon Journal*, September 9, 1940.

———. "Harter Defeats Schroy by Over 5,000." *Akron Beacon Journal*, November 5, 1941.

———. "He's Ready: Youth, Training Give Bliss Background for GOP Spot." *Akron Beacon Journal*, October 21, 1945.

———. "Last 2-Booth Count Decides Mayors' Race." *Akron Beacon Journal*, November 7, 1951.

———. "Patterson Gets 36095 votes; Labor Candidates Take 4 Seats in Council." *Akron Beacon Journal*, November 3, 1937.

———. "Ray Bliss Declines to Run." *Akron Beacon Journal*, November 9, 1945.

———. "Says Davey Liquor Agents Are Aiding Schroy's Drive." *Akron Beacon Journal*, October 20, 1937.

———. "Schroy Elected." *Akron Beacon Journal*, November 8, 1939.

———. "See Bliss Being Groomed for Spot in Taft Plans." *Akron Beacon Journal*, February 12, 1951.

———. "Slusser Has Habit of Winning by 10,000 in Mayoral Elections." *Akron Beacon Journal*, November 6, 1949.

———. "Slusser Wins by 9,812 Votes." *Akron Beacon Journal*, November 3, 1943.

———. "Slusser Wins Second Term." *Akron Beacon Journal*, November 7, 1945.

———. "Young GOP Crowd Annihilates Rivals." *Akron Beacon Journal*, December 21, 1941.

Havel, Robert J. "Bliss Acclaims Nixon's Victory as Phenomenal." *Cleveland Plain Dealer*, November 10, 1968.

Hawbaker, Becky Wilson. "Taking 'the Pulse of Democracy': George Gallup, Iowa, and the Origin of the Gallup Poll." *Palimpsest* 74 (1993): 98–113.

Herrnson, Paul S. *Party Campaigning in the 1980s*. Cambridge, MA: Harvard University Press, 1988.

———. "Party Leadership and Party Organizational Change." In *Politics, Professionalism, and Power: Modern Party Organization and the Legacy of Ray C. Bliss*, edited by John C. Green. Lanham, MD: University Press of America, 1994.

Hershey, William. "Down on the Farm with John Galbreath." *Akron Beacon Journal Beacon Magazine*, January 24, 1982.

———. "For Truman the Luck Started Here." *Akron Beacon Journal*, September 24, 1992.

———. "The Party's Not Over." *Akron Beacon Journal*, June 7, 1981.

———. "Trump's Nuts and Bolts Guy." *Akron Beacon Journal*, January 21, 2017.

Hess, David. "Bliss Closed GOP Sex-Quota Debate." *Akron Beacon Journal*, September 11, 1973.

———. "Could That Frown Be Real, Mr. Bliss?" *Akron Beacon Journal*, October 11, 1968.

Hess, Stephen, and David Broder, *The Republican Establishment*. New York: Harper and Row, 1967.

Hinman, George L., Series J.2. Nelson A. Rockefeller Personal Papers, Politics. Rockefeller Archive Center, Sleepy Hollow, NY.

Hirsh, Lou. "Politics Program Planned in Honor of Bliss." *The Buchtelite*, August 13, 1981.

Hissam, Michael B. "C. William O'Neill and the 1958 Right-to-Work Amendment." Senior honors thesis, Ohio State University, 2005.

Hoyt, Robert E. "Bliss Shy As GOP Raves." *Akron Beacon Journal*, January 7, 1961.

———. "Rocky over Nixon? Unlikely, Says Bliss." *Akron Beacon Journal*, June 9, 1960.

Huckshorn, Robert J. *Party Leadership in the States*. Amherst: University of Massachusetts Press, 1976.

Hughes, L. Patrick. "When All the Experts Got It Wrong: Harry Truman's Upset Presidential Victory, 1948." http://www.austincc.edu/lpatrick/his1302/WhenAllTheExperts1.html.

Hutchison, Louise. "Team Play Wins Elections, Bliss Tells Women." *Chicago Tribune*, April 16, 1969.

J

Jackson, James S. "URW Bitterly Assail Davey." *Akron Beacon Journal*, September 13, 1937.

Jaycox, Betty. "An Evening of Pure 'Bliss.'" *Akron Beacon Journal*, January 20, 1969.

Johnson, Thomas A. "Governor Lauded by Rights Leader." *New York Times*, August 7, 1968.

Jones, Alfred W. *Life, Liberty, and Property: A Story of Conflict and a Measurement of Conflicting Rights.* Akron, OH: University of Akron Press, 1999.

Jordan, Gene. "GOP's Ray Bliss Easing Out of Politics." *Columbus Dispatch Magazine*, July 6, 1980.

K

Kenworthy, E. W. "Nixon Telegram Endorses Bliss." *New York Times*, January 18, 1969.

Kessel, John H. "Ray Bliss and the Development of the Ohio Republican Party." In *Politics, Professionalism, and Power: Modern Party Organization and the Legacy of Ray C. Bliss*, edited by John C. Green. Lanham, MD: University Press of America, 1994.

———. "Road to the Mansion: A Study of the 1956 Gubernatorial Campaign in Ohio." PhD diss., Ohio State University, 1958, 311.

Kleindienst, Richard D., Collection. Richard Nixon Presidential Library and Museum, Yorba Linda, CA.

Klinkner, Philip A. "A Comparison of Out-Party Leaders: Ray Bliss and Bill Brock." In *Politics, Professionalism, and Power: Modern Party Organization and the Legacy of Ray C. Bliss*, edited by John C. Green. Lanham, MD: University Press of America, 1994.

———. *The Losing Parties: Out-Party National Committees, 1956–1993.* New Haven, CT: Yale University Press, 1994.

Knepper, George W. *Akron, City at the Summit.* Tulsa, OK: Continental Heritage Press, 1981.

———. *Ohio and Its People.* Kent, OH: Kent State University Press, 1989.

———. *Summit's Glory: Sketches of Buchtel College and The University of Akron.* Akron, OH: University of Akron Press, 1990.

Knight, John S. "Goldwater as Nominee Gives GOP New Vigor." *Akron Beacon Journal*, July 19, 1965.

Knippenburg, O. F. "State Demos Swipe GOP's Prize Recipe." *Dayton Daily News*, August 20, 1967.

Kotzbauer, Robert. "All's Not Peaceful in the GOP Camp." *Akron Beacon Journal*, April 8, 1961.

———. "Bliss Acclaimed as Goldwater Derides 'Frontier.'" *Akron Beacon Journal*, February 2, 1962.

———. "Bliss Chooses 6 to Help Recruit Workers for GOP." *Akron Beacon Journal*, July 25, 1962.

———. "Bliss Removes Personal Roadblock for Taking National GOP Helm." *Akron Beacon Journal*, June 23, 1964.

———. "Bliss Wants to Change the Subject." *Akron Beacon Journal*, January 29, 1961.

———. "Won't Stay as State GOP Leader, Bliss Announces." *Akron Beacon Journal*, January 21, 1965.

Krock, Arthur. "Party Platform for All: Republicans' Draft Viewed as Allowing the Candidate to Run in All Directions." *New York Times*, August 7, 1968.

L

Lawrence, W. H. "Eisenhower and Nixon Are Renominated." *New York Times*, August 22, 1956.

Leach, Paul R. "Bliss Considered by GOP for National Chairman." *Akron Beacon Journal*, March 29, 1953.

Leonard, Lee. "Ohio GOP Has Weakened." *Sandusky Register*, August 17, 1981.

————. "Old Pro Retires from Panel." *Sarasota Herald-Tribune*, July 19, 1980.

Lichtenstein, Nelson. *Walter Reuther: The Most Dangerous Man in Detroit.* New York: Basic Books, 1997.

Lightner, Richard E. "Democrats Win Reapportionment Board Control." *Akron Beacon Journal*, November 4, 1970.

The Laurel of Phi Kappa Tau. "Twenty Minutes with Chairman Bliss." September 1978.

M

Madden, Richard L. "Lindsay Chosen by Acclamation at GOP Meeting." *New York Times*, May 28, 1965.

Maher, Richard L. "Schorr's Wings Clipped by Ohio GOP." *Cincinnati Enquirer*, December 9, 1952.

Maidenburg, Ben. "... But at Least It Started on Time." *Akron Beacon Journal*, August 7, 1968.

————. "Why Nixon Fired Bliss as GOP Chairman." *Akron Beacon Journal*, August 7, 1981.

Mansfield News-Journal. "Wesleyan Sets 'Republican Day' in Delaware Thursday." March 20, 1949.

Mann, Clyde. "10-Year Republican Rule Broken as 81,433 Ballot." *Akron Beacon Journal*, November 4, 1953.

————. "Bender Endorsement Seen Causing Rift in Ohio GOP Party." *Akron Beacon Journal*, January 8, 1954.

————. "Bliss and Hanhart Again Party Chiefs." *Akron Beacon Journal*, May 18, 1954.

————. "Bliss Blames RTW for GOP Debacle." *Akron Beacon Journal*, November 5, 1958.

————. "Bliss 'Farm System' Gives GOP Surplus of Able Candidates." *Akron Beacon Journal*, January 23, 1955.

————. "Bliss Hailed as GOP's Top Leader." *Akron Beacon Journal*, November 6, 1954.

————. "Bliss Ignored in Strategy." *Akron Beacon Journal*, July 15, 1952.

————. "Bliss Rips Lausche as 'Straddler.'" *Akron Beacon Journal*, June 26, 1956.

————. "Bliss Says Nixon Holds His Fire." *Akron Beacon Journal*, May 17, 1960.

————. "Bliss Takes Self out of Top GOP Picture." *Akron Beacon Journal*, April 2, 1959.

————. "Bliss to Have 'Experts' Aid GOP County Chiefs." *Akron Beacon Journal*, January 28, 1959.

————. "Compensation Bills Deadlock Broken by Bliss' Efforts." *Akron Beacon Journal*, July 3, 1955.

————. "'Demotion' Irritates C. J. Brown." *Akron Beacon Journal*, August 7, 1960.

————. "GOP Party Job Not for Me—Bliss." *Akron Beacon Journal*, April 1, 1953.

————. "Krenzler Pushing to Fill Ray Bliss' Shoes—Sometime." *Akron Beacon Journal*, February 17, 1957.

————. "Mild Rebellion within Ohio GOP Soon Quelled." *Akron Beacon Journal*, July 26, 1956.

————. "Name Bliss One of GOP Strategists." *Akron Beacon Journal*, September 7, 1952.

————. "Ohioans Still Grumbling." *Akron Beacon Journal*, July 29, 1960.

————. "O'Neill Pay Raise Switch 'Shocks' Leaders of GOP." *Akron Beacon Journal*, April 7, 1957.

————. "O'Neill's Campaign Damaged by Rumors He Would Oust Bliss." *Akron Beacon Journal*, January 29, 1956.

————. "Ray Bliss: He Believes in Peace." *Akron Beacon Journal*, February 17, 1957.

————. "Ray Bliss in Middle of Battle over GOP Senate Nomination." *Akron Beacon Journal*, January 3, 1954.

————. "Saxbe Claims Bliss Goes Out If Bender Wins Nomination." *Akron Beacon Journal*, March 13, 1954.

————. "Saxbe Jolts Ohio Peace Hope." *Akron Beacon Journal*, January, 14, 1954.

————. "Saxbe to Run against Bender." *Akron Beacon Journal*, January 13, 1954.

Marchione, Marilynn. "The Glitter Fades for Old Washington Hands." *Akron Beacon Journal*, January 18, 1981.

Mazo, Earl. "Burch's Resignation Split the Goldwater Bloc." *New York Times,* January 14, 1965.
———. "Eisenhower Proposes a Revamped National Organization to Lead Republican Party." *New York Times,* January 6, 1965.
———. "Goldwater Asks for Unity in GOP." *New York Times,* January 22, 1965.
McCartney, James. "Lindsay's Victory in New York Gives GOP Shot in Arm." *Akron Beacon Journal,* November 3, 1965.
———. "Showdown at the DC Corral." *San Francisco Chronicle,* April 28, 1974.
McCrary, Lacy, and Joe Rice. "Bliss Approached to 'Take Over.'" *Akron Beacon Journal,* June 14, 1970.
McDiarmid, Hugh C. "The Gilligan Interlude, 1971–73." In *Ohio Politics,* edited by Alexander P. Lamis. Kent, OH: Kent State University Press, 1994.
McGaffin, William, and James McCartney. "How Goldwater Was Forced to Accept Bliss for Burch." *Akron Beacon Journal,* January 13, 1965.
McMahon, Patrick. "Charge State Aids Schroy; New Deal Club Hits Judge." *Akron Beacon Journal,* October 14, 1937.
———. "Patterson Hits at 'Hobgoblins.'" *Akron Beacon Journal,* October 12, 1937.
McMullan, John. "Ohio Delegation's Release Kills Last Scranton Bid?" *Akron Beacon Journal,* July 10, 1964.
Mears, Walter R. "'Bliss-For-Chairman' Move Is Rolling." *Akron Beacon Journal,* January 8, 1965.
Menefee-Libey, David. "Embracing Campaign-Centered Politics at the Democratic Headquarters." In *Politics, Professionalism, and Power: Modern Party Organization and the Legacy of Ray C. Bliss,* edited by John C. Green. Lanham, MD: University Press of America, 1994.
Meyer, Philip E. "GOP Gets Fund-Raising Ideas from Dollar Backers." *Akron Beacon Journal,* August 20, 1965.
Mitten, Ray. "Bliss Seeks Large Vote." *Akron Beacon Journal,* June 19, 1949.
Morehead, Robert. "The Test Tube City." *Nation's Business,* February 1938.
Muller, Will. "Ohio's Republican Chairman Converts Gimmicks into Votes." *Detroit News,* May 28, 1957.

N
Naughton, James N. "Ballot Security Is Goal of Bliss." *Cleveland Plain Dealer,* October 12, 1968.
Nelson, Daniel. "The CIO at Bay: Labor Militancy and Politics in Akron, 1936–1938." *Journal of American History* 31 (1984): 567–68.
———. "The Great Goodyear Strike of 1936." *Ohio History* 92 (1983): 6–36.
Nelson, Jack. "Bliss Ducks Questions on Racism, Birch Society." *Los Angeles Times,* September 26, 1965.
News Bulletin of Ohio Chamber of Commerce. "Nation Has Eyes on Ohio Right to Work Campaign—Verity." June 1958.
New York Post. "Bliss Agrees to Stay as Chairman." January 11, 1969.
New York Times. "$800,000 Miami Bid for '68 Convention of GOP Is Highest." February 22, 1967.
———. "Determined Republican: Raymond Charles Bliss." January 13, 1965.
———. "GOP's Site Selection Panel Picks Miami Beach." July 27, 1967.
———. "Inauguration Seating Arrangement." January 20, 1969.
———. "Nixons Greet Republicans by the Hundreds." April 14, 1969.
———. "To Politics with Love." May 15, 1965.
Newsweek. "Ohio's Ray Bliss: The GOP Picks a Chairman." January 25, 1965.
Nichols, Kenneth. *Yesterday's Akron: The First 150 Years.* Miami, FL: E. A. Seemann Publishing, 1976.
Nixon, Richard. "Letter Accepting Resignation of Ray C. Bliss as Chairman of the Republican National Committee." February 17, 1969. *The American Presidency Project.* http://www.presidency.ucsb.edu/ws/?pid=2395.

———. *RN: The Memoirs of Richard Nixon*. New York: Simon and Schuster, 1978.

———. White House Recordings. Miller Center. University of Virginia, Charlottesville, VA.

O

O'Dea, Suzanne. *Madam Chairman: Mary Louise Smith and the Republican Revival after Watergate*. Columbia: University of Missouri Press, 2012.

Ogden, Daniel M., Jr., and Arthur L. Peterson. *Electing the President*. San Francisco: Chandler, 1968.

Ohio Republican News. "Ray C. Bliss: Ohio National Committeeman Bliss Goes on the Record." June 25, 1976.

Ohio Secretary of State. "Articles of Incorporation for Tower Agencies, Inc." Last modified January 31, 2017. https://www5.sos.state.oh.us/ords/f?p=100:7:0::NO:7:P7_CHARTER_NUM: 204608.

Ohio State Journal. "Sabotage Seen in Office Blast." April 15, 1932.

Otten, Alan L., and Charles B. Seid. "The Minor Masterpiece of Ray C. Bliss." *Reporter*, February 10, 1965.

P

Patterson, James T. *Grand Expectations: The United States, 1945–1974*. Oxford: Oxford University Press, 1996.

———. *Mr. Republican: A Biography of Robert A. Taft*. Boston: Houghton Mifflin, 1972.

Pearson, Drew, and Jack Anderson. "The Claude Kirk Mystique—Or Could It Be Mistake." *Akron Beacon Journal*, August 7, 1968.

Perlstein, Rick. *Nixonland: The Rise of a President and the Fracturing of America*. New York: Scribner, 2008.

Perry, James M. *The New Politics: The Expanding Technology of Political Manipulation*. New York: Clarkson N. Potter, 1968.

Peterson, Arthur L. "Ray C. Bliss: Leader or Manager?" In *Politics, Professionalism, and Power: Modern Party Organization and the Legacy of Ray C. Bliss*, edited by John C. Green, 85. Lanham, MD: University Press of America, 1994.

Petit, Mary Loretta. "Charles Dick of Akron, Politician." Master's thesis, Catholic University of America, 1948.

Phillips, Cabell. "GOP Loss Is Laid to the Big Cities." *New York Times*, February 26, 1961.

Pitney, John J., Jr. "Republican Alternatives to the Great Society." In *Politics, Professionalism, and Power: Modern Party Organization and the Legacy of Ray C. Bliss*, edited by John C. Green, 205–17. Lanham, MD: University Press of America, 1994.

Poidomani, Mary Grace. "Bliss Not Accustomed to Defeat." *Akron Beacon Journal*, August 7, 1981.

Poorman, Paul A. "Bliss' Forte: He Looked Forward." *Akron Beacon Journal*, August 9, 1981.

Price, Mark J. "Local History: The Great Temple." *Akron Beacon Journal*, August 27, 2007.

R

Rabb, Charles. "Nixon May Kiss Off Bliss for a More-Blistery Boss." *New York Daily News*, November 18, 1968.

Rice, Joe. "After 20 Yrs.—Ayres Falls." *Akron Beacon Journal*, November 4, 1970.

———. "Bliss Gives Big Lift to GOP Fund Drive." *Akron Beacon Journal*, August 13, 1970.

———. "Bliss Gives Ohio GOP Something to Cheer About." *Akron Beacon Journal*, July 9, 1970.

———. "Bliss to GOP Heads: 'We're Down, Not Out.'" *Akron Beacon Journal*, August 14, 1970.

———. "No Longer Boss, But Ray Bliss Still Keeps Busy." *Akron Beacon Journal*, August 20, 1972.

———. "Quarterback Styles Differ—But GOP Games the Same." *Akron Beacon Journal*, June 18, 1969.

———. "Ray Bliss to Assist State GOP Drive." *Akron Beacon Journal*, July 8, 1970.

———. "Sen. Scott Praises Bliss, Sees GOP Senate Control." *Akron Beacon Journal*, May 23, 1969.

Riesel, Victor. "Bliss-Krieg of Cities Won Race for Nixon." *Tampa Tribune*, November 23, 1968.

Rigueur, Leah Wright. *The Loneliness of the Black Republican: Pragmatic Politics and the Pursuit of Power.* Princeton, NJ: Princeton University Press, 2014.

Ronan, Thomas P. "Bliss Pledges Aid to Lindsay's Race." *New York Times*, May 15, 1965.

———. "Lindsay Says He Will Run against Wagner to Halt 'Decline and Fall' of City." *New York Times*, May 14, 1965.

S

Sandusky Register. "GOP Architect Ray Bliss, 73, Praised in Death." August 7, 1981.

Saxbe, William B. *I've Seen the Elephant.* Kent, OH: Kent State University Press, 2000.

Semple, Robert B., Jr. "GOP Governors Will Press Convention Fight." *New York Times*, December 14, 1967.

———. "Nixon, Sworn, Dedicates Office to Peace; Offers a Role to Young and Disaffected and a Chance to 'Black as Well as White.'" *New York Times*, January 21, 1969.

Shadegg, Stephen. *What Happened to Goldwater?* New York: Holt, Rinehart, and Winston, 1965.

Silverman, Alvin. "2 Whistle Stops Put Back for Ike." *Cleveland Plain Dealer*, September 23, 1952.

Smith, Daly. "Dennis Shaul 'Sounds Like a Republican.'" *Akron Beacon Journal*, October 28, 1971.

———. "Nixon Wire Hails Bliss on Birthday." *Akron Beacon Journal*, December 11, 1971.

———. "Shaul Defeated by 4,194 Votes." *Akron Beacon Journal*, November 3, 1971.

Smith, Reed. "GOP Gives Clevelander 58,000 Lead." *Akron Beacon Journal*, May 5, 1954.

Smith, Richard Norton. *Thomas E. Dewey and His Times.* New York: Simon & Schuster, 1984.

Spencer, Thomas T. "Auxiliary and Non-Party Politics: The 1936 Democratic Presidential Campaign in Ohio." *Ohio History Journal* 90 (1981): 114–28. http://resources.ohiohistory.org/ohj /browse/displaypages.php?display[]=0090&display[]=114&display[]=128.

Stacy, Harold A. "Bliss Pledges New GOP Formula as He Takes Over Party Reins." *Columbus Dispatch*, February 10, 1949.

Stone, Barbara S. "The John Birch Society: A Profile." *Journal of Politics* 36, no. 1 (1974): 184–97.

Strouse, Don. "I Like to Do Things People Say Can't Be Done." *Akron Beacon Journal*, January 31, 1953.

Sutliff, Ray C. "Bliss Would Be GOP Chief, If—." *Akron Beacon Journal*, January 8, 1961.

———. "I. S. Myers Defeats Earl Cox for Mayor." *Akron Beacon Journal*, November 7, 1933

———. "Myers Challenges Old Adage: 'They Never Come Back.'" *Akron Beacon Journal*, October 17, 1933.

———. "Ray Bliss Named to Zoning Board." *Akron Beacon Journal*, January 9, 1934.

———. "Vital Decisions on City Election Near for GOP Leaders." *Akron Beacon Journal*, May 17, 1959.

T

Thimmesch, Nick. *The Condition of Republicanism.* New York: W. W. Norton, 1968.

Thompson, Kenneth W, ed. *The Nixon Presidency*, vol. 1. Lanham, MD: Rowman & Littlefield, 1987.

Time. "Man behind the Desk." November 23, 1962.

Toledo Blade. "Briley for Senator." October 11, 1962.

U

United Press International. "Obituaries: Bliss Rebuilt Republicans with Nixon." August 7, 1981.

Usher, Brian. "A Bliss Dream to Become an Asset for Akron." *Akron Beacon Journal*, August 9, 1981.

————. "Bliss Warns of Dewey-Like Overconfidence." *Akron Beacon Journal*, July 15, 1980.

————. "GOP 'Sage' Bliss Devoted Life to Party." *Akron Beacon Journal*, August 6, 1981.

————. "Ray Bliss' Message Finds Receptive Ears in Ohio GOP." *Akron Beacon Journal*, September 21, 1980.

————. "Summit GOP Chief Lost a Mentor in Bliss." *Akron Beacon Journal*, August 9, 1981.

Usher, Brian, and Michael Cull. "A Man Named Rhodes." *Akron Beacon Journal*, March 5, 1978.

Usher, Brian, and Marilynn Marchione. "Politicians, Friends Bid Farewell to Bliss." *Akron Beacon Journal*, August 12, 1981.

V

Vance, William. "And No Hitting in Clinches." *Akron Beacon Journal*, June 18, 1967.

————. "Bliss in Akron—Mum on Ouster Report." *Akron Beacon Journal*, December 3, 1968.

————. "Bliss' Political Chums in Dark on Resignation." *Akron Beacon Journal*, February 19, 1969.

————. "Here's the Story behind the Story of Ray Bliss." *Akron Beacon Journal*, February 23, 1969.

————. "Nixon Owes Bliss Explanation—Waddell." *Akron Beacon Journal*, November 20, 1969.

————. "No Bliss on the Far Right." *Akron Beacon Journal*, July 9, 1967.

————. "Ohio Dems Take Bliss Handbook as 1970 Guide." *Akron Beacon Journal*, July 30, 1967.

————. "Ohioans Going Away Mad?" *Akron Beacon Journal*, August 9, 1968.

————. "Ray Bliss Will Resign as GOP Chief April 15." *Akron Beacon Journal*, February 18, 1969.

————. "We Won a Couple Just the Same: Bliss." *Akron Beacon Journal*, April 9, 1969.

Van Riper, Frank. *Glenn: The Astronaut Who Would Be President.* New York: Empire Books, 1983.

W

Waldron, Martin. "Curfew Ordered in Most of Miami." *New York Times*, August 10, 1968.

Washington Post. "Bliss Agrees to Stay as Chairman." January 11, 1969.

Washington Star. "Bliss Won't Intervene in Women's Election." May 9, 1967.

Weaver, Warren, Jr.. "GOP Governors Dodge Bliss Issue." *Akron Beacon Journal*, December 7, 1968.

————. "Miami Beach Tops Nominating Sites." *New York Times*, April 4, 1967.

Wieland, Dennis E. "The Lives and Times of the Wielands." Unpublished family history.

Weinraub, Bernard. "Ray Bliss Dies in Ohio at 73; Rebuilt GOP After '64 Rout." *New York Times*, August 7, 1981.

White, F. Clifton. *Suite 3505: The Story of the Draft Goldwater Movement.* New Rochelle, NY: Arlington House, 1967.

White, Theodore. *The Making of the President 1960.* New York: Atheneum, 1962.

————. *The Making of the President 1964.* New York: Harper Collins, 1965.

————. *The Making of the President 1968.* New York: Atheneum, 1969.

White, William S. *The Taft Story.* New York: Harper and Row, 1954.

Whited, Charles. *Knight: A Publisher in the Tumultuous Century.* New York: Dutton, 1988.

Wicker, Tom. "Goldwater Aftermath." *New York Times*, January 16, 1965.

————. *One of Us: Richard Nixon and the American Dream.* New York: Random House, 1991.

Williams, R. Hal. *Realigning America: McKinley, Bryan, and the Remarkable Election of 1896.* Lawrence: University Press of Kansas, 2010.

Wilson, H. Earl. "Cox, Making Third Fight for Mayor's Chair, Believes Long War against Bosses Will Yield Him Coveted Prize." *Akron Beacon Journal*, October 18, 1931.

Wirt, Frederick M. "The Organization Man in Politics: Ray Bliss and the 1960 Election." In *Politics, Professionalism, and Power: Modern Party Organization and the Legacy of Ray C. Bliss*, edited by John C. Green, 65. Lanham, MD: University Press of America, 1994.

Wise, David. "GOP Unhappy over New Barry Club?" *Akron Beacon Journal*, June 15, 1965.

Witkin, Richard. "Liberals Choose Lindsay to Lead a Fusion Ticket; Beame Joins the Contest." *New York Times*, June 29, 1965.

Z

Zaidan, Abe. "Arshinkoff Wins Election to Head GOP in Summit." *Akron Beacon Journal*, June 28, 1978.

———. "Bliss to Leave Board of Elections." *Akron Beacon Journal*, November 22, 1978.

———. "Bliss: No Full-Time Role in Nixon Drive." *Akron Beacon Journal*, May 17, 1972.

———. "Bliss Sees GOP's Rebirth, Calls Ford a Team Player." *Akron Beacon Journal*, August 9, 1974.

———. "Ray Bliss: The 'Retired' Mr. GOP Will Still Keep a Hand in Politics." *Akron Beacon Journal*, April 20, 1969.

———. "Rhodes' View, Voters Now 'Owe Him One.'" *Akron Beacon Journal*, March 26, 1978.

———. "Roses and Strudel for Bliss." *Akron Beacon Journal*, April 18, 1969.

Zaidan, Abe, and Ronald D. Clark, "They're Ready for a Victory Party." *Akron Beacon Journal*, August 18, 1976.

Ziegler, Mel. "Kirk Gets a Cushiony Job in Blissful Breeze Batting." *Miami Herald*, July 28, 1968.

Zimmerman, Richard G. "Rhodes's First Eight Years, 1963–1971." In *Ohio Politics*, edited by Alexander P. Lamis, 59. Kent, OH: Kent State University Press, 1994.

Index

A

Abernathy, Ralph, 227–28

Adams, Sherman, 90

AFL-CIO, 105, 127, 132, 198, 322

Agnew, Spiro T., 228–29, 232, 235, 258, 270, 286, 287

Akron Bar Association, 54

Akron Beacon Journal: on Akron politics, 35–36, 41, 56, 64, 70; as Akron's sole newspaper, 45; anti-gambling crusade of, 41; on Bliss and Goldwater, 138; on Bliss and Ohio chairmanship, 51–52, 83, 92, 125, 135; on Bliss and Young Republicans, 212–13; on Bliss as potential RNC chairman, 76, 115, 126, 156; on Bliss as RNC chairman, 165, 169, 175, 191; Bliss, coverage of in, 15–16, 40–41, 50, 51–52, 69, 110, 259; on Bliss, efforts to unseat, 263, 265; on Bliss in politics after chairmanship, 284, 285, 286, 290, 291, 298, 299, 301, 305; Bliss reading of, 201; Bliss's relations with, 24, 35, 38, 52; and Bliss's resignation, 267, 271–72, 273, 274–76, 282; endorsements by, 22, 35, 282–83, 295, 309; involvement in Akron politics by, 22–24, 35, 45, 282–83; John S. Knight at, 23–24, 30, 35, 41, 45, 315; and mayoral campaign, 1965, 186–87, 188; and mayoral campaign, 1971, 282–83; and May Queen fiasco, 15–16; on Nixon/Bliss tensions, 205, 230–31, 239, 246, 254–55; on presidential campaign, 1976, 295; on Republican convention, 1964, 140, 142; on Summit County politics, 106, 107, 160, 309; on University of Akron, 15–16, 304, 319;

rivalry with *Columbus Dispatch*, 130; on state chairmanship, controversy regarding, 92

Akron Chamber of Commerce, 61, 97, 106–7

Akron City Council, 38–39, 41, 64, 106, 180, 309, 312

Akron City Hospital, 294, 316

Akron Labor Council, 187, 302

Akron Law School. *See* University of Akron, law school

Akron, Ohio: *Akron Beacon Journal* in, 45; Bliss family in, 5–7; Bliss in after chairmanship, 274, 288; Bliss in with Ellen, 109; Bliss returning to post-chairmanship, xv, 1, 272, 274–75, 231, 272, 275, 277, 281, 288; Bliss's experience in, 77, 93, 163, 200, 278; Bliss's home in 61, 86, 136, 145, 159, 184, 208; as Bliss's hometown; xv, 1, 32, 37, 50, 65, 103, 128, 189, 199, 214, 271, 285, 315; Bliss's visits to, 184, 188, 208, 244; economy of, 2–3, 305; Harris, Herman in, 54; high society of, 259; history, 2–4, 9, 19, 305; Ku Klux Klan in, 20–21; labor movement in, 29–31, 32–36, 84; mayoral campaign of 1937 in, 29, 30–31, 32–36, 37; mayoral campaign of 1941 in, 39; mayoral campaign of 1943 in, 41, 45; mayoral campaign of 1947 in, 48, 56; mayoral campaign of 1949 in, 48, 50, 64, 70; mayoral campaign of 1953 in, 78; mayoral campaign of 1959 in, 103, 106; mayoral campaign of 1965 in, 185–88, 189, 190, 209; mayoral campaign of 1971 in, 282–83, 295; mayoral campaign of 1979 in, 311; mayoral campaigns of the early 1930s in, 22–23, 27, 38; national

387

183; as potential vice-presidential candidate, 299; as president, 291, 292; president, appointment as, 290; vice-president appointment as, 287
Fowler, George, 210
Free Society Association, 168, 173, 177

G

Galbreath, John H. W., 99, 104, 244
Gallup, George H., 27, 66
Gallup Poll, 27, 28
Gardner, Donfred, 15, 16
Garrett Jr., Thaddeus A., 188, 227
Garrigan, Ed, 106
Georgia, 151, 237, 270, 295
Germany, 5, 6, 315
Gilligan, John J., 198, 237, 280–81, 292, 302
Gillmor, Paul, 308
Glenn, John H., 134–35, 280
Goldwater, Barry: and Bliss, 126, 138–39, 141, 143, 146–47, 168; Civil Rights Act opposition to, 210; as conservative, 139, 147, 155–56, 178, 181, 328; and "draft Goldwater committee," 138, 173, 212; and Free Society Association, 168, 173, 177; independence from the party, xiv, 147; and John Birch Society, 168, 182; in Ohio, 146, 147; Lindsay, John and, 190; opposition to, 141–42, 145–46; as party leader, 158, 164–65; presidential campaign, loss of, xiii–xiv, 1, 147–48, 186; and presidential campaign of 1960, 117; presidential campaign of, 1964, 139, 141–42, 150, 204, 219, 237, 286–87; on Republican Coordinating Committee, 177; rhetoric of, 181; RNC chairman, selection of, 143, 149–54, 156; RNC, operatives of in, 164, 172–74; supporters of, 128, 138, 141, 145–46, 149, 170, 192, 211, 280, 294; Schlafly, Phyllis, and, 214
Good, Josephine: on 1968 convention, 217–18, 222, 228; on Bliss's personality, 202; on Bliss's respect for staff, 206; on Bliss's personal habits, 173; history at Republican headquarters, 172; relationship with Bliss, 172–73, 202; on Republican Coordinating Committee, 179–80; work for Bliss, 172–73, 216–17
Goodrich, Benjamin Franklin, 2

Goodyear Tire and Rubber Company, 2, 29–30, 281, 301–2
Gore, Al, 323
Gosman, Robert F., 269
Gray, Theodore (Ted), 160
Great Depression, 19, 22–23, 29, 109
Great Society, 180, 234–35, 327
Greeley, Horace, 9
Green, John C., 320
Group Research, Inc., 182
Gulmon, G. W., 211
Guzzetta, Dominic, 304, 316, 320

H

Haldeman, H. R. (Bob): and Bliss after chairmanship, 285; and Bliss, efforts to unseat, 248–49, 251, 253, 260–61, 264–65
Hall, Leonard W., 76, 88, 90, 111, 286
Hames, Tim, 326, 328
Hanhart, Eugene H., 101
Hanna, Marcus (Mark), 19–20, 35, 39, 51
Harding, Warren, 20
Harris, Herman B., 53–54
Harsha, William, 121, 123
Harter, Dow W., 41
Harter, George J., 39, 41
Hartley, Fred A., 95
Harvard University, 54, 282
Hayes, W. W. (Woody), 122
Herbert, Victor, 187
Herrnson, Paul S., 326
Hickel, Walter, 263
Hill, Hugh, 316
Hilltop Party (University of Akron), 13–17
Hinman, George L., 136
Hook, Charles R., 99
Hoover, Herbert, 21, 23
Huber, Walter, 68,
Huckshorn, Robert, 278, 326
Hummel, Edward J., 51
Humphrey, Hubert H., 175, 222, 234, 235, 237, 258
Humphreys, Robert, 88

I

Illinois, 236–37
Independent Order of Odd Fellows, 20–21